Criminal Justice The

Criminal Justice Theory examines the theoretical foundations of criminal justice in the modern era, whilst also considering legal philosophy and ethics, explaining criminal behaviour, and discussing policing, the court process and penology in the context of contemporary socio-economic debates.

Throughout the book a realist theoretical thread acts as a guide interlinking concepts of social progress, conflict and carceral models of criminal justice, whilst also recognising our collusion in the creation of an increasingly pervasive culture of socio-control that now characterises contemporary society.

The complex theoretical issues tackled in this book are addressed in an accessible style, making this a relevant and comprehensive introduction to criminal justice theory for students on a wide range of undergraduate criminal justice modules. It will also be a helpful guide for those commencing postgraduate studies in the disciplines of criminal justice, criminology and law.

Roger Hopkins Burke is Criminology Subject Leader at Nottingham Trent University where he teaches criminological theory and juvenile justice to both undergraduates and postgraduates. His numerous publications include *Zero Tolerance Policing* (Perpetuity Press, 1998), *Hard Cop/Soft Cop* (Willan Press, 2004), *Young People, Crime and Justice* (Willan Press, 2008) and *An Introduction to Criminological Theory* (2001, 2005, 2009).

Criminal Justice Theory

An introduction

Roger Hopkins Burke

Routledge
Taylor & Francis Group

LONDON AND NEW YORK

First published 2012
by Routledge
2 Park Square, Milton Park, Abingdon, Oxon, OX14 4RN

Simultaneously published in the USA and Canada
by Routledge
711 Third Avenue, New York, NY 10017

Routledge is an imprint of the Taylor & Francis Group, an informa business

British Library Cataloguing in Publication Data
A catalogue record for this book is available from the British Library

Library of Congress Cataloging-in-Publication Data
Burke, Roger Hopkins.
Criminal justice theory : an introduction / by Roger Hopkins-Burke.
p. cm.
Includes bibliographical references and index.
1. Criminal justice, Administration of–Philosophy. 2. Criminology.
3. Corrections–Philosophy. 4. Police administration–Philosophy. I. Title.
HV7419.B87 2011
364.01–dc23
2011018288

ISBN 13: 978–0–415–49096–2 (hbk)
ISBN 13: 978–0–415–49097–9 (pbk)
ISBN 13: 978–0–203–88051–7 (ebk)

Typeset in Times New Roman by Keystroke, Station Road, Codsall, Wolverhampton

MIX
Paper from
responsible sources
FSC® C004839

Printed and bound in Great Britain by the MPG Books Group

For Kristan, Thomas and Oliver

Contents

1 Introduction

Modernity and criminal justice

This is a book about criminal justice theory. Students of criminal justice and the law – and in reality other disciplines as well – are invariably overwhelmed by the word 'theory' which they seem to subconsciously associate with the esoteric or even the mythical and scary 'rocket science' with the outcome being an inherent resistance to the subject matter. Theory nevertheless in reality means 'explanation' and is simply about how and, most importantly, 'why' we do some things and in the form that we do.

There seems to be no academic consensus as to what exactly constitutes a 'criminal justice theory' but this text approaches the task by explaining from different, often competing, but sometimes complementary, perspectives why the various components of the 'criminal justice system' operate in the way that they do and in whose interest. This book thus considers the theoretical underpinnings of criminal justice and its institutions and in doing so considers the areas of legal philosophy and ethics, explaining criminal behaviour (criminological theory), policing, the court process, punishment or penology and youth justice. The theories discussed are significantly all the products of an era encompassing approximately the past three centuries which has come to be termed the modern age and it is a time period which has its origins in a period of great intellectual ferment and activity known as the European Enlightenment.

The European Enlightenment and the rise of the modern age

The European Enlightenment involved the development of a whole range of thought concerning the nature of human beings, their relationship with each other, institutions, society and the state, and in doing so, provided the guiding ideas of the modern age. This is not to say that all of these ideas have stood the test of time and circumstance, but before the eighteenth century, the human world and the ideas that underpinned it are distinctly less recognisable to modern observers than those which emerged and struggled to gain acceptance in that tumultuous period.

Many of the ideas of the Enlightenment stressed commonalities among people and, in doing so, threatened the social domination of the aristocracy and the established Church. Before this time the common people had been encouraged by the church to simply accept their lot in life but with the rise of Protestantism and the 'Protestant ethic' people came to expect success for hard work in this world and not to have to wait until the 'afterlife'. Consequently, many people could now identify a direct connection between hard work and success, while assumptions about the natural superiority of the powerful aristocracy, and their right to economic wealth and political power, came to be challenged.

Writers of the Enlightenment period were concerned with exploring social conditions and thus, in the late eighteenth century, John Howard wrote *The State of the Prisons in England and Wales*, Immanuel Kant produced his great essay *Fundamental Principles of the Metaphysics of Morals* and Jeremy Bentham presented his *Introduction to the Principles of Morals and Legislation*. Inspired by such ideas and responding to dramatically changing economic and political circumstances, revolutions occurred in the American colonies and in France, giving rise to political systems that would embrace the new conceptions of individual rationality and free will. These revolutions moreover prompted changes in ideas concerning human rights that were championed in many European countries by the merchant, professional and middle classes and these developments introduced significant changes in the nature of systems of government, administration and law.

The eighteenth century was thus a period of enormous and significant change. The authority of the old aristocracies was being seriously questioned, both because of their claims to natural superiority and their corrupt political practices. A new and increasingly powerful middle class was benefiting from the profits of trade, industry, and agricultural rationalisation and in the interests of the latter the enclosure movement dispossessed many of the rural poor from access to common lands and smallholding tenancies. This movement caused great hardship to many of the rural poor yet, at the same time, produced a readily available pool of cheap labour to satisfy the demands of the Industrial Revolution. As a result of these changes, societies were becoming increasingly industrialised and urbanised, with previous standard forms of human relationships based on familiarity, reputation and localism yielding to more fluid, often anonymous interactions which posed significant problems for existing forms of social control.

Traditional conceptions of property and ownership were disrupted by these social changes and the enclosure movement provides a good example. In the interests of maximising the economic viability of agricultural land, many landowners fenced in previously open tracts of common land and this process gradually deprived ordinary people of what had been their customary rights to use common land and its resources such as game, fish, firewood, food plants and fruits. These changes created popular resentment among the poorer sections of the largely rural society and seriously jeopardised the agricultural and rural power base of the traditional aristocracy. The plight of the poor was, moreover, in sharp contrast to the wealth of the newly affluent classes which was displayed in the streets of the growing urban areas, in close proximity to the dispossessed who had migrated to the towns in order to find employment. The rich, even though they tended to reside in separate parts of the new towns and cities from the poor, were nonetheless no longer as geographically isolated in their everyday affairs. Those employed in harsh circumstances in manufacturing or processing, or not employed at all, were at best tempted and at worst provoked. Koestler and Rolph (1961: 34) observe: 'all foreign visitors agreed that never before had the world seen such riches and splendour as displayed in London's residences and shops – nor so many pick-pockets, burglars and highwaymen'.

Criminal justice in the pre-modern era

In pre-modern Europe, criminal behaviour had been primarily explained for over a thousand years by notions of spiritualism and demonology – where criminals were said to be possessed by demons who forced them to do things beyond their control – and legal systems during that era were founded on these religious explanations of crime. Little law was written or codified and that which did exist was applied erratically, via judicial discretion and whim, and was targeted predominantly by the powerful aristocracy against the significantly less powerful general population. Those accused of crimes often faced secret accusations, torture and closed trials with arbitrary and harsh sanctions applied to the convicted. The emphasis of punishment was on the physical body of the accused, the bulk of the population possessing little else on which the power to punish could be exercised (Foucault, 1977). Generally there were few written laws and those which did exist were applied mainly to those who were not of the aristocracy.

Punishments inflicted on those found guilty of contravening criminal codes in the pre-modern period were thus extremely severe and brutal. Foucault (1977: 3) provides an account of a form of public execution reserved for the greatest of all crimes under the French *ancien régime*, regicide:

> The flesh will be torn from the breasts, arms, thighs and calves with red-hot pincers, his right hand, holding the knife with which he committed the said parricide, burnt with sulphur, and, on those places where the flesh will be torn away, poured molten lead, boiling oil, burning resin, wax and sulphur melted together and then his body drawn and quartered by four horses and his limbs and body consumed by fire.

Torture was in general use in all of Europe except England, where judicial torture was only available under a special warrant issued by the Crown. In the 100 years from 1540 to 1640 only 89 of these were issued, for offences ranging from treason to horse stealing. In England after 1640, the use of torture appears to have declined. Langbein (1974) argued that general changes in the laws of evidence and proof rendered torture 'unnecessary' in the legal process. It had been previously necessary in order to ensure a secure conviction to have a confession of guilt and/or two eyewitnesses. One eyewitness, or a strong probability of guilt, was insufficient for the courts, thus torture had to be used to secure a confession. Gradually this strict law of proof was relaxed and it was no longer necessary to use torture in order to obtain a conviction. It was thus no longer essential to the successful functioning of the criminal justice system.

Punishment nevertheless frequently involved torture and furthermore the death sentence was very common. In some jurisdictions the possibility of being tortured to death remained a penal option into the nineteenth century but in England penal torture was not used except in exceptional cases for treason. Scotland retained, at least in legal theory, although certainly not in practice, hanging, drawing and quartering for treason until 1948. Punishments such as whipping were, however, common while over 200 offences, such as shooting a rabbit, carried a sentence of death by hanging. Imprisonment was rarely used as a punishment.

Prisons were most commonly places for holding suspects and offenders prior to trial or punishment, except in cases of debt when they were used to hold debtors until their financial affairs could be settled. It would appear that the powerful in society, who framed and administrated the law, enacted and exercised the criminal codes on the premise that it was only the threat of savage and cruel punishments, delivered in public and with theatrical emphasis, that would deter the dangerous, generally materially dispossessed classes who constituted 'the mob' of whom they were mortally afraid.

From the seventeenth to the early nineteenth century the affluent classes, led by the rural English aristocracy, sought to protect their increasing property interests through the exercise of the criminal law. Vast numbers of property crimes were thus made punishable by death, giving this particular sudden increase in legislation the title 'The Bloody Code'. Capital statutes (those which allow for the use of the death penalty) were enacted en masse in the hope that such punishments would strike fear into the hearts of potential malefactors and serve to deter them from offending. In England, the standard form of execution was by hanging in public which was a highly theatrical and symbolic ritual. It was anticipated that such dramatic, public punishment would serve to restore the majesty of the law and those in whose interests it was exercised.

Each eighteenth-century statute permitted a 'branching out' to cover a host of related offences. Radzinowicz (1948) shows how in this way the standard punishment for murder (execution) also became applicable to stealing turnips, writing threatening letters, being found armed or disguised in a forest, stealing from a rabbit warren, poaching, forgery, picking pockets, cutting down a tree, impersonating an outpatient of Greenwich Hospital, damaging a fishpond, or 'consorting with gypsies'. For this last offence 13 people were hanged at one assize (local court sitting).

It is estimated that by 1800 there were more than 250 capital offences and in the early eighteenth century public executions took place every six weeks with five to 15 people hanged on each occasion (Lofland, 1973). Koestler and Rolph (1961) attribute this flood of savage legislation to three major factors. First, there was England's lead in the Industrial Revolution which meant that there were no precedents for jurists to consider in terms of foreign experience. Indeed, other countries in this period were reducing the rigours of criminal punishment under the influence of the Enlightenment. Second, they identify a traditional British dislike of certain kinds of authority, notably political authority, as illustrated by works such as Burke's *Reflections on the Revolution in France* of 1790 and the Liberal Reform Movements which both vigorously promoted the ultimate sovereignty of the individual.

This British wariness of state interference with individual civil liberties was to a large extent the barrier to the provision of alternative forms of crime control, such as the establishment of a modern, centralised, state directed and controlled police force, as had been developed in France. At this time Britain maintained a highly localised and largely inefficient network of police and watch organisations which were completely breaking down under the chaos of their informality and the new demands for order brought on by the growth of towns and cities. There was nevertheless substantial resistance to efforts to establish a regular professional police force and this came from almost all classes of society, and appears to have been based on a deeply held suspicion and fear that such a force would become state-funded 'spies' on the population. Despite some specialist, local and private provision, the first formal professional police force was not established in England until 1829 and that after considerable resistance and as a result of a carefully brokered political and constitutional compromise.

Third, there was the English state and notably the judiciary. In this period England was ruled by an oligarchy based freely on wealth, preoccupied by the sanctity of the property that comprised that prosperity and with their status-based authority in the nation. The legislators and enforcers of the law were prominent members of this oligarchy and their influence was diffused throughout the country by their local structures of magistrates' benches drawn from the 'squirearchy' of the local gentry.

This observation is well illustrated by the way in which the judges of England dealt with the 'Waltham Black Act'. This was a piece of legislation passed through Parliament, with hardly any debate, in order to introduce new powers and vigour to deal with what was perceived by the aristocracy to be a local crime crisis. The Act was engineered to permit judges to extend the use of the death penalty to punish a whole range of generally minor property offences. Even when faced with protests from reformers, the senior judges, who sat in Parliament, replied firmly in the words of the Chief Justice of the Common Peace, Lord Wynford: Nolemus legus Angliae mutari (We do not wish the laws of England to be changed).

Many judges advocated the extension of capital legislation and their interpretations of existing law established precedents to be followed in subsequent cases. This was a one-way process, making every aggravation of the law irreversible, but this extension of capital legislation and judicial precedent had remarkably little effect on levels of property crime. Many years later, Lord Justice Devlin reflected:

> The judges of England have rarely been original thinkers or great jurists. Many have been craftsmen rather than creators. They have needed the stuff of morals to be supplied to them so that out of it they could fashion law. When they have to make their own stuff their work is inferior.
>
> (Quoted in Koestler and Rolph, 1961: 55)

It was nevertheless the gradual permeation of Enlightenment ideas that was to provide the moral basis to soften the rigour of the draconian Bloody Code.

Despite the vast numbers of offences for which the death penalty could be exercised, and the fact that many thousands were hanged for what might today be regarded as extremely minor offences, the full weight of the law was not always applied. Clemency and leniency, permitted at the discretion of the judge, were used by the rural aristocracy, who also sat as judges and 'Justices of the Peace' (JPs), to demonstrate their power over the 'lower orders'. Evidence of 'respectability' by way of the provision of references from a benevolent landowner, evidence of significant religious observance and piety, or the simple whim of a JP could lead to an offender being handed a lesser sentence. Such discretion allowed transportation to a colony, a non-fatal, if brutal, corporal punishment, or even release, to take the place of hanging (Thompson, 1975; Hay *et al.*, 1975; Hay, 1981).

Social contract theory and utilitarianism

The late seventeenth and eighteenth centuries saw an explosion in writings critical of established religious dictates and interpretations of the nature of the world. Some of these writers were devout, if critical, Christians, some were committed to a distinctly secular view of the world, others deferred to the prevailing religious ideas of the time, often to avoid conflict with established authority. The two major sets of ideas which underpinned this change were *social contract theories* and *utilitarianism*.

Social contract theories

The essence of social contract theories is the idea that legitimate government is the artificial product of the voluntary agreement of free moral agents and that there is no such thing as 'natural' political authority as asserted by the monarchical regimes which preceded and contested the development of the Enlightenment. An influential version of this approach, developed by the philosopher John Locke, could be summarised by his assertion that 'voluntary agreement gives political power to governors' (Locke 1970, originally 1689).

Social contract theories were to undergo something of a revival in the last quarter of the twentieth century, both in the study of politics and economics and as justifications for government policies such as those introduced by Prime Minister Margaret Thatcher in the UK. However, the 'golden age' of social contract theories was the period 1650–1800 and while there are influential precursors of these theories in the works of Ancient Greek philosophy, and later in medieval thought, the 'high points' of the approach are generally considered to begin with Thomas Hobbes and his book *Leviathan* (Hobbes, 1968, originally 1651).

Social contract theories are generally based on the notion that people are able to exercise their *will* freely – or *voluntaristically* – and were probably influenced by parallel developments in Christian theology. From this religious perspective, for a 'good act' to be performed the actor has to knowingly and willingly perform the act and know that it is 'good'. Hence a 'good' form of politics requires the moral assent and volition of individuals. The individual emphasis of this approach was compounded by the growing influence of the individualistically oriented forms of Christianity promoted by the 'Protestantism' that had earlier emerged following the Reformation and which had provided a practical criticism of the established Catholic versions of Christianity, prior to the Enlightenment.

Given the influence of religion on politics, it was predictable that the Protestant view of individual moral autonomy should emerge from theology and moral philosophy into the political arena, providing an intellectual basis for social contract theories. Protestantism thus questioned the automatic 'excellence' of established church institutions and they now required the authorisation and voluntary acquiescence of individuals.

This perspective came to be applied to the authority of states, the basis of whose authority was generally associated with that of churches. Hence, after the seventeenth century the idea of the state as an intrinsically 'good' institution came to be subjected to revisionist arguments that insisted that its power should be *legitimised* by the free assent of its subjects. The influence on contemporary thought of seventeenth-, eighteenth-, and early nineteenth-century writers such as Hobbes, Locke and Rousseau, who raised criticisms of the exercise of arbitrary powers by monarchs, established churches and aristocratic interests, provides the theoretical foundations for specific attacks on previous legal systems and practices. It is to these writers that we now turn our attention.

Thomas Hobbes (1588–1678) emphasised that it is the exercise of human free will that is the fundamental basis of a legitimate social contract. Compliance can be enforced by the fear of punishment, but only if entry into the contract and the promise to comply with it has been freely willed, given and subsequently broken. Hobbes held a rather negative view of humanity and proposed a need for social institutions – the origins of the very idea of modern criminal justice systems – to support social contracts and to enforce laws. He claimed that in a 'state of nature' – or without outside intervention in their lives – people would be engaged in a 'war of all against all' and life would tend to be 'nasty, brutish and short'. He thus proposed that people should freely subject themselves to the power of an absolute ruler or institution – a 'Leviathan' – which, as the result of a political-social contract, would be legitimately empowered to enforce the contracts that subjects make between themselves (Hobbes, 1968).

John Locke (1632–1704) had a more complex conception of what people are like 'in the state of nature' and argued that there is a natural law that constitutes and protects essential rights of life, liberty and property: key assumptions that, subsequently, were to significantly shape the constitutional arrangements of the USA. Locke proposed that the Christian God has presented all people with common access to the 'fruits of the earth', but at the same time individual property rights can be legitimately created when labour is mixed with the produce of the land, for example by cultivating crops or extracting minerals. People nevertheless have a natural duty not to accumulate more land or goods than they can use and if this natural law is observed then a rough equality can be achieved in the distribution of natural resources. Unfortunately, this natural potential towards egalitarianism had been compromised by the development of a money economy that has made it possible for people to obtain control over more goods and land than they can use as individuals.

Locke saw the transition from a state of nature to the development of a political society as a response to desires, conflict and ethical uncertainty brought about by the growth of the use of money and the material inequalities that consequently arose. The expansion of political institutions is thus necessary to create a social contract to alleviate the problems of inequality generated by this distortion of natural law. For Locke, social contracts develop through three stages. First, people must agree unanimously to come together as a community and to pool their natural powers in order to act together to secure and uphold the natural rights of each other. Second, the members of this community must agree, by a majority vote, to set up legislative and other institutions. Third, the owners of property must agree, either personally or through political representatives, to whatever taxes that are imposed on them.

Locke rejected Hobbes' view that people should surrender themselves to the absolute rule of a Leviathan and argued, in contrast, that people gain their natural rights to life and liberty from the Christian God and hold them effectively in trust so they are not, therefore, theirs to transfer to the arbitrary power of another. He moreover argued that government is established in order to protect rights to property and not to undermine them and cannot, therefore, legitimately take or redistribute property without consent. It is not the task of human legislation to replace natural law and rights but to give them the precision, clarity and impartial enforceability that are unattainable in the state of nature.

Although Locke had a relatively optimistic view of human potential in the state of nature, he nevertheless observed the inevitable potential for conflict and corruption that occurs with the increasing complexity of human endeavour and the 'invention' of money. If natural rights are to be preserved, what is required is the consensual development of institutions to clarify, codify and maintain these rights to life, liberty and property. In short, these institutions should constrain all equally in the interests of social harmony (Locke, 1970).

Jean-Jacques Rousseau (1712–1778) was a severe critic of some of the major aspects of the emerging modern world arguing that the spread of scientific and literary activity led to moral corruption. He emphasised that human beings had evolved from an animal-like state of nature in which isolated, somewhat stupid individuals lived peacefully as 'noble savages'. Rousseau (1964, originally 1762) had claimed that humans were naturally free and equal, animated by the principles of self-preservation and pity. It was when they came together into groups and societies, engaging in communal activities that gave rise to rules and regulations, that the 'natural man' evolved into a competitive and selfish 'social man', capable of rational calculation and of intentionally inflicting harm on others. Rousseau thus had a pessimistic view of social change and was unconvinced that the human species was progressing. Civilisation was not a boon to humanity; it was 'un-natural' and would always be accompanied by costs that outweighed the benefits.

With his later work, Rousseau (1978, originally 1775) appeared a little more optimistic about the future of humanity but he still asserted that at the beginning of history people were admirable, fundamentally equal, free individuals and that moral corruption and injustice arose as people came to develop more complex forms of society and become dependent on one another, thus risking exploitation and disappointment. He was, however, now prepared to propose political solutions to the moral corruption of society, arguing the necessity of establishing human laws that consider all individuals equally and give each a free vote on the enactment of legislation.

Rousseau developed the concept of the *general will*, observing that in addition to individual self-interest, citizens have a collective interest in the well-being of the community. Indeed, he traced the foundations of the law and political society to this idea of the 'general will' – a citizen body, acting as a whole, and freely choosing to adopt laws that will apply equally to all citizens.

Rousseau's work presented a radical democratic challenge to the French monarchical *ancien régime* proposing that it was the 'citizen body' – not kings – that were 'sovereign' and government should represent their interests. It was only in this way that individuals could freely vote for, and obey, the law as an expression of the common good, without contradicting their own interests and needs.

Rousseau considered that he had resolved the dilemma of human selfishness and collective interests posed by Hobbes. Moreover, he had done this without denying the potential existence of a positive and active form of civic freedom, based on self-sacrifice for a legitimate political community.

Social contract theories provide an overwhelming critique of pre-modern forms of government and are highly relevant to the development of the rational actor model of crime and criminal behaviour that we will encounter in the following chapter. First, there is the claim that human beings once lived in a state of 'innocence', 'grace' or 'nature'. Second, there is the recognition that the emergence of humanity from its primitive state involved the application of *reason* – an appreciation of the meaning and consequences of actions – by responsible individuals. Third, the human 'will' is recognised as a psychological reality, a faculty of the individual that regulates and controls behaviour, and is generally free. Fourth, society has a 'right' to inflict punishment although this right has been transferred to the political state, and a system of punishments for forbidden acts, or a 'code of criminal law'.

Thus, human beings are viewed as 'rational actors', freely choosing to enter into contracts with others to perform interpersonal or civic duties. Laws can legitimately be used to ensure compliance if they have been properly approved by citizens who are party to the social contract.

Utilitarianism

A further major intellectual contribution to the development of the rational actor model was the philosophical tradition termed *utilitarianism*. Essentially this philosophy assesses the rightness of acts, policies, decisions and choices by their tendency to promote the 'happiness' of those affected by them. The two most closely associated adherents and developers of the approach were the political philosophers Jeremy Bentham and John Stuart Mill.

Jeremy Bentham (1748–1832) proposed that the actions of human beings are acceptable if they promote happiness, and they are unacceptable if they produce the opposite of happiness. This is the basis of morality. His most famous axiom is the call for society to produce 'the greatest happiness of the greatest number'. 'Happiness' is understood to be pleasure and unhappiness is pain, or the absence of pleasure. The moral principle arising from this perspective is that if individuals use their reason to pursue their own pleasure then a state of positive social equilibrium will naturally emerge.

For Bentham, pleasures and pains were to be assessed, or 'weighed', on the basis of their intensity, duration and proximity. Moreover, such a calculus was considered to be person-neutral, that is, capable of being applied to the different pleasures of different people. The extent of the pleasure – or the total number of people experiencing it – was also a part of the calculation of the rightness of the outcome of an act. The overall aim was to provide a calculation whereby the net balance of pleasure over pain could be determined as a measure of the rightness of an act or policy.

John Stuart Mill (1806–1873) generally accepted the position of Bentham including his emphasis on hedonism as the basic human trait that governs and motivates the actions of every individual. Mill nevertheless wanted to distinguish qualities – as well as quantities – of pleasures, and this posed problems. For it is unclear whether a distinction between qualities of pleasures – whether one can be considered more worthwhile than another – can be sustained or measured. Mill emphasised, first, that pure self-interest was an inadequate basis for utilitarianism, and suggested that we should take as the real criterion of good, the social consequences of the act. Second, he proposed that some pleasures rank higher than others, with those of the intellect superior to those of the senses. Importantly, both social factors and the quality of the act were seen as important in seeking an explanation for human behaviour.

Mill has proved to be a formidable and influential philosophical force but it is Bentham who has had the greatest impact on the development of the rational actor model of crime and criminal behaviour. He essentially provided two central additions to social contract theory. First, there is his notion that the principal control over the unfettered exercise of free will is that of fear; especially the fear of pain. Second, there is the axiom that punishment is the main way of creating fear in order to influence the will and thus control behaviour.

Modern societies

The notion of the modern involved a secular rational tradition which can be summarised in the following four origins we observed above. First, there was the emergence of humanist ideas and Protestantism in the sixteenth century.

Previously the common people had been encouraged by the established church to unquestioningly accept their position in life and look for salvation in the afterlife. It was with the rise of the 'protestant ethic' that people came to expect immediate material success in return for hard work in this world. At the same time, assumptions about the natural superiority – or the divine right – of the powerful aristocracy came to be questioned. Second, there was the scientific revolution of the seventeenth century where our understanding of the world around us was first explained by reference to natural laws. Third, there was the eighteenth-century philosophical Enlightenment where it was proposed that the social world could similarly be explained and regulated by natural laws. Political systems should be developed that embraced new ideas of individual rationality and free will. Indeed, inspired by such ideas and responding to dramatically changing economic and political circumstances, revolutions occurred in the American colonies and in France. These were widely influential and ideas concerning human rights were championed in many European countries by the merchant, professional and middle classes. Subsequently, there were to be significant changes in the nature of systems of government, administration, law and criminal justice. Fourth, there was the increasingly evident power of industrial society and the prestige afforded to scientific explanation in the nineteenth and twentieth centuries that seemed to confirm the superiority of the modernist intellectual tradition over all others (Harvey, 1989).

The key characteristics that epitomise the idea of modern society can be identified in three main areas. First, in the area of economics there was the development of a market economy which involves the growth of production for profit, rather than immediate local use, the development of industrial technology with a considerable extension of the division of labour and wage labour which became the principal form of employment. Second, in the area of politics there was the growth and consolidation of the centralised nation-state and the extension of bureaucratic forms of administration, systematic forms of surveillance, control and criminal justice, the development of representative democracy and political party systems. Third, in the area of culture there was a challenge to tradition in the name of rationality with the emphasis being on scientific and technical knowledge. The modern world – and the increasingly bureaucratised institutions that came to characterise it – was consequently a very different place from its pre-modern predecessor. Not surprisingly, therefore, modern explanations of crime and criminal behaviour – and the nature of criminal justice interventions that were introduced in order to combat crime – were different from those that had existed in pre-modern times.

Four models of criminal justice development

This book explains from different theoretical perspectives why it is that the various components of the 'criminal justice system' or 'criminal justice process' have come to operate in the way that they do and in whose interests they function in modern societies. Four different models of criminal justice development are thus now outlined, in which the various criminal justice theories that we will encounter in this book can be located and which provide different explanations for how, why and in whose interests the law and the agencies of the criminal justice system have developed during the past 300 years or the modern period. These models of criminal justice development are: (1) the orthodox social progress model; (2) the radical conflict model; (3) the carceral surveillance society model; and (4) the left realist hybrid model.

The orthodox social progress model

The orthodox social progress model is – as its name suggests – the standard non-critical explanation which considers the development of law and the criminal justice system to be predominantly non-contentious. These institutions operate neutrally in the interests of all. The concept of progress in history is the idea of an advance that occurs within the limits of the collective morality and knowledge of humanity and its environment. It is an idea often associated with the Western notion of a straight linear direction as developed by the early Greek philosophers Aristotle and Plato and which was to influence the later Judeo-Christian doctrine. The idea spread during the Renaissance in Europe between the fourteenth and sixteenth centuries and this marked the end of the static view of history and society that had been characteristic of feudalism. By the eighteenth and nineteenth centuries – and during the great Industrial Revolution that was to transform western Europe and instigate the rise of modern society – belief in progress was to become the dominant paradigm non-critically accepted by most people.

Social progress is defined as the changing of society toward the ideal and was a concept introduced in early nineteenth-century social theories especially those of social evolutionists like Auguste Comte (1798–1857) and Herbert Spencer (1820–1903). The former was a philosopher and social visionary and is perhaps best known for giving a name to the discipline of sociology that he nevertheless outlined rather than practised. Central to his thought was his search in chaotic times – exemplified by the major transition from predominantly agrarian to urban societies throughout western Europe – for principles of cultural and political order that were consistent with the apparent forward march of society. Spencer was the major theorist of social evolutionism and held the view that human characteristics are inherited and it was this aspect of his work that was to be a major influence on the development of the predestined actor model of crime and criminal behaviour we will encounter in the next chapter. Spencer went much further than the natural scientist Darwin and explained evolution as the product of the progressive adaptation of the individual character to the 'social state' or society; his major contribution to the development of sociology is his recognition that human beings develop as part of a process of interaction with the social world they inhabit.

The orthodox social progress model of modern criminal justice development in the modern era should thus be seen in this evolutionary context. From this perspective, it proposed that the development of modern societies, their laws and criminal justice systems is the product of enlightenment, benevolence and a consensual society where the whole population shares the same core values and which develops an increasingly progressive humanitarian response to crime and disorder. Cohen (1985) observes that from this liberal perspective the impetus for change is seen to come from developments in ideals, visions, theories, intentions and advances in knowledge. All change is 'reform' and, moreover, this is a term without any negative connotations. All reform is motivated by benevolence, altruism, philanthropy and humanitarianism with the collective outcome of a succession of reforms being progress. Theories of criminal justice – and other associated disciplines such as criminology and psychology – provide the scientific support or knowledge base to inform the particular reform programme, and changes occur when the reform vision becomes more refined and ideas more sophisticated.

Thus, for example, the orthodox social progress perspective on the development of the public police service observes the emergence, expansion and consolidation of a bureaucratic professionalised service to be part of a progressive humanitarian development of institutions considered necessary to respond to crime and disorder in the interests of the whole of society (Reith, 1956). It is observed that the effectiveness of the pre-modern system of policing had been based on stable, homogeneous and largely rural communities where people knew one another by name, sight and/or reputation. During the eighteenth century such communities had begun to break down in the face of the rapid transition to an industrial economy while at the same time the unpaid and frequently reluctant incumbents of posts such as the parish constable and the watch failed to carry out their duties with great diligence. Many employed substitutes who were more often than not ill-paid, ignorant and too old to be effective in their duties. The local watch was also often demoralised, drunk on duty and did little to suppress crime.

The fast-expanding towns and cities were increasingly becoming a haven for the poor and those dispossessed of their land as a result of the land enclosures we encountered above, while the rookeries, slum areas and improvised shelters for the poor grew rapidly in the eighteenth century as the urban areas expanded to serve the labour needs of the growing industrial machine. These areas were extremely overcrowded, lacked elementary sanitation, and were characterised by disease, grinding poverty, excessive drinking and casual violence. Prostitution and thieving were everywhere (Emsley, 1996, 2001). From the orthodox social progress perspective the establishment of the first professional police service in 1829 and its subsequent development occurred in the interest of all groups and classes in society who needed protection from the criminality and disorder in their midst.

Similarly, contemporary notions of childhood and adolescence were formed or socially constructed,[1] to use sociological language, at the outset of the modern era. Children and increasingly their families were disciplined, controlled and placed under surveillance because motivated entrepreneurial philanthropists had genuine humanitarian concerns about poor urban children and young people at risk from the numerous dangers on the streets, including criminality and a failure to find God, and were keen to do something about this problem in the interests of the whole of society and not least of the children and the parents themselves.

Cohen (1985) further observes that, in terms of the orthodox social progress model, criminal justice institutions do not actually 'fail' to achieve their aims and objectives, which might seem to be almost self-evident to the neutral observer. Instead they adapt and modify themselves in the face of changing scientific knowledge and social circumstances. This vision is nevertheless not complacent. The system is recognised to be flawed in practical and even moral terms; bad mistakes are seen to be made and abuses to occur. From the social progress perspective all these problems can be solved, nevertheless, over time, with the provision of more resources (invariably more money), better trained staff and improved facilities. Thus, all can be humanised and improved with the application of scientific principles and reason.[2]

Cohen (1985) observes that the orthodox social progress model is a contemporary variant of Enlightenment beliefs in progress and its supporters and adherents are the genuine heirs to the nineteenth-century reform tradition. It is in many ways the most important model, not least because it represents taken for granted mainstream opinion and is thus the orthodox view held by most. There is, nonetheless, a more recent, radical, cynical, ambivalent, critical variant to this liberal reform story which has emerged from the mid-1960s onwards. Yet, while critical of the purist version of that history it can still be conceptualised in the liberal reform tradition, not least because of its tendency to propose orthodox solutions to even major significant failure. Cohen (1985: 19), in his discussion of the development of the penal system in modern society, observes the extent of that failure:

> The message was that the reform vision itself is potentially suspect. The record is not just one of good intentions going wrong now and then, but of continual and disastrous failure. The gap between rhetoric and reality is so vast that either the rhetoric itself is deeply flawed or social reality resists all such reform attempts.

This revisionist variant of the orthodox social progress model thus tells a less idealist account than the purist history. Ideas and intentions are still important and to be taken seriously, but not as the simple products of humanitarian caprice or even advances in knowledge. They are functional solutions to immediate social changes. Rothman (1971) discusses the establishment and development of the asylum in the USA at the end of the eighteenth century and in doing so provides the original revisionist variant of the social progress model. He observes that in the aftermath of the War of Independence there emerged a new restless, dispossessed, socially mobile and potentially dangerous population while there was a simultaneous widespread sense that the old traditional modes of social control based on small self-policing local communities were now seriously outdated. The asylum was conceived as a microcosm of the perfect social order, a utopian experiment in which criminals and the insane could be isolated from bad influences and would be changed by subjection to a regime of discipline, order and regulation.

This goal of changing the individual was clearly based on a very optimistic worldview on the nature of humanity but there was, however, soon to be a widespread proliferation in these institutions. By the late nineteenth century it was clear that they had failed in their honourable, rehabilitative intentions and had degenerated into mere custodial institutions. Rothman nevertheless observes that regardless of their failure and widespread derogatory criticisms these institutions were retained and sustained because of their functionality and the enduring power of the rhetoric of benevolence. They kept a dangerous population off the streets. Rothman (1980) develops his argument further by observing degeneration in closed institutions in the early decades of the twentieth century which occurred regardless of the introduction of a progressive reform package. The outcome of this disappointment was a search for alternatives, which was to lead to the ideal of individual treatment, the case-by-case method and the introduction of psychiatric doctrines and attempts to humanise all closed institutions. But yet again none of the programmes turned out the way their designers had intended. Cohen (1985: 20) observes that:

> Closed institutions hardly changed and were certainly not humanized; the new programmes became supplements, not alternatives, thus expanding the scope and reach of the system; discretion actually became more arbitrary; individual treatment was barely attempted, let alone successful. Once again, however, failure and persistence went hand in hand: operational needs ensured survival while benevolent rhetoric buttressed a long discredited system, deflected criticism and justified 'more of the same'.

For Rothman the crucial concept is that of 'convenience', which does not, in reality, undermine the original vision or 'conscience' but actually aids in its acceptance. The managers of the system and their staff come to actively embrace the new programmes and use them to their advantage. A useful political alliance is thus developed between the reformers and the managers and this allows the system to survive even though it appears to be a total failure. Rothman (1980) observes that it is essential that we have a critical understanding of the origins of the original reform vision, the political interests behind them, their internal paradoxes and the nature of their appeal, for this creates a story that is far more complicated than terms such as 'reform', 'progress', 'doing good', 'benevolence' and 'humanitarianism' suggest. This revisionist account provides a significantly more critical account than the simplistic purist version of the orthodox social progress model but it nevertheless remains a liberal model that still believes that things can be improved if we learn the correct lessons from history and research. The radical conflict model to which we now turn our attention goes much further and identifies an inherent problematic contradiction in the very nature of capitalist society.

The radical conflict model

Proponents and supporters of the social progress model – whether in its purist or revisionist form – nevertheless fundamentally agree that society is characterised by consensus. Proponents of the radical conflict model, in contrast, argue that society is inherently conflict-ridden. Max Weber (1864–1920) had influentially argued that conflict is intrinsic in society and arises from the inevitable battle within the economic market place – between different interest groups with different levels of power – over the distribution of scarce material resources. The radical conflict model of criminal justice development is heavily influenced by the work of Karl Marx (1818–1883) who – in a simplified account of a complex and highly contested materialist philosophy[3] – goes significantly further than Weber and argues that economic inequality is inherent in society with the outcome being an inevitable conflict between antagonistic irreconcilable social classes. Those who own and control the capitalist mode of production are also in the final analysis in control of the political and civil institutions in society which, in turn, are used to maintain and sustain the capitalist system in the interests of the rich and powerful, to the disadvantage of the poor and powerless or for that matter anyone not owning capital.

From the radical conflict perspective, it is proposed that the story of the development of the criminal justice system during the modern era is neither what it appears to be, nor, for that matter, can it be considered to be in any way a 'failure'. For the new control system served more than adequately the requirements of the emerging capitalist order for the continued repression of recalcitrant members of the working class and, at the same time, continued to persuade everyone (including the reformers themselves) that these changes were fair, humane and progressive.

It is thus argued from this perspective that the professional police were from their very formation at the beginning of the modern period 'domestic missionaries' with an emphasis on the surveillance, discipline and control of the rough and dangerous working-class elements in society in the interests of the capitalist class (Storch, 1975); while contemporary 'hard' strategies such as zero tolerance policing which are ostensibly targeted at socially excluded groups in society are simply a continuation of that tradition (see Crowther, 1998, 2000a, 2000b; Hopkins Burke, 1998a, 2004a). At the same time, children and their families were disciplined and controlled from the early nineteenth century in the interests of an industrial capitalism which required a fit, healthy, increasingly educated, trained, but always obedient workforce (Hopkins Burke, 2008). The motor force of history is thus the political economy and the requirements of the dominant mode of production which in the modern era is capitalism. Ideology is only important in that it succeeds in passing off as fair, natural and just, a system which is basically coercive and unfair. It is only the outside observer, uncontaminated by false consciousness, who can really know what is going on.[4]

Rusche and Kirchheimer (1968, originally 1938) provide the earliest version of the radical conflict model and they begin from the principle that changes in the mode of production correspond with changing dominant forms of punishment in society. Hence, the origins and development of penal systems were determined by and, therefore, must be studied in terms of, primarily economic and fiscal forces. Their central argument is that in societies where workers are scarce and work plentiful, punishment is required to make the unwilling work, and when there is a surplus of labour (or a reserve army) harsh punishments are used to keep the workless under control. The status of the labour market thus determines the form and severity of punishment. The reformed prison renders docile the non-compliant members of the working class, it deters others; it teaches habits of discipline and order; it reproduces the lost hierarchy; it repairs defective humans to compete in the market place and rehabilitation is used in the interests of capitalism. Increasingly, the state takes on a more and more active role in guiding, coordinating and planning a criminal justice system which can achieve a more thorough, rationalised penetration of the subject population.

Melossi and Pavarini (1981) take this argument further and argue that the functional connection between the prison and society can be found in the concept of discipline. The point is to create a socially safe proletarian who has learned to accept being propertyless without threatening the very institution of property. The capitalist organisation of labour shapes the form of the prison as it does other institutions and nothing can change this. The control system continues to replicate and perpetuate the forms necessary to ensure the survival of the capitalist social order.

Ignatieff (1978) produces a rather different 'softer' version of the radical control model and in doing so rejects the rather simplistic straightforward 'economic determinism'[5] and 'left functionalism'[6] of the purist version above and observes the 'complex and autonomous structure and philosophical beliefs' which led reformers to conceive of the penitentiary. It is these beliefs and not the functional necessity of the economic system nor the 'fiction of a ruling class with a strategic conception of its functional requirements' which explains why the penitentiary was adopted to solve the 'crisis in punishment' in the last decades of the eighteenth century. Motives were complex. Driven by a perceived disintegration of the society they valued, the reformers sought a return to what they imagined to be a more stable and orderly society. They may well have acted out of political self-interest but also out of religious belief and a sense of guilt about the condition of the lower orders.

This revisionist version of the radical conflict model is very similar to that presented by Rothman but there are crucial differences. Ignatieff observes organised philanthropy to be a new strategy of class relations and both the property nature of crime and the role of the prison in containing the labour force are essential to his account. He argues that the new disciplinary ideology of the penitentiary – with its attempt to isolate the criminal class from the rest of the working class – was a response to the crisis years of industrialisation. There was thus a specific class problem to be solved and not a vague sense of unease about 'social change'. Cohen (1985: 24) observes that from this perspective:

> The point of the new control system – reforming the individual through punishment, allocating pain in a just way – was to devise a punishment at once

so humane and so just that it would convince the offender and the rest of society of the full moral legitimacy of the law.

In this way the system was far from the failure suggested by the orthodox social progress model but, quite the contrary, it was remarkably successful. The carceral surveillance society model takes these arguments further.

The carceral surveillance society model

We have seen that supporters of the orthodox social progress model propose that the development of modern societies, their laws and criminal justice systems is the product of enlightenment, benevolence and a consensual society which develops an increasingly progressive humanitarian response to crime and disorder. Advocates of the radical conflict model essentially reject the consensual view and observe, in contrast, an inherently conflict-ridden society with the development of the criminal justice system as a mode of social control and repression functioning in the interests of the capitalist order. Proponents of the carceral society model do not totally disregard these arguments but consider the situation to be far more complex than that explained by both the social progress and radical conflict models.

It is clear that from the beginning of the modern period many – if not most – philanthropists had genuine humanitarian concerns about those involved – or at risk of involvement – in crime and disorder on the streets. They moreover acted with the best of humanitarian intentions but without fully understanding the full (especially long-term) consequences of their actions. The labelling theorist Howard Becker (1963) helps us to understand further not only the notion of the motivated philanthropist but also the invariably obscure consequences – intentional or unintentional – of their actions. He argues that rules of conduct – including criminal laws – are made by people with power and enforced upon people without power. Thus, rules are made by the old for the young, by men for women, by white people for ethnic minorities, by the middle class for the working class. These rules are invariably imposed upon their recipients against their will and own best interests and are legitimised by an ideology that is transmitted to the less powerful in the course of primary and secondary socialisation. As an outcome of this process, most people internalise and obey the rules without realising – or questioning – the extent to which their behaviour is being decided for them.

Becker observes that some rules may be cynically designed to keep the less powerful in their place but others have simply been introduced as the outcome of a sincere – albeit irrational and mistaken – belief on the part of high-status individuals that the creation of a new rule will be beneficial for its intended subjects. Becker termed the people who create new rules for the 'benefit' of the less fortunate 'moral entrepreneurs'. Hopkins Burke (2008) observes that this account has resonance with the story of how philanthropic entrepreneurs came to define different categories of children and youth as acceptable and non-acceptable to respectable society while, at the same time, developing strategies to ensure their surveillance, control, discipline and tutelage with the intention of reconstructing the non-acceptable in the form of the acceptable. But, yet again, this account is too simplistic. It is clear that not only did many of these philanthropists have little idea of the actual or potential consequences of their actions but they might well have become extremely concerned had they recognised that final reality. Indeed, this predominantly liberal labelling perspective fails to take into account the complexities of power and the outcomes of strategies promoted by agencies at the mezzo level of the institution that often enjoy autonomy from the political centre and implemented by those working at the micro-level of the front-line who often enjoy considerable discretion in the criminal justice field. It is thus the notion of the carceral surveillance society devised by Michel Foucault (1980) and developed notably among others by Jacques Donzelot (1980), Stanley Cohen (1985) and David Garland (2001) that helps us to make sense of this situation and provide the fundamental basis of the carceral surveillance society model.

Foucault observed that the prison is a form of social and political control with significant consequences for the whole of society and is not just an institution which controls crime and criminal behaviour. He observes how the eighteenth century witnessed 'the great confinement' (Foucault, 1971), where whole groups of problematic people were categorised and confined in institutions in order to educate and discipline them for their regeneration as useful citizens. We thus were to see the reform of prisoners (in prisons), the education of children (in schools), the confinement of the insane (in psychiatric hospitals) and the supervision of industrial workers (in factories) as part of an emerging 'carceral society'. Prison, for example, is an institution of power and regulation which is thrust upon a population with a corresponding shift in emphasis from punishment that targets the body (in pre-modernity) to one which focuses on the mind (modernity) with the intention not to take vengeance on the criminal act but to alter the behaviour of the criminal. Thus, the prison was to become concerned with the personality of the offender, seeking to explain why it was that the individual had committed the crime with the purpose of intervention and the ending of any future disobedience. The outcome was to be the proliferation of experts, such as social workers, psychiatrists and criminologists, becoming central components within the criminal justice process.

From this Foucauldian perspective, power is not simply conceptualised as the privilege of an all-powerful state, although that which it does both possess and wield is clearly very significant. Strategies of power are in reality pervasive throughout society with the state only one location of the points of control and resistance. Foucault (1971, 1976) observes that particular areas of the social world – and he uses the examples of, law, medicine, sexuality – are colonised and defined by the norms and control strategies a variety of institutions and experts devise and abide by. He argues that these networks of power and control are governed as much by the knowledge and concepts that define them as by the definite intentions of groups.

Power and knowledge are seen to be inseparable. Humanism, good intentions, professional knowledge and the rhetoric of reform are neither in the idealist sense the producers of change nor in the materialist sense the mere product of changes in the political economy. They are inevitably linked in a power/knowledge spiral. Thus forms of knowledge such as criminology, psychiatry and philanthropy are directly related to the exercise of power, while power itself creates new objects of knowledge and accumulates new bodies of information.

The state, for its part, is implicated in this matrix of power-knowledge, but it is only part of the story, for in this vein it has been argued that within civil society there are numerous 'semi-autonomous' realms and relations – such as communities, occupations, organisations, families – where surveillance and control are present but where the state administration is technically absent. These semi-autonomous arenas within society are often appropriately negotiated and resisted by their participants in ways that, even now, the state has little jurisdiction.

The carceral society model is thus founded on the work of Michel Foucault and, while complementary to the conflict model, recognises that power is both diffuse and pervasive in society. Agents and experts at all levels of the social world have both access to and control of power and although this is invariably exercised in the overall interests of the capitalist class in the long run, those involved in its application at the micro, mezzo and macro levels are not always aware of their contribution to the 'grand design'. Cohen (1985) observes that the 'great incarcerations' – which put thieves into prison, lunatics into asylums, conscripts into barracks, workers into factories, children into school – are to be seen as part of a grand design. Property had to be protected, production had to be standard-ised by regulations, the young segregated and inculcated with the ideology of thrift and success, the deviant subjected to discipline and surveillance. The mode of discipline that was represented by the prison belonged to an economy of power quite different from that of the direct, arbitrary and violent rule of the sovereign in the pre-modern era. Power in capitalist society had to be exercised at the lowest possible cost – economically and politically – and its effects had to be intensive and extended throughout the social apparatus in order to gain control of those populations resistant and previously invisible to the disciplinary control matrix.

The left realist hybrid model

Hopkins Burke (2004a, 2008, 2009) has developed the left realist hybrid model which essentially provides a synthesis of the orthodox social progress, radical conflict and carceral surveillance society models, but with the additional recognition of *our* interest and collusion in the creation of the increasingly pervasive socio-control matrix of the carceral society. It is heavily influenced by left realism – an eclectic and now influential criminological perspective (Hopkins Burke, 2009) – which recognises that crime is a real problem for ordinary and invariably poor people who are targeted by the criminal element living in their own communities and from whom they require a protection that has not always been recognised or forthcoming (Lea and Young, 1984; Matthews and Young, 1986, 1992; Young, 1994, 1997).

Hopkins Burke has subsequently employed the left realist perspective in a historical context to demonstrate that the general public has always had an interest in the development of social progress (orthodox social progress model) but this has invariably conveniently coincided with the requirements of capitalism (radical conflict model) and which has invariably contributed unwittingly to the con-struction of the disciplinary control matrix that constrains the actions and rights of all. First, in order to explain the development of the public police service from the beginning of the nineteenth century, it is recognised, from this perspective, that crime was as real a problem for ordinary people at the time as it is now, and that the respectable working class has always required protection from the criminal elements in their midst whether these were termed the 'rough working classes' (nineteenth century) or a socially excluded underclass (twenty-first century) (Hopkins Burke, 2004b). Second, this historical variant on the left realist thesis has helped explain the increasing surveillance and control of young people on the streets and elsewhere from the nineteenth century to the present day (Hopkins Burke, 2008). Third, it is observed that in a complex, fragmented, dangerous society it is we the general public – regardless of social class location, gender or ethnic origin – that have a material interest, or an enthusiasm, for the development of the carceral surveillance matrix that restricts the civil liberties or human rights of some individuals or groups (Hopkins Burke, 2004c).

The left realist hybrid perspective readily accepts the carceral society thesis that disciplinary strategies are invariably implemented by philanthropists, moral entrepreneurs, professional agents and practitioners who rarely seem to recognise how their often humble discourse contributes to the grand overall disciplinary control matrix. Thus, the bourgeois child tutelage project of the nineteenth, and early twentieth century we will encounter later in this book can clearly be viewed in that context.

Proponents of the radical conflict model argue that definitions of crime and criminality are class-based with the public police service agents of a capitalist society targeting the activities of the socially excluded, while at the same time ignoring the far more damaging behaviour of corporate capitalism (see Scraton and Chadwick, 1996). Left realists consider the situation to be more ambiguous, crucially recognising that crime is a real problem for ordinary people and that it is therefore appropriate that the criminal justice system – of which the police service is a key institution – should seek to defend the weak and oppressed (see Lea and Young, 1984; Matthews and Young, 1986; Young, 1997; Hopkins Burke, 1998a, 2004a).

Observed from a left realist perspective it is apparent that from soon after the introduction of the new police in the mid-nineteenth century there was a widespread – and admittedly at times tacit and fairly grudging – acceptance and support for this body. The police may well have targeted criminal elements within the working class and they might on occasion have taken the side of capital in trade disputes, but at the same time their moralising mission on the streets coincided conveniently with the increasing enthusiasm for self-betterment among the great majority that has been described from differing sociological perspectives as 'embourgeoisement' (Goldthorpe, 1968–1969) and 'the civilising process' (Elias, 1978, 1982).

The left realist hybrid perspective thus does not dismiss the orthodox social progress, radical conflict or carceral models of criminal justice development but instead produces a synthesis of the three. For it seems self-evident that the police are an essential necessity in order to deal with conflicts, disorders and problems of coordination necessarily generated by any complex and materially advanced society (Reiner, 2000) and hence there is a widespread demand for policing throughout society. Studies have shown that while during the nineteenth century prosecutions for property crime emanated overwhelmingly from the more affluent groups, the poorer sections of society also resorted extensively to the law as victims (see Storch, 1989; Philips and Storch, 1999; Emsley, 1996; Taylor, 1997; Miller, 1999). Indeed, at crucial times these poorer groups had considerable interest in the maintenance of the status quo and the isolation of a growing criminal class. For example, with the end of the Crimean War the prospect of a footloose army of unemployed soldiers returning – at the very time that transportation to the colonies had ended – meant that 'an organised race of criminals' would be roaming the countryside looking for criminal opportunities and from whom all would need protection (Steedman, 1984; Hopkins Burke, 1998c, 1999b).

Thus, while working-class antagonism may have been exacerbated by police intervention in recreational activities and labour disputes, a close reading of the issues suggests a more complex situation than previously supposed (Hart, 1978). There seems to be little doubt that the police were closely linked with the general increase in orderliness on the streets of Victorian society (Gatrell, 1980; Taylor, 1997) and this was again widely welcomed. Indeed, it has been argued that the crucial way in which the police affect law enforcement is not by the apprehension of criminals – for that depends on many factors beyond their control – but by symbolising the existence of a functioning legal order, by having a visible presence on the street and being seen to be doing something (Gatrell, 1980). It is a discourse that coincides neatly with a consistent widespread contemporary public demand for police on the streets frequently expressed in contemporary crime surveys and regardless of the academic policing orthodoxy that has repeatedly stated the service on its own can have little effect on the crime rate (Hopkins Burke, 1998a, 1998b, 2004a, 2004b).

The left realist hybrid variation on the carceral society model proposes that there are further interests involved in the creation of the disciplinary control matrix and those significantly are ours and those of our predecessors. This hybrid model accepts that the orthodox social progress, radical conflict and carceral surveillance society models are to some extent legitimate for there were and are a multitude of motivations for both implementing and accepting the increasing surveillance and control of a potentially dangerous population on the streets and elsewhere. For the moralising mission of the entrepreneurial philanthropists and the reforming zeal of the liberal politician and administrator corresponded conveniently with those of the mill and mine-owners and a government which wanted a fit healthy fighting force, but it also coincides with the ever-increasing enthusiasm for self-betterment among the great majority of the working class. Those who were resistant to that moralising and disciplinary mission – the 'rough working' class of the Victorian era – have subsequently been reinvented in academic and popular discourse as the socially excluded underclass of contemporary society, with the moral panics of today a reflection of those of the past and demands for action remarkably similar. The radical conflict perspective nevertheless demands some prominence in the left realist hybrid model of criminal justice development because significantly everyone in the nineteenth century – and certainly all of us today – are subject to the requirements and demands of the economy. Attempts at self-improvement or embourgeoisement were always constrained and restricted by the opportunities provided by the economy – healthy or otherwise – and this will always be the case as recent events following the virtual collapse of the worldwide banking system have shown. Children and young people were increasingly disciplined and controlled throughout the nineteenth – and first half of the twentieth – century in a form that was functional and appropriate to the needs of mass modern society and an industrial capitalism which required an abundant, healthy and increasingly skilled workforce. With the fragmentation of that modernity and the subsequent retreat from mass industrialism that was to occur in the last quarter of the twentieth century, the requirements for young people were to change accordingly (Hopkins Burke, 1999a, 2008).

Attempts to control the financial services industry, which is a central component of contemporary post-industrial capitalist societies such as the UK and increasingly the USA, have certainly been popular in the past with a general population which has been the victim of financial incompetency/malpractice/criminality. However, these controls which challenge the practices of market capitalism have not been that successful and only time will tell whether further attempts following the great international banking disaster of 2008–2009 will be any more effective. At the time of the financial scandals at Enron and WorldCom in the USA in 2002 the great economist J.K. Galbraith, then aged 93, observed that large modern corporations – as manipulated by what he terms the 'financial craftsmen' at Enron and elsewhere – have grown so complex that they are almost beyond monitoring and effective control by their owners, the shareholders (Cornwell, 2002). Noting the sheer scale of the inadequacy of the accountancy profession and some of its prominent members in the aforementioned scandals, Galbraith observed the need for the strongest public and legal pressure to get honest competent accounting as part of a greater corporate regulation and public control of the private sector. He argued that steps must be taken so that boards of directors, supine and silent for so long, are competent to exercise their legal responsibility to their shareholders.

Public motivation for the increased policing of the financial services industry, in particular the investment arm of banking, is both apparent and unquestionably understandable in view of the activities of this sector of the economy, particularly but not exclusively in the USA and the UK at the end of the first decade of the twenty-first century, which range from gross incompetence to unequivocal criminality. Other policing, surveillance and control intrusions into various parts of the social world are at first sight equally non-problematic and acceptable both to the general public and informed opinion. Taken individually, they may seem both inoffensive and supportable by most law-abiding right-thinking people; taken collectively they are part of an impressive matrix of social control that restricts our freedom, as the following examples clearly demonstrate.

The freedom of the authorities to access information on our private lives has grown considerably in recent years. Data from a wide range of sources – the Office for National Statistics, the National Health Service, the Inland Revenue, the VAT office, the Benefits Agency, our school reports – can now be collated into a file on a citizen, without a court order showing why this should be the case. Legislative proposals in recent years have included phone and e-mail records to be kept for seven years, the extension of child curfews, keeping DNA of those acquitted of crimes and 'ex-suspects', restrictions on travel of those convicted of drug offences, the extension of compulsory fingerprinting for those cautioned of a recordable offence and public authorities authorised to carry out speculative searches of the DNA database (Wadham and Modhi, 2003). The Social Security Fraud Act 2001 allows for the compilation of a financial inventory from our bank accounts, building societies, insurance companies, telecom companies and the Student Loan Company, while every number on our phone bills may be reverse searched for an address. There may be no evidence that we are involved in fraud for us to be investigated, we may merely belong to a demographic group of people that the authorities feel is 'likely' to be involved in fraud.

The left realist hybrid model of criminal justice development thus proposes that in a complex contemporary society we all have interests in – and indeed a considerable enthusiasm for the introduction of – constraints and restrictions that are placed on particular activities and which restrict the civil liberties or human rights of some individuals or groups in the apparent greater interest. Taken together collectively these many individual restrictions contribute significantly to the ever-expanding and pervasive disciplinary control surveillance matrix that constrains the lives of all in the carceral society.

Four models of criminal justice development summarised

Four models or different ways of theorising the development of criminal justice have been introduced in this chapter. First, the orthodox social progress model proposes that the development of modern societies, their laws and criminal justice systems is the product of enlightenment, benevolence and a consensual society where the whole population share the same core values and which develops an increasingly progressive humanitarian response to crime and disorder. Theories of criminal justice – and other disciplines such as criminology and psychology – provide the scientific support or knowledge base to inform the particular reform programme, and changes occur when the reform vision becomes more refined and ideas more sophisticated. The revisionist variant of the orthodox social progress model tells a less idealist account where the ideas and intentions of the reformers are still seen to be important but where changes occur as functional solutions to immediate social changes. It provides a more critical account than the purist version but nevertheless remains a liberal model which still believes that things can be improved if we learn the correct lessons from history and research and apply them.

Second, the radical conflict model of criminal justice development challenges the notion of a consensual society implicit in the orthodox model and, in contrast, proposes that society is inherently characterised by conflict. From this perspective, the developing criminal justice system has successfully served the requirements of the emerging capitalist order by allowing for the continued repression of non-compliant members of the working class while this oppressive reality is hidden from the general population and the impression given that the changes introduced were fair, humane and progressive. In reality the changes introduced have always been in the interests of the capitalist economy and its maintenance. A revisionist 'soft' variant of the radical conflict model proposes that changes in the development of criminal justice did not simply occur because of the functional requirements of capitalism for the motives of those involved were many and complex. Thus, reformers may well have ultimately acted out of political self-interest but benevolent motives and genuine concerns about the welfare of the target population were also involved.

Third, proponents of the carceral society model of criminal justice development consider both the social progress and radical conflict models to be too simplistic and – while recognising the strengths of each and in particular complementary to the latter – recognise that power is both diffuse and pervasive in society. Agents and experts at all levels of the social world have both access to and control of power and although this is invariably exercised in the overall interests of the capitalist class, those involved in its application at the micro and mezzo levels are not always aware of their contribution to the 'grand design'.

Fourth, the left realist hybrid model of criminal justice development does not completely dismiss the social progress, radical conflict or carceral surveillance society models but recognises at least partial strengths of each and produces a synthesis of the other three while at the same recognising the interest and collusion of the general public – and that means *us* – in the creation of the increasingly pervasive socio-control matrix of the carceral society. It is moreover influenced by left realist criminology which recognises that crime and disorder is a real problem for poor people who are targeted by – and are the principal victims of – a criminal element living in their own communities and from whom they require a protection that has not always been recognised or forthcoming. This model proposes that the general public has since the beginnings of the modern era always had an interest in the development of social progress that has conveniently coincided with the requirements of capitalism and have invariably contributed unwittingly to the construction of the disciplinary control matrix. It is accepted that each of the other perspectives are to some extent legitimate for there were and are a multitude of motivations for both implementing and accepting the increasing surveillance and control of a potentially dangerous population on the streets and elsewhere.

The structure of this book

It is the purpose of this book to explain why it is that the various components of the 'criminal justice system' or 'criminal justice process' operate in the way that they do and in whose interests it functions as a whole. The various criminal justice theories that are introduced in the following chapters are thus located in the context of the four models of criminal justice development that were outlined above.

The second chapter considers those various theories which have sought to explain crime and criminal behaviour in the modern era. Three models of criminal behaviour are identified. The first, the rational actor model, proposes that human beings are rational creatures who choose to become involved in criminality, just like they would any other activity, in this case, after calculating the rewards to be obtained from illegality and having taken into account the likelihood of getting caught and punished. The second, the predestined actor model, rejects the rational actor emphasis on free will and replaces it with the doctrine of determinism. From this *positivist* standpoint, criminal behaviour is explained in terms of factors, either internal or external to the human being, that cause, or determine, people to act in ways over which they have little or no control. The third, the victimised actor model, proposes, with increasingly radical variants, that the criminal is in some way the victim of an unjust and unequal society. There follows a discussion of integrated theories of crime and criminal behaviour which seek, as the name suggests, integration of different theories both within one of the models of crime and criminal behaviour, or across model boundaries, with the intention of providing a more comprehensive explanation of criminality.

The third chapter considers the philosophers of law who are concerned with providing a general philosophical analysis of law and legal institutions. There are broadly three categories of modernist legal philosophy. First, analytic jurisprudence provides an analysis of the essence of law in order to understand what differentiates it from other systems of norms such as ethics. Second, normative jurisprudence involves the examination of normative, evaluative and otherwise prescriptive issues about the law, such as restrictions on freedom, obligations to obey the law, and the justifications for punishment. Critical theories of law, such as critical legal studies and feminist jurisprudence, provide a third radical category of modernist legal philosophy while, finally, there is a consideration of Islamic jurisprudence – or Sharia law – which is increasingly providing a significant radical challenge to the Western tradition of legal philosophy in contemporary post-industrial societies.

The fourth chapter explores the development of policing from the beginnings of the modern era in the context of the four models of criminal justice development. It is observed that the history of the public police service can be legitimately explained to some extent by both the orthodox social progress and the radical conflict models. It is nevertheless the carceral surveillance society model that recognises policing to be both pervasive and insidious throughout contemporary fragmented society and thus 'hard' and 'soft' policing styles – and these can involve not only the public police service, but the private security industry or social work agencies – are all part of the contemporary all-seeing multiple agency corporate crime industry. The left realist hybrid model goes further and observes that crime – or public disorder – has always been a real problem for ordinary people and the respectable working class has always required protection from the criminal elements in their midst, whether these were termed the 'rough working classes' in the past or a socially excluded underclass in contemporary society.

The fifth chapter considers the legal process in modern society and this has its foundations in the very beginning of modern society. Thus, in pre-modern European society there had been very little codified or written law and that which did exist was applied erratically, via judicial discretion and whim. This all nevertheless changed with the advent of the modern world and the introduction of increasingly bureaucratised criminal justice institutions and a rationalised process for responding to criminality. Again it appears, at first sight, that these developments can best be conceptualised in the context of the social progress model of criminal justice development but it nevertheless becomes apparent that the criminal justice process provides a control function in society and there are clearly interest groups involved. Our attention is thus alerted to the radical conflict model and the argument that progress has occurred in the interests of capitalism but it becomes even more apparent that the situation is more complex and our attention thus turns to the carceral surveillance society model and the left realist hybrid model.

The sixth chapter discusses the philosophy and theory of punishment in modern societies. Punishment is viewed by most theorists to be both necessary and just and thus can be again clearly conceptualised in the context of the social progress model for there appears to be no – or at least limited – sectional interest unfairly influencing policy and its implementation. The radical conflict model nevertheless proposes that rules or laws are introduced and enforced ultimately in the interests of the rich and powerful in capitalist society; the carceral surveillance society model develops that thesis and recognises the multiple ambiguities and diffusion of power in complex societies and the role and material interests of experts and front-line practitioners with professional discretion in the introduction of laws and their enforcement; while the left realist hybrid model goes further and recognises the interest of the general public in these developments.

The seventh chapter considers the development of a separate criminal justice to deal with children and young people and it is observed that in order to make sense of the contemporary system it is essential to locate the discussion in an historical context because the debates, discourses and political solutions that emerged in the past are very similar to those of today. It is shown that contemporary notions of childhood and adolescence were socially constructed at the outset of industrial modernity and children and their families were subsequently disciplined and controlled not least in the interests of an industrial capitalism which required a fit, healthy, increasingly educated, trained and obedient workforce. Reality was again more complex than proposed by proponents of the radical conflict model, while the orthodox social progress perspective which proposes these disciplinary strategies to be the actions of motivated entrepreneurial philanthropists with genuine concerns about poor urban children and young people is, while at least partially correct, also too simplistic. It is argued that both the carceral surveillance society and left realist hybrid models recognise the role of moral entrepreneurs, professional agents, practitioners and, in the latter case, the general public, in the development of a surveillance and intervention system to target miscreant children and young people as part of the disciplinary control matrix, ultimately in the interests of capitalism.

The eighth and concluding chapter reconsiders the nature of the criminal justice system in contemporary fragmented societies – thought by some influential commentators and theorists to be inherently characterised by a *post*modern condition – in the context of the four models of criminal justice development and the fast-expanding carceral surveillance society which is seen to be an inevitable response to the present-day risk society and the simultaneous introduction of new modes of governance and social control.

2 Explaining crime and criminal behaviour

The previous chapter discussed four models which have each sought to explain the development of criminal justice in the modern era and in whose interest its various agencies operate. This chapter considers the various different ways in which crime and criminal behaviour has been variously explained during the modern period and it is divided into four sections. The first three sections consider a different model – or tradition – which has been developed during the modern era to explain crime and criminal behaviour.[1] Different explanations, or theories, can generally be located in terms of one of these models and in this chapter these are introduced chronologically in order of their emergence and development within the context of their particular model of criminal behaviour. The fourth section considers more recent attempts to integrate theories both within the different models and across model boundaries with the purpose of developing a more rigorous explanatory tool. We start by considering the rational actor model of crime and criminal behaviour.

The rational actor model

The rational actor model of crime and criminal behaviour can be broadly conceptualised in the context of the social progress model of criminal justice development and central to this tradition is the notion that people have free will and make the choice to commit crime in very much the same way as they choose to indulge in any other form of behaviour. Its emergence in the late eighteenth century was heavily influenced by the social contract theories and utilitarianism we encountered in the previous chapter and which had provided the basis of modernist political thought.

It is the ideas of the Classical School of Criminology or Criminal Justice associated with Cesare Beccaria in Italy and Jeremy Bentham in England that provide the central theoretical foundations of the rational actor tradition and, from this perspective, it is argued that people are rational creatures who seek pleasure while trying to avoid pain. Consequently, the level of punishment inflicted on them must outweigh any pleasure that might be derived from a criminal act in order to deter them from committing further transgressions. Thus, the punishment meted out to the individual should be proportionate to the crime committed and all people, regardless of social position or status, should be treated equally by the law. These notions, which, at first sight, seem to be equitable and attractive, provide the essential foundations of legal systems in modern societies. In short, it is proposed that all human beings are capable of committing criminal behaviour once they have made the choice to do so and have not been deterred from taking this course of action. In its purist sense this model does not consider criminals to be a distinct category of humanity from non-criminals. We all have the potential to be criminals or at least commit criminal acts. Some of us will do so.

The rational actor model went into a sudden decline as an explanatory model of criminal behaviour and was out of favour for much of the twentieth century. It had become increasingly apparent to observers in the criminal courts that many people – for example, children, 'idiots' and the insane – do not enjoy the capacity of perfect rational decision-making which is presumed by the model. Thus from the nineteenth century onwards the purist variant of the model became incrementally compromised as more and more 'experts' were increasingly allowed into the court to plead for mitigation for the defendant on the grounds of their limited responsibility. The outcome was that sentences became more individualised, were dependent on the perceived degree of responsibility of the offender and on individual mitigating circumstances. The neo-Classicists thus responded by retaining the central rational actor model notion of free will, but with the significant modification that certain circumstances may be less conducive to the unfettered exercise of free choice than others.

The rational actor tradition was to be revived and revitalised with the rise of the political 'new right' – populist or neo-conservatives – both in the USA (epitomised by the presidency of Ronald Reagan) and the UK (the Conservative governments led by Margaret Thatcher) during the last quarter of the twentieth century. This emerging body of thought was highly critical of both the then orthodox predestined actor model that we will encounter below, with its prescriptions of treatment rather than punishment, and the even more radical 'victimised' actor model, the focus of the third section of this chapter, with its propositions of forgiveness and non-intervention (Morgan, 1978; Dale, 1984; Scruton, 1980, 1985).

These rational actor model revivalists argued that crime would be reduced if the costs of involvement in criminal activity – that is, the certainty of punishment – were to be increased so that involvement in legal activities was more attractive than criminal activity (Wilson, 1975; Wilson and Herrnstein, 1985; Felson, 1998). Moreover, these 'right realists' were dismissive of those who denied the existence of crime as a real problem and, in contrast, observed a real evil that victimises ordinary, often poor, people and which requires a rigorous response. Furthermore, they argued that the focus should be less on simple breaches of the criminal law but more on regulating street life and incivilities, such as prostitution, begging, gang fights, drunkenness and disorderly conduct, which may not in themselves be so very harmful, but which in aggregate are detrimental to the community and therefore need to be controlled (see Hopkins Burke, 1998b, 2004b; Karmen, 2004). James Q. Wilson (1975: 21) observes the individualistic nature of offending and adopts a utilitarian explanation for human action:

If the supply and value of legitimate opportunities (i.e. jobs) was declining at the very time that the cost of illegitimate opportunities (i.e. fines and jail terms) was also declining, a rational teenager might well have concluded that it made more sense to steal cars than to wash them.

The implication of this utilitarian argument would seem to support both increasing the benefits of 'non-crime' (by providing more and better jobs) and increasing the costs of crime (by the use of imprisonment). Wilson nevertheless concentrates on the latter half of the equation and these 'right realist' crime control strategies thus place far more emphasis on the stick than the carrot. For Wilson (1975) the proposed solution involves catching and successfully processing more offenders, by increasing police effectiveness, and improving the consistency of the criminal justice system. Wilson and Herrnstein (1985) lament the irrationality of the criminal justice system, which they argue reflects the view of judges that prison fails to act as a deterrent and, in support of their argument, they cite the low proportion of recidivists who are sent to prison. They thus call for fixed-term sentences for offences, regardless of the age of the offender and other attributes, such as the scope for rehabilitation. Differential sentences for the same crime reflect a wish to change the behaviour of the offender and this causes a moral dilemma. Those perceived less likely to re-offend receive shorter sentences, which in practice means that young, poor black offenders from unstable family backgrounds are sent to prison for longer than older, white middle-class offenders from stable family backgrounds who have committed the same offence.

Three categories of contemporary rational actor theories came to prominence with the rediscovery of the rational actor model. In the first category, modern deterrence theories address the principles of certainty, severity and promptness in terms of the administration of criminal justice (Zimring and Hawkins, 1973; Gibbs, 1975; Wright, 1993). The deterrence doctrine proposes that in order to deter, punishment must be both swift and certain; the notion of swiftness concerns the celerity with which sanctions are applied after the commission of a crime, while certainty refers to the probability of apprehension and punishment. If the punishment applied is severe, certain and swift, people will rationally calculate that there is more to be lost than gained from offending. Certainty is seen to be more effective in deterring crime than the severity of punishment administered: for the more severe the available punishment, the less likely it is to be applied; while, on the other hand, the less certain the punishment, the more severe it will need to be to deter crime (Akers, 1997).

Deterrence is said to affect the willingness to become involved in criminal behaviour in one of two ways. First, in the case of 'general deterrence' the punishment of offenders by the state is seen to serve as an example to the general population who will be frightened into non-participation in criminal behaviour (Zimring and Hawkins, 1973). Second, in the case of 'specific deterrence', it is proposed that the apprehended and punished offender will themselves refrain from further offending because they realise that they are certain to be caught and severely punished.

Even if punishment does deter actual and potential offenders effectively, a number of ethical objections can be raised against the use of sentences for this purpose. Beyleveld (1978) suggests that the types of punishment and length of sentences needed to deter a potential offender will vary substantially between different people, different crimes and different circumstances. Therefore, in order to deter crime, it might well be necessary to set sentences at a level totally out of all proportion to the seriousness of the offence (Wright, 1982) and this is at odds with the central rational choice actor model concept that the punishment should fit the crime. Moreover, when a particular offender has not been deterred from committing a crime then he or she *must* receive the threatened punishment and the consequences of this may be simply counterproductive (Wright, 1982).

In the second category, contemporary rational choice theories propose that people make decisions to act based on the extent to which they expect that choice to maximise their profits or benefits and minimise the costs or losses. Hence, decisions to offend are based on the expected effort and reward compared to the likelihood and severity of punishment and other costs of crime (Becker, 1968; Cornish and Clarke, 1986). From this perspective, becoming involved in crime is the outcome of a career decision; it is a chosen way of life, a way of making your living, it is one of a range of available options. There is no need to search for complex cultural, structural, biological or psychological explanations of crime and criminal behaviour.

There are five key propositions of the rational action perspective which can be identified. First, most criminals are normal, reasoning people and the mode of reasoning used by all adults, with perhaps the exception of the mentally ill, is rational. Second, rationality is a mode of thinking in which individuals are able to accurately distinguish between *means* and *ends*. They can thus identify what they want and the ways that are available to them for obtaining those ends. Third, for each of the different means *available* to them, rational actors are also able to calculate the likely costs they could incur (things they do not want to happen) and benefits they might receive (how many or how much of their ends they can achieve) from following a particular course of action. Fourth, if the benefits outweigh the costs, then *do it*. If the costs outweigh the benefits, then *don't do it*. Fifth, from the perspective of rational choice theory, it is not necessary to consider prior causes, antecedents and structures. All that matters are the rational judgements and calculations confronting a given person, with their particular set of ends and preferences, in a given situation.

Earlier and less developed variants of rational choice theory had tended to follow these key propositions and compared the decision-making process adopted by offenders with straightforward economic choice (Becker, 1968). A more sophisticated and highly influential variant was to be introduced subsequently by Clarke and Cornish who define crime as 'the outcome of the offender's choices or decisions, however hasty or ill-considered these might be' (Clarke, 1987: 118). In other words, offenders invariably act in terms of a *limited* or *bounded* form of rationality. They will not always obtain all the facts needed to make a wise decision and the information available will not necessarily be weighed carefully but they do have the capacity to make calculations and decisions based on the extent of their knowledge and personal reasoning capacity. It is an approach that avoids the inherent tendency within the predestined actor model that we will encounter below to treat criminals as a category of humanity set apart from law-abiding citizens. Crime is simply rational action performed by fairly ordinary people in response to particular pressure, opportunities and situational inducements (Hough *et al.*, 1980; Trasler, 1986).

Clarke (1987) is nevertheless not entirely dismissive of the predestined actor tradition and suggests that most of the factors seen as predisposing an individual to offend can be interpreted in terms of their influence on offender cognitive decision-making. This suggestion that individuals respond to situations in different ways because they bring with them a different history of psychological conditioning is considered below.

In the third category, routine activities theories propose that the likelihood of a crime taking place increases when there are one or more motivated persons present, a suitable target or potential victim available, and an absence of capable, invariably informal, guardians to deter the offender. Cohen and Felson (1979) observe that the fundamental changes in daily activities related to work, school, and leisure since the Second World War have placed more people in particular places at specific times. This has both increased their accessibility as targets of crime and kept them away from home as guardians of their own possessions and property. Felson (1998) thus places less emphasis on the significance of formal guardians – such as the police – because he has reached the conclusion that crime is a private phenomenon largely unaffected by state intervention but stresses the natural crime prevention and deterrence that occurs in the informal control system, the 'quiet and natural method by which people prevent crime in the course of daily life' (Felson, 1998: xii–xiii). Ordinary people, we, friends, family, or even strangers are the most likely capable guardians.

Akers (1997) argues that routine activities theory is merely a way of explaining why people become victims of crime and fails to explain why some people engage in criminal behaviour while others do not. There is a taken-for-granted assumption that such people exist and that they commit crimes in certain places and at times when the opportunities and potential victims are available. The theory tells us absolutely nothing about who these people are and their moti-vations for engaging in criminal activities. The predestined actor model offers numerous suggestions.

The predestined actor model

Proponents of the predestined actor model fundamentally reject the rational actor emphasis on free will and replace it with the doctrine of determinism. It can nevertheless still be conceptualised in terms of the orthodox social progress model of criminal justice development and indeed many, if not most, proponents and supporters of this perspective would consider this to be an issue of neutral science beyond the realms of the political. From this *positivist* standpoint, criminal behaviour is explained in terms of factors, either internal or external to the human being, that cause – or *determine* – people to act in ways over which they have little or no control. The individual with certain characteristics or living in a particular environment is predestined to be a criminal.

There are three basic formulations of the predestined actor model: biological, psychological and sociological. All nevertheless incorporate the same fundamental assumptions, and although each variant is discussed separately, it will become increasingly apparent that they are not mutually exclusive. Thus, for example, biologists came to embrace sociological factors, while at times it is often difficult to differentiate between biological and psychological explanations.

Three factors can be identified as being central to the emergence of the predestined actor model. First, science replaced theology as the central explanation of the essence of humanity. In particular, the theory of evolution proposed that human beings were subject to the same natural laws as all other animals (Darwin, 1871). Second, there was development of *social* evolutionism and the view that human beings develop as part of a process of interaction with the world they inhabit (Spencer, 1971, originally 1862–1896). Third, there was the philosophical doctrine of positivism and the idea that we may only obtain legitimate knowledge of human nature and society – and thus can only explain human behaviour – by recourse to the methods of the natural sciences (Comte, 1976, originally 1842).

Biological positivism

The biological variant of the predestined actor model has its origins in the early theories of 'the Italian School' where the central focus is on the notion that the criminal is a physical type distinct from the non-criminal (Lombroso, 1875; Ferri, 1895; Garofalo, 1914) and which was in complete contrast to the prevailing orthodoxy of the rational actor model. Both the methodology they employed and clearly some of their findings appear to be highly simplistic by the standards of today but they nevertheless established an enduring scientific tradition that has become increasingly sophisticated over the years but has nevertheless remained ultimately flawed.

Inherited criminal characteristics theories considered that criminal behaviour is a biological predisposition inherited from criminal parents in the same way as physical characteristics such as hair and eye colour and evidence to support that proposition was subsequently obtained from three sources: the study of criminal families (Dugdale, 1877; Goddard, 1914; Goring, 1913), twins (Lange, 1930; Christiansen, 1968, 1975; Dalgard and Kringlen, 1976; Cloninger and Gottesman, 1987; Rowe and Rogers, 1989; Rowe, 1990) and adopted children (Hutchings and Mednick, 1977; Mednick *et al.*, 1984). None of these theories were ultimately able to establish inherited biological characteristics as the cause of criminality because they failed to rule out environmental factors or the transmission of values through upbringing. There is nevertheless still a *possibility* that some people may be genetically endowed with characteristics that render them more likely to 'succumb to crime' (Hutchings and Mednick, 1977: 140).

Genetic structure theories have sought to identify crucial sex chromosome abnormalities as causes of crime. Thus, the possession of an extra female chromosome (X) in males was associated with increased female, often effeminate, characteristics while an extra (Y) chromosome was associated with extra maleness among men (Klinefelter *et al.*, 1942; Price and Whatmore, 1967; Ellis, 1990). Associations with criminality causation were nevertheless impossible to establish because it was found that there are thousands of perfectly, normal and harmless people in the general population who have an extra sex chromosome. Geneticists have been subsequently cautious in claiming that human behaviour is primarily determined by inherited characteristics but the discovery that some personality traits can be explained by a genetic component (Jones, 1993) does greatly strengthen the possibility that some criminal behaviour can be explained by a genetic susceptibility triggered by environmental factors.

Criminal body-type theories have direct antecedents in the early Italian School tradition of seeking to establish links between different categories of physical build and criminality, and although the studies became increasingly sophisticated (Hooton, 1939; Sheldon, 1949; Glueck and Glueck, 1950; Gibbons, 1970; Cortes and Gatti, 1972) they all ultimately fail to establish whether their research subjects were offenders because of their build and disposition, or simply because their physique and dispositions – in some cases associated with poverty and deprivation – are socially conceived to be associated with offending by the criminal justice system.

Neurological and brain injury theories address neurological conditions that supposedly *cause* criminal behaviour but there is little evidence that such incapacitations actually lead to criminal behaviour. There have been cases reported, but these are very rare, and studies suggest that the original personality and social background of the person are of greater significance. A brain injury might, however, accentuate an underlying trend to aggression if it occurs in a specific area of the brain (Mark and Ervin, 1970; Mednick and Volavka, 1980; Volavka, 1987).

Biochemical theories are similar to the altered biological state theories below but the former involve substances, or chemical processes, already present in the body while the latter involve the introduction of outside agents. Sexual hormones are produced by the pituitary, adrenal, gonad, pancreas and thyroid glands and they control, and are themselves controlled by, certain anatomical features that affect the thresholds for various types of responses and have extensive feedback loops with the central nervous system. Studies suggest a causal relationship between hormones and criminal behaviour arguing that either an excess or underproduction of hormones can lead to emotional disturbance followed by criminal behaviour (Schlapp and Smith, 1928; Dalton, 1961, 1964; Rose, Bernstein, Gorden and Catlin, 1974; Keverne, Meller and Eberhart, 1982; Olwens, 1987; Schalling, 1987; Virkkunen, 1987; Ellis and Crontz, 1990; Baldwin, 1990; Fagan, 1990; Fishbein and Pease, 1990; Pihl and Peterson, 1993).

Blood sugar levels or low blood sugar levels – sometimes related to diabetes mellitus – may result in irritable, aggressive reactions, and may culminate in sexual offences, assaults, and motiveless murder (see Shah and Roth, 1974). Shoenthaler (1982) discovered that by lowering the daily sucrose intake of young offenders it was possible to reduce the level of their antisocial behaviour. Adrenaline sensitivity theories propose a relationship between adrenaline and aggressive behaviour. Hare (1982) found that when threatened with pain, criminals exhibit fewer signs of stress than other people.

Altered biological state theories link behavioural changes with the introduction of an external chemical agent. Allergies and diet theories propose a link between irritability and aggression that may lead individuals in some circumstances to commit criminal assault (Printz *et al.*, 1980; Virkkunen, 1987; Lesser, 1980; Pihl, 1982; Raloff, 1983).

Substance abuse is usually brought about by the intake of drugs in the widest sense. Some of these drugs are legal and freely available such as alcohol, which is drunk, and glues and lighter fluids, which are inhaled. The medical profession prescribes some such as barbiturates, while others – such as cannabis, amphetamines, LSD, MDA or 'Ecstasy', opiates (usually cocaine or heroin) – are only available illegally.

The use of alcohol has probably much closer links with crime and criminal behaviour than most other drugs – with the contemporary exception of crack cocaine and possibly heroin – and this is at least partially explained by alcohol being legal, readily available and in extremely common usage. In short, alcohol has long been associated with antisocial activity, crime and criminality (Saunders, 1984; Flanzer, 1981; Deluca, 1981; Collins, 1986, 1988; Fagan, 1990; Rada, 1975; Lindqvist, 1986; Goodwin *et al.*, 1973; Ramsay, 1996; Abram, 1989; Gottfredson, 1984; Mott, 1990; Hodge, 1993; Mirrlees-Black, 1999).

Illegal drug taking does not have as long an association with criminal behaviour as alcohol consumption and it was only at the beginning of the twentieth century that drugs were labelled as a major social problem and came to be regulated. Drugs are chemicals and once taken alter the chemical balance of the body and brain and this can clearly affect behaviour but the way that this occurs varies according to the type and quantity of the drug taken (see Fishbein and Pease, 1990; Pihl and Peterson, 1993). The biological effects of cannabis and opiates such as heroin tend to reduce aggressive hostile tendencies, while cocaine and its derivative crack are more closely associated with violence.

Some see both alcohol and drug misuse as intrinsically wrong and thus in need of punishment; others see them as social and personal problems requiring understanding and treatment. The first solution has generally been applied in the case of (illegal) drugs, while the second has tended to be more acceptable in the case of (legal) alcohol (Institute of Alcohol Studies, 2005; Department of Health, 2005).

Central to the biological variant of the predestined actor model of crime and criminal behaviour is the perception that criminality arises from some physical disorder within the individual offender and it is proposed that by following a course of treatment – such as surgical intervention, for example castration, chemotherapy and electro-control – rather than punishment individuals can be cured of the predisposing condition that causes their criminality but this should not in any way be considered to be a soft option (Hopkins Burke, 2009).

Psychological positivism

Psychological positivism directs the search for the causes of crime to the 'criminal mind' or 'personality' and for purist proponents of this perspective there are patterns of reasoning and behaviour that are specific to offenders and these remain constant regardless of their different social experiences. There are three broad categories of psychological theories. The first category – psychodynamic theories – has its origins in the highly influential work of Sigmund Freud (1920, 1927) and his notion of psychosexual development, based on the idea of a number of complex stages of childhood psychic development which if disrupted can lead to neuroses or severe difficulties in adults, including involvement in criminal behaviour. Essential to the successful development of the child is the influence of the parents and, importantly, many of these influences are unconscious. Unconscious conflicts or tensions are seen to *determine* all actions and it is the purpose of the conscious (or ego) to resolve these tensions by finding ways of satisfying the basic inner urges by engaging in activities sanctioned by society.

The subsequent psychodynamic tradition was concerned with elaborating on the development of the ego and thus subsequently latent delinquency theory proposed that the absence of an intimate attachment with parents could lead to later criminality (Aichhorn, 1925; Healy and Bronner, 1936), while maternal deprivation theory – which was to have a major and lasting influence on the training of social workers – proposed that a lack of a close mother/child relationship in the early years of life could lead to later criminal behaviour (Bowlby, 1952). Others have nevertheless argued that it is the nature and quality of child-rearing practice that is the crucial causal link to later behavioural patterns (Glueck and Glueck, 1950; McCord, 1959; Bandura and Walters, 1959; Hoffman and Saltzstein, 1967; Rutter, 1981) while others propose that much criminality is a product of 'broken families' (Burt, 1945; Mannheim, 1948; Wootton, 1959; West, 1969; Pitts, 1986; Kolvin *et al.*, 1990; Farringdon, 1992). Others note that the 'broken home' is not a homogeneous category and thus a range of different factors need to be considered (Bowlby, 1952; Mannheim, 1955; Tappan, 1960); while Nye (1958) and Gibbens (1963) found that offending is more likely to occur among children from intact but unhappy homes where they can witness and be involved in conflict.

The second category – behavioural learning theories – has its origins in the notion that all behaviour is learned from an external stimulus (Skinner, 1938). Criminals thus develop abnormal, inadequate, or specifically criminal personalities or personality traits that differentiate them from non-criminals. These theories – based on the concept of conditioned learning – propose that there are dimensions of personality that can be isolated and measured and thus criminal behaviour predicted (Eysenck, 1970, 1977; Smith and Smith, 1977; McEwan, 1983; McGurk and McDougall, 1981) although little evidence has been found to support these suppositions (Farrington, 1994).

Antisocial personality disorder researchers have proposed that similar techniques can be used to detect individuals who are 'psychopaths' but there is little agreement as to exactly what characteristics consistently constitute the condition and there has been little success in predicting future dangerousness (Cleckley, 1976; Hare, 1980; Feldman, 1977; Hare and Jutari, 1986; Hollin, 1989; Kozol *et al.*, 1972). Monahan (1981) comprehensively reviewed the clinical techniques used for predicting violent behaviour and concluded that it can only be done within very restricted circumstances arguing that it is not possible to predict violence over an extended period or when a person is moving from one situation to another, for example, being released from prison.

Researchers have subsequently moved away from trying to predict future violent behaviour towards the more general possibility that individuals might engage in any form of offending behaviour (Vold *et al.*, 1998). Most of this research has focused on juveniles rather than adults with the strongest predictor of later offending behaviour found to be early childhood problem behaviours such as disruptive classroom conduct, aggressiveness, lying and dishonesty (Loeber and Dishion, 1983). The stability of these behavioural problems over time suggests that these people may have certain personality characteristics associated with antisocial behaviour even if they do not show up in personality tests. In recent years personality typing – or offender profiling – has been used, particularly in the USA, to help detect particular types of criminals and it is a method found to have been most useful in the detection of serial murders (Holmes and De Burger, 1989; Omerod, 1996).

The third category – cognitive learning theory – is explicitly critical of the determinist nature of the previous two traditions and the predestined actor perspective (Tolman, 1959; Piaget, 1980; Skinner, 1981). This social learning theory emphasises that behaviour may be reinforced through expectations that are learned by watching what happens to other people but ultimately the person will choose what they will learn and how. Social learning theory thus proposes that behaviour is learned through watching what happens to other people and then making *choices* to behave in a particular way and it is in this way that psychology can be seen to have moved away from its roots in the predestined model to incorporate notions from the rational actor model.

An early proponent of the notion that crime is normal learned behaviour was Gabriel Tarde (1843–1904) who argued that criminals are primarily normal people who, by accident of birth, are brought up in an atmosphere in which they learn crime as a way of life. His 'laws of imitation' are essentially a cognitive theory in which the individual is said to learn ideas through association with others and behaviour (including criminal behaviour) follows.

Edwin Sutherland (1947) argued that criminal behaviour occurs when individuals acquire sufficient sentiments in favour of offending with which they outweigh their association with non-criminal tendencies. Those associations or contacts that have the greatest impact are those which are frequent, early in point of origin, or the most intense. Sutherland argued that it was not necessary to explain why a person has particular associations as this involved a complex of social interactions and relationships, but maintained that it was the existence of differential social organisation that exposed people to varied associational ties. Differential association theory retains, in contrast to other psychological explanations, a dominant sociological argument that it is the primary groups to which people belong which exerts the strongest influence on them.

Sutherland (1940) significantly used differential association theory as an explanation of white collar or corporate crime observing that the main focus of criminology had previously been on offenders from the lower classes while ignoring the enormous quantities of crime committed by businessmen. Others have provided empirical support for this position. Geis (1968) examined evidence given to hearings into the illegal price-fixing activities of businesses in the USA and found that people taking up new posts tended to find such activities an established practice and thus became routinely involved as part of learning their new job. Baumhart (1961) had similarly found unethical behaviour on the part of businessmen to be influenced by superiors and peers with both researchers suggesting that the learning process is reinforced by 'rewards' and 'punishments'. Clinard (1952) nevertheless observed that differential association does not explain why it is that some individuals exposed to the same processes do not deviate and proposed that the theory should be adapted to consider personality traits, although we might consider that the social control theories we will encounter below provide a more satisfactory explanation.

Others have supported the view that crime is normal learned behaviour and have sought to explain that this knowledge acquisition does not have to take place in intimate personal groups and can take place through direct interactions with the environment, including the various and increasing forms of media, independent of associations with other people, through the principles of operant learning (Akers, 1985, 1992).

In conclusion, psychological explanations of criminality have firm foundations in the predestined actor model with both the psychodynamic and behaviourist traditions implying that there is such a thing as the criminal mind or personality which in some way determines the behaviour of the individual. The causes are dysfunctional, abnormal emotional adjustment or deviant personality traits formed in early socialisation and childhood development with the inevitable outcome being that the individual is destined to become a criminal. The only way that destiny can be avoided is through the identification of the predisposing condition and the provision of some form of psychiatrist intervention.

The more recent cognitive learning approach involves a retreat from the purist predestined actor model approach. First, there is recognition of the links between the psychology of the individual and important predisposing influences or stimuli available in the social environment. Second, criminals are now seen to have some degree of choice. They can choose to imitate the behaviours of others or they can choose not to. There may be a substantial range of factors influencing their decision and these may suggest to the individual that in the particular circumstances – when the opportunity arises – criminal behaviour is a rational choice to make. Thus we can see the links between more recent cognitive learning theories and contemporary variants of the rational actor model. In short, the active criminal can in favourable circumstances make the choice to change their behaviour and cease offending or alternatively the individual living in circumstances where criminal behaviour is the norm can choose not to take that course of action. In this case, crime is not inevitably destiny.

Sociological positivism

Sociological variants of the predestined actor model explain crime as being a product of the social environment, which provides cultural values and definitions that govern the behaviour of those who live within them. Deviant or criminal behaviour is that which occurs when an individual, or a group of individuals, behaves in accordance with definitions that conflict with those of the dominant culture.

Emile Durkheim, the founding father of academic sociology in France and a major social theorist working at the turn of the twentieth century, observed that it was not just the psychological and biological versions of the predestined actor model that were unable to provide an adequate explanation of social action; he was also strongly opposed to those theoretical ideas – social contract theory and utilitarianism – that had provided the foundations of the rational actor model. A society that is divided into different interest groups on an unequal basis is not one in which 'just contracts between individuals and society could be made' (Durkheim, 1933, originally 1893: 202).

In *The Division of Labour in Society*, first published in 1893, Durkheim described the processes of social change that accompanies the industrial development of society, arguing that earlier forms of society had high levels of mechanical solidarity, while the more developed industrial societies are characterised by an advanced stage of 'organic' solidarity.[2] Societies with high levels of mechanical solidarity are characterised by the conformity of the group where individuals hold common attitudes and beliefs that bind them to each other. It is a form of social solidarity that at first sight appears attractive, suggesting popular notions of the close-knit community, but at the same time places significant restrictions on the capacity of individuals to develop a sense of personal identity or uniqueness. Moreover, such societies have a very intense and rigid collective conscience where members hold very precise shared ideas of what is right and wrong. The law is used as an instrument to maintain uniformity, and punishment performs the necessary function of reinforcing the moral consensus – or worldview – of the group. Durkheim significantly claims that a society with no crime would be abnormal because the imposition of sufficiently tight controls that make criminality impossible would seriously restrict the potential for innovation and social progress.

Durkheim argues that with greater industrialisation societies develop greater levels of organic solidarity where there is a more developed division of labour and different groups become interdependent on each other. Social solidarity relies less on the maintenance of uniformity between individuals, and more on the management of the diverse functions of different groups, although a certain degree of uniformity remains essential. Durkheim argues that the division of labour is a progressive phenomenon that does not bring about the inevitable collapse of morality but instead the emergence of a new *content* for the collective conscience. In societies dominated by mechanical solidarity the emphasis is on the obligation of the individual to society; with organic formations, the focus is increasingly on the obligation of society to the individual person. Although there is now an emphasis on the rights of individuals it is not proposed that altruism – that is, self-sacrifice for others – will disappear. On the contrary, moral individualism is *not* unregulated self-interest but the imposition of a set of reciprocal obligations that binds together individuals (Durkheim, 1933). In short, Durkheim regarded the cohesion of nineteenth-century *laissez-faire* society, with its wholly unregulated markets, its arbitrary inequalities, and its restrictions on social mobility and its 'class' wars, as a dangerous condition. Thus, such imperfect social regulation will lead to a variety of different social problems, including crime and deviance.

Durkheim provides a threefold typology of deviants. The first is the biological deviant whose behaviour is explained by physiological or psychological malfunctioning and who can be present in any division of labour. The other two are linked to the nature and condition of the social system and are present in those societies that are characterised by an abnormal or forced division of labour. Thus, the second typology, the functional rebel, is a 'normal' person who is responding to a pathological, unequal society, rebelling against the existing, inappropriate and unfair division of labour and indicating the existence of strains in the social system. Such a person expresses the true 'spontaneous' or 'normal' collective consciousness as opposed to the artificial 'forced' or 'pathological' one currently in operation (Taylor *et al.*, 1973). The third typology, the skewed deviant, involves those who have been socialised into a disorganised pathological society and for whom involvement in criminality is normal learned behaviour; this is the most influential of his three categorisations of criminal behaviour.

Durkheim proposed two central arguments to explain the growth of crime and criminal behaviour in modern industrial societies. First, such societies encourage a state of unbridled 'egoism', or individualism', which is contrary to the maintenance of social solidarity and conformity to the law. Second, the likelihood of inefficient regulation is greater at a time of rapid modernisation, or social change, because new forms of control have not evolved sufficiently to replace the older and now less appropriate means of maintaining solidarity. In such a period, society is in a state of normlessness or 'anomie', a condition characterised by a breakdown in norms and common understandings and which can help facilitate involvement in criminal behaviour.

Sociologists working at the University of Chicago during the early part of the twentieth century also concluded that the existence of crime and criminal behaviour in conditions of unremitting urban poverty could not simply be explained in terms of biological predisposition and the criminal mind. Crime made more 'sense' when viewed as a social problem and it was argued that the poor are not simply born into a life of crime but driven by the conditions of their social environment. By changing their surroundings it would be possible to reverse the negative effects of the city and transform these people into law-abiding citizens.

Robert Park (1921) proposed that the development and organisation of the city is neither random nor idiosyncratic but patterned; human communities, like plants, live together symbiotically. In other words, different kinds of human beings share the same environment and are mutually dependent on each other. Patterns of change in the city are comparable to changes in the balance of nature. At the time, the human population in US cities was migratory, rather than fixed, with new immigrants moving into the poor areas and replacing the previous inhabitants as they moved out to the suburbs.

Ernest Burgess (1928) argued that as cities expand in size, the development is patterned socially and they grow radially in a series of concentric zones or rings. Burgess outlined five different zones and proposed that a competitive process decided how people were distributed spatially amongst these: commercial enterprises were thus located in the central business district (or loop) in close proximity to the transport systems; in contrast, the most expensive residential areas were in the outer commuter zones or suburbs, away from the bustle of the city centre, the pollution of the factories and the homes of the poor.

It was the 'zone in transition' – containing rows of deteriorating tenements and often built in the shadow of ageing factories – that was the particular focus of study. The outward expansion of the business district led to the constant displacement of residents. As the least desirable living area, the zone was the focus for the influx of waves of immigrants who were too poor to reside elsewhere. Burgess observed that these social patterns weakened family and communal ties and resulted in 'social disorganisation' and it was this thesis that was influentially presented as the primary explanation of criminal behaviour.

Shaw and McKay (1972, originally 1931) observed that it was the very nature of neighbourhoods – not the nature of the individuals who lived within them, regardless of their social origin or ethnicity – that regulated involvement in crime and they were to influentially emphasise the importance of neighbourhood organisation in allowing or preventing offending behaviour by children and young people. They observed that in more affluent communities, parents fulfilled the needs of their offspring and carefully supervised their activities, but in the zone of transition, families and other conventional institutions – schools, churches and voluntary associations – were strained, if not destroyed, by rapid urban growth, migration and poverty. Left to their own devices, young people in this zone were not subject to the social constraints placed on their contemporaries in the more affluent areas and were more likely to seek excitement and friends in the streets of the city. Shaw and McKay concluded that disorganised neighbourhoods help produce and sustain 'criminal traditions' that compete with conventional values and can be 'transmitted down through successive generations of boys, much the same way that language and other social forms are transmitted' (Shaw and McKay, 1972: 174).

Later anomie or strain theories develop the positivist sociological tradition to propose that most members of society share a common value system that teaches us both the things we should strive for in life and the approved way in which we can achieve them. Without reasonable access to the socially approved means, people will nevertheless attempt to find some alternative way, including criminal behaviour, to resolve the pressure to achieve (Merton, 1938).

Robert Merton followed the Chicago School sociologists in rejecting individualistic explanations of criminality but took his sociological argument a step further than Durkheim. Whereas his predecessor had considered human aspirations to be natural, Merton argued that they are usually socially learned while, at the same time, there are social structural limitations imposed on access to the means to achieve these goals. His work therefore focuses upon the position of the individual within the social structure rather than on personality characteristics and in his words, 'our primary aim lies in discovering how some social structures exert a definite pressure upon certain persons in the society to engage in nonconformist conduct' (Merton, 1938: 672).

Merton distinguished between *cultural goals* and *institutionalised means*: the former are those material possessions, symbols of status, accomplishment and esteem that established norms and values encourage us to aspire to, and are, therefore, socially learned; the latter are the distribution of opportunities to achieve these goals in socially acceptable ways. Merton observes that it is possible to overemphasise either the goals or the means to achieve them, and it is this which leads to social strains, or 'anomie'.

Deviant, especially criminal, behaviour results when cultural goals are accepted, for example, and people would generally like to be financially successful, but where access to the means to achieve that goal is limited by the position of a person in the social structure. Merton outlined five possible reactions, or adaptations, that can occur when people are not in a position to legitimately attain internalised social goals.

Conformity is a largely self-explanatory adaptation where people tend to accept both the cultural goals of society and the means of achieving them. Even if they find their access to social mobility to be limited, they still tend not to 'deviate'. Merton claimed that in most societies this is the standard form of adaptation, for if this were not the case society would be extremely unstable.

Retreatism is the least common adaptation and involves those who reject both social goals *and* the means of obtaining them and these are true 'aliens', they are 'in the society but not *of* it' (Merton, 1938: 677). It is a category of social 'drop-outs' that includes among others drug addicts, psychotics, vagrants, tramps and chronic alcoholics.

Merton identifies many similarities between the third adaptation, *ritualists*, and 'conformists', with an example of the former being a person who adheres to rules for their own sake. Those in rule-bound positions in the armed services, social control institutions or public service may be particularly susceptible to this form of adaptation where the emphasis is on the means of achievement rather than the goals.

Innovation, the usual focus for the student of crime and criminal behaviour, involves those who are keen to achieve the standard goals of society, wealth, fame or admiration, but, probably due to blocked opportunities to obtain these by socially approved means, embark on novel, or innovative, routes. Many 'innovative' routes exist in complex organic societies, so much so that in some cases innovators can be considered indistinguishable from 'conformists', for example, the sports, arts and entertainment industries frequently attract, develop and absorb 'innovators'. The innovator nevertheless overemphasises the goals of achievement over the means. Thus, conventionally regarded success may be achieved by any means that seem appropriate to the innovator including crime and criminal behaviour.

Rebellion involves those who not merely reject but also wish to change the existing social system and its goals and thus reject both the socially approved means and goals of their society.

Three main criticisms of anomie theory can be identified. First, it has been accused of being a self-acknowledged 'theory of the middle range' that does little to trace the origins of criminogenic circumstances (Taylor *et al.*, 1973). Second, there is the notion that cultural goals and values are known and shared by all members of society (Lemert, 1972). Third, there is the assumption that it is the 'lower classes' who are most likely to suffer from frustrated aspirations and who are subject to strain and commit criminal or deviant acts. Later criminological studies nevertheless reveal that not only is there a great deal more deviant behaviour in society but anomie theory has also made a major contribution to explaining white collar and business crime (Etzioni, 1961; Box, 1983; Staw and Szwajkowski, 1975; Gross, 1978; Braithwaite, 1984) while others have demonstrated its value for explaining 'hate crimes' (Perry, 2001; Hopkins Burke and Pollock, 2004).

There are different deviant subculture explanations of crime and criminal behaviour but all share a common perception that some social groups have values and attitudes that enable or encourage delinquency. Albert Cohen (1955) argued that adolescent gang members invariably steal for the fun of it, not the acquisition of financial reward, and take pride in their acquired reputations for being tough and 'hard'. The gang – or subculture – offers possibilities for *status* and the acquisition of respect that are denied elsewhere. Involvement in gang culture is, to use contemporary terminology, simply cool. Cohen noted that although society is stratified into socio-economic classes it is the norms and values of the middle class that are dominant and employed to judge the success and status of everybody in society. The young working-class male nevertheless experiences a different form of upbringing and is unlikely to internalise these norms and values. He is thrust into a competitive social system founded on alien middle-class norms and values with the outcome that he experiences a deficit of respect and *status frustration*.

Walter Miller (1958) develops this theme and argues that offending is simply the product of long-established traditions of working-class life and it is the very structure of that culture that generates offending behaviour not conflicts with middle-class values. The *focal concerns* of young males in working-class society

– toughness, smartness, excitement, fate and autonomy – combine in several ways to produce criminality. Those who respond to such concerns automatically violate the law through their behaviour and, thus, the very fact of being working class places the individual in a situation that contains a variety of direct incitements towards deviant conduct. Implicit in this formulation is a significant attack on the notion that subcultures originate as a response to lack of status or thwarted aspirations. On the contrary, delinquency is simply a way of life and a response to the realities of their particular lives.

Cloward and Ohlin (1960) propose that it is necessary to have two theories in order to fully explain adolescent criminal behaviour: first, there is a need for a 'push' theory to explain why it is that large numbers of young people offend, and second, a 'pull' theory to explain the continuance of this behaviour and how it becomes passed on to others. The originality of their work lies in their use of a combination of anomie theory (Merton) to explain the 'push' and differential association theory (Sutherland) to explain the 'pull'. They moreover recognise that there is a discrepancy between the aspirations of working-class adolescent males and the opportunities available to them. Thus, when an individual recognises that membership of a particular ethnic group or social class and/or lack of a suitable education has seriously restricted their access to legitimate opportunities, they will blame an unfair society for this failure and withdraw their belief in the legitimacy of the social order. It is this awareness that leads to a rejection of conventional codes of behaviour.

Cloward and Ohlin followed Cohen in stressing that individuals have to actively seek out and join with others who face the same problems and together these young males will devise a collective solution to their predicament for, surrounded by hostile adults, they need all the support that they can get from each other. Moreover, they need to develop techniques to neutralise the guilt they feel and this is easier to achieve as the member of a like-minded group.

Underlying this reformulation of anomie theory is the assumption that illegitimate routes to success are freely available to those individuals who 'need' them. Cloward and Ohlin combine the cultural transmission theory of Shaw with the differential association theory of Sutherland to create an 'illegitimate opportunity structure' concept that parallels the 'legitimate opportunity structure' of Merton. From this theory the existence of three separate delinquent subcultures was predicted. First, *criminal* delinquent subcultures are said to exist where there are available illegitimate opportunities for learning the motivations, attitudes and techniques necessary in order to commit crimes. Second, a *conflict* subculture exists where adolescent males, denied access to the legitimate opportunity structure because of their social class, ethnic origin, etc., have no available criminal opportunity structure and, in this scenario, young males work off their frustrations by attacking people (assault), property (vandalism) and each other (gang fights). Third, *retreatist* subcultures tend to exist where drugs are freely available and membership is composed of those who have failed to gain access to either the legitimate or criminal subcultures. These young males retreat into drug misuse and alcoholism and are considered to be 'double failures'.

A number of specific criticisms of the US deviant subculture tradition can be identified. First, descriptions of the 'typical' offender where they are portrayed as being in some way different from non-offenders and driven into offending behaviour by grim social and economic forces beyond their control are seriously problematic. There is simply no attempt to explain why it is that many if not most young males faced with the same 'problems of adjustment' *do not* join delinquent gangs. Second, virtually all deviant subculture explanations consider adolescent offending to be a gang phenomenon where in reality this is a very doubtful proposition. A lot of adolescent offending behaviour is a solitary activity or involves, at the most, two or three young males together. Third, none of these explanations takes into account the roles of authority figures – the police, parents, social workers and teachers – in labelling these young people as offenders. Fourth, no adequate explanations are provided of how it is that many young males appear to simply outgrow offending behaviour. Fifth, no explanation is provided for the offending behaviour of adolescent females. Sixth, there is an inherent assumption that offending is the preserve of the young male lower working classes and this is clearly not the case.

The deviant subculture concept has nevertheless been subsequently successfully applied to the study of business or corporate crime where these were found to be sometimes acceptable and endorsed by group norms with certain types of illegal activity seen as normal by those involved (Aubert, 1952; Braithwaite, 1984); hate crimes, for being part of a particular ethnic group with its additional transmitted traditions and mechanical solidarities can undoubtedly act as a particular focus for collective belonging and provide both the fulcrum for the actualisation of hate crime behaviour and protection against it (Hopkins Burke and Pollock, 2004); and police canteen culture where working in a hard, hostile environment has brought serving officers together and rather inevitably led to them looking inwards to the group for a supportive shared worldview (Hopkins Burke, 2004a).

The US deviant subcultural tradition has been widely accused of being overly determinist in its apparent rejection of free-will and it is the work of David Matza that provides a link with the non-determinist theories that follow. Matza (1964) proposes that delinquency is simply a *status* and delinquents are *role players* who intermittently act out a delinquent role. These young men are perfectly capable of engaging in conventional activity and, therefore, the alleged forces that compel them to be delinquent are somehow rendered inactive for most of their lives. They simply 'drift' between delinquent and conventional behaviour. The young person is neither compelled to engage in, nor committed, to delinquent activity but freely chooses it sometimes and on other occasions does not do so.

Matza accepts the existence of subcultures whose members engage in delinquency but, on the other hand, denies the existence of a specific deviant subculture. Theories that propose the existence of such a subculture assume that this involves a contra culture, one that deliberately runs counter to the values of the dominant culture. Matza argues that this position is seriously problematic. First, there is the implication that the young person does not experience feelings of guilt and this is not the case. Second, there is an assumption that young offenders have no respect for conventional morality whereas, in reality, most young people involved in offending behaviour recognise the legitimacy of the dominant social order and the validity of its moral standards. Third, it is argued that young offenders define all people outside their 'delinquent subculture' as a potential victim whereas they distinguish special groups, mostly other delinquents, as legitimate targets to victimise. Fourth, it is proposed that delinquents are immune from the demands of the larger culture whereas, in reality, the members of these supposed 'delinquent subcultures' are invariably *children* and cannot escape from disapproving adults and their condemnation of delinquent behaviour.

Later deviant subculture theorists – with clear theoretical foundations in the victimised actor model – propose that involvement in particular subcultures, whether these be 'mainstream' (where working-class *boys* learn the skills to later survive the mind-numbing tedium of working-class jobs) (Willis, 1977) or 'spectacular' (where young people acquire certain musical and sartorial tastes), is determined by wider socio-economic factors (thus, for example, the aspiring social climbers 'the mods' were products of the self-confident full employment years of the 1960s while 'the punks' were an outcome of the widespread unemploy-ment and despair of the late 1970s) (Hebdige, 1976, 1979; Brake, 1980, 1985). Postmodern approaches develop that perspective but recognise an element of albeit limited and constrained choice of subcultural belonging for some young people (Hopkins Burke and Sunley, 1996, 1998).

The victimised actor model

The victimised actor model proposes, with increasingly radical variants, that the criminal is in some way the victim of an unjust and unequal society and this perspective can thus be clearly conceptualised in terms of the radical conflict model of criminal justice development. From this perspective, it is the behaviour and activities of the poor and powerless sections of society that are targeted and criminalised while the sometimes dubious activities of the rich and powerful are either simply ignored or not even defined as criminal.

There are two identifiable factors central to the emergence of the victimised actor model. First, there emerged during the mid-twentieth century within the social sciences an influential critique of the predestined actor model of human behaviour. Thus, symbolic interactionism (Mead, 1934), phenomenology (Schutz, 1962) and ethnomethodology (Garfinkel, 1984) all questioned the positivist insistence on identifying and analysing the compelling *causes* that drive indi-viduals towards criminal behaviour while at the same time being unable to describe the social world in a way that is meaningful to its participants. Positivists were observed to have a restricted notion of criminality that was based on a tendency to accept the conventional morality of rules and criminal laws as self-evident truths and where a particular action is defined as a crime because the state has decreed it to be so. Second, there developed a critique of the orthodox predestined actor model notion that society is fundamentally characterised by consensus. Pluralist conflict theorists proposed that society consists of numerous interest groups all involved in an essential struggle for material resources with other groups (Dahrendorf, 1958); while more radical theories, informed by various inter-pretations of Marxist social and economic theory, simply view social conflict as having its roots in fundamental discord between social classes (Taylor *et al.*, 1973).

Social reaction – or labelling – theories (Lemert, 1951; Kitsuse, 1962; Becker, 1963; Piliavin and Briar, 1964; Cicourel, 1968) propose that no behaviour is inherently deviant or criminal, but only comes to be considered so when others confer this label upon the act. Thus, it is not the intrinsic nature of an act, but the nature of the social reaction that determines whether a 'crime' has taken place. Central to this perspective is the notion that being found out and stigmatised, as a consequence of rule-breaking conduct, may cause an individual to become committed to further deviance, often as part of a deviant subculture.

The essence of this position is neatly summarised in a well-known passage by Becker (1963: 4) who, unlike most other labelling theorists, was concerned with the creators and enforcers of criminal labels and categories:

> Social groups create deviance by making the rules whose infraction con-stitutes deviance, and by applying those rules to particular people and labelling them as outsiders. From this point of view . . . the deviant is one to whom the label has been successfully applied; deviant behaviour is behaviour that people so label.

Becker argued that rules, including criminal laws, are made by people with power and enforced upon people without power. Thus, even on an everyday level, rules are made by the old for the young, by men for women, by whites for blacks and by the middle class for the working class. These rules are often imposed upon the recipients against their will and their own best interests and are legitimised by an ideology that is transmitted to the less powerful in the course of primary and secondary socialisation. As a result of this process, most people internalise and obey the rules without realising – or questioning – the extent to which their behaviour is being decided for them.

Becker also argues that some rules may be cynically designed to keep the less powerful in their place while others may have simply been introduced as the outcome of a sincere – albeit irrational and mistaken – belief on the part of high-status individuals that the creation of a new rule will be beneficial for its intended subjects. Becker termed the people who create new rules for the 'benefit' of the less fortunate 'moral entrepreneurs'.

Becker noted two closely interrelated outcomes of a successful 'moral crusade': first, there is the creation of a new group of 'outsiders', those who infringe the new rule; second, a social control agency emerges charged with enforcing the rule and with the power to impose labels on transgressors, although more often this simply means an extension of police work and power. Eventually the new rule, control agency and 'deviant' social role come to permeate the collective consciousness and are taken for granted with the outcome being the creation of negative stereotypes of those labelled 'deviant'.

The labelling perspective has also been applied at a group level and the concept of 'deviancy amplification' suggests that the less tolerance there is to an initial act of group deviance, the more acts that will be defined as deviant (Wilkins, 1964). The process continues through a media campaign that whips up a frenzy of popular societal indignation or a 'moral panic' about a particular activity that is seen to threaten the very fabric of civilisation. For example, 'lager louts', 'football hooligans', 'new age travellers', 'ravers' and even 'dangerous dogs' have all been the subjects of moral panics in the recent past in the UK. Once labelled as such, those engaged in the particular activity become ostracised and targeted as 'folk devils' by the criminal justice system reacting to popular pressure (Young, 1971; Cohen, 1973).

Among the critics of the labelling perspective are those who argue that they simply do not go far enough. By concentrating their attention on the labelling powers of front-line agents of the state working in the criminal justice system, they ignore the capacity for powerful groups to make laws to their advantage and to the disadvantage of the poor and dispossessed. Conflict and radical theorists seek to address these issues. Both sets of theorists argue that laws are formulated to express the values and interests of the most powerful groups in society while at the same time they place restrictions on the behaviour and activities commonly engaged in by the less powerful, thus disproportionately 'criminalising' the members of these groups. The more radical variants propose that it is the very conditions generated by the capitalist political economy that generate crime (Vold, 1958; Turk, 1969; Quinney, 1970; Chambliss, 1975). These latter ideas were further developed in the UK in the late 1960s and early 1970s by the 'new criminologists' who sought an explanation of criminal behaviour based on a theoretical synthesis of Marxism and labelling perspectives (Taylor *et al.*, 1973; Hall *et al.*, 1978).

Criticisms of radical criminology have arisen from three primary sources. First, traditional Marxists have questioned the manipulation of this theoretical tradition to address the issue of crime (Hirst, 1980). Second, there was the important recognition by the populist conservatives, or right realists, that most predatory street crime is committed by members of the poorer sections of society against people in a similar class location and this recognition changed the whole nature of political debate on the crime problem. Third, there was the increasing recognition of this latter reality by sections of the political left and the consequent development of a populist socialist response that will be discussed below.

Feminists have considered the gendered nature of criminality and propose that it is men who are the dominant group in an unequal society and it is they who make and enforce the rules and laws to the detriment of women, and some again argue – in the case of Marxist and socialist feminists – that these processes also operate in the interests of the reproduction of capitalism. Feminists moreover challenge the until recently orthodox psycho-biological predestined actor model explanations of female criminality where women are seen to be the poor victims of their biological destiny (Smart, 1977; Heidensohn, 1985) and have produced significant critiques of traditional 'malestream criminology' in four critical areas.

First, there is the 'female emancipation leads to crime debate' where it is argued that increases in often aggressive female crime during the late 1960s and early 1970s could be explained by the influence of the emerging women's liberation movement (Adler, 1975; Simon, 1975). Box and Hale (1983) merely observe an historical overlap between women's liberation and the increase in female criminality.

Second, there is the invalidation of the 'leniency hypothesis' of Pollak (1950) which had proposed that women are treated more leniently by the criminal justice system for reasons of 'chivalry'. Farrington and Morris (1983) nevertheless found that court leniency towards women was an outcome of their lesser criminal records, while Carlen (1983) found that Scottish Sheriffs justified imprisonment more readily for female offenders whom they viewed as having 'failed' as mothers and were thus 'double deviants'. Downes and Rock (1998: 285–286) conclude that rather than being treated leniently by the courts, 'women – by comparison with men – are under-protected and over-controlled'.

Third, there is the emergence of gender-based theories where some feminist writers have modified the 'control theory' we will encounter below, to argue that the reason why there are so few women criminals is because of the formal and informal controls that constrain them within male dominated society. Heidensohn (1985) proposes that in order to understand more about the transmission of gender inequality and the control of women by familial roles, it is necessary to consider the practical and ideological constraints imposed on them by family life.

Fourth, there was the recognition and redefinition of previously non-problematic activities such as domestic violence and intrafamilial child molestation as serious crimes that need to be taken seriously (Hanmer and Saunders, 1984; Dobash and Dobash, 1992).

Finally, feminist discourse has encouraged a small but growing group of male writers to 'take seriously' the issue of 'masculinities' and the idea that 'maleness' is itself a social construction and that there are different ways of being a man with some variants more likely to become involved in – invariably violent – criminal behaviour (Connell 1987, 1995; Messerschmidt 1993; Jefferson, 1997).

Critical criminology is one of two contemporary variants of the radical conflict tradition in criminology but the only one with unequivocal roots in the victimised actor model. There are a number of different versions but in general critical criminologists define crime in terms of oppression where it is members of the working class, women and ethnic minority groups who are the most likely to suffer the weight of oppressive social relations based upon class division, sexism and racism.

Critical criminologists focus their attention on both the crimes of the powerful and those of the less powerful. Crime is viewed to be associated with broad processes of the political economy that affect both groups but in quite different ways. For the powerful, there are the pressures associated with the securing and maintenance of state and corporate interests in the context of global capitalism. In the case of the less powerful, criminal behaviour is seen to be the outcome of the interaction between the marginalisation, or exclusion from access to mainstream institutions, and criminalisation by the state authorities, with particular attention paid to the increasing racialisation of crime, in which the media and police, in the 'war against crime' and public disorder, target certain invariably ethnic minority communities. In short, critical criminologists link offending behaviour to a social context that is structurally determined by the general allocation of societal resources and by the specific nature of police intervention in the lives of its citizens (Cohen, 1980; Box, 1983; Scraton, 1985; Sim *et al.*, 1987; Scraton and Chadwick, 1996).

Critical criminologists have nevertheless been criticised by the other contemporary wing of the radical tradition – the populist socialists or 'left realists' whom we will encounter below – who consider them to be 'left idealists' with romantic notions of criminals as revolutionaries or latter-day 'Robin Hoods' stealing from the rich to give to the poor, while failing adequately to address the reality that much crime is committed by the poor on their own kind. Critical criminologists have nonetheless widened the horizons of the discipline to embrace the study of zemiology or social harms such as sexism, racism, imperialism and economic exploitation which, it is argued, could and should be included as the focal concern of criminological investigation as these are seen to be far more damaging to the fabric of society than those restricted activities which have been defined as criminal (Schwendinger and Schwendinger, 1970; Shearing, 1989; Tifft, 1995).

Integrated theories

There are three ways in which theories – or explanations of crime and criminal behaviour, in this case – can be developed and evaluated. First, each theory can be considered on its own merits, that is, there is a consideration of whether or not it provides a plausible explanation of the observed phenomena. Second, there can be a process of theory competition where there is a logical and comprehensive examination of two different perspectives and a consideration of which one most successfully fits the data at hand (Liska, 1987). The third way is by theoretical integration where the intention is to identify commonalities in two or more theories in order to produce a synthesis that is superior to any one individual theory. Thus, integrated theories of crime and criminal behaviour seek, as the name suggests, the integration of different theories both within one of the models outlined above, or across model boundaries, with the intention of providing a more comprehensive explanation of criminality (Farnsworth, 1989).

This section thus considers some recent attempts at theoretical integration within criminological theory. We should note that different integrated theories can be located in the context of any of the models of criminal justice development but in general the overall intention of developing a more powerful explanatory criminological tool tends to place them in the predominantly apolitical orthodox social progress model and in this way they represent a high point in the progressive modernist project.

Thus, socio-biological theories have sought a synthesis of biological and socio-logical explanations of crime and criminal behaviour in an attempt to overcome the failure of earlier biological theories to account for environmental factors. Bio-social theorists argue that the biological characteristics of an individual are only part of the explanation of criminal behaviour and factors in the physical and social environment of the offender are also influential. It is argued that all individuals must learn to control natural urges toward antisocial and criminal behaviour (Mednick and Christiansen, 1977; Mednick *et al.*, 1987). Environmentally influenced behaviour explanations also address those incidents where outside stimuli such as drug and alcohol use have instigated or enhanced a propensity towards certain forms of behaviour (Fishbein and Pease, 1996).

The socio-biological perspective has been developed by the 'right realist' criminological theorists Wilson and Herrnstein (1985), who have developed a theory combining gender, age, intelligence, body type and personality factors and have considered these in the context of the wider social environment of the offender. They propose that the interplay between these factors provides an explanation of why it is that crime rates have increased both in periods of economic boom and recession, observing that the relationship between the environment and the individual is a complex one. They suggest that:

> Long-term trends in crime rates can be accounted for primarily by three factors. First, shifts in the age structure of the population will increase or decrease the proportion of persons – young males in the population who are likely to be temperamentally aggressive and to have short horizons. Second, changes in the benefits of crime . . . and in the cost of crime will change the rate at which crimes occur, especially property crimes. . . . Third, broad social and cultural changes in the level and intensity of society's investment (via families, schools, churches, and the mass media) inculcating an internalized commitment to self control will affect the extent to which individuals at risk are willing to postpone gratification, accept as equitable the outcomes of others, and conform to rules.
>
> (Wilson and Herrnstein, 1985: 437)

Among the most contentious socio-biological criminological theories to emerge in recent years have been those that propose that rape has evolved as a genetically advantageous behavioural adaptation. Thornhill and Palmer (2000) argue that the underlying motivations of rapists evolved because they were at one time conducive to reproduction and observe that the overwhelming majority of rape victims are of childbearing age and suggest that this perception is significant in the victims chosen by rapists. Women, they argue, have evolutionary-psycho-logical adaptations that protect their genes from would-be rapists and they cite a study that claims victims of childbearing age suffer more emotional trauma from rape than older women.

Environmental theories are part of a long established tradition with their foundations firmly located in the sociological version of the predestined actor model. Later British area studies were to incorporate notions from the victimised actor model, primarily a consideration of the effects of labelling individuals, groups of residents, and particular neighbourhoods as different or bad (Damer,

1974; Gill, 1977). Later North American studies sought to incorporate the discipline of geography to provide a more sophisticated analysis of the distribution of crime and criminals (Brantingham and Brantingham, 1981). However, this should not be conceived as simply a geographical determinist account where the environment *causes* individuals or groups to become involved in criminal behaviour. For, in adopting the recognition that crime happens when the four elements of a law, an offender, a target and a place coincide, the perspective is brought into contact with contemporary rational actor model theories (Cohen and Felson, 1979). Environmental management theories certainly presuppose the existence of a rational calculating individual whose activities can be restricted or curtailed by changing his or her surroundings (Wilson and Kelling, 1982).

Social control theories again have a long and distinguished pedigree with their origins in both the rational actor and predestined actor models of crime and criminal behaviour (Hobbes, 1968; Durkheim, 1951; Freud, 1927) with both social and psychological factors having been employed in order to explain why it is that many people conform to the norms of society while others deviate and become involved in criminal activities. Early social theory had proposed that inadequate forms of social control were more likely during periods of rapid modernisation and social change because new forms of regulation could not evolve quickly enough to replace declining forms of social integration (Durkheim, 1951). This argument was developed by early social control theorists, such as the Chicago School, who proposed that social disorganisation causes a weakening of social control making crime and deviance more *possible*, but others attached more importance to individual psychological factors (Nye, 1958; Matza, 1969; Reckless, 1967). The highly influential later social control theories are based on the fundamental assumption that individuals become involved in criminal acts when their bonds to society are weakened or broken (Hirschi, 1969).

Hirschi (1969) identified four elements of the social bond – *attachment, commitment, involvement* and *belief* – but unlike other control theorists who had emphasised the internal psychological dimension of control, these terms were employed in a much more sociological sense. The idea that norms and attitudes can be so deeply internalised as to constitute part of the personality is simply rejected and the bonds of an individual to conventional society are considered much more superficial and precarious. First, *attachment* refers to the capacity of individuals to form effective relationships with other people and institutions, in the case of adolescents, with their parents, peers and school. Second, *commitment* refers to the social investments made by the individual to conventional lines of action that could be put at risk by engaging in deviant behaviour. Third, *involvement* again refers not to some psychological or emotional state but to the more mundane reality that a person may be too busy doing conventional things to find time to engage in deviant activities. Fourth, *beliefs* are not – as we might expect – a set of deeply held convictions but rather a set of impressions and convictions in need of constant reinforcement. These four variables, although independent, are also highly interrelated and are theoretically given equal weight: thus each helps to prevent law-breaking activities in most people. In an attempt to remedy identified defects in social control theory, different writers and researchers have sought subsequently to integrate the theory with other perspectives.

First, a model expanding and synthesising strain, social learning and control theories begins with the assumption that individuals have different early social-isation experiences and that these lead to variable degrees of commitment to, and integration into, the conventional social order (Elliot *et al.*, 1979).

Second, an integration of control theory with a labelling/conflict perspective – from the victimised actor tradition – seeks to show how the 'primary' deviants of the self-report studies become the largely economically disadvantaged and minority group 'secondary' deviants of the official statistics. It is shown that differential policing practices and institutional biases at different stages of the criminal justice system all operate in favour of the most advantaged sections of society and to the detriment of its less favoured citizens which, it is argued, is an outcome of the selective targeting of the most disadvantaged groups in society by the criminal justice system, acting in the interests of powerful groups (Box, 1981, 1987), which of course is a radical conflict model of criminal justice development argument.

Third, a further highly influential approach builds upon and integrates elements of control, labelling, anomie and subcultural theory and proposes that criminal subcultures provide emotional support for those who have been negatively labelled, stigmatised and rejected by conventional society. Braithwaite (1989) proposes a positive process of shaming – that is, one that shames the act and not the person – and claims that individuals are more susceptible to shaming when they are enmeshed in multiple relationships of *interdependency* and, furthermore, societies shame more effectively when they are *communitarian*. It is such societies or cultures – constituted of dense networks of individual interdependencies characterised by mutual help and trust – rather than individualistic societies that are, it is argued, more capable of delivering the required more potent shaming and moreover shaming that is reintegrative.

Both Box and Braithwaite have sought to rescue the social control theory perspective from its emphasis on the individual – or more accurately family – culpability that had made it so popular with conservative governments both in the UK and the USA during the 1980s. Box (1981, 1987) located his radical reformu-lation within the victimised actor model but it is the notion of 'reintegrative shaming' developed by Braithwaite that has been central to the populist socialist perspective that we encounter below.

Gottfredson and Hirschi (1990) subsequently sought to produce a 'general theory of crime' that combines rational actor notions of crime with a predestined actor model (control) theory of criminality. In accordance with the former, crime is defined as acts of force or fraud undertaken in pursuit of self-interest, but it is the predestined actor notion of – or lack of – social control that provides the answer as to exactly who it is who will make the choice to offend when appropriate circumstances arise.

There have been three recent developments in the social control theory tradition. First, power control theory developed by John Hagan (Hagan *et al.*,

1985, 1987, 1990; Hagan, 1989) combines social class and control theories of criminal behaviour in order to explain the effects of differential familial control on gender differences in crime. Hagan *et al.* (1987) argue that parental position in the workforce affects patriarchal attitudes in the household and these, in turn, result in different levels of control placed on boys and girls in the home. Moreover, differing levels of control affect the likelihood of the children taking risks and ultimately becoming involved in deviant behaviour.

Second, control balance theories define deviancy as simply any activity which the majority find unacceptable and/or disapprove of and which occurs when a person has either a surplus or deficit of control in relation to others: those whose position in society allows them to exert more control over others and their environment than is exerted over them enjoy a control surplus; a control deficit arises where people are controlled more by others than they are able to control. Any control imbalance, either surplus or deficit, is likely to lead to deviancy (Tittle, 1995, 1997, 1999, 2000).

Third, differential coercion theory observes that coercion has multiple sources – including families, schools, peer relations and neighbourhoods – and then specifies how each of these coercive experiences fosters criminal involvement. Colvin (2000) uses the term differential because individuals vary in the extent to which they are exposed to coercion and it is a central premise of his perspective that criminal involvement will be positively related to the degree of duress experienced by individuals.

'Left realism' emerged in the latter years of the twentieth century as a direct response to two closely related factors. First, there was the reaction among some key radical criminologists on the political left to the perceived idealism of critical criminology and its inherent apology for criminals and criminal behaviour, we saw above, and second, there was the rise of the populist conservatives and their 'realist' approach to dealing with the reality of crime. Thus, 'left realists' came to acknowledge that crime is a real problem that seriously impinges on the quality of life of many poor people and must therefore be addressed. From this perspective, a comprehensive solution to the crime problem – a 'balance of intervention' – is proposed (Young, 1994). On the one hand, crime must be tackled and criminals must take responsibility for their actions; but, on the other hand, the social conditions that encourage and make involvement in crime for many a rational choice must also be tackled.

Left realism is thus an integrated theory of crime but rather an approach that recognises that there is something to be said for most theories of crime and for most forms of crime prevention with the distinct suggestion that insights can be incorporated from each of the three models of crime and criminal behaviour. It is a strategy that was to become very influential with the 'New Labour' government elected in the UK in 1997 which was, as demonstrated by the oft-quoted remark of Prime Minister Tony Blair first made while previously the Shadow Home Secretary, 'tough on crime, tough on the causes of crime' (Hopkins Burke, 2008, 2009).

Being 'tough on crime' suggests that offenders should take responsibility for their actions and is in theoretical accordance with the prescriptions of the rational actor model. Taking a tough stance on the causes of crime suggests nevertheless a targeting of both those individual and structural factors that in some way encourage criminality and is thus in accordance with not only the predestined actor model but *also* rooted most firmly in the victimised actor model. The theoretical justification for that governmental approach – and it is one that sets it apart from its political opponents and predecessors in government – is demonstrated by the following realist case study of an apparently criminal 'underclass'.

First, the behavioural perspective, which is normally associated with the populist or neo-conservatives in the contemporary rational actor model tradition, argues that state welfare erodes individual responsibility by giving people incentives not to work and provide for themselves and their family. Furthermore, it is observed that those 'controls' that stop individuals and communities from behaving badly, such as stable family backgrounds and in particular positive male role models as proposed by the social control theory tradition (Hirschi, 1969), have ceased to exist for many members of this identified 'underclass' (Murray, 1990, 1994).

Second, structural explanations, which are normally associated with sociological variants of the predestined actor model, critical criminologists and left idealists, observe the collapse of the manufacturing industry, traditional working-class employment and the subsequent retreat of welfare provision in modernist societies as providing the structural pre-conditions for the creation of a socially excluded class (Dahrendorf, 1985; Campbell, 1993; Jordan, 1996; Crowther, 1998).

Third, a left realist process model proposes that we should not dismiss either of the other two perspectives for we need to identify and address the structural pre-conditions for the emergence of a socially excluded underclass while at the same time we need to consider the behavioural subcultural strategies developed by those finding themselves located in that socio-economic position (Hopkins Burke, 1999a).

Postscript

It has been explained earlier that each of the theories introduced in this book – and, indeed, their particular host model or explanatory tradition – have a common central characteristic: that is, each is a product of what has come to be termed the modern age. Prior to the rise of modernity, religion and other forms of pre-scientific knowledge had crucially influenced explanations of crime and, at that time, criminal justice and its administration was non-codified, capricious, invariably brutal and at the cynical discretion of the agents of monarchical regimes. In contrast, modern societies are secular, industrialised, rationalised, codified and rule-bound with at least some pretence to widely participative democracy. Science is the dominant – and for a long time unchallenged – form of knowledge and thus crime and criminal behaviour has been invariably explained by reference to scientific discourses or theories while, at the same time, there has been a wider modernist faith in reason which stretches back from the great liberals of the twentieth century to beyond the Enlightenment philosophers of the eighteenth century, to the Ancient Greeks.

In the last decades of the twentieth century there were to be increasing doubts about the sustainability of the modernist project in an increasingly fragmented and diverse social world and this is a situation that some social scientists came to refer to as the postmodern condition (see Lyotard, 1984; but also Baudrillard, 1988; Bauman, 1989, 1991, 1993). This fragmentation of modernity was to pose significant problems for criminology and the criminal justice system and it is an issue to which we will return in the final chapter of this book.

3 The philosophy of law and legal ethics

In the previous chapter we considered the different ways in which crime and criminal behaviour has been variously explained during the modern era and beyond, with reference to the four different models of criminal justice development which provide the theoretical underpinnings of this book. In this chapter we will consider the philosophers of law who are concerned with providing a general philosophical analysis of law and legal institutions and locate these debates within the context of the different models of criminal justice development.

Issues in legal philosophy range from abstract conceptual questions about the nature of law and legal systems to normative questions about the relation between law, morality and the justification for various legal institutions. Topics in legal philosophy tend to be more abstract than related topics in political philosophy and applied ethics. Thus, for example, the question of whether capital punishment is morally permissible falls under the heading of applied ethics but the issue of whether the institution of punishment can be justified falls under the heading of legal philosophy.

There are broadly three categories of modernist legal philosophy. First, analytic jurisprudence provides an analysis of the essence of law in order to understand what differentiates it from other systems of norms such as ethics. Second, normative jurisprudence involves the examination of normative, evaluative and otherwise prescriptive issues about the law, such as restrictions on freedom, obligations to obey the law, and the justifications for punishment. We should observe that both analytic and normative jurisprudence can be broadly conceptualised in the context of the orthodox social progress model of criminal justice development which recognises an incremental evolutionary process that is the outcome of enlightenment and benevolence in a widely consensual society.

Critical theories of law, such as critical legal studies and feminist jurisprudence, provide a third category of modernist legal philosophy, which can be widely conceptualised in the context of the radical conflict model of criminal justice development which proposes that society is essentially conflict-ridden and the criminal justice system operates in the interests of the reproduction of capitalism and the economic and politically dominant groups in society. Indeed, it is possible to see the incrementally increasing body of legislation which has, in recent years, placed significant restrictions on our freedoms and civil liberties in the context of the carceral society *and* left realist hybrid models of criminal justice development, which identify the increasingly pervasive socio-control matrix of the carceral society but which in the final analysis nevertheless operate in the interests of the preservation and reproduction of capitalist society. Finally, we consider Islamic jurisprudence, or Sharia law, which is increasingly providing a significant radical challenge to the Western tradition of legal philosophy in contemporary post-industrial societies and indeed, in its more radical forms, the modernist enterprise itself.

Analytic jurisprudence

The principal objective of analytic jurisprudence has been to provide an account of what distinguishes law as a system of norms from other systems such as ethics. John Austin (1995, originally 1833: 11) observes that analytic jurisprudence seeks 'the essence or nature which is common to all laws that are properly so called' and is concerned with establishing the necessary conditions required for the existence of law and what distinguishes it from non-law in every possible world.

The analytic jurisprudence task is usually considered to be the analysis of the concepts of law and the legal system but there is nevertheless some confusion as to both the value and character of conceptual analysis in the philosophy of law. Brian Leiter (1998) observes that the philosophy of law is one of the few philosophical disciplines which considers conceptual analysis to be its principal concern: others take a naturalistic perspective, incorporating the tools and methods of the sciences. Brian Bix (1995) nevertheless identifies four different purposes that can be served by conceptual claims: (1) to track linguistic usage; (2) to stipulate meanings; (3) to explain what is important or essential about a class of objects; and (4) to establish an evaluative test for the concept-word. Bix proposes that conceptual analysis in law is primarily concerned with (3) and (4).

Conceptual analysis of law thus remains an important, if somewhat controversial, project in contemporary legal theory and conceptual theories of law can be divided into two main categories: first, those that argue there is a conceptual relation between law and morality, and second, those that deny that there is any such relationship. Ronald Dworkin is usually characterised as having developed a third theory not least because it is unclear what his position is on the presence or absence of a conceptual relationship between law and morality.

Natural law theory

All variations of natural law theory subscribe to the *overlap thesis* which emphasises an essential close relationship between the concepts of law and morality. Thus, from this perspective the concept of law cannot be fully articulated without some reference to moral notions. John Finnis (1980: 3) observes that when we attempt to explain what the law is we inevitably make assumptions about what is 'good':

It is often supposed that an evaluation of law as a type of social institution, if it is to be understood at all, must be preceded by a value-free description and analysis of that institution as it exists in fact. But the development of modern jurisprudence suggests, and reflection on the methodology of any social science confirms, that a theorist cannot give a theoretical description and analysis of social facts, unless he also participates in the work of evaluation, of understanding what is really good for human persons, and what is really required by practical reasonableness.

The overlap thesis appears at first sight to be unambiguous but it has nevertheless been interpreted in a number of different ways. The strongest variant can be found in the classical naturalism of Thomas Aquinas[1] and William Blackstone[2] which the latter describes in the following terms:

> This law of nature, being co-eval with mankind and dictated by God himself, is of course superior in obligation to any other. It is binding over all the globe, in all countries, and at all times: no human laws are of any validity, if contrary to this; and such of them as are valid derive all their force, and all their authority, mediately or immediately, from this original.
>
> (Blackstone, 1979: 41)

Blackstone outlines in the above passage the two claims that constitute the fundamental theoretical core of classical naturalism. First, there can be no legally valid standards that conflict with the natural law. Second, all valid laws derive what force and authority they have from the natural law. Quite simply, from this perspective, an unjust law is no law at all.

In seventeenth-century Europe entire branches of the law were supposedly founded on natural law but its influence declined significantly during the nineteenth century and this was the outcome of two formidable forces. First, the ideas associated with legal positivism, which we will encounter below, were to provide a considerable opposition to natural law thinking. Second, the idea that in moral reasoning there can be no rational solutions – the so-called non-cognitivism in ethics[3] – introduced a profound scepticism about natural law. Thus, if we cannot objectively know what is right or wrong, natural law principles are little more than subjective opinion. They can be neither right nor wrong.

The twentieth century was to see a revival of interest in natural law theory not least with the post-Second World War recognition of human rights and their expression in declarations such as the Charter of the United Nations and the Universal Declaration of Human Rights, the European Convention on Human Rights and the Declaration of Delhi on the Rule of Law of 1959. Natural law is not now perceived as a 'higher law' in the constitutional sense of invalidating ordinary law but as a benchmark against which to measure positive law. Legal theory has moreover advanced the cause of natural law theory.

Lon Fuller (1964) developed a secular natural law approach which regards law as having an 'inner morality'. He rejects the idea that there are necessary moral constraints on the content of law and argues that a legal system has the specific purpose of 'subjecting human conduct to the governance of rules'. There is thus a necessary connection between law and morality. Fuller proposes that the law is necessarily subject to a *procedural* morality that consists of the following eight principles:

1   the rules must be expressed in general terms;
2   the rules must be publicly promulgated;
3   the rules must be prospective in effect;
4   the rules must be expressed in understandable terms;
5   the rules must be consistent with one another;
6   the rules must not require conduct beyond the powers of the affected parties;
7   the rules must not be changed so frequently that the subject cannot rely on them;
8   the rules must be administered in a manner consistent with their wording.

Fuller argues that no system of rules that fails minimally to satisfy these principles of legality can achieve the essential purpose of the law. Thus, for example, a system of rules that fails to satisfy (2) or (4) cannot guide behaviour because people will not be able to determine what the rules require. Fuller (1964: 39) concludes that his eight principles are 'internal' to law in the sense that they are built into the existing conditions for law: 'a total failure in any one of these eight directions does not simply result in a bad system of law; it results in something that is not properly called a legal system at all'.

John Finnis (1980) provides a contemporary natural law theory and argues that the naturalism of Aquinas and Blackstone should not be construed as a conceptual account of the existence of conditions for law. He argues that the classical naturalists were not concerned with giving a conceptual account of legal validity but were more concerned with explaining the moral force of law. Thus, 'the principles of natural law explain the obligatory force (in the fullest sense of "obligation") of positive laws, even when those laws cannot be deduced from those principles' (Finnis 1980: 23–24).

Finnis argues that the essential function of law is to provide a justification for state coercion. An unjust law can be legally valid, but cannot provide an adequate justification for the use of state coercive power and is hence not obligatory in the fullest sense. Thus, an unjust law fails to realise the moral ideals implicit in the concept of law. An unjust law is legally binding, but is not fully law.

Finnis proposes that the overriding rationale of natural law theory is to establish 'what is good for human persons'. We cannot pursue human goods until we have a community: the authority of a leader derives from their serving the best interests of the community. Hence, should the leader enact unjust laws they would lack direct binding legal authority because they militate against the common good. From this perspective, principles of justice are no more than the general requirement that a person should foster and promote the common good in their community.

The central claims of natural law are nevertheless rejected by legal positivists who deny that the legal validity of a norm *necessarily* depends on its substantive moral qualities.

Legal positivism

The term 'positivism' derives in the legal sense from the Latin *positum* which refers to the law as it is laid down or posited. The core of legal positivism is the view that the validity of any law can be traced to an objectively verifiable source. Legal positivists hence reject the natural law perspective view that law exists independently from human enactment. From this perspective, the law as laid down should be kept separate, for the purpose of study and analysis, from the law as it ought morally to be. Thus, a clear distinction must be made between 'ought' (that which is morally desirable) and 'is' (that which actually exists). It nevertheless does not follow that a legal positivist is indifferent to moral questions: most criticise the law and propose means to reform it and this normally involves moral judgements.

Legal positivism is broadly comprised of three theoretical commitments. First, there is the *social fact thesis* – which is also known as the *pedigree thesis* – and which proposes that it is a necessary truth that legal validity is ultimately a function of certain kinds of social facts. Second, there is the *conventionality thesis* which emphasises the conventional nature of the law and which claims that the social facts which give rise to legal validity are authoritative in virtue of some kind of social convention. Third, the *separability thesis* proposes that there is no overlap whatsoever between the notions of law and morality.

The social fact thesis is heavily influenced by the utilitarian legal thought of Jeremy Bentham (1970, originally 1789) who sought to subject the common law to reason and attempted to demystify the law. Bentham argued that appeals to natural laws are nothing more than 'private opinion in disguise' or 'the mere opinion of man self-constituted into legislatures'. The indeterminacy of the common law is endemic: unwritten law is intrinsically vague and uncertain and cannot provide a reliable, public standard that can reasonably be expected to guide behaviour. Bentham observed that the chaos of the common law had to be dealt with systematically and the answer lay quite simply in codification. Legal codes would significantly diminish the power of judges and their task would thus consist less of interpretation but be one of administration.

John Austin (1995) observes – in accordance with the then contemporary influential social contract theory we encountered in the previous chapter – that the principal distinguishing feature of a legal system is the presence of a sovereign who is habitually obeyed by most people in society. Austin proposes that a rule R is legally valid (that is, it is a law) in a society S if, and only if, R is commanded by the sovereign in S and is backed up with the threat of a sanction. The relevant social fact that confers validity is promulgation by a sovereign willing to impose a sanction for non-compliance. Austin's identification of commands as the hallmark of law leads him to a more restrictive definition of law than that adopted by Bentham who sought to formulate a single, complete law which sufficiently expresses the legislative will.

The central feature of jurisprudence is, according to Austin, the notion of the law as a command of the sovereign. Anything that is not a command is not law. Only general commands count as law: only commands emanating from the sovereign are 'positive laws'. Moreover, this insistence on law as commands requires the exclusion of customary, constitutional and public international law from the field of jurisprudence because no specific sovereign can be identified as the author of their rules.

Bentham and Austin established the foundations for modern legal positivism but their ideas have been subsequently refined, developed and even rejected by contemporary legal positivists such as H.L.A. Hart, Hans Kelsen and Joseph Raz.

H.L.A. Hart (1994) conceives law as a social phenomenon that can be understood only by describing the actual social practices of a community. He observes that in order for the community to survive there is a need for certain fundamental rules that he calls the 'minimum content of natural law'. These arise out of our natural condition which is characterised by four essential features. First, there is the issue of *human vulnerability* for we are all susceptible to physical attacks. Second, there is an issue of *approximate equality* for even the strongest of us must sleep at times. Third, there is the issue of *limited altruism* for we all need food, clothes, and shelter and they are all in limited supply. Fourth, there is the issue of *limited understanding and strength of will* for we cannot be relied upon to cooperate with our fellow human beings.

These human frailties thus require the enactment of rules to protect persons and property and to ensure that promises are kept. Hart argues that Austin accounts, at most, for just one kind of rule: that is, primary rules that require or prohibit certain kinds of behaviour. This is a perspective – Hart argues – which overlooks the presence of other primary rules that confer upon citizens the power to create, modify, and extinguish rights and obligations in other persons. Hart thus observes that the rules governing the creation of contracts and wills cannot plausibly be characterised as restrictions on freedom that are backed by the threat of a sanction for non-compliance. We might nevertheless observe that Austin's perspective is more appropriate in the case of criminal law.

More significantly, Hart argues that Austin overlooks the existence of secondary meta-rules that have as their subject matter the primary rules themselves and which distinguish mature legal systems from primitive variants:

[Secondary rules] may all be said to be on a different level from the primary rules, for they are all *about* such rules; in the sense that while primary rules are concerned with the actions that individuals must or must not do, these secondary rules are all concerned with the primary rules themselves. They specify the way in which the primary rules may be conclusively ascertained, introduced, eliminated, varied, and the fact of their violation conclusively determined.

(Hart, 1994: 92)

Hart distinguishes three types of secondary rules that mark the transition from primitive forms of law to mature legal systems. First, there is the *rule of recognition*, which 'specif[ies] some feature or features possession of which by a suggested rule is taken as a conclusive affirmative indication that it is a rule of the group to be supported by the social pressure it exerts' (Hart, 1994: 92). This rule thus determines the criteria by which the validity of all the rules of a legal system is decided. Second, there is the *rule of change*, which enables a society to add, remove and modify valid rules. Third, there is the *rule of adjudication*, which provides a mechanism for determining whether a valid rule has been violated. This rule is usually associated with a further power to punish the wrongdoer or compel them to make restoration. Hart therefore takes the view that every society with a advanced legal system necessarily has a rule of recognition that articulates criteria for legal validity that include provisions for making, changing and adjudicating law. Hence, law is, to use Hart's famous phrase, 'the union of primary and secondary rules' (Hart, 1994: 107).

Hart's variation on the social fact thesis thus proposes that a proposition P is legally valid in a society S if and only if it satisfies the criteria of validity contained in a rule of recognition that is binding in S. The conventionality thesis implies that a rule of recognition is binding in S only if there is a social convention among officials to treat it as defining standards of official behaviour. Thus, for Hart (1994: 113) the 'rules of recognition specifying the criteria of legal validity and its rules of change and adjudication must be effectively accepted as common public standards of official behaviour by its officials'.

In its most general form, the separability thesis proposes that law and morality are conceptually distinct and this particular abstract formulation can be interpreted in a number of ways. Klaus Füsser (1996), for example, interprets it as making a meta-level claim that the definition of law must be entirely free of moral notions. This interpretation implies that any reference to moral considerations in defining the related notions of law, legal validity, and the legal system is inconsistent with the separability thesis.

More commonly, the separability thesis is interpreted as making only an object-level claim about the existence conditions for legal validity. Hart (1994: 181–182) proposes that it is no more than the 'simple contention that it is in no sense a necessary truth that laws reproduce or satisfy certain demands of morality, though in fact they have often done so'. Insofar as the object-level interpretation of the separability thesis denies it is a necessary truth and that there are moral constraints on legal validity, it implies the existence of a possible legal system in which there are no moral constraints on legal validity.

All positivists agree that it is possible to have a legal system without moral constraints on legal validity but there are conflicting views as to whether it is possible to have legal systems *with* such constraints. According to inclusive positivism – also known as incorporationism and soft positivism – it is possible for the rule of recognition in a society to incorporate moral constraints on the content of law. Hart (1994: 250) maintains that:

[T]he rule of recognition may incorporate as criteria of legal validity conformity with moral principles or substantive values . . . such as the Sixteenth or Nineteenth Amendments to the United States Constitution respecting the establishment of religion or abridgements of the right to vote.

Hans Kelsen (1967) developed a complex 'pure theory of law' and presented a subtle and profound account of the way in which we should understand law, which he insists we should do by conceiving of it as a system of 'oughts' or *norms*. He concedes that the law also consists of legal acts as determined by these norms but the essential character of law derives from the latter which include judicial decisions and legal transactions such as contracts and wills. He observes that even the most general norms describe human conduct.

Kelsen argues that legal theory is less a science than physics or chemistry and thus we need to purge it of the impurities of morality, psychology, sociology and political theory. He proposes a sort of ethical cleansing under which our analysis is directed to the norms of positive law: those 'oughts' that declare that if certain conduct (X) is performed, then a sanction (Y) should be applied by an official to the offender. His 'pure' theory thus excludes that which we cannot objectively know and that includes the moral, social or political functions of law. Law has but one purpose and that is the monopolisation of force (Kelsen, 1991).

Joseph Raz (1979) is an exclusive – or what is sometimes termed 'hard' positivist – who subscribes to the *source thesis* which proposes that the existence and content of law can always be determined by reference to its sources without recourse to moral argument. He maintains that the identity and existence of a legal system may be tested by reference to three elements: efficacy, institutional character, and sources. From this perspective, law is founded on the idea that legality does not depend on its moral merit which is in contrast to the position taken by H.L.A. Hart – who is considered a soft positivist – who acknowledges that content or merit may be included or incorporated as a condition of validity and is thus considered an 'incorporationist'.

Raz argues that the law is autonomous: we can thus identify its content without recourse to morality. Legal *reasoning*, on the other hand, is not autonomous: it is an inevitable, and desirable, feature of judicial reasoning. The existence and content of every law may be determined by a factual enquiry about conventions, institutions, and the intentions of participants in the legal system. Thus, the answer to the question 'what is law?' is always a fact and never a moral judgement. Raz is an 'exclusive' positivist because the reason we regard the law as authoritative is the fact that it is able to guide our behaviour in a way that morality cannot do. In other words, the law asserts its primacy over all other codes of conduct. Law is the ultimate source of authority. A legal system is thus quintessentially one of authoritative laws. It is the claim of authority that is the trademark of a legal system.

Ronald Dworkin and law as interpretation

The foundations of legal positivism were shaken during the 1970s by the ideas of the American jurist Ronald Dworkin who in 1969 succeeded H.L.A. Hart as Professor of Jurisprudence at Oxford. The dominance of legal positivism – especially in the UK – was over the next three decades subjected to a comprehensive onslaught in the form of a complex theory of law which was at the same time both controversial and highly influential. Dworkin's concept of law continues to exert considerable authority, especially in the USA, whenever contentious moral and political issues are debated.

Dworkin significantly contends that the law contains a solution to almost every problem and this is a viewpoint very much at variance with the traditional positivist perception that, when a judge is faced with a difficult case to which no statute or previous decision applies, he or she exercises discretion and decides the case on the basis of what seems to him or her to be the correct answer. Dworkin, in contrast, shows how a judge does not make law but rather interprets what is already part of the legal materials. It is through his or her interpretation of these materials that voice is given to the values to which the legal system is committed.

Dworkin (1977) thus rejects the social fact thesis proposed by positivism because there are some legal standards the authority of which cannot be explained in terms of social facts. He argues that in deciding hard cases, for example, judges often invoke moral principles that do not derive their *legal* authority from the social criteria of legality contained in a rule of recognition. Since judges are bound to consider such principles when they are relevant, they must be characterised as law. Dworkin (1977: 44) concludes that 'if we treat principles as law we must reject the positivists' first tenet, that the law of a community is distinguished from other social standards by some test in the form of a master rule'. He later proposed that adjudication is and should be interpretive:

> Judges should decide hard cases by interpreting the political structure of their community in the following, perhaps special way: by trying to find the best *justification* they can find, in principles of political morality, for the structure as a whole, from the most profound constitutional rules and arrangements to the details of, for example, the private law of tort or contract.
>
> (Dworkin, 1982: 165)

Dworkin observes that there are two elements of a successful judicial interpretation. First, since an interpretation is successful insofar as it justifies the particular practices of a particular society, it must *fit* with those practices in the sense that it coheres with existing legal materials defining the practices. Second, since an interpretation provides a *moral justification* for those practices, it must present them in the best possible moral light. Thus, Dworkin (1982: 171) argues, a judge should strive to interpret a case in roughly the following way:

> A thoughtful judge might establish for himself, for example, a rough 'threshold' of fit which any interpretation of data must meet in order to be

'acceptable' on the dimension of fit, and then suppose that if more than one interpretation of some part of the law meets this threshold, the choice among these should be made, not through further and more precise comparisons between the two along that dimension, but by choosing the interpretation which is 'substantively' better, that is, which better promotes the political ideals he thinks correct.

Dworkin is thus of the view that the legal authority of a binding principle derives from the contribution it makes to the best moral justification for the legal practices of a society considered as a whole. Thus, a legal principle maximally contributes to such a justification if and only if it satisfies two conditions: (1) the principle coheres with existing legal materials; and (2) the principle is the most morally attractive standard that satisfies (1). The correct legal principle is the one that makes the law the best it can be morally.

Dworkin later expands the scope of his 'constructivist' view beyond that of adjudication to encompass the realm of legal theory. He distinguishes conversational interpretation from artistic/creative interpretation and argues that the task of interpreting a social practice is more like artistic interpretation:

> The most familiar occasion of interpretation is conversation. We interpret the sounds or marks another person makes in order to decide what he has said. Artistic interpretation is yet another: critics interpret poems and plays and paintings in order to defend some view of their meaning or theme or point. The form of interpretation we are studying – the interpretation of a social practice – is like artistic interpretation in this way: both aim to interpret something created by people as an entity distinct from them, rather than what people say, as in conversational interpretation.
>
> (Dworkin, 1986: 50)

Furthermore, artistic interpretation, like judicial interpretation, is constrained by the dimensions of fit and justification. Thus, 'constructive interpretation is a matter of imposing purpose on an object or practice in order to make of it the best possible example of the form or genre to which it is taken to belong' (Dworkin, 1986: 52).

The point of any general theory of law is, therefore, to interpret a very complex set of related social practices that are 'created by people as an entity distinct from them' and, for this reason, Dworkin argues that the project of putting together a general theory of law is inherently constructivist:

> General theories of law must be abstract because they aim to interpret the main point and structure of legal practice, not some particular part or department of it. But for all their abstraction, they are constructive interpretations: they try to show legal practice as a whole in its best light, to achieve equilibrium between legal practice as they find it and the best justification of

that practice. So no firm line divides jurisprudence from adjudication or any other aspect of legal practice.

(Dworkin, 1986: 90)

Dworkin argues that the relationship between jurisprudence and adjudication is so close that the former is no more than the most general part of the latter and thus proposes that 'any judge's opinion is itself a piece of legal philosophy' (Dworkin, 1986: 90).

Dworkin, therefore, rejects not only the social fact thesis of positivism but also what he considers to be its underlying presuppositions about legal theory. Hart (1994) has nevertheless responded by distinguishing two perspectives from which a set of legal practices can be understood. A legal practice can, therefore, be understood from the 'internal' point of view of the person who accepts that practice as providing legitimate guides to conduct, as well as from the 'external' point of view of the observer who wishes to understand the practice but does not accept it as being authoritative or legitimate. Hart understands his theory of law to be both descriptive and general in the sense that it provides an account of fundamental features common to all legal systems that, in itself, presupposes a point of view that is external to all legal systems. For this reason, he regards his project as:

> A radically different enterprise from Dworkin's conception of legal theory (or 'jurisprudence' as he often terms it) as in part evaluative and justificatory and as 'addressed to a particular legal culture', which is usually the theorist's own and in Dworkin's case is that of Anglo-American law.
>
> (Hart, 1994: 240)

Hart is of the opinion that the theoretical objectives of Dworkin are fundamentally different from those of positivism, which, as a theory of analytic jurisprudence, is largely concerned with conceptual analysis. For his part, Dworkin conceives his work to be conceptual but not in the same sense that Hart regards his work:

> We all – at least all lawyers – share a concept of law and of legal right, and we contest different conceptions of that concept. Positivism defends a particular conception, and I have tried to defend a competing conception. We disagree about what legal rights are in much the same way as we philosophers who argue about justice disagree about what justice is. I concentrate on the details of a particular legal system with which I am especially familiar, not simply to show that positivism provides a poor account of that system, but to show that positivism provides a poor conception of the concept of a legal right.
>
> (Dworkin, 1977: 351–352)

These differences between Hart and Dworkin have led many legal philosophers – most recently Bix (1996) – to suspect that they are not really taking inconsistent positions at all. Indeed, there remains an issue as to whether the work of Dworkin should be construed as falling under the rubric of analytic jurisprudence.

Normative jurisprudence

Freedom and the limits of legitimate law

Laws limit the autonomy of human beings by restricting their freedom. Criminal laws remove certain behaviours from the range of behavioural options available to the individual or group by penalising them with imprisonment and, in some cases, death. Civil laws similarly require people to take certain precautions not to injure others and to honour their contracts. Given that human autonomy deserves *prima facie* moral respect, the question arises as to what are the limits of the legitimate authority of the state to restrict the freedom of its citizens. John Stuart Mill (1906, originally 1869: 12–13) provides the classic liberal answer in the form of the harm principle:

> [T]he sole end for which mankind are warranted, individually or collectively, in interfering with the liberty of action of any of their number is self-protection. The only purpose for which power can rightfully be exercised over any member of a civilized community against his will is to prevent harm to others. His own good, either physical or moral, is not a sufficient warrant. Over himself, over his own body and mind, the individual is sovereign.

Mill left the notion of harm underdeveloped but he is most frequently interpreted as meaning only physical harms and more extreme forms of psychological harm. It is a view – or something similar to it – which enjoys widespread currency among the public but it has generated considerable controversy among philosophers of law and political philosophers. Many argue that Mill simply understates the limits of legitimate state authority over the individual and they, in contrast, claim that the law may be used to enforce morality, to protect the individual from him or herself and in some cases to protect individuals from offensive behaviour.

Legal moralism is the view that the law can legitimately be used to prohibit behaviours that are in conflict with the collective moral judgements of society even when those behaviours do not result in physical or psychological harm to others. From this perspective, the freedom of the individual or group can be legitimately restricted simply because it conflicts with the collective morality of society. Thus, legal moralism implies that it is permissible for the state to use its coercive power to enforce this collective morality. The most famous legal moralist is Patrick Devlin, who argues that a shared morality is essential to the existence of a society:

> [I]f men and women try to create a society in which there is no fundamental agreement about good and evil they will fail; if, having based it on common agreement, the agreement goes, the society will disintegrate. For society is not something that is kept together physically; it is held by the invisible bonds of common thought. If the bonds were too far relaxed the members would drift apart. A common morality is part of the bondage. The bondage is part of the price of society; and mankind, which needs society, must pay its price.
>
> (Devlin, 1965: 10)

Insofar as human beings cannot lead a meaningful existence outside society, it follows, from this perspective, that the law can be used to preserve the shared morality as a means of preserving society itself.

H.L.A. Hart (1963) argues that Devlin overstates the extent to which the preservation of a shared morality is necessary for the continuing existence of a society. Devlin concludes that the necessity of a shared social morality makes it permissible for the state to legislate sexual morality (in particular, to legislate against same-sex sexual relations), but Hart (1963: 50) argues it is implausible to think that 'deviation from accepted sexual morality, even by adults in private, is something which, like treason, threatens the existence of society'. While enforcement of certain social norms protecting life, safety, and property is likely to be essential to the existence of a society, a society can survive a diversity of behaviour in many other areas of moral concern which have surrounded controversies such as abortion and homosexuality in recent years.

Legal paternalism is the view that it is permissible for the state to legislate against what Mill calls self-regarding actions when it is necessary to prevent individuals from inflicting physical or severe emotional harm on *themselves*. Gerald Dworkin (1972: 65) describes a paternalist interference as an 'interference with a person's liberty of action justified by reasons referring exclusively to the welfare, good, happiness, needs, interests or values of the person being coerced'. Thus, for example, a law requiring the use of a helmet when riding a motorcycle is a paternalistic interference insofar as it is justified by concerns for the safety of the rider.

Dworkin argues that Mill's view that a person 'cannot rightfully be compelled to do or forbear because it will be better for him' (Mill, 1906: 13) precludes paternalistic legislation to which fully rational individuals would agree. According to Dworkin, there are goods, such as health and education, that any rational person needs to pursue for his or her own good, no matter how that good is conceived. Dworkin thus concludes that the attainment of these basic goods can be legitimately promoted in certain circumstances by using the coercive force of the state.

Dworkin offers a hypothetical consent justification for his limited legal paternalism and takes the view that there are a number of different situations in which fully rational adults would consent to paternalistic restrictions on freedom. For example, a fully rational adult would consent to paternalistic restrictions to protect him or her from making decisions that are 'far-reaching, potentially dangerous and irreversible' (G. Dworkin, 1972: 80). He nonetheless identifies three limits to legitimate paternalism. First, the state must show that the behaviour governed by the proposed restriction involves the sort of harm that a rational person would want to avoid. Second, based on the calculations of a fully rational person, the potential harm involved should outweigh the benefits of the relevant behaviour. Third, the proposed restriction should be the least restrictive alternative for protecting against the harm.

Joel Feinberg (1985) argues that the harm principle does not provide sufficient protection against the wrongful behaviours of others, as it is inconsistent with many criminal prohibitions we take for granted as being justified. If the only legitimate use of the state's coercive force is to protect people from harm caused by others, then statutes prohibiting public sex are impermissible because it might be offensive but does not cause harm to others, certainly in the sense proffered by Mill. Feinberg thus argues that the harm principle must be augmented by the offence principle, which he defines as follows:

> It is always a good reason in support of a proposed criminal prohibition that it would probably be an effective way of preventing serious offense (as opposed to injury or harm) to persons other than the actor, and that it is probably a necessary means to that end.
>
> (Feinberg, 1985: 82)

With the term 'offense', Feinberg intends a subjective and objective element: the former consists in the experience of an unpleasant mental state (for example, shame, disgust, anxiety, embarrassment); the latter consists in the existence of a wrongful cause of such a mental state.

The obligation to obey law

Natural law critics of positivism (for example, Fuller, 1958) frequently complain that if positivism is correct, there cannot be a moral obligation to obey the law qua law. As Feinberg (1979: 55) observes:

> The positivist account of legal validity is hard to reconcile with the [claim] that valid law as such, no matter what its content, deserves our respect and general fidelity. Even if valid law is bad law, we have some obligation to obey it simply because it is law. But how can this be so if a law's validity has nothing to do with its content?
>   The idea is this: if what is essential to law is just that there exist specified recipes for making law, then there cannot be a moral obligation to obey a rule *simply because it is the law*.

Contemporary positivists, in general, accept the idea that positivism is inconsistent with an obligation to obey law qua law (cf. Himma, 1998) but argue that the mere status of a norm as law cannot give rise to any moral obligation to obey that norm. While there might be a moral obligation to obey a particular law because of its moral content (for example, laws prohibiting murder) or because it solves a coordination problem (for example, laws requiring people to drive on one side of the road), the mere fact that a rule is law does not provide a moral reason for doing what the law requires.

Indeed, arguments for the existence of even a *prima facie* obligation to obey law (that is, an obligation that can be outweighed by competing obligations) have largely been unsuccessful. Arguments in favour of an obligation to obey the law roughly fall into four categories: (1) *arguments from gratitude*; (2) *arguments from fair play*; (3) *arguments from implied consent*; and (4) *arguments from general utility*.

The *argument from gratitude* begins with the observation that all persons, even those who are worst off, derive some benefit from the enforcement of the law by the state. From this perspective, a person who accepts benefits from another person thereby incurs a duty of gratitude towards the benefactor and thus the only plausible way to discharge this duty towards the government is to obey its laws. However, as M.B.E. Smith (1973: 953) observes, 'If someone confers benefits on me without any consideration of whether I want them, and if he does this in order to advance some purpose other than promotion of my particular welfare, I have no obligation to be grateful towards him.' In short, since the state does not give its citizens a choice with respect to such benefits, the mere enjoyment of them cannot give rise to a duty of gratitude. John Rawls (1964) argues that there is a moral obligation to obey law *qua* law in societies in which there is a mutually beneficial and just scheme of social cooperation. What gives rise to a moral obligation to obey law qua law in such societies is a *duty of fair play*: fairness requires obedience of persons who intentionally accept the benefits made available in a society organised around a just scheme of mutually beneficial cooperation. There are nevertheless a couple of problems here. First, this argument does not establish the existence of a content-independent obligation to obey law: the obligation arises only in those societies that institutionalise a just scheme of social cooperation. Second, even in such societies, citizens are not presented with a genuine option to refuse those benefits. For example, I cannot avoid the benefits of laws ensuring clean air. But accepting benefits one is not in a position to refuse cannot give rise to an obligation of fair play.

The *argument from consent* grounds an obligation to obey law in some sort of implied promise. It is clearly the case that we can voluntarily assume obligations by consenting to them or making a promise; on the other hand, most citizens never explicitly promise or consent to obey the laws. For this reason, proponents of this argument attempt to infer consent from such considerations as continued residence and acceptance of benefits from the state. Nevertheless, acceptance of benefits one cannot decline no more implies consent to obey law than it does duties of fair play or gratitude. Moreover, the prohibitive difficulties associated with emigration preclude an inference of consent from continued residence.

Finally, the *argument from general utility* grounds the duty to obey the law in the consequences of universal disobedience. Since, according to this argument, the consequences of general disobedience would be catastrophic, it is wrong for any individual to disobey the law. Thus, no person may disobey the law unless everyone may do so. In response, Smith (1973: 966) observes that 'we will have to maintain, for example, that there is a prima facie obligation not to eat dinner at five o'clock, for if everyone did so, certain essential services could not be maintained'.

The justification of punishment

Punishment is unique among putatively legitimate acts in that its purpose is to inflict discomfort on the recipient. Thus, an act that is incapable of causing a person minimal discomfort cannot be characterised as a punishment. In most contexts, the commission of an act for the purpose of inflicting discomfort is morally problematic because of its resemblance to torture. For this reason, institutional punishment requires a moral justification sufficient to distinguish it from other practices of purposely inflicting discomfort on other people.

Justifications for punishment typically take five forms: (1) retributive; (2) deterrence; (3) preventive; (4) rehabilitative; and (5) restitutionary. The retributive justification justifies punishing a person because they committed an offence that deserves the punishment. From this perspective, it is morally appropriate that a person who has committed a wrongful act should suffer in proportion to the magnitude of their wrongdoing. The problem, however, is that the mere fact that someone is deserving of punishment does not imply it is morally permissible for the state to administer punishment. It would be wrong for me, for example, to punish someone else's child even though their behaviour might deserve it.

In contrast to retributivist theories that look back to a wrongful act committed in the past as justification for punishment, utilitarian theories look forward to the beneficial consequences of punishing a person. There are three main lines of utilitarian reasoning. According to the deterrence justification, punishment of a wrongdoer is justified by the socially beneficial effects that it has on other persons. From this perspective, punishment deters wrongdoing by persons who would otherwise commit wrongful acts. The problem with the deterrence theory is that it justifies punishment of one person on the basis of the impact that it will have on other people. The idea that it is permissible to deliberately inflict discomfort on one person because doing so may have beneficial effects on the behaviour of other persons appears inconsistent with the Kantian philosophical principle that it is wrong to use people as a mere means.[4] The preventive justification for punishment argues that incarcerating a person for wrongful acts is justified insofar as it prevents that person from committing wrongful acts against society during the period of incarceration. The rehabilitative justification argues that punishment is justified in virtue of the effect that it has on the moral character of the offender. Each of these justifications suffers from the same logical flaw: prevention of crime and the rehabilitation of the offender can be achieved without the deliberate infliction of discomfort that constitutes punishment. For example, prevention of crime might require detaining the offender, but it does not require incarceration in an environment that is as unpleasant as those typically found in prisons.

The restitutionary justification focuses on the effect of the wrongful act committed by the offender to the detriment of the victim. Other theories of punishment conceptualise the wrongful act as an offence against society but the restitutionary theory sees wrongdoing as an offence against the particular victim. Thus, from this perspective, the principal purpose of punishment must be to make the victim whole to the extent that this can be done: 'the point is not that the offender deserves to suffer; it is rather that the offended party desires compensation' (Barnett, 1985: 289). Accordingly, a criminal convicted of wrongdoing should be sentenced to compensate their victim in proportion to the loss suffered by the victim. The problem with restitutionary theory is that it fails to distinguish between compensation and punishment. Compensatory objectives focus on the victim, while punitive objectives focus on the offender. The philosophical justifications for punishment are merely introduced in this section but are discussed in greater depth in Chapter 6 of this book.

Critical legal theory

Legal realism

Legal or American realism originated in the USA and was inspired by John Chipman Gray and Oliver Wendall Holmes and reached its apex in the 1920s and 1930s through the work of Karl Llewellyn, Jerome Frank, and Felix Cohen. The realists eschewed the conceptual approach of the positivists and naturalists in favour of an empirical analysis that sought to show how practising judges *really* decide cases (see Leiter, 1998) although they were inherently legal positivists.

The realists were deeply sceptical of the increasingly popular notion that the creation of judicial legislation is a rarity. While not entirely rejecting the idea that judges can be constrained by rules, the realists maintained that the judiciary creates new law through the exercise of law-making discretion considerably more often than is commonly supposed. It is furthermore argued that the decisions of judges are guided far more frequently by political and moral intuitions about the facts of the case – instead of legal rules – than is acknowledged by positivist and naturalist theories.

Legal realism originated in response to legal formalism which itself was a particular model which incorporates legal reasoning with syllogistic reasoning.[5] The formalist model proposed that the legal outcome (that is, the holding) logically follows from the legal rule (major premise) and a statement of the relevant facts (minor premise). Realists argue that formalism understates judicial law-making abilities insofar as it represents legal outcomes as *entailed* syllogistically by applicable rules and facts. For if legal outcomes are logically implied by propositions that are binding on judges, it therefore follows that the latter lack the legal authority to reach conflicting outcomes.

Legal realism is broadly characterised by the following claims: (1) the class of available legal materials is insufficient to logically entail a unique legal outcome in most cases worth litigating at the appellate level (*the local indeterminacy thesis*); (2) in such cases, judges make new law in deciding legal disputes through the exercise of a law-making discretion (*the discretion thesis*); and (3) judicial decisions in indeterminate cases are influenced by the political and moral convictions of the judge and not by legal considerations. Though (3) is logically independent of (1) and (2), (1) seems to imply (2): insofar as judges decide legally indeterminate cases, they must be creating new law.

It is important to note the relationship between legal realism, formalism and positivism. While formalism is often thought to be compatible with positivism, in reality legal realism is not only consistent with positivism but also presupposes the truth of all three of the core theses of positivism. Indeed, the realist acknowledges that law is essentially the product of official activity, but argues that judicial law-making occurs more frequently than is commonly assumed. But the idea that law is essentially the product of official activity presupposes the truth of positivism's conventionality, social fact, and separability theses. Though the preoccupations of the realists were empirical (that is, attempting to identify the psychological and sociological factors influencing judicial decision-making), their implicit conceptual commitments were actually positivistic in reality.

Critical legal studies

The critical legal studies (CLS) movement attempts to expand the radical aspects of legal realism into a Marxist critique of mainstream liberal jurisprudence and can be clearly conceptualised in the context of the radical conflict model of criminal justice development. CLS theorists argue that the realists understate the extent of indeterminacy. Whereas the latter propose that indeterminacy is local in the sense that it is confined to a certain class of cases, CLS theorists argue that law is radically – or globally – indeterminate in the sense that the class of available legal materials rarely, if ever, logically/causally entails a unique outcome. They also emphasise the role of ideology in shaping the content of the law and in liberal democracies this necessarily reflects 'ideological struggles among social factions in which competing conceptions of justice, goodness, and social and political life get compromised, truncated, vitiated, and adjusted' (Altman, 1986: 221). The inevitable outcome of such struggles is a profound inconsistency permeating the deepest layers of the law which gives rise to radical indeterminacy. If the law is inconsistent, a judge can justify any number of conflicting outcomes.

Central to the CLS critique of liberal jurisprudence is the idea that radical indeterminacy is inconsistent with liberal conceptions of legitimacy. According to these traditional liberal conceptions, the role of the judge is to interpret, and not make, the law. For democratic ideals imply that law-making must be left to legislators who, unlike appointed judges, are accountable to the electorate. But if law is radically indeterminate, then judges nearly always decide cases by making new law, which is thus inconsistent with liberal conceptions of the legitimate sources of law-making authority.

The CLS indentifies in the law a form of 'hegemonic consciousness' which is a term borrowed from the writings of the Italian Marxist Antonio Gramsci (1977–1978), who observed that social order is maintained by a system of beliefs which are accepted as 'common sense' and part of the natural order – even by those who are actually subordinated to it. Thus, these ideas are treated as eternal and necessary whereas they really reflect only the transitory, arbitrary interests of the dominant elite. Moreover, the ideas are 'reified', a term used by Marx, and refined by the Hungarian Marxist György Lukács (1970), to refer to the manner in which ideas become material things, and are portrayed as essential, necessary, and objective when, in fact, they are contingent, arbitrary and subjective. Furthermore, legal thought is, following the work of Sigmund Freud (1920), a form of denial, in that it affords a way of coping with contradictions that are too painful for us to hold in our conscious mind. It therefore denies the contradiction between, on the one hand, the promise of equality and freedom, and on the other, the reality of oppression and a hierarchical social order.

Law and economics

The law and economics movement argues for the value of economic analysis in the law both as a description about how courts and legislators behave and as a prescription for how such officials should behave. The legal economists, led by Richard Posner, argue that the content of many areas of the common law can be explained in terms of its tendency to maximise preferences:

> [M]any areas of law, especially the great common law fields of property, torts, crimes, and contracts, bear the stamp of economic reasoning. It is not a refutation that few judicial opinions contain explicit references to economic concepts. Often the true grounds of decision are concealed rather than illuminated by the characteristic rhetoric of judicial opinions. Indeed, legal education consists primarily of learning to dig beneath the rhetorical surface to find those grounds, many of which may turn out to have an economic character.
>
> (Posner, 1992: 23)

Posner (1992: 23) subscribes to the so-called efficiency theory of the common law, according to which 'the common law is best (not perfectly) explained as a system for maximizing the wealth of society'.

Posner takes the normative view that law should strive to maximise wealth. It is the proper goal of the statutory and common law to promote wealth maximisation and this can best be done by facilitating the mechanisms of the free market. This normative perspective combines elements of utilitarian analysis with a Kantian respect for autonomy. On the utilitarian side, markets tend to maximise wealth and the satisfaction of preferences. In a market transaction with no third-party effects, wealth is increased because all parties are made better off by the transaction. Otherwise there would be no incentive to consummate the transaction and no one is made worse off.

On the Kantian side, the law should facilitate market transactions because these best reflect autonomous judgements about the value of individual preferences. At least ideally, individuals express and realise their preferences through mutually consensual market transactions consummated from positions of equal bargaining power. Thus, market transactions tend, ideally, to be both efficient (because they tend to maximise wealth without harmful third-party effects) and just (because all parties are consenting).

Outsider jurisprudence

Outsider jurisprudence is concerned with providing an analysis of the ways in which law is structured to promote the interests of white males and to exclude females and ethnic minorities. For example, one principal objective of feminist jurisprudence is to show how patriarchal assumptions have shaped the content of laws in a wide variety of areas: property, contract, criminal law, constitutional law, and civil rights law. Additionally, feminist scholars challenge traditional ideals of judicial decision-making according to which judges decide legal disputes by applying neutral rules in an impartial and objective fashion. Feminists have, of course, always questioned whether it is possible for judges to achieve an objective and impartial perspective, but now question whether the traditional model is even desirable (Smart, 1993; Lacey, 1998).

Critical race theory is likewise concerned to locate the ways in which assumptions of white supremacy have shaped the content of the law at the expense of ethnic minorities. These theorists show how the experience, concerns, values, and perspectives of people from ethnic minorities are systematically excluded from mainstream discourse among practising lawyers, judges, and legislators. Finally, such theorists attempt to show how assumptions about race are built into most liberal theories of law (Harris, 1990; Delgado and Stefanic, 1997).

Islamic jurisprudence and Sharia law

Islamic jurisprudence and Sharia law are becoming increasingly significant concepts in post-industrial Western societies because of the relatively recent widespread immigration of people from Islamic countries and the increasing conversion of a growing minority within those societies. Islamic jurisprudence and Sharia law cannot however be conceptualised in terms of the four models of criminal justice development that provide the theoretical underpinnings of this book because in their purist form both pre-date and indeed provide a radical external challenge to the Western Enlightenment and modernist tradition, although the more liberal and reformed variants seek some accommodation with contemporary secular society and its belief systems.

Sharia law governs all aspects of the life of a Muslim and has its origins in a combination of sources including the *Qur'an* (the Muslim holy book),[6] the *Hadith* (sayings and conduct of the prophet Muhammad) and *fatwas* (the rulings of Islamic scholars). Sharia is the word of God and its interpretation by learned expert scholars and Islamic jurisprudence is based on notions of the absolute *divine* truth and would thus appear, at first sight, to be incompatible with the social constructionist ideas of modernity where all four models of criminal justice development propose that laws are constructed in terms of the value systems and interests of human beings. The concept of natural law that we encountered above does have its origins in early Christian theology but the Christian Bible does not profess to be the literal word of God and theology has been far less influential in criminal justice matters since the Protestant reformation and certainly since the

rise of modernity. Fundamentalist Islamic jurisprudence continues to unambiguously accept that the Qur'an is the word of God or Allah although judicial
interpretation – and hence social construction – does play a significant part, as we
shall discover in the following discussion of the origins and prescriptions of Sharia.

There are four main schools of Sharia law, which range from the more liberal
to the conservative. First, *Hanbali* is the most conservative and fundamentalist
school which is used in Saudi Arabia and some states in northern Nigeria. Second,
Hanifi is the most liberal school and is relatively open to modern ideas. Third,
Maliki is based on the practices of the people of Medina during the lifetime of the
Prophet Muhammad. Fourth, *Shafi'i* is a conservative school that emphasises
the opinions of the companions of the Prophet Muhammad in the seventh century.
However, what applies within one school does not necessarily apply in the others;
for example, the Maliki law school accepts evidence of pregnancy as proof that
an unmarried woman has either committed adultery or been raped but the other
schools do not accept this (Iman, 2001).

For over a century Islamic law had gone into a forced decline in its previous
homeland, but growing independence from the West during the past quarter of a
century has seen the restoration of a sometimes more fundamental interpretation of
all traditions. The Constitutional Rights Foundation (2009) explains:

> In the 19th century, many Muslim countries came under the control or influ-
> ence of Western colonial powers. As a result, Western-style laws, courts, and
> punishments began to appear within the Sharia. Some countries like Turkey
> totally abandoned the Sharia and adopted new law codes based on European
> systems. . . . Modern legislation along with Muslim legal scholars who are
> attempting to relate the will of Allah to the 20th century have reopened the
> door to interpreting the Sharia. This has happened even in highly traditional
> Saudi Arabia, where Islam began. . . . Since 1980, some countries with
> fundamentalist Islamic regimes like Iran have attempted to reverse the trend
> of westernization and return to the classic Sharia.
>
> (Constitutional Rights Foundation, 2009)

Within Sharia law, there are a group of '*haram*' offences which carry severe
punishments and these include pre-marital sexual intercourse, sex by divorced
persons, adultery, false accusation of unlawful intercourse, drinking alcohol, theft
and highway robbery. Haram sexual offences can carry a sentence of stoning to
death or severe flogging.

Sharia law has been adopted in various forms by many countries, ranging from
a strict interpretation in Saudi Arabia and northern states of Nigeria, to a relatively
liberal interpretation in much of Malaysia. Sharia law is intended to be only
applicable to Muslims. Christians and other non-Muslims are supposed to be
exempt from the provisions of the law but this is a provision that is not universally
followed in countries where it is in place (Johansen, 1993).

The philosophy of Sharia – ' the clear path '

> For each We have appointed a divine law and a traced-out way. Had God willed, He could have made you one community. But that He may try you by that which He has given you. So vie one with another in good works. Unto God you will all return, and He will then inform you of that wherein you differ.
>
> (Qur'an, 5:48)

For Muslims, life did not begin at birth, but a long time before that, before even the creation of the first man. It began when God created the souls of everyone who would ever exist and asked them, 'Am I not your Lord?' and they all replied, 'Yea'. God decreed for each soul a time on earth so that He might try them. Then, after the completion of their appointed terms, He would judge them and send them to their eternal destinations: either one of endless bliss, or one of everlasting grief. This life, then, is a journey that presents to its wayfarers many paths. Only one of these paths is clear and straight. This for believers is the path of the Sharia (Ansari, 1992).

In Arabic, Sharia means 'the clear, well-trodden path to water', and in Islam, it is used to refer to the matters of religion that God has legislated for His servants. The linguistic meaning of Sharia reverberates in its technical usage for just as water is vital to human life, so the clarity and uprightness of Sharia is the means of life for souls and minds (Ansari, 1992).

Muslims believe that throughout history, God has sent messengers to people all over the world, to guide them to the straight path that would lead them to happiness in this world and the one to follow. All messengers taught the same message about belief – the Qur'an teaches that all messengers called people to the worship of the One God – but the specific prescriptions of the divine laws regulating the lives of people have varied according to the needs of his people and time. The Prophet Muhammad[7] is considered to be the final messenger and his Sharia represents the ultimate manifestation of the divine mercy (Humphreys, 1991).

The Sharia regulates all human actions and puts them into five categories: obligatory, recommended, permitted, disliked or forbidden. Obligatory actions must be performed and when done with good intentions are rewarded. The opposite is forbidden action. Recommended action is that which should be done and the opposite is disliked action. Permitted action is that which is neither encouraged nor discouraged and most human actions fall into this last category. The ultimate worth of actions is based on intention and sincerity, as mentioned by the Prophet, who said, 'Actions are by intentions, and one shall only get that which one intended'. The Sharia covers all aspects of human life and classical manuals are often divided into four parts: laws relating to personal acts of worship, laws relating to commercial dealings, laws relating to marriage and divorce, and penal laws (Ansari, 1992).

Legal philosophy

Muslims believe that God sent prophets and gave books to humanity to show them the way to happiness in this life and success in the hereafter. This is encapsulated in the believer's prayer, stated in the Qur'an, 'Our Lord, give us good in this life and good in the next, and save us from the punishment of the Fire' (2:201).

The legal philosophers of Islam explain that the aim of Sharia is to promote human welfare and that this is evident in the Qur'an, and teachings of the Prophet. The scholars explain that the welfare of humans is based on the fulfilment of necessities, needs and comforts (Ansari, 1992).

Necessities are matters which worldly and religious life are dependent upon and their omission leads to unbearable hardship in this life, or punishment in the next. There are five necessities: preservation of religion, life, intellect, lineage and wealth. These ensure individual and social welfare in this life and the hereafter. The Sharia protects these necessities by ensuring their establishment and then by preserving them. First, to ensure the establishment of religion, God made belief and worship obligatory, and to ensure its preservation, the rulings relating to the obligation of learning and conveying the religion were legislated. Second, to ensure the preservation of human life, God legislated for marriage, healthy eating and living, and forbade the taking of life and laid down punishments for doing so. Third, God permitted that sound intellect and knowledge be promoted, and has forbidden that which corrupts or weakens it, such as alcohol and drugs. He also imposed preventative punishments in order that people stay away from them, because a sound intellect is the basis of the moral responsibility that humans were given. Fourth, marriage was legislated for the preservation of lineage, and sex outside marriage was forbidden. Punitive laws were thus put in place in order to ensure the preservation of lineage and the continuation of human life. Fifth, God made it obligatory to support oneself and those one is responsible for, and placed laws to regulate the commerce and transactions between people, in order to ensure fair dealing and economic justice, and to prevent oppression and dispute.

Needs and comforts are the things people seek in order to ensure a good life, and to avoid hardship, even though they are not essential. The spirit of the Sharia with regards to needs and comforts is summed up in the Qur'an, 'He has not placed any hardship for you in religion' (22:87), and 'God does not seek to place a burden on you, but that He purify you and perfect His grace upon you, that you may give thanks' (5:6). Therefore, everything that ensures human happiness, within the spirit of Divine Guidance, is permitted in the Sharia (Kamali, 1991).

Sources of the Sharia

The primary sources of the Sharia are thus the Qur'an and the example of the Prophet Muhammad. Muslims believe that the Qur'an was revealed to the Prophet gradually over a period of 23 years and the essence of its message is to establish the oneness of God and the spiritual and moral need of man for God. This need is fulfilled through worship and submission, and has ultimate consequences in the hereafter. The Qur'an is thus believed to be the word of God and it ensures the worldly and next-worldly welfare of humanity. It is thus fundamental to Islamic belief and law.

The role of the Prophet is expounded in the Qur'an. 'We have revealed the Remembrance [Qur'an] to you that you may explain to people that which was revealed for them' (16:44). Following the guidance and the example of the Prophet was made obligatory, 'O you who believe, obey God and obey the Messenger' (4:59) and 'Verily, in the Messenger of God you have a beautiful example for those who seek God and the Last Day, and remember God much'. The Prophet himself instructed, 'I have left two things with you which if you hold on to, you shall not be misguided: the Book of God and my example' (4:42).

There are two agreed-upon derived sources of Sharia: scholarly consensus (*ijma'*) and legal analogy (*qiyas*). The basis for scholarly consensus being a source of law is the Qur'anic command to resolve matters by consultation, as God stated, 'Those who answer the call of their Lord, established prayer, and whose affairs are by consultation' (42:38). Scholarly consensus is defined as being the agreement of all Muslim scholars at the level of juristic reasoning (*ijtihad*) in one age on a given legal ruling. Given the condition that all such scholars have to agree to the ruling, its scope is limited to matters that are clear according to the Qur'an and Prophetic example, upon which such consensus must necessarily be based. When established, though, scholarly consensus is decisive proof. It is thus incorrect to say that social construction and interpretation play no part in Islamic jurisprudence.

Legal analogy is thus a powerful tool to derive rulings for new matters that arise in a forever changing world. For example, drugs have been deemed impermissible, through legal analogy from the prohibition of alcohol that is established in the Qur'an. Such a ruling is based on the common underlying effective cause of intoxication. Legal analogy and its various tools enable the jurists to understand the underlying reasons and causes for the rulings of the Qur'an and Prophetic example (*sunna*) and this helps when dealing with ever-changing human situations in contemporary society and allows for new rulings to be applied most suitably and consistently (Burton, 1990).

The basic principles of Sharia law

The basic principles of Sharia law are thus to see that the will of God is done on earth as it is in Heaven (as in the Christian Lord's Prayer). Muslims believe that the whole principle of God's will is to bring about compassion, kindness, generosity, justice, fair play, tolerance, and care in general, as opposed to tyranny, cruelty, selfishness and exploitation. Sharia rules are intended to bring about those ends (Kamali, 1991).

Sharia supporters argue that the usual criticisms of their legal philosophy – that it is inherently cruel with regards to execution (including the stoning of women found guilty of adultery), flogging and cutting off hands – totally ignore all the extenuating circumstances that would lead to these penalties not being applied.

Such punishments are known as *hadd* penalties or the extreme limit of the penalty. Thus, if a person was sentenced to having a hand cut off, he or she should not be sent to prison and/or be fined as well. Muslims recognise that people who regard these practices as cruel are extremely unlikely to be persuaded otherwise but argue that the cutting off of the hand for theft is a very powerful deterrent. Muslims appear to care less for the criminal than they do for the victim of crime and, moreover, offences such as adultery and murder are perceived very differently in Islamic societies than they are in Western modern societies.

Thus, within contemporary (post)modern societies, adultery is seen to have become commonplace because of sexual freedoms with much of the emphasis being on the attainment of sexual satisfaction. In Muslim societies, in contrast, there is far less emphasis on sex, where it is usually regarded as a weakness that can lead to all sorts of problems and where family is seen to be far more important. The notion of a million unborn children per year being aborted,[8] and the existence of single mothers, is abhorrent to Muslims and their beliefs (Johansen, 1993).

Sharia law allows the death penalty for murder but its supporters regard it as more compassionate than Western modernist law in one respect at least. After judicial judgement has been made, appeals are allowed to the family of the murdered victims, and they are begged to be merciful. In Islam, it is always regarded as the pinnacle of mercy to forgive a murderer, even though one may have the right to take his/her life in reprisal. Capital punishment is nevertheless accepted in accordance with the teachings of the Qur'an (6:151), 'Take not life, which God has made sacred, except by way of justice and law. Thus does He command you, so that you may learn wisdom.'

Muslims accept that capital punishment is a most severe sentence but one that may be commanded by a court for crimes of suitable severity. They argue that while there may be more profound punishment at the hands of God in the afterlife, there is also room for an earthly punishment. Methods of execution in Islamic countries vary and can include beheading, firing squad, hanging and stoning, and in some countries public executions are carried out to heighten the element of deterrence. Each case is nevertheless to be considered individually, with extreme care, and the court is fully able to impose more lenient sentences as and when they see fit.

In Islamic law, the death penalty is appropriate for two groups of crime. First, in the case of *intentional murder* where the family of the victim is given the option as to whether or not to insist on a punishment of this severity. Second, in the case of *fasad fil-ardh* ('spreading mischief in the land') where Islam permits the death penalty for anyone who threatens to undermine authority or destabilise the state. What constitutes the crime of 'spreading mischief in the land' is open to interpretation but crimes such as the following are usually included: treason/apostasy (when one leaves the faith and turns against it); terrorism; piracy of any kind; rape; adultery; and homosexual activity (Burton, 1994).[9]

Whilst Islam remains firmly committed to the retention of capital punishment, there is a small but growing abolitionist Islamic view encompassing the three following issues. First, the Ulamas (those who are learned in Islamic law, constitution and theology) do not always agree on the interpretation or authenticity of the sacred texts. Neither do they agree on the social context in which these texts should be applied. Second, Sharia law is often used by repressive powers that attack women and the poor. Third, there are incidences of states summarily executing those who are accused whilst denying them access to a lawyer. These acts are in reality in total contradiction to the concept of Islamic justice.

It is clear that there are emerging liberal and modern tendencies within Islamic jurisprudence that are at least tentatively embracing ideas and notions that have incrementally developed within modernist thought and jurisprudence. The fundamental beliefs of Islamic legal philosophy, namely that the Qur'an contains the word of God and establishes the legal foundations which are to be obeyed by all devout Muslims, are not challenged and this puts Islam at least potentially at odds with modernist jurisprudence in the contemporary Western world. We have nevertheless seen that there are crucial elements of interpretation, and indeed social construction, within Islamic jurisprudence that provide the potential and possibility of rapprochement with Western modernist legal thought. Much will depend on the nature of the particular Islamic state and its position on a spectrum between liberal and conservative.

4   Policing modern society

All modern societies use some form of state-sponsored professionalised police force in order to control crime and to contribute to public order but as Gary Marx (2001) observes the organisational conditions under which they operate vary greatly between liberal democratic and non-democratic societies, even though there are similarities in the control function of policing. He identifies the following three components as essential to a definition of a police force in a liberal democratic modern society. First, it is subject to the rule of law embodying values respectful of human dignity, rather than the wishes of a powerful leader or political party. Second, it can intervene in the life of citizens only under limited and carefully controlled circumstances. Third, it is accountable to the general public for its actions.

Marx (2001) observes that it is an ongoing common myth that it is only the police force or service that stands between total chaos and social order in a democratic society. Social order has multiple sources which include socialisation to norms, a desire to have others think well of us, reciprocity, self-defence and the design of the physical environment. He nevertheless acknowledges that the police are an important factor with their significance increasing with the heterogeneity and size of a society as well as with the more recent globalisation. A defining characteristic of the police is their mandate to legally use force and to deprive citizens of their liberty and we might observe that this power is bound to generate opposition from those who are subject to it and it also offers great temptations for police abuse and maltreatment on behalf of the authorities controlling them. Thus, law enforcement in modern democratic societies requires a delicate balancing act between 'hard' and 'soft' strategies, as we will observe later in this chapter.

The meaning of the word 'police' has changed over the past five centuries and has its origins in the term 'polity' which means the form of government of a political body. In Europe in the fifteenth century it referred broadly to matters involving life, health and property and there was no distinct police force or service. Policing was done intermittently by the military, and society was largely 'unpoliced' except at a very local community level. It was with the formation of modern states with clear national borders, beginning in the eighteenth century, that the term police began to refer to the specific functions of crime prevention and order maintenance. It was then only a small step to identify the word police with the personnel (Johnson, 1992). With the expansion of the law over the next several centuries, police also came to be increasingly concerned with the prevention of public dangers such as crime and disorder and the prevention or redress of breaches of law. They also themselves came to be more controlled by the law (Lane, 1967; Critchley, 1978; Fogelson, 1977).

The above discourse can be very much located in the context of the social progress model of criminal justice development. Thus from this orthodox perspective the modern police service developed in response to progressive benevolent and humanitarian concerns in a complex, changing, albeit significantly challenging society, but ultimately in the interests of all its citizens. This chapter will show that the reality has been both more ambiguous and complex, and will be divided into four parts. First, we will consider the incremental development of policing from its origins in pre-modern society until the twenty-first century. Second, we explore more closely the relationship between policing and contemporary society from the end of the Second World War to the present day. Third, there will be a discussion of significant policing issues in contemporary society. Fourth, there will be a brief review of these debates in the context of the four models of criminal justice development.

A brief history of the police

Crowther (2007) observes that the emergence of the modern police service in England in the early nineteenth century can only be understood with reference to the system of policing in place before that time. Moreover, we should note that early government institutions and the philosophies on which they are founded throughout the 'new world' (including the USA and Australasia) invariably have their roots in Britain and this is particularly the case with law enforcement. It thus should be seen that this pre-modern history is for many in modern societies worldwide a shared history.

A rather simplistic account suggests that before the Industrial Revolution, which occurred in Britain approximately between the years 1750 and 1830, society was predominantly constituted of relatively small rural homogeneous communities, which were largely self-policing. The Saxons had developed a system of tythings, a group of 10 families, headed by a tythingman. When a crime was committed in the local community, all adult males (12+) had to produce a culprit or else pay a fine themselves. The tythings themselves were grouped into hundreds, headed by a hundredman, who ran the court of the hundred to administer and adjudicate on proceedings. Above the hundredman was the county shire-reave or sheriff who was appointed by the King and when necessary could muster the *posse comitatus*, which was a gathering of all able-bodied men in the county. Anyone in the community could be called upon when the 'hue and cry' was raised to join in the pursuit of a felon.

Following the Norman conquest of Britain in 1066 changes were made to the system of collective peacekeeping and the frankpledge system was introduced, under which all but the most powerful men and their households were bound together by mutual responsibility to keep the peace. The Normans also introduced the office of constable, which was originally a high military rank and a royal appointment; and order maintenance was to become increasingly centralised with the creation of sheriffs' courts which dealt with many offences (Rawlings, 2001). Towards the end of the twelve century, as Normans and Saxons gradually integrated, this centralised system was relaxed and by the following century the title of constable was transferred to the lowly Saxon tythingman as a prototype parish constable and the unpopular sheriff's court had been replaced by the local manorial courts.

The Statute of Winchester 1285 reaffirmed the principle of local responsibility for peacekeeping and revived the Saxon custom of the 'hue and cry' – which imposed a peacekeeping responsibility on everyone – backed by an assize of arms, which meant every male between 15 and 60 had to keep to hand weapons appropriate to his social rank to assist in the pursuit of felons. The Statute also introduced the system of the watch and ward in order to supplement the constable system. All able-bodied townsmen had to serve their turn of duty in the watch and their role was to warn and protect the community rather than track down law-breakers (Wilson, 1963). This marks the first distinction between urban and rural peacekeeping and this development may have arisen because of a growing realisation that the rapidly expanding towns of the thirteenth century were more difficult to police than rural communities. The Statute was important because it established the legal framework for policing for almost the next 800 years (Critchley, 1978).

The first Justices of the Peace (JPs) were appointed following the Justices of the Peace Act 1361. These were local landowners, men of position and authority who had police, judicial and administrative authority in their local area. Constables were placed under the authority of the JPs as their unpaid executive agents appointed by the manorial courts on a rotary basis from all eligible citizens.

Critchley (1978) observes that while the Statute of Winchester had tended to decentralise law enforcement and peacekeeping and place the responsibility in the hands of local citizens, the Act of 1361, in contrast, centralised and concentrated law enforcement in the hands of the property-owning classes. Significantly, these two conflicting tendencies of centralisation and decentralisation came to permeate the entire history of British domestic policing.

This fourteenth-century system of policing, based on JPs, constables and the watch – which placed an onus on all citizens to assist constables and help maintain the peace – remained in place for 500 years. But from the mid-eighteenth century the series of fundamental changes that were to occur in society, and from which emerged the beginnings of the modern era, was to lead to the eventual breakdown of the traditional system of policing which had served society well.

The breakdown of 'the old police'

The effectiveness of the pre-modern policing system was based and dependent upon the existence of stable, homogeneous and largely rural communities characterised by high levels of mechanical solidarity (Durkheim, 1933, originally 1893) where people knew one another by name, sight and/or reputation. During the eighteenth century such communities began to break down in the face of the rapid transition to an industrial economy based increasingly on organic solidarity where there is a more developed division of labour, less reliance on maintaining uniformity between individuals, and more on the management of the diverse functions of different groups with different worldviews (Durkheim, 1933). At the same time, the unpaid and frequently reluctant holders of posts such as the parish constable and the watch failed to carry out their duties with great diligence. Many employed substitutes who were more often than not ill-paid, ignorant and too old to be effective in their duties while the local watch was often demoralised, drunk on duty and did little to suppress crime.

The fast-expanding towns and cities were increasingly becoming a haven for the poor and those dispossessed of their land as a result of the land enclosures.[1] The rookeries, slum areas and improvised shelters for the poor grew rapidly in the eighteenth century as the urban areas expanded to serve the labour needs of the growing industrial machine. These areas were extremely overcrowded, lacked elementary sanitation, and were characterised by disease, grinding poverty, excessive drinking and casual violence. Prostitution and thieving were invariably the only realistic means of survival (Emsley, 2002).

In addition to the increasingly serious problem of ordinary crime and lawlessness – thieving, violence and vice – the urban poor constituted a serious threat to public order. The example of the French Revolution had led to the ruling classes becoming extremely wary of the impoverished mob on their doorstep. This fear was accentuated by the recognition of the English tradition whereby the crowd exercised a degree of power by protesting or rioting, often in a non-political fashion, against local grievances to restore traditional rights eroded by economic and social change. In this way the poor posed a threat to the seats of both local and national power, which were often close to where they lived. In the eyes of the propertied and the powerful something had to be done for the protection of individual lives and property and for collective security (Emsley, 1996).

In the sixteenth century, during a period of widespread social disruption and poverty, savage penalties had been imposed on the perpetrators of what would now be regarded as fairly minor property crimes. By the early eighteenth century penalties such as hanging, mutilation or transportation to the colonies were being imposed for an extensive list of petty crimes. It was a strategy pursued with the intention of protecting life and property from the depredations of the poor, who were at the time being herded into locally run workhouses. Indeed at the beginning of the nineteenth century, apart from such crimes as treason, murder, piracy, arson, stealing, rape, sodomy and breaches of various game laws, it was a capital offence to send a letter demanding money with a fictitious name, to impersonate a Chelsea Pensioner, to make false entry in the books of the Bank of England, to strike a Privy Councillor and to damage Westminster Bridge, to name but a few examples. Although often the sentence was not carried out, executions were still common-place, even for children. For instance in 1801 a boy aged 13 was hanged for breaking into a house and stealing a spoon and in 1808 two sisters aged 8 and 11 were hanged (Hibert, 1987).

The continuing rise in property crimes demonstrated that such a harsh penal code was not merely unjust but clearly inadequate while the traditional agents of authority were failing to achieve their goals of protecting life and property. The growth of the teeming and anonymous urban environment dissipated the individualistic, charismatic exercise of power by judges and powerful individuals, compromising the exercise of local power that had typified the face-to-face relationships of smaller less complex societies. The injustice of severe penalties for minor crimes also discouraged juries from reaching guilty verdicts in an increasing number of cases where guilt was clearly obvious. The culmination of all these changes led to increasing pressure for reform of 'the old system'.

The growing call for reform

The first influential advocates of reform were the Fielding brothers. The older brother Henry Fielding was appointed Chief Magistrate of Bow Street in 1748 and from this position he attempted to address the corrupt state of justice and influence the level of crime. He wrote a series of pamphlets on these issues and established himself as a leading thinker on crime and penal policy. However, perhaps his most important initiative in the evolution of the police was the establishment of a small body of thief takers at Bow Street who evolved into the famous 'Bow Street Runners'. He died in 1754 and was succeeded by his brother John, who carried on his work.

In the summer of 1780 London was abandoned to mob violence during the Gordon Riots[2] and William Pitt, influenced by the work of the Fielding brothers, attempted to introduce legislation to establish a police force in London. The Bill was bitterly opposed and failed (Critchley, 1978) but a similar Bill was successfully introduced to establish a police force in Dublin. On Friday 29 September 1786 the first modern police force in the British Isles began patrolling the streets of Dublin.[3]

The next major advocate for reform was Patrick Colquhoun, a self-made entrepreneur and a former provost of Glasgow, who spent much of his 25 years as a London magistrate promoting reform of the police. Colquhoun used techniques which are very common today, but which were rare at the time, such as employing statistics to illustrate arguments. He also wrote lengthy treatises arguing for a well-regulated police and publicly supported the activities of the French police who were generally seen as the antithesis of what was needed in England and Wales. Colquhoun advocated the separation of police and judicial powers, the creation of a central board to consist of five commissioners under the control of the Home Secretary, and in every parish a nucleus of professional police headed by a high constable and assisted by a parochial chief constable (Rawlings, 2001).

Colquhoun's most influential contribution to the debates of the time was his *Treatise on the Commerce and Police of the River Thames* published in 1800. The Port of London docks had become the centre of international trade and they had also become the centre of very large losses resulting from criminal activity. In 1798 Colquhoun estimated the docks were plundered to the extent of £506,000, a huge sum in those days. This finding encouraged the West India Merchants to introduce a Marine Police Establishment, which was to have such a dramatic impact on the level of crime that the force became a model for preventative policing (Radzinowicz, 1956).

Despite the efforts of Colquhoun, other advocates of reform such as Jeremy Bentham and Luke Chadwick and three successive parliamentary committees (1816, 1818 and 1822), there was still strong opposition to reform. The 1822 committee argued:

> It is difficult to reconcile an effective system of police with that perfect freedom of action and exemption from interference, which are the great privileges and blessings of society in this country, and your Committee think that the forfeiture or curtailment of such advantages would be too great a sacrifice for improvements in police or facilities in detection of crime, however desirable in themselves, if abstractly considered.
>
> (Cited in Critchley, 1978: 47)

A further Select Committee in 1828 was nevertheless to recommend the establishment of an Office of Police under the direction of the Home Secretary and to be funded partly from public funds and partly by a local rate. Significantly, the City of London, which had been a fierce opponent of the 'old system' of policing, was to be exempt from the provisions of the legislation. Robert Peel, the Home Secretary, was to introduce a Parliamentary Bill the following year and the Metropolitan Police was established (Emsley, 1996).

The Metropolitan Police Act 1829

The Metropolitan Police Act 1829 established two commissioners of police who were to be responsible for the administration of the force and to be appointed by the Home Secretary. The force was to be composed of a 'significant number of fit and able men'. The constables would be sworn in by local justices and have the powers of a constable at common law. The legislation was successfully passed without any significant opposition, largely because it excluded the City of London, on 19 July 1829. Remarkably, perhaps, it was to remain the governing statute of the Metropolitan Police until the Police Act 1964.

Most of the police officers were recruited from among the upper end of the working class and were commanded by middle-class officers. The new body was soon established as a semi-professional occupational group; they were rigidly disciplined and many recruits were dismissed for improper behaviour in the formative years.

At first, the 'New Police' were very unpopular among *all* sections of society and they were referred to by a range of derogatory terms: 'Crushers', 'Peel's Bloody Gang', 'Blue Locusts', 'Jenny Darbies', 'Raw Lobsters' and 'Blue Drones', to name but a few (Reiner, 2000). Within a year there were calls for their abolition and early crowd control techniques merely fuelled the hostility. In response to this widespread opposition two parliamentary committees were established in 1833 to investigate the conduct of the new police. The first committee exonerated the police. The second, established in the aftermath of clashes between the police and political demonstrators at Cold-Bath Fields – where a policeman had been killed and the inquest had reached a verdict of 'justifiable homicide' – according to Critchley (1978) turned public opinion towards the police. However, as late as 1838, a scathing indictment of the new police was published by Captain W. White in his *Police Spy, Or the Metropolitan Police: Its Advantages, Abuses and Defects* where he documents the very high labour turnover of the new force and how the majority who left the force left on grounds of corruption, brutality and sexual assault. White also argues that the main activities of the new force were politically orientated and not motivated by crime prevention.

There is nevertheless evidence to suggest that the force had a considerable impact on the level of crime and perceptions of public safety in some areas of London and it was these observations that were to encourage the increasingly influential middle classes to come to accept the force, concluding that they had nothing to fear from them. The police also began to realise that the middle classes were their principal allies and focused upon protecting them from victimisation from the poorer sections of society. It thus has been argued that the police were simply used to control the 'dangerous classes', generally the poor with little stake in society, and Bunyan (1978: 63) provides us with the following description:

> In London the success of the new police was partly in combating crime and political opposition and partly in convincing the bourgeoisie that, unlike the French police whose arbitrary powers were feared, the London police did not threaten their liberty. The only people whose liberty was curtailed were those who broke the law; that is, largely members of the working class who offended against the property and persons of the bourgeois class.

Following the establishment of the London Metropolitan Police Force and their gradual acceptance by the upper and middle classes there ensued 140 years of expansion and rationalisation.

1829–1870: the formation of the new police

The Metropolitan Police Force was established in 1829 but in the rest of the country the old systems prevailed and many argued that the success of the police in London would displace crime from the city to other areas. Consequently, these arguments were the basis for the establishment of police forces outside the metropolis although the extent to which the displacement argument was valid is debatable. The first major piece of legislation was the Municipal Corporations Act 1835 which allowed large boroughs to establish a 'Watch Committee' comprising local councillors and magistrates to oversee a police force along the Metropolitan

Police lines. The decision to implement the legislation was nevertheless left to the discretion of the local council and consequently not many did. The Metropolitan Police Act had abolished the old system based on parish constables, the watch and beadles from London, but the Municipal Corporations Act did not abolish these institutions and many of the old watchmen and parish constables were re-employed. The Metropolitan Police were forbidden from accepting gratuities from the public but outside London such policies were dependent on the discretion of the local Watch Committee.

The 1830s witnessed public order problems associated with the Chartist movement and these events provided considerable motivation towards further expansion of the police throughout the country. Following a Royal Commission, the County Police Act 1839 was passed, which permitted counties to form police forces but again it was left to the discretion of the individual county council as to whether they adopted the legislation. Eight of the 56 counties in England and Wales established police forces in 1839, a further 12 in 1840, four in 1841 and four more counties over the next 15 years. In 1839 the City of London finally succumbed to political and public pressure and established the City of London Police Force (Critchley, 1978).

With the introduction of these reforms there were now two forms of policing in existence in England and Wales. First, there were the Metropolitan Police in London, and outside the capital hundreds of small forces controlled by local magistrates. Second, there were large rural areas where the old pre-modern system of policing was still in existence.

The new police forces which had been established outside London were nevertheless insufficiently integrated or controlled to meet the challenges proffered by a growing industrialised economy, for the general population in urban areas was growing rapidly and becoming increasingly refined in terms of reading and writing and political sophistication. The Chartist movement for political reform grew rapidly from 1837 to 1848, causing considerable unease among the established economic and political interests.

In order to contain what many considered to be potentially revolutionary activity, the police had to be rationalised and made accountable to some kind of central control and coordination. The Metropolitan Police from its inception – as is still the case today – was responsible to the Home Secretary but other forces were subject to the control of local magistrates. The next important legislative initiatives thus tackled these issues and introduced a degree of rationalisation and centralisation. The most important reform was the County and Borough Police Act 1856, which made the establishment of full-time police forces compulsory throughout the country, made provision for central government to pay a quarter of the cost of local police forces and importantly established an Inspectorate of Constabulary. The latter was charged with making annual inspections of each force and providing written reports for the Home Secretary.

Many of the new local forces were too small and inefficient to adequately perform their designated roles; they had poor record keeping and a high labour turnover. There was however little potential for inter-force cooperation between these forces because of intense local rivalry but the next range of reforms was introduced in order to tackle these very problems.

1870–1920: internal reforms and consolidation

The second half of the nineteenth century was characterised by the further consolidation of the police throughout the country. The Municipal Corporations (New Charters) Act 1877 placed checks and restrictions on the formation of small forces. The Local Government Act 1888 abolished independent police forces in towns with a population under 10,000, the outcome of this reform being a reduction in the number of forces from 231 in 1880 to 183 nine years later. Critchley (1978) observes that this policy of reducing the number of small forces was one which survived every change of government.

Bunyan (1978) argues that it was during this period that we can identify three significant changes to the police. First, there was an increasing extension of police activity in working-class areas. Second, there were internal reforms such as the introduction of record keeping and improvements in pay and conditions. Third, the detection of crimes was initiated with the establishment of the Criminal Investigations Department.

Identified and defined criminal activity appeared to be the preserve of certain sections of the working class and it was claimed that the detection of crime would only be possible through a thorough understanding of the culture of this group. It was thus necessary to patrol the areas in which these people lived. Not surprisingly this strategy led to a hostile reaction from some of those under surveillance and there were many reports of policemen being physically attacked by disgruntled residents. It can nevertheless be argued that by patrolling these areas the police came to protect 'respectable' working-class people from the ravages of society and in particular the rougher elements in their midst at the time, and we revisit this argument below.

During this period there were improvements in the quality of record keeping, a degree of managerial rationalisation and the introduction of science. The Criminal Records Office at Scotland Yard was established in 1871 with the use of fingerprinting introduced in 1894. In 1917 the first women police officers were appointed in the face of much male police – and indeed public – hostility.

There was considerable internal dissent about the poor pay and conditions, with police officers receiving on average the wage of an unskilled labourer. For this remuneration they were expected to work a seven-day week, for an average day of 10 to 12 hours, and they would often patrol 20 miles plus in a day. They were expected to wear their uniform at all times, not to associate with civilians and to attend church (Critchley, 1978).

There was extensive initial public resistance to the criminal investigation branch because the image of police officers operating out of uniform to many revived fears of 'state spies' on the continental model. It was nevertheless recognised within the police service that the need for a force dedicated to the tracking down of criminals and thus building on the private investigative tradition was essential. As early as 1842 the Metropolitan Police had established a detective force consisting of two inspectors and six sergeants and this had slowly expanded to a complement of 15 officers by 1867. Their practices were copied by some other forces but, nevertheless, remained unpopular with Parliament and the public.

The issue came to prominence with the notorious 'Detective Case' in 1877, when three out of the four chief inspectors of the Metropolitan Police Detective Branch were convicted of corrupt practices concerning race-course gambling. A Home Office inquiry was established and one of its recommendations was the creation of a more disciplined and accountable detective branch. In 1878 the Criminal Investigations Department (CID) was established with some 250 officers, and by 1884 this had expanded to 800 and included the Special Irish Branch, which was created to counter Irish Republican activity.

1920–1994: centralisation and technological change

The period from 1920 saw a succession of attempted and successful initiatives by the Home Office to further centralise and rationalise the number of police forces. The Desborough Committee recommended the abolition of forces in towns with less than 100,000 inhabitants, but in 1922 a Bill to force amalgamations among small forces was defeated by fierce opposition from local authorities.

The following year the Home Office pressed the view to a Royal Commission that county forces should have at least 250 officers and a borough should have a complement of 300. The successful implementation of this policy would have meant a reduction in the number of forces of 50 per cent. The Commission, however, did not accept the Home Office recommendation. In 1932 a House of Commons Select Committee recommended that there should be no non-county borough forces in areas with a population under 30,000 but on the eve of the Second World War in 1939 there were still a total of 183 police forces in England and Wales. The Home Secretary was, however, given increasing powers during the war years and a number of amalgamations were forced through in military-sensitive areas.

After the war the Police Act 1946 forced the pace of amalgamations, abolished non-county borough forces and gave executive powers to the Home Secretary to enable him or her to require amalgamations if he or she considered it to be in the public interest. When the legislation was implemented on 1 April 1947, 45 non-county borough forces were immediately abolished and by the end of this series of amalgamations completed by 1960 there were a total of 125 forces in England and Wales (Critchley, 1978). The next phase of rationalisation and centralisation would follow the Willink Royal Commission and the Police Act 1964.

From the 1930s there was an increasing expansion in the use of technology and more sophisticated forms of training by the police. During the 1930s and 1940s the police increasingly used cars and motorcycles, partly as a result of their increased role in policing road traffic. In addition, forensic laboratories were intro-duced to help in the detection of crimes. The first police dogs were deployed in 1934 and their numbers grew rapidly throughout the 1940s and 1950s. During this period a National Police College was established as well as recruitment training centres for new recruits. In addition central promotion exams were introduced and negotiating machinery for pay bargaining.

There was also the establishment of specialist police squads during this period. In the 1950s a number of specialist detective branches were established to combat specific crime problems such as vice, murder and organised crime. This period also saw the initiation of the first specialist traffic squads.

By the end of the 1950s the police were facing a crisis. They were under-staffed, there was a serious problem of being unable to retain trained personnel and there were increasing cases of malpractice coming to public notice at a time of constant increase in the crime figures. It was in response to these problems that the Home Secretary established a Royal Commission under the auspices of Henry Willink which reported in 1962 and culminated in the Police Act 1964.

The Willink Commission was probably the most thorough and important investigation of the police ever undertaken. The Commission made a number of important recommendations. First, there should be more amalgamations and the minimum size of a force should be a complement of 500 officers. Second, the Home Secretary should be given greater powers to oversee and control forces outside London. Third, a Chief Inspector of Constabulary should be appointed and should be given wider powers of inspection than those established in 1856. Fourth, the old Watch Committees should be renamed Police Authorities and be constituted of two-thirds elected local authority councillors and one-third magistrates. These recommendations were largely embodied in the Police Act 1964.

The outcome of these reforms was to strengthen and increase central government control over the police service, strengthen the powers and operational discretion of individual Chief Constables, seriously weaken local control over policing and to produce a higher degree of rationalisation and uniformity over the force. The amalgamations which followed the implementation of the 1964 legislation combined with the local government reorganisation that occurred in the early 1970s and eventually led to the current number of 43 'home' forces that exist in England and Wales.

The period from 1964 to the mid-1990s was to see further advances in the processes of centralisation and increasing civilianisation. Loveday (1995) argued that since the implementation of the Police and Magistrates' Courts Act 1994 the police have ceased to be local forces and have effectively become a state force. The Police and Magistrates' Courts Act 1994 continued the long-term trend of increasing Home Office control and slimmed down and reduced the powers of police authorities, increased the power of individual Chief Constables and ensured that local forces have to meet national objectives. The implementation of the legislation was the culmination of a turbulent few years for the police service with the Sheehy Report (1993), the Police Reform White Paper (1993), and the initial publication of the Police and Magistrates' Courts Bill – which was much more radical than the final Act.

Policing and social context since the Second World War

The golden age of British policing 1945–1970

The period following the Second World War has been described as a 'golden age of British Policing' (Emsley, 2009). Thus, by the 1950s, a police officer was regarded as a semi-skilled working-class job, and one whose terms and conditions had gradually improved, although the force always had vacancies. Following the war, the role of the police was to nevertheless change. The arrival of mass-produced motor cars created new crimes to investigate and 'traffic offences' brought the police into conflict with the respectable middle classes, often for the first time. The police too had cars which meant a steady decline in the foot patrol but, in general, relations with the wider public were harmonious, certainly more so than in the period of social turmoil before the war. With the exception of the criminal class, or those with a radical political disposition, the 1950s saw the police officer at the height of respectability. Culturally, this was reflected in the Dixon of Dock Green image, popularised in the film *The Blue Lamp* and the subsequent television series, and whilst this image was romanticised, like all stereotypes it contained a degree of truth.

Wider social, political, and economic changes were responsible for creating the 'golden age of British Policing'. In the 1950s, Britain had seemingly entered an era of progress and prosperity for all, an era that would have been unthinkable to those who had lived through the 1930s, or to those who had experienced the savage butchery of the Second World War. The political truce between capital and labour in the post-war era was to produce social stability and cohesion, which consequently improved the relationship between working-class communities and the police. The fear of the pre-war 'red menace' or communist threat had dissipated and by the 1960s few people took seriously the idea that the British working classes were the agents of proletarian revolution. Instead of revolution, which had been genuinely feared by the ruling elites during the 1920s and 1930s, the working class were now en-masse participants in the new consumer society.

Modern market economies had now appeared for the first time to deliver satisfaction and security for the majority of citizens. The average British house was equipped with refrigerators, washing machines, telephones and television sets. Young people, or 'teenagers', occupied their time buying pop records and devouring a steady diet of popular culture invariably originating from the USA. By the late 1960s, most people owned a car and new markets in tourism meant that ordinary working-class people could for the first time travel beyond the British Isles. The workers of the modernist Western world appeared to have far more to lose than just their chains.

The golden age ends 1970–1985

The golden age did not last long, for new challenges and problems were to emerge which had been, in reality, apparent even during the good times. The police, who were an inherently conservative institution, were slow to respond to the challenges of change, particularly the social and cultural changes of the 1960s (Emsley, 2009). Sexist and homophobic attitudes were common amongst 1960s British police officers whilst racism was endemic. The police did not welcome the era of 'multi-culturalism', which transformed British social and cultural life; for many 'immigrant' meant 'criminal' and while a tiny fraction of the 'minority ethnic' community may have joined the service they were often subjected to systematic racist taunts from fellow officers (Reiner, 2000).

Cultural attitudes towards young people changed in the 1960s, particularly amongst those who had benefited from the expansion of higher education. Britain had adopted the welfare/treatment model as an intervention strategy in youth justice and it was an approach that had given credence and opportunities to social workers and other public sector professionals who were proud of their liberal attitudes towards young people. The police were hostile to 'welfarism', with many rank and file police officers dismissive of 'social workers' as 'do-gooders', and the Children and Young Person's Act 1969 was a pivotal piece of legislation which was strongly opposed by the police (Hopkins Burke, 2008).

By the end of the 1970s, crime rates were rising dramatically and crime was now a political issue for the first time in many years. The spectre of poverty had returned, or was 'rediscovered', and a crisis in the international financial markets brought with it the return of (mass) unemployment; meanwhile the disastrous and architecturally ugly public housing projects of the 1960s had recreated the modern equivalent of the slum, or 'inner-city' areas. The age of prosperity was coming to an end, and so too was the age of welfarism (Hopkins Burke, 1998b).

Margaret Thatcher fought the British General Election in 1979 on a strong law and order platform with authoritarian political discourse dominating the Conservative Party campaign and reference made to a 'moral crisis' that appeared to engulf the nation. According to a narrative, which was well received by people from all social classes, welfarism was to be seen not as a solution to social problems, but as an unmistakable part of the problem. The discourse had shifted from 'blaming society' towards personal responsibility, law and order, and punishment. Most police officers welcomed this shift and the Police Federation began to relish a Tory victory in the 1979 election. On her first day in office, Margaret Thatcher increased the pay of police officers, with the service being nicknamed by the press as 'Maggie's Boys'. Nevertheless, despite generous pay increases and other entitlements, the police were to pay another price. The era of harmonious community relations was now over and the 'golden age of British policing' was little more than a distant memory. Class war was to return to the streets of Britain as 'Maggie's Boys' were called upon to defeat the National Union of Mineworkers.

The miners' strike 1984–1985

The miners' strike 1984–1985 seemed to be a return to the pre-war years of social chaos and instability. The police were central to government plans to defeat the miners and officers began to look increasingly like a strong-arm instrument of an authoritarian state. Enormous numbers of police officers were moved around the country in what effectively became a national force while the security services undoubtedly played a significant part in the operations (Emsley, 2009). The purpose of what was to become a very successful policing strategy was to disrupt the pickets and to guarantee that imported coal made its way through the picket lines. Moreover, the police ensured that strike breakers were escorted into work in order to maintain production. Police officers, now equipped with a riot shield and fitted with flameproof overalls with a vestured helmet and usually on horse-back, went to war against the very communities they were sworn to protect. In what effectively became scenes resembling a civil war, the police were willed on by a ruthless government determined to succeed at any cost. When the strike ended in 1985 it was evident that the police had played a definitive role in defeating the NUM. The scars of the strike would last a generation, and for some people a lifetime. The defeat of the miners opened up a whole new era in politics and policing (Emsley, 2009).

Consensus and conflict: British policing 1985–present

In the aftermath of the miners' strike, the reputation of the police had been damaged in working-class communities, particularly in the former heartlands of industrial labour. At the turn of the twentieth century they were called 'the blue drones' or 'blue locusts' (Storch, 1975); by the 1980s they were known in some working-class communities as the 'pigs' or the 'scum' (Emsley, 2009). The miners' strike had shattered the social consensus that had existed in the post-war decades. Social life in Britain was dramatically altered, and by the end of the decade it was obvious to most political commentators that the era when organised industrial labour could be a significant force in British politics was finished. There was to be an irretrievable fragmentation within the former working class resulting in deep social division (Hopkins Burke, 1999b).

Traditional political loyalties were transformed as elements of the working classes bought their way into the new meritocracy and took an 'upward strategy', whilst others languished on the scrap heap and joined the swelling ranks of the 'underclass' ostensibly following a 'downward' strategy (Hopkins Burke, 1999c). Those who prospered were thus referred to as the 'upwardly mobile' as they could look forward to owning their own homes and living in private estates and buying shares in the privatised utilities. Political consciousness in some sections of the working class drifted to the right and this was linked to the emergence of the 'underclass' we encountered at the conclusion to the last chapter, which was characterised as a dangerous sub-group of amoral wasters who lived off the welfare state and were habitually criminal.

The political discourse encouraged by the populist press was one in which 'hard working tax payers' resented subsidising an 'underclass' that apparently lived on public welfare as a matter of choice. The welfare state, seen in the decades of post-war prosperity as providing emergency aid for those who truly needed it, was now commonly regarded as being abused by a hard core who lived on social welfare as a way of life. Consequently, many skilled workers now found themselves at least potential supporters of the political right.

Policing the underclass

The issue of policing the 'underclass' became one of the dominant themes in British policing in the 1990s, with the service receiving support and sympathy from both the public and politicians alike (Crowther, 1998, 2000a, 2000b). The police were to spend much of their time dealing with the everyday affairs of those living on the margins of society whose lifestyles were labelled 'dysfunctional' and 'chaotic', and high levels of crime were to become commonplace, a taken for granted part of life in the inner-city.

In the 1990s, the British public accepted a trade off between the provision of security and the loss of certain civil liberties. As a consequence, more powers were given to the police, and certain communities experienced an almost permanent police presence, alongside CCTV and other crime-fighting measures. Whilst intellectuals on the left talked about the 'occupation of poor communities by the police', the measures adopted by New Labour often had popular support, with 'more police on the street' becoming a repeated slogan stemming from working-class communities. This is a point to which we will return in the concluding section of this chapter.

Policing contemporary society

The bureaucratisation of policing

We saw in the first section of this chapter that the establishment of the state-sponsored police service or force was incrementally inevitable but the issue remains as to whether it had to take the form that it did. Thus, it can be argued that the emergence of a police bureaucracy in Britain was not inevitable but dependent on the vision of the political elite as to what an orderly disciplined society should be like (Hopkins Burke, 2004b). In many parts of the UK this vision of social order and authority was contested and from the outset each new policing service had to struggle to establish the legitimacy to exist; while a wide range of other individuals and groups – the old parish constables, gamekeepers and private watchmen, the docks and railway police, and the increasingly expanding private security industry – continued to operate (Emsley, 2001).

Thus, from their inception, the new public police service was never the only organisation undertaking police work in British society; new forms were negotiated with different audiences and multiple versions were produced, 'each with particular symbolic and instrumental meanings for specific groups' (McLaughlin, 2001: 75). What differentiated the new police from their predecessors and competitors was that they were from the outset an instrument of government. Political opposition obliged the nineteenth-century policing reformers to drop all hopes of creating a national service on the continental model and, consequently, an assortment of forces gradually took to the streets alongside those other individuals and groups performing policing functions. A progressive rationalisation and *de facto* nationalisation nevertheless took place throughout the twentieth century and to the present day as the local response to the increasing threats posed by public order (including terrorism) and crime appeared inadequate to the task. Moreover, the extensive expansion in demands placed on the public police service has increasingly stretched their resources, however much these may have expanded. An influential Audit Commission report (1996a) placed crime control as central to the police function which it observed to be: (a) responding appropriately to crime, other incidents and emergencies; (b) maintaining public order and tackling anti-social behaviour; (c) reassuring the public through a visible police presence; and (d) forging links with local communities to reduce problems of crime and nuisance.

Police effectiveness and the growth in police business

The contemporary police service has been regularly and roundly criticised for its apparent failure to produce value for money, but this has invariably always been the case. The level of recorded crime in England and Wales has risen at an average of 5.1 per cent per annum ever since 1916 and over the last two decades of the twentieth century the rise had been particularly sharp (although the figures have fallen back a little during the early twenty-first century). In 1979 there were around 2.4 million offences recorded but by 1992 the figure had reached over 5.4 million with offences against property constituting three-quarters of the total (Wilson *et al.*, 2002: 47); meanwhile the British Crime Survey has consistently shown that these official crime figures significantly underestimate the real incidence of crime.

At the same time, the police clear-up rate for England and Wales has fallen from 40 per cent in 1980 to 23.5 per cent by 2003 (Home Office, 2003) and these are mean averages that conceal considerable local variations. The Audit Commission (1999) reported that the police fail to solve as many as 92 per cent of burglaries and less than half of street robberies (although detection rates for more serious crimes are far better and have remained consistently high). However, while crime rates have risen and clear-up rates fallen, governments have not kept the police short of resources. Between 1979 and the early 1990s budgets rose in real terms by almost 90 per cent and by 1998 total expenditure on the police stood at £7.21 billion.

While there has been a considerable decrease in police effectiveness as measured by crime clear-up rates during the past half century, this reality has coincided with a huge increase in public expectations and demands for the wide range of services they provide. Five broad and closely inter-linked developments can be detected that have accelerated the growth in these expectations on which the police cannot realistically be expected to deliver.

The first broad development has been the *increase in criminal opportunities* that has occurred as a result of the increasing affluence in British society since the end of war-time rationing and the beginning of the consumer society circa 1955. Two interlocking aspects of that development are explained by Felson (1998)[4] and his notion of 'opportunity theory', where he observes that a huge increase in the number of high value portable domestic products attractive to criminals has occurred at the very same time there has been a considerable *decrease* in informal capable guardians, such as ourselves, with the great expansion in dual income households that invariably leave homes unoccupied for long periods.

The second development has been the *increase in motivated offenders* notably ignored in earlier variants of contemporary opportunity theories. Mike Sutton (1995, 1998) has argued persuasively that it is the existence of stolen goods markets that provides the crucial stimulus for theft; much of the motivation for seeking out those markets is invariably provided by the large increase in drug addiction in recent years. Bennett, Holloway and Williams (2001), in a study conducted for the British Home Office, detected a considerable correlation between heroin and crack cocaine use and offending behaviour, finding that those who used both drugs regularly spent on average £290 a week or £15,000 a year, were rarely employed and invariably needed to steal to fund their habit.

The third development is the increasing embourgeoisement or *civilising process*, observed earlier in this book, whereby standards of acceptable behaviour change over time. Elias (1978, 1982) – in what constitutes a sociological history of manners – observes a progressive moderation and discipline of personal behaviour that centres on a restraint in emotions and the possibilities for embarrassment and shame. Although this linear variant social progress model has been criticised for ignoring the class-based nature of social manners by proponents of the radical conflict model (see Slaughter, 2003), it has become increasingly persuasive in view of the expansion of white-collar employment and the often enforced accompanying changes in acceptable behaviour particularly those, popularly termed 'political correctness', endemic in the extensive public sector.

The fourth development has been the *increasing social construction of crime* and the *criminalisation* of a whole range of new offences, many associated with technological innovations; for example, consider the number of criminal offences associated with the motor car and there are many more than the simple theft of the vehicle. Computer crime was unknown until relatively recently but now provides widespread and very varied criminal opportunities. There are offences where computers are the *objects of crime*, for example, they can be damaged or stolen; they provide a *criminal environment*, for the illegal downloading or unauthorised copying of programmes or films; and they can be the *instrument of the criminal act* in the case of downloading or distributing pornography.

Other recently defined offences are closely linked with the notion of the civilising process and include domestic violence, stalking and date rape. Twenty-five years ago the then Metropolitan Police Commissioner, Kenneth Newman, dismissed domestic violence as 'rubbish work' akin to dealing with stray dogs and not worthy of police time (Hopkins Burke, 2004a). Following a concerted campaign by feminists to put the issue firmly at the top of the policing agenda it is now almost universally taken seriously by the service, although Martin (2003) observes that it has become a popular offence with detectives under considerable pressure to obtain convictions because of the relative ease in detecting the offender.

The fifth development is the *increasing complexity of society*. The public police service is very much a product of modern mass societies characterised by moral certainty and confidence in the capacity of grand social and political theories (see Hopkins Burke, 2009). Such societies have sought to develop social and economic programmes that satisfy the different and often antagonistic class interests in society and have been in the recent past relatively successful, not least in the 25 years following the Second World War. The role of the church, education system, and mass media have all been cited at various times as helping to develop and maintain an invariably conservative social consensus (see Althusser, 1969; Anderson, 1968). Others have – as we have seen above – noted the disciplinary role of the public police service in the pursuit of those goals (see for example, Bunyan, 1976; Cohen, 1979; Scraton, 1985; Storch, 1975). Essential to that disciplinary and missionary project had long been the nature and – often unintended – outcomes of recruitment policies.

Sir Robert Peel had decided from the outset of the Metropolitan Police in 1829 that his officers should come from the unskilled and semi-skilled working class and this policy became the orthodoxy with the other 'new police' forces. Emsley (2001) notes that many of the early recruits had joined as a temporary measure to alleviate a period of unemployment and had little idea what the job would entail. He observes that many loathed the rigorous discipline, the night work and the exhausting and physically dangerous nature of the job; a hard physical existence that contributed significantly to the development of a tough, masculine culture that came to dominate the service. Indeed, these were essential behavioural traits for dealing with authentic police business of the time, the rougher elements of their own social class.

This tough working-class police culture, or 'canteen culture' as it has been subsequently termed (see Holdaway, 1983; Fielding, 1988; Reiner, 2000), transmitted and adapted to changing circumstances across the generations, was undoubtedly *relatively* non-problematic during the relatively consensual modern era. The disciplinary missionary intervention against the rougher elements of the working class had undoubted support from most elements of society including essentially the socially aspiring respectable elements of that class who lived cheek-by-jowl with the roughs and sought protection from them.

It was with the fragmentation of modernity which was to accelerate, in particular, during the final quarter of the twentieth century – a situation termed by some the postmodern condition (see Lyotard, 1984) – that this macho-police occupational culture was to become increasingly problematic in a society consisting of myriad interest groups as diverse as major industrialists and financiers, small business proprietors, the unemployed and dispossessed, wide-ranging gender and sexual preference interests, environmentalists, the homeless and the socially excluded. In this complex social formation, the objective reality, or competing objective realities, of modernity, has been replaced with the multiple realities or moral ambiguities of the postmodern condition and it has become increasingly the role of the contemporary police service to intervene and arbitrate in the disputes and conflicts that inevitably occur in such societies. Crucially, the moral certainties of the dominant mono-cultural occupational police culture are inappropriate in this greatly changed world.

The issue of police occupational culture is important because of the inherent discretion available to an officer in the course of their job. In essence they must transform the 'written law' into 'law in action' and in doing so they act as key decision-makers or gatekeepers to the criminal justice system (McLaughlin, 2001). Under the guidance and control of experienced officers, new recruits are socialised into the real world of practical police work, while junior officers develop their own commonsense theories of 'justice', crime causation and solutions and come to distinguish between 'real' police work ('feeling collars' and 'getting figures') and 'rubbish' or 'dead-end' work (the rest) (Young, 1991). In order to do their job 'objectively' officers depersonalise the public by 'stereo-typing', separating and labelling them into categories deemed worthy of police assistance: the community – and the 'others', the 'toe-rags', 'slags', 'scrotes', 'scum' and 'animals'. Some have argued that these stereotypes drive the day-to-day nature and pattern of police work (Smith and Gray, 1985; Young, 1991, 1993). Certainly, these malevolent attitudes towards the public in general and particular groups are the source of many conflictual and counterproductive encounters with the public.

It is clear that taken together these five broad societal developments – the increase in criminal opportunities and motivated offenders, the increasing embourgeoisement and lower tolerance of criminal activities and social disorder, alongside the great expansion in the number of criminal offences on the statute book at a time of increasingly complex social relations – have increased public expectations of the police service to an extent that they have been unable to meet and have thus led to widespread support for more rigorous policing strategies such as 'zero tolerance', originally introduced in New York City during the mid-1990s and later in the UK.

Zero tolerance policing and 'broken windows theory'

The New York City zero tolerance policing strategy – and other variants intro-duced most notably in other cities in the USA and the UK (see Dennis, 1997; Hopkins Burke, 1998a, 2004a) – is theoretically informed by the 'broken windows' thesis which proposes that just as an unrepaired broken window is a sign that nobody cares and leads to more damage, minor incivilities – such as begging, public drunkenness, vandalism and graffiti – if unchecked and uncontrolled, produce an atmosphere in a community in which more serious crime will flourish (Wilson and Kelling, 1982). Over time, individuals may feel that they can get away with minor offences and this encourages them to commit more serious offences, or at least does not discourage them.

Proponents of such policing strategies, for example Bratton in New York City (see Bratton, 1997) and Mallon of the Cleveland Constabulary in the UK (see Dennis and Mallon, 1997; Romeanes, 1998), adapted the 'broken windows' thesis and argued that a positive police presence targeting petty offenders on the streets can lead to substantial reductions in the level of crime. They pointed to the success of experiments in their own areas, where there were large reductions in the crime figures during the mid-to-late 1990s, to support those assertions (Dennis, 1997; Hopkins Burke, 1998a).

The introduction of zero-tolerance-style policing was to receive far from universal support and criticisms were to predominantly focus on two closely linked radical conflict model arguments. First, it was argued that such strategies are reminiscent of the failed military-style 'hard' policing measures introduced by metropolitan forces in inner-city neighbourhoods in the UK during the 1970s and early 1980s. 'Swamp 81' and the subsequent disorders in Brixton, south-west London, are considered to be the defining events. Observing the inequity of primarily targeting the poor, the socially excluded and the large numbers of ethnic minority members over-represented within those groups with the simultaneous potential to incite serious disorder in the streets, opponents of 'hard' policing styles were to demand a return to community-style 'soft' policing strategies introduced following the Scarman Report into the Brixton disorders (Scarman, 1982) (see Morgan, 1997; Read, 1997; Pollard, 1997; Currie, 1997; Bowling, 1998a, 1998b; Crowther, 1998; Wadham, 1998).

Second, no clear evidence supporting a direct causal link between 'hard' policing styles and any apparent decline in the crime figures has been identified. Substantial reductions in the crime figures in all major cities in the USA were widely noted regardless of whether or not any policing initiatives, 'hard' or 'soft', had been introduced. It was argued that demographic factors, a substantial decline in the use of crack cocaine and a general disinclination towards criminal behaviour among certain – invariably ethnic – groups of young people were the real reasons for this decline (see Blumstein and Wallman, 2000).[5] The 7,000 extra police officers recruited during the Bratton/Giuliani strategic policing offensive in New York City were not widely deemed to have had a significant impact (see Hopkins Burke, 1998b).

Hopkins Burke (1998b) was to nevertheless make two significant observations. The first observation is that there is a widespread general consumer demand in society for a highly visible police presence on the streets and most significantly this existed across all ethnic and interest group divisions. Eli Silverman (1998) noted a considerable demand among black communities in the poorer neighbourhoods of New York City for the same levels of policing as in the affluent white areas. George Kelling and Caroline Coles (1996) meanwhile had clearly implied in their seminal text – forensically examining the ambiguities and contradictions between the rights of individuals and those of communities in the policing of incivilities – that widespread public support for recently implemented 'hard' policing styles in various locations in the USA had come from a wide range of victimised and fearful citizens in all social classes and ethnic groups.

Recognition of the ambiguous nature of 'hard' policing strategies – and acknowledgement of legitimate widespread popular support – was to subsequently come from two eminent criminologists in the UK previously identified with the radical conflict model, Jock Young and Kevin Stenson. Young (1999) observed that liberal criticisms of the targeting of street incivilities and the protection of actual and potential victims from these activities seemed incongruous considering the demand from similar groups for zero tolerance of such activities as domestic violence. Hopkins Burke (2004b) observes that we might note a similar and virtually unquestionable enthusiasm for zealously seeking out and eradicating child abuse and school bullying. Stenson (2000) concurs that the targeting of illegal economies and bullies in some run-down working-class housing estates often on the periphery of towns and cities is very much in the interest of the wider community.

A key theme to emerge out of that first significant observation, and by implication present in the work of Stenson and Young, is the notion of (moral) ambiguity. Controlling and policing diverse fragmented societies, where there are a multitude of interest groups, with their own often incompatible but legitimate viewpoints on a whole range of activities – where moral ambiguity and multiple truths prevail over moral certainty, consensus and absolute truth – provides a not inconsequential challenge both to politicians needing to build often complex electoral coalitions and to the police who invariably need to adjudicate between these different interest groups. Crime control is, on the other hand, an issue with very widespread public support even among those oppressed groups whom the authorities apparently overly-target and this is a perspective that can clearly be identified in the context of the left realist hybrid model of criminal justice development. Thus, zero tolerance policing styles have been widely popular in the areas in which they have been introduced but less so with most liberal criminologists and commentators. There is, therefore, considerable moral uncertainty, indeed ambiguity, around issues of crime control, due process, civil liberties and human rights.

Thus, there may well be a widespread populist enthusiasm for a proactive confident visible police service on the streets but, at the same time, this is dependent on a service perceived to be acting professionally, interceding as a neutral arbiter in societal problems. 'Hard' policing strategies need to be sensitive to the policing requirements of the particular community in order to gain, and significantly retain, widespread support and legitimacy. Indeed, as noted above, there are crucial difficulties in sustaining widespread political support over an extended period, essentially because pressure to reduce crime has coincided in some areas with an escalation in levels of unprofessional behaviour and in some cases instances of outrageous brutality committed against members of those very ethnic minority communities seeking quality policing (Silverman, 1998). The outcome has been a spiral of decline in police community relationships that has dealt an almost terminal blow for the legitimacy of robust interventions (Hopkins Burke, 2002).

The second significant observation made by Hopkins Burke (1998b) was that of an extremely convenient convergence between two significant and influential policing discourses. On the one hand, there was an influential liberal/libertarian criminal justice perspective widely supported by academic orthodoxy which proposed that the police should withdraw from whole areas of the social world in order that they did not further criminalise groups of dispossessed unfortunates. On the other hand, there were the material concerns of senior police management with the problem of managing perceived inadequate resources. This seemingly unlikely alliance between albeit implicit supporters of the orthodox social progress and radical conflict visions of the world appears to have provided a most convenient justification for doing very little regardless of levels of widespread public support (Hopkins Burke, 1998b).

Conclusions: pervasive policing and public demand

Hopkins Burke (2004a) shows that while the public police service retains a virtual monopoly on the legitimate use of coercion in society and apparently 'hard' and coercive interventions such as 'zero tolerance', other generic policing strategies such as diversionary schemes for young offenders and the work of the probation service appear to incorporate 'softer' styles. A closer examination nevertheless often betrays an ambiguity and confusion as to what can be considered 'hard' or 'soft' with the invariable reality that both are simply part of an all-seeing multiple-agency corporate crime industry that is pervasive throughout society with 'softer' and more subtle measures preferred to more coercive measures as a more insidious form of social control.

This tension between the rights of both individuals and the wider community, and at the same time between minority communities and the wider society, is central to debates about the policing of contemporary fragmented and diverse multicultural post-industrial societies. Debates about differentiation and diversity are themselves the product of a moral certainty or confidence in the economic and cultural dominance of the post-industrial West. Such certainty has been traditionally stronger among those 'in-groups' who are part of the paid employment-based consumption sectors in these societies. 'Out-groups' currently termed the underclass, or the excluded, have always been treated with suspicion and been the central focus of police business. However, near universal acceptance of the legitimacy of such social systems has been engendered in no small part by the obvious empirical evidence all around us that has shown the real possibility of transition from 'out-group' to 'in-group' status.

The history of the past 200 years in Western societies – or the modernist era – has shown that many of the material aspirations of the respectable working class have been realised and that many – if not most – of this group would now consider themselves to be middle class. Classical Marxists are nevertheless quite right to observe that the traditional social relations of capitalism remain intact and that this new embourgeoisement, or civilising process, obscures the reality that the vast majority of people remain fundamentally workers who have nothing to sell in the market place other than their labour power, legitimately that is, and that the labour market is a fast changing entity where skills in high demand yesterday may well be superfluous today or perhaps tomorrow. At the time of writing, we are currently experiencing the greatest economic downturn in at least a century where there has been subsequently a major assault upon the middle-class employment sector – in particular, that in the public sector – where more and more people are being absorbed into a proletarianised net of social exclusion, formerly the preserve of the manual working classes.

There is little legitimate doubt that mature global capitalism requires, and perhaps far more importantly is extremely dependent on, a highly educated workforce. There is a vast literature that recognises that the emergence of welfare states in such societies has been, at least in part, in response to organised working-class demands. More recent developments such as widespread home and share ownership and private pensions are a clear indication of the greater rewards expected by an educated, skilled and valuable workforce, with corresponding changes to the nature of its political representation. This process is exemplified in Britain by the transition from 'old' Labour via 'popular' conservatism or 'Thatcherism' to New Labour. With such material gains, and the improved education that has brought this about, come improved expectations of 'rights' and civil liberties. Thus, we have all come to expect respect, decency and professionalism from public servants with whom we have dealings and the state-sponsored police service and other branches of the criminal justice system are no exception. These expectations are in no doubt part of the increasing civilising process and resultant pressures have contributed to the great increase in police business.

Rights and liberties at one time – while at least theoretically the prerogative of all Englishmen – were in the main matters of concern for a small propertied and relatively affluent percentage of the population. The great majority of us were controlled and disciplined and policed by the demands of long hours of hard physical toil either paid or unpaid. The increasing process of embourgeoisement led to the expansion of civil rights to whole sections of the population not previously considered entitled to them such as English*women* and children. In the case of the former, a husband no longer enjoys the right, nay the duty as was considered legislatively appropriate in the late nineteenth century, to discipline his wife with a stick, as long as the aforesaid instrument was constituted of a thickness no larger than the thumb of her husband, but he is now considered by the criminal justice system to be not just a criminal but increasingly a *serious* criminal. At the same time, we have progressively demanded the right to a peaceful and victimless existence. Thus, in a world where criminal opportunities are forever increasing and victimisation is widespread, public support for rigorous, indeed 'hard', policing strategies has been popular as long as these are not perceived to be getting in the way of our civil liberties. At the same time, a simultaneous component of the growth of the 'crime control industry' (Christie, 1993) has been an apparent increase in the number of civil, or more recently human, rights lawyers who have been eager to ensure that those socially excluded members of society who come into more regular contact with the criminal justice system have their rights safeguarded.

Thus we can observe a constant tension between, on the one hand, a demand for our human rights – and in many cases this stretches to a requirement for a minimal intervention in our often hedonistic and sometimes at least technically criminal lifestyles where the use of recreational drugs is involved – and, on the other hand, a demand for a peaceful and secure existence which we expect governments and their agents to deliver, a 'schizophrenia of crime' (Hopkins Burke, 2007) that we will encounter further in the concluding chapter. It is clear that these two demands cannot be easily reconciled but what does become increasingly clear is that the incremental development of pervasive generic policing throughout society, with an oft confused ambiguity between 'hard' and 'soft' multi-agency policing strategies, is part of an expanding insidious form of social control that has come about with at least our implicit agreement and this goes well beyond the public police service.

Policing and the four models of criminal justice development

This section critically reflects on the history and development of policing in the context of the four models of criminal justice development: (1) the orthodox social progress model; (2) the radical conflict model; (3) the carceral surveillance society model; and (4) the left realist hybrid model.

Policing and the orthodox social progress model

At first sight, it is would seem self-evident that the history of the public police service, from pre-modernity and throughout the modernist era, can be explained by the orthodox social progress model of criminal justice development with its notions of a progressive humanitarian response to social problems in the interests of all social groups in society. We have seen that the effectiveness of the pre-modern system had been based on stable, remarkably similar, predominantly rural communities where people knew each other and their activities extremely well.

It was during the eighteenth century that the pre-modern system came under significant challenge from three closely interlinked sources. First, the traditional rural communities and their long established social order had begun to break down in the face of the rapid transition to an industrial economy. Second, the amateur nature of the response, the unpaid parish constable and the voluntary watch, was to prove increasingly inadequate to the task of policing communities and individuals were indeed invariably unwilling to do so. Third, the fast-expanding towns and cities were increasingly becoming a haven for the poor and the landless who occupied extremely overcrowded slums ridden with disease, crime and violence (Emsley, 1996, 2001).

From the orthodox social progress perspective the establishment of the first professional police service in 1829 and its subsequent development occurred in the interest of all groups and classes in society who needed protection from the criminality and disorder in their midst. Admittedly, there had been initial opposition from across the social spectrum but for very different reasons. Affluent groups felt that the police were a burden on the taxpayer and they were not part of the established way of life. The middle classes were concerned about perceived threats to civil liberties and the imposition of an intrusive centralised system of social control similar to the continental model. Working-class opposition was based on the perception that the police were in place in order to enforce ruling-class interests. Nevertheless, over the course of the next 130 years or so, the police came to be accepted by most of the population with perhaps the exception of the socially excluded underclass (Crowther, 2000a, 2000b).

Policing and the radical conflict model

Proponents of the radical conflict perspective argue that the professional police were from their very formation at the beginning of the nineteenth century 'domestic missionaries' with an emphasis on the surveillance, discipline and control of the rough and dangerous working-class elements in society and from the very outset these were implemented in the interests of the capitalist class (Storch, 1975). In the same way, contemporary 'hard' strategies such as zero tolerance policing which are ostensibly targeted at socially excluded groups in society are very much a continuation of that tradition (see Crowther, 1998, 2000a, 2000b; Hopkins Burke, 1998a, 2004a).

Proponents of the radical conflict model argue that definitions of crime and criminality are class-based and the public police service are simply agents of a capitalist society which targets the activities of the socially excluded while at the same time ignoring the far more damaging behaviour of corporate capitalism (see Scraton and Chadwick, 1996).

Policing and the carceral surveillance society model

The carceral surveillance society model is, as we have seen, a perspective which is complementary to the radical conflict model but at the same time there is a significant recognition that the issue of power in society is one of some complexity. From this post-structuralist[6] perspective, power is not just the preserve and possession of an all-powerful monolithic state but is both diffuse and pervasive throughout society with agents and experts at all levels of the social world having both access to and control of power. This power is inevitably, in the final analysis, exercised in the overall interests of the dominant class in a capitalist mode of production – hence its compatibility with the radical conflict model – but those who are involved in its application at the micro, mezzo and macro levels of society are not always aware of their often obtuse contribution to the 'grand design' of the disciplinary control matrix that constrains and restrains us all in society.

Hopkins Burke (2004a) observes, in the theoretical context of the carceral surveillance model, that policing is both pervasive and insidious throughout contemporary fragmented society. 'Hard' and 'soft' policing styles – regardless of whether conducted by the public police service, the private security industry or social work agencies – are all part of the contemporary all-seeing multiple agency corporate crime industry. As the Italian communist Antonio Gramsci

(1977–1978) and more recently the radical US criminologist Austin Turk (1969) have both observed, societies adopt coercive or 'hard' policing measures when they are under threat from internal or external 'enemies'. Such measures are nevertheless invariably unpopular with the public if used indiscriminately and for extended periods and it could therefore become more difficult to control society. Thus, 'softer' and more subtle measures are preferred as a more insidious form of social control.[7] In reality, both 'hard' and 'soft' measures are invariably used concurrently and compatibly in pursuit of the same crime and social control goal (Hopkins Burke, 2004a).

The carceral surveillance society model explains the incremental increase in multiple hard and soft policing strategies as the inevitable response to the many and varied crime and social control challenges presented by the fragmentation and complexity of our contemporary world which is discussed in more detail in the concluding chapter. Challenges are both internal (intra-national) and external (inter-national) and these are all underpinned by a widespread and inherent moral ambiguity where old norms, values and understandings of right and wrong are under challenge or indeed superseded.

Policing and the left realist hybrid model

We saw in the first chapter that the left realist hybrid model developed by Hopkins Burke (2004a, 2008, 2009) essentially provides a synthesis of the orthodox social progress, radical conflict and carceral surveillance society models but which additionally and significantly recognises *our* interest and collusion in the creation of the increasingly pervasive socio-control matrix of the carceral surveillance society. It is a model heavily influenced by left realism, a criminological per-spective we encountered in the previous chapter and which identifies crime to be a real problem for poor people targeted by the criminal element living in their own communities and from whom they require a protection that has not always been forthcoming (Lea and Young, 1984; Matthews and Young, 1986, 1992; Young 1994, 1997).

Hopkins Burke has subsequently developed the left realist perspective in a historical context to show that the general public has always had an interest in the development of social progress (orthodox social progress model) which has invariably conveniently coincided with the requirements of capitalism (radical conflict model) and which has contributed invariably unwittingly to the con-struction of the disciplinary control matrix that constrains and restrains the actions and rights of all and this is the basis of the left realist hybrid model of criminal justice development. Thus, in order to explain the development of the public police service from the beginning of the nineteenth century, it is recognised that crime was as real a problem for ordinary people at the time as it is now, and that the respectable working class has always required protec-tion from the criminal elements in their midst, whether these were termed the 'rough working classes' (nineteenth century) or a socially excluded underclass (twenty-first century) (Hopkins Burke, 2004b).

Significantly, in the contemporary, complex, fragmented, dangerous society we currently inhabit it is we the general public – regardless of our social class location, gender or ethnic origin – that have a fundamental interest in the development of the carceral surveillance matrix that restricts the civil liberties or human rights of some individuals or groups (Hopkins Burke, 2004c). It is moreover a discourse that coincides neatly with a consistent, widespread, contemporary public demand for police on the streets, frequently expressed in contemporary crime surveys but which has been contrary to the prevailing, widely influential, academic policing orthodoxy which has repeatedly stated that the service on its own can have little effect on the crime rate (Hopkins Burke, 1998a, 1998b, 2004a, 2004b).

5 The legal process in modern society

The legal process in modern society has its foundations in the beginnings of modernity and was a response to the pre-modern world where there had been very little codified or written law and that which did exist was applied erratically, via judicial discretion and whim. This was all to change with the advent of the modern world and the introduction of increasingly bureaucratised criminal justice institutions and a rationalised process for responding to criminality.

The modern legal process has its origins in the work of Cesare Beccaria (1738–1794) who we saw in the second chapter provided the theoretical foundations for the rational actor model of crime and criminal behaviour where it is proposed that individuals have free will and choose to become involved in criminal behaviour in the same way that they might choose any other course of action.[1] In common with many of his contemporary intellectuals, and inspired by the social contact theories we encountered in the first chapter, Beccaria was strongly opposed to the many inconsistencies that existed in government and public affairs in the pre-modern era and his major text was essentially the first attempt at presenting a systematic, consistent and logical penal system and this can be summarised in the following 13 propositions. First, in order to escape social chaos, each member of society must surrender part of their liberty to the sovereignty of the nation-state. Second, to prevent or discourage individuals from infringing the liberty of others by breaking the law, it is necessary to introduce punishments for such breaches. Third, 'the despotic spirit', or the tendency to offend, is in everyone and we are all capable of criminal behaviour. Criminals are thus not a separate category of humanity from non-criminals. Fourth, available punishments should be decided by the legislature (or our elected representatives) and not by the courts. Fifth, the judiciary should only impose punishments established by the law in order to preserve consistency and the certainty of punishment. Sixth, the seriousness of the crime should be judged not by the intentions of the offender but by the harm that it does to society. Seventh, the punishment must be proportionate to the crime committed and should be set on a scale, or a tariff, with the most severe penalties corresponding to offences which caused the most harm to society. The most serious crimes are those which threaten the stability of society. Eighth, punishment which follows promptly after a crime is committed will be more just and effective. Ninth, punishment has to be certain to be effective. Tenth, laws and punishments have to be well publicised so that people are well aware of them and the consequences if they were to transgress. Eleventh, punishment is imposed for the purpose of deterrence and therefore capital punishment is unnecessary and should not be used. Twelfth, the prevention of crime is better than punishment. Thirteenth, activities which are not expressly prohibited by law are not illegal and are therefore permissible.

These ideas have had a profound effect on the development and establishment of the modern criminal law and, while they may not be expressed in quite the same way, it is easy to detect resonances of these views in any popular discussion on crime. The doctrine of free will is built into many legal codes and has strongly influenced popular conceptions of justice.

This chapter commences with a brief examination of the role of the different agencies and processes of what many refer to as the criminal justice system. There are of course clear, invariably significant, differences between the systems in different countries and thus while many of the examples cited here refer to England and Wales they are indicative of institutions in other modern societies although readers are advised to consult other sources for the details of criminal justice institutions in other locations. The criminal justice process is the process by which people who have transgressed against the criminal law are dealt with by the state, It is made up of a series of stages which a person charged with a criminal offence must go through in order to be convicted.

In this chapter we will examine and analyse some of the issues surrounding the pre-trial process including the investigation of crime, the prosecution process and remand decisions. These issues illustrate the fundamental problem of the criminal justice process which attempts to reconcile the rights of suspects, defendants and offenders with those of wider society and its interests.

At first sight, it would appear that the development and establishment of the criminal justice process can be best conceptualised in the context of the social progress model of criminal justice development with its fundamental notions of a progressive humanitarian response to social problems in the interests of all social groups in society. It nevertheless becomes increasingly apparent that the criminal justice process has a control function in society and there are clearly interest groups involved. Thus, our attention is alerted to the radical conflict model of criminal justice development and the argument that this progress has occurred – at least in the last instance – in the interests of the capitalist economy. However, it becomes even more apparent with further investigation that the situation is more ambiguous and complex and our attention thus turns to the carceral surveillance society model where it is recognised that power is both diffuse and pervasive throughout society, with agents and experts at all levels of the social world having both access to and control of power of differing levels of magnitude although it is recognised that in the final analysis this power is invariably exercised in the overall interests of the capitalist economy. These agents are, moreover, invariably unaware of their contribution to the 'grand design' of the disciplinary control matrix that constrains and restrains us all in society and it is thus the left realist hybrid model that significantly recognises our interest and collusion in the creation of the mechanisms, policies and strategies which collectively contribute to the increasingly pervasive socio-control matrix of the carceral surveillance society. Thus, it is we the general public that have significant interests in the increasing development of the criminal justice process or system. Durkheim (1933, originally 1893) and later Foucault (1977), in a very different way, have argued that crime is functional – and thus useful – to society, although of course harmful and unwelcome. The former famously argues that crime can bring social solidarity in societies such as our own which are characterised by anomie or normlessness, atomisation and individualism. It is the condemnation of crime and criminals that can bring unity among people living in otherwise fragmented and privatised worlds against an enemy within – or least nearby – our communities. Foucault (1977) observes that if there were no crime or social disorder there would be no need for the various agencies of the criminal justice process or, for that matter, the extensive private security and voluntary sectors. There is thus a 'crime control industry' which like any other enterprise seeks to expand and develop in terms of its own invariably material interests (Christie, 1993) and which in the UK employs in excess of 400,000 people (Crowther, 2007). These models of criminal justice development should thus be kept in mind as we proceed to consider the working of different elements of the criminal justice process.

Criminal justice agencies

The criminal justice process is made up of a number of agencies who have discrete but connected roles and hence the assumption that there is indeed 'a system'. Christie (1977) observes that early communities tended to respond to criminal behaviour by bringing together the offender and victim and solving any dispute between them, but it is with the emergence of modern societies that there is the incremental creation of complex criminal justice systems with a parallel change of orientation. It is now the state that takes a lead in determining the treatment of a suspect. Thus, in England and Wales, the police and subsequently the Crown Prosecution Service (CPS) determine whether a case is prosecuted, judges and juries determine whether those charged are found innocent or guilty, and judges usually determine the sentence for those found guilty within a framework of legal guidance. The original victim of the crime does not perform any of these functions. Crowther (2007: 51) observes that 'basically, the system is based on the argument that the state is victim of the offence, and accordingly the state assumes responsibility for the correction or amendment of the harm caused'.

We observed in the previous chapter that the police have a number of roles but a central one is their contribution to social control and the maintenance of law and order. The police are crime fighters when they enforce the law through stop and search, making arrests, detaining, interviewing and interrogating suspects, and observing and monitoring a range of suspects and offenders. Crime fighting is all about the police using their legitimate right to coerce or use force against law- and rule-breakers on behalf of the state (Crowther, 2007). The police are invariably the first contact point with the criminal justice process for people who have allegedly broken the criminal law or are victims of crime and it is they who are responsible for recording and investigating crime and arresting and detaining suspects. The police provide subsequent stages of the process with information about the offence, the circumstances which surrounded it and details about the defendant. The stage of the process therefore plays an integral role in how the case proceeds and plays a large part in the prosecution and conviction of offenders.

The Crown Prosecution Service (CPS) was established in 1986 by the Prosecution of Offences Act 1985 and its function is 'to take over the conduct of all criminal cases against both adults and juveniles which are instituted by or on behalf of the police' (Zander, 1988: 212). It is thus the CPS which, after a suspect has been charged with a criminal offence, conducts all criminal proceedings in the magistrates' courts and which briefs counsel for Crown Court proceedings. Once a person has been charged by the police or information put against them, the papers are sent to the appropriate branch office of the CPS where the evidence is reviewed by the Crown Prosecutor and a decision is made whether or not to continue the proceedings. The CPS makes decisions to proceed based on two criteria: evidential and public interest. The first involves assessing whether or not the evidence is sufficient to provide a realistic prospect of conviction and the second whether it is in the public interest to proceed. If it is not then the CPS have an obligation to discontinue (Uglow, 1995).

The CPS is, both in conception and law, an independent agency with exclusive power to decide whether or not to continue proceedings. In theory, it operates to provide the accused with a further form of procedural safeguard, in that their case is considered independently by an agency whose primary objective is not that of securing as many convictions as possible.

The CPS nevertheless has a contradictory role. On the one hand, it is responsible for prosecuting the guilty and its success is measured by the number of cases it prosecutes while, on the other hand, it has a role in protecting the interests of the accused to prevent wrongful convictions. Its independence is compromised by the fact that it has no investigative powers and relies on the police for information about the case which thus enables the latter to ensure that the information they pass on provides a justification for the necessity and desirability of a prosecution (Sanders and Young, 2006).

The fundamental role of the courts in all modern societies is to decide whether or not a defendant is guilty and, if so, to impose the appropriate sentence. They also make other key decisions such as remand and mode of trial decisions. There are several different types of courts within the English criminal justice process and the two most important are the magistrates' courts and the Crown Courts.

Magistrates' courts are the 'work horses' of the criminal justice process and deal with at least 95 per cent of all criminal cases (Uglow, 1995). This is the lower court, where sentences are administered by magistrates who are charged with trying more minor offences which include summary offences and some either-way offences. The majority of sentencers in the magistrates' court are lay magistrates who are unpaid and not professionally trained in the law and consequently they are unable to conduct cases alone and must be part of a three-member bench assisted by a legally qualified clerk to the court. A small percentage of magistrates are professionally qualified in law and these full-time salaried stipendiaries have the power to try cases alone. But not all magistrates' courts have a stipendiary magistrate and they tend to be concentrated in the large urban areas.

All defendants first appear in the magistrates' courts and if the offence is minor all of the proceedings will take place in that jurisdiction. If the offence is indictable only, it will be sent to the Crown Court for trial. But if it is an either-way offence, magistrates have to make a decision about where the case should be heard. One of the criteria for such decisions is the likely sentence as the lower courts have limited sentencing powers although they do have the power to commit offenders to the higher court for sentencing. Summary and either-way offences begin with the charge being read to the court. If the defendant pleads guilty then no trial needs to take place and the magistrate will instigate the procedures required for sentencing. If a not guilty plea is submitted, a trial must take place and if the magistrates find the defendant guilty they will decide on a suitable sentence following the advice of the clerk (Walker, 1985).

Crown Courts were established by the Courts Act 1971 and are controlled by professional, legally trained, government appointed judges who are responsible for all questions of procedure and law and determine the appropriate sentence if an offender is found guilty. Four different types of judge are involved in the operation of the Crown Court. First, *High Court Judges* undertake the most important and serious criminal cases, for example treason, murder and genocide. Second, *Circuit Judges* preside over the majority of cases and are full-time, salaried individuals appointed by the Crown. Third, *Recorders* are part-time judges who have previously worked in other areas of the law and who are normally lawyers with at least ten years' experience. Fourth, *Deputy Circuit Judges* and *Assistant Recorders* were created to enable the court to function efficiently at times when there is a backlog of cases or an unexpected increase in business (Wasik, 2001).

The Crown Court hears cases of a more serious nature than those tried in the lower court involving indictable offences and the more serious triable either-way offences. Each trial is preceded by a committal hearing where the magistrates decide whether there is sufficient evidence to proceed to the higher court and where the defence has the opportunity to request that the case be dismissed. If the defendant enters a not guilty plea, a trial takes place in the presence of a jury of twelve men and women who are randomly selected from the general public and it is they who decide if the defendant is innocent or guilty, though they may be directed by the presiding judge. Once the offender has been found guilty, the judge passes sentence (Wasik, 2001). Therefore, one of the primary distinctions between the two courts is that in the higher court 'the judge decides questions of law and the jury decide issues of fact . . .' while in the lower court, sentencers must be '. . . the arbiters of both law and fact' (Sprack, 1992: 75).

Triable either-way offences include theft, burglary and criminal damage and as the name suggests can be dealt with in either the lower or higher courts. The decision as to where these offences are tried is dependent on the magistrates and the accused. Magistrates can 'refuse jurisdiction' (Sprack, 1992: 74) and require the case to be sent to the higher court and this decision is usually dependent on the perceived seriousness of the offence. Defendants also have the right to insist on trial by jury, but in most cases offenders opt for a trial in the lower court simply because of the speed of proceedings and the 'ceiling' placed on the sentences that magistrates can impose (Uglow, 1995: 138).

The role of the probation service is to provide pre-sentence reports to the court, bail facilities, information to the CPS about the defendant to inform the bail decision, supervision of offenders sentenced to community sentences, and supervision of offenders released on licence from prison. Youth Offending teams have some of the same responsibilities in relation to juveniles and youths (Hopkins Burke, 2008). The role of the prison service is to hold securely those remanded in custody or sentenced to terms of imprisonment by the courts.

All of the above agencies of the criminal justice process have national coordinating bodies and work within a national remit. They nevertheless all have a decentralised structure which, in the main, is regionally based and, as a consequence, the way in which the criminal law is implemented varies in different geographical locations. Other agencies and individuals are not statutory organisations. These include defence lawyers whose role it is to represent defendants, protect their rights and put their point of view throughout the process; voluntary agencies such as victim support; campaigning groups such as the Howard League for Penal Reform, the Prison Reform Trust and the National Council for the Care and Rehabilitation of Offenders (NACRO).

Criminal justice 'system' or 'process'

A major debate has taken place among academics as to whether or not the criminal justice process can be viewed as a 'system'. The main work in this area was produced by the British Home Office (Pullinger, 1985; Feeney, 1985) and centred around the reality that each part of the process and the agencies involved are all interdependent and closely related while no stage can be viewed in isolation as the policies and practices it follows have consequences for other components. Pullinger (1985: 18) argues that 'In order to study the criminal justice system at any point it is necessary to be aware of the interdependence of its component parts. Changes at any point have repercussions elsewhere.'

Important decisions are taken throughout the criminal justice process and what happens at any one stage is dependent upon another. For example, the workload of the CPS depends on the decisions of the police as to whether or not to charge a suspect, decisions made by the CPS about whether or not to prosecute offenders determine the workload of the courts, and the decisions of the court affect the workload of the prison service and the probation service. As a result, it is important to view each stage and agency in the context of the criminal justice process as a whole. Feeney (1985: 10) observes that 'what one criminal justice agency does is likely to affect and be affected by other agencies and . . . a detailed knowledge of the kinds of interactions that are likely to take place is essential for undertaking system improvements'.

Thus, changes which are made to any component affect other stages of the process and the agencies involved. As a result, any proposals for change must take account of the process as a whole and examine the impact of those changes on other parts of the system. Hence, the criminal justice process, if it is to run efficiently and effectively, must be viewed as a system.

No one denies that the stages and processes of criminal justice are inter-connected but many commentators (for example, Cavadino and Dignan, 2006) argue that the process cannot be viewed as a system because it is simply dys-functional. It is made up of different agencies, all of which have different and sometimes competing objectives and exercise wide and unaccountable discretion-ary powers. The agencies work in isolation and there is a lack of communication and cooperation both between stages and agencies. The outcome is a criminal justice process which is ill coordinated and as Feeney (1985: 8) observes, the research in this area has:

> expos[ed] a great deal of divergence in the way that agencies approach particular problems and show[s] that the policies followed by one agency often undermine or [are] at cross purposes with those followed by other agencies. It also demonstrate[s] just how complex and interdependent the various parts of the system actually are.

This debate has been useful for it helps to explain why some reforms have different outcomes from those that were intended. It also illustrates that these issues must be considered to enable changes to succeed and have the intended outcome. In addition, it has emphasised the importance of cooperation and communication between agencies in the criminal justice process. This point was highlighted by the Royal Commission (Runciman, 1993) and Lord Justice Woolf (Woolf Report, 1991) who commented on the lack of cooperation and communication between criminal justice agencies and recognised the need for effective planning and communication within the criminal justice process on both a national and a local level. To this end, both national and area consultative committees were established to provide a forum for debate.

The criminal justice process in context

The criminal justice process has to be observed in the context of the wider social, political and economic environment in which it operates. At a micro level how defendants and offenders are perceived and dealt with is significantly influenced by their own social and economic circumstances. At a macro level, broader political objectives affect the policies which are proposed and implemented. For example, criminal justice policy between 1979 and 1997 was informed, at least in part, by three fundamental political policies: reducing the level of public expenditure, seeking to provide services (for example, community care and punishment) in the community, and privatisation. These objectives brought about significant changes in the criminal justice system: the introduction of privately run prison establishments and prison escort services and the provision of a greater number of 'community sentences' are clear examples. The importance of ideology and fundamental principles is strikingly apparent by the fact that the New Labour government elected in 1997 signalled their intention to stop any further private prisons becoming operational despite no evidence that they provided a poorer service than state run prisons (Bottomley *et al.*, 1996) but subsequently once elected accepted the status quo.

The importance of the media in issues relating to crime and criminal justice policy cannot be ignored. Editions of every newspaper and television news programme are full of stories about crime and there has been a dramatic increase in the number of documentaries and drama programmes which relate to the issue. The public has never had so much information about crime and the criminal justice process but, at the same time, the media also play a significant role in heightening public concern and contributing to policy debates. The role of the media is important because it is the main source of the public knowledge about crime. Crime sells newspapers but the incidents reported are selected on the criterion of newsworthiness. Thus, media coverage tends to focus on unusual crimes which involve novelty, drama or titillation (Schlesinger and Tumber, 1994; Jewkes, 2005). In this way, newspaper crime reports tend to provide a distorted picture of crime with these stories often reported in a sensationalised manner.

One of the most important and significant influences on issues relating to criminal justice is its politicisation. Law and order is high on the political agenda and its increasing importance partly reflects public concern about increasing levels of crime that have occurred since the 1970s, while the fact that it has become a significant issue also raises public awareness. One of the consequences of this was a high rate of change in criminal justice policy under the Conservatives between 1979 and 1997 with no fewer than five new Criminal Justice Acts and a great deal of other legislation which fundamentally changed areas of criminal justice practice.

The new legislation touched every criminal justice agency and involved the creation of new offences (for example, aggravated vehicle taking), new sentencing options (for example, combination orders) and new procedures. Much of this legislation was criticised on the grounds that it had been a response to specific cases, which, although causing a great deal of public concern, were rare and unusual (see Hucklesby, 1993), and the government was accused of producing uninformed 'knee-jerk' legislation without any awareness of its impact on existing legislation, criminal justice agencies, offenders or the process as a whole. Despite a change in government in 1997, the rapid changes in criminal justice law did not decrease and the significant New Labour flagship criminal justice legislation, the Crime and Disorder Act, became law as early as 1998.

In addition to legislative changes there were two Royal Commissions, one in 1981 (Phillips, 1981) and another in 1993 (Runciman, 1993), which examined various aspects of the criminal justice process. Both were established after public confidence in the criminal justice process had declined due to specific, and, in the case of the Runciman Commission (1993), numerous, miscarriages of justice. The Royal Commission on Criminal Procedure (Phillips, 1981) was established after the wrongful conviction of three people for the murder of Maxwell Confait (Sanders, 1994: 1). Its remit was to study police powers which had been found to be haphazard and piecemeal and it recommended that there should be a balance between the powers of the police and the rights of suspects and that the investigation and prosecution of crime should be overseen by separate agencies. Its recommendations resulted in the Police and Criminal Evidence Act 1984 and the Prosecution of Offences Act 1985 which aimed to reduce the risk of further miscarriages of justice. The Royal Commission on Criminal Justice 1993 was nevertheless established in similar circumstances after a string of miscarriages of justice which indicated a further deepening of the crisis in the criminal justice process.

The report which followed was accepted by the political and legal establishment but was condemned by many on the grounds that it endorsed many changes in the criminal justice process which would reduce the protections afforded to suspects and defendants, such as extending police questioning before charge, the introduction of plea-bargaining and the advance disclosure of the defence to the prosecution (see McConville and Bridges, 1994). McConville and Bridges (1994: xv) observe that 'the Commission . . . helped to effect a dramatic reversal in the political climate over criminal justice, from a situation of crisis engendered by miscarriages of justice to one of triumphal "law and orderism"'.

The situation did not change with the election of the New Labour government in 1997 since when more than 50 Acts of Parliament were to be passed which contained the words 'crime' 'justice' or 'police' with an estimated 4,300 new criminal offences created or an average of 28 new offences per day. This constant law-making occurred in a political environment where the government consistently spoke of the need to 'rebalance' the criminal justice system towards the victim and away from the defendant. The unfortunate implication of this rebalancing exercise was that it seems that one had to either be on the 'side' of the criminal or of the victim. The policy driver for many new laws seemed to be a need to show that 'something was being done' whether or not there was a genuine gap in the law that needed addressing. As well as creating a myriad of new offences this approach can prove problematic for enforcement agencies who have to devote time, energy and resources to ensuring that they are up to date with new laws, powers and procedures.

Adversarial and inquisitorial criminal justice processes

The English, Welsh, Scottish and Northern Irish criminal justice processes, and those of other common law jurisdictions such as Australia, Canada and the US, are based on adversarial principles whereas most of the legal systems in the rest of Europe, for example, France and Germany, are based upon inquisitorial values. Whether the legal system of a country is based on adversarial or inquisitorial principles depends on their particular 'history, culture and underlying ideology' (Sanders and Young, 2006).

A major focus of the Royal Commission 1993 (Runciman, 1993) was on whether or not the English and Welsh criminal justice process should become more inquisitorial for it was thought that this might provide superior protection to the accused and prevent further miscarriages of justice. It nevertheless concluded that it was inappropriate to adopt a more inquisitorial method but *parts* of the process could be improved by moving more in that direction.

Under an adversarial system it is the role of the prosecution to bring the case to court and prove that the defendant is guilty. The case is prepared by the prosecution and defence and the judge acts as an independent arbitrator. It is their role to listen to the evidence, ensure that correct procedures are followed and make the final decisions in the case. In contrast, under an inquisitorial system, the judge takes a central role and examines a dossier about the case in advance of the trial so that they can 'master' the details and afterwards decide which witnesses should be called and talk to them. The prosecution and defence lawyers have only a subsidiary role, in contrast to the adversarial process, where it is the lawyers who take centre stage and decide which witnesses to call and what to ask them. The adversarial process places a great emphasis on the day in court where the judge and jury turn up with no prior knowledge of the case, whereas under an inquisitorial process the judge is involved in the collection and selection of evidence (Uglow, 1995).

Sanders and Young (2006) observe that traditionally adversarial systems have been characterised as about the determination of 'proof' whereas inquisitorial processes are about discovering the 'truth'. They nevertheless argue that this distinction is too simplistic as both systems are about ascertaining the truth but this is found in different ways. Adversarial processes are based on the assumption that 'the truth is best discovered by powerful statements on both sides of the question' (Sanders and Young, 2006: 8) and it is recognised that the circumstances surrounding the commission of the offence are open to interpretation. A judge is thus provided with two versions of events before deciding which one is the 'truth'. In the case of the inquisitorial processes, in contrast, there is a real possibility that alternative scenarios will not be investigated because the investigator may favour one particular interpretation. The defence are thus often uncertain as to whether or not the prepared dossier includes all the relevant material which may help the suspect. Sanders and Young (2006: 8–9) later observe that:

> There is also a danger that a trial judge, having formed an initial view of the case based on a reading of the dossier, will give too much weight to evidence adduced at the trial which is consistent with the pre-existing theory, and too little to that which conflicts with it. . . . So while inquisitorial systems are rightly portrayed as involving searches for the truth, the way in which that search is conducted can shape the 'truth' that is proclaimed in court.

On the other hand, the adversarial process may also not find the 'truth' as one or both parties may not present relevant evidence and/or one side, invariably the defence, may have limited access to resources and expertise (Sanders and Young, 2006: 9).

There are further fundamental differences between the adversarial and inquisitorial processes. The former is founded on the fundamental premise that the state must prove its case against the accused who is considered to be innocent until proven guilty beyond reasonable doubt and in this way defendants are protected from the abuse of state power. This safeguard is also achieved by, for example, the provision of defence solicitors, who enable the accused to challenge the prosecution, and the creation of strict procedures for the collection of evidence and the establishment of guilt, which must be adhered to. These safeguards are often lacking in inquisitorial processes as the state is seen as neutral (Sanders and Young, 2006) but there is evidence to suggest that abuses do occur under such systems (Leigh and Zedner, 1992).

Models of the criminal justice process

A number of different theoretical models have been introduced during the past 40 years in order to explain the operation of the criminal justice process. These have been formulated in an attempt to explain the difference between what the law says should happen (the rhetoric of the law) and how the criminal justice process operates in practice (the practical operation of the law). This is what is often termed the difference between the 'law in books' and the 'law in action'.

Criminal justice agencies and the individuals who work for them have wide discretionary powers and this situation arises partly because of the way that the criminal law is framed and to some extent because every law needs to be interpreted to fit the circumstances of individual cases. This discretion significantly enables variation in practices and decision-making to occur and it thus means that procedures and decisions do not necessarily equate with the letter of the law.

The criminal justice process models of Herbert Packer

Herbert Packer (1969) sought to explain the difference between the law in books and its practical operation. He observes that the criminal justice process:

> can be described, but only partially and inadequately, by referring to the rules of law that govern the apprehension, screening, and trial of persons suspected of crime. It consists at least as importantly of patterns of official activity that correspond only in the roughest kind of way to the prescriptions of procedural rules . . . we are just beginning to be aware how rough the correspondence is.
> (Packer, 1969: 149)

Michael King (1981) later pertinently observes that his predecessor had attempted to:

> develop a framework for the understanding of the relationship between rules and behaviour within the criminal justice system, for without such a framework it is fruitless to talk of reforming the system by changing formal rules. In the past there has been a tendency . . . to assume that changes in the law and legal procedures will result automatically in desired changes in the

way the system operates in practice. Too often the good intentions of the reformers have been thwarted by the capacity of interest groups to interpret and adapt would-be reforms so that they fit neatly into existing patterns of behaviour. On other occasions reforming the rules has led to unforeseen and undesired changes in the behaviour of those that operate the system.

(King, 1981: 3)

There is thus a gap between what should happen and what does actually happen, and the various agencies involved in the criminal justice process have the capacity to undermine legal changes if they disapprove of them. This can happen because of the high level of discretion afforded to these groups by the law. In reality, all laws need to be interpreted to fit individual cases: hence the ability to adapt them.

Packer produced two models of the criminal justice process. The first, the *crime control model*, can be characterised as an assembly line which moves people along with the minimum of difficulty towards the final outcome (sentence), while the second, the *due process model*, can be conceptualised as an obstacle course where each stage of the process is a hurdle whereby, if it is hit, the person drops out of the race and consequently does not complete the process. These two models are ideal types[2] in the sense that they are two ends of a continuum, that is to say they are two extremes and, in reality, most processes will fall somewhere between the two extremities. Packer nevertheless argues that most cases will lean more to one extreme than the other.

The crime control model explains the primary function of the criminal justice process to be the repression of criminal conduct. Crime is controlled through the punishment of the offender and inherent in this objective is the idea of retribution and deterrence. The level of punishment inflicted should be in accordance with the 'deserts principle', that is, in relation to the extent of the harm caused by the offence and the blameworthiness of the offender, and its success is measured in terms of a high rate of apprehension and conviction. To achieve these results, the system must be efficient in its capacity to apprehend, try, convict and dispose of a high proportion of those offenders whose offences become known. This measure of success ultimately requires an emphasis on speed and finality of the decisions, especially in an environment where large numbers are involved with only limited resources to deal with them. Speed, in turn, depends on informality and uniformity and results in the condonement of extra-judicial practices or a disregard of legal controls which King (1981: 9) observes:

> [is] the tendency for the imposition of formal rules of procedure and evidence designed for the defendant's protection to be perceived as having little value but rather as presenting obstacles in the way of processing defendants or 'ceremonial rituals' which do not advance the progress of the case.

Consequently, laws, rules and procedures to protect defendants have little value as they are seen as obstacles to the repression of crime. Of equal importance is an efficient process with uniform, routine and stereotyped administrative procedures which allow the process to run smoothly and quickly. Hence the analogy to an assembly line where defendants move along without any obstacles towards the final conclusion.

The criminal justice process is thus perceived as a screening process in which each successive stage involves routinised operations whose success is measured by their tendency to bring cases to a successful conclusion. Implicit in this scenario is the notion that the innocent are screened out at an early stage and those that are guilty are quickly and efficiently processed through the system. Thus, a presumption of guilt exists for those who are caught up in the system, as it is assumed that the screening processes of the police and the prosecutors are reliable indicators of probable guilt and will eject from the system those persons who are innocent at an early stage.

The due process model, in contrast, proposes that the primary function of the criminal justice process is one of arbitrator of the conflicts which arise between individual citizens and the state. The latter is seen as the upholder of the rule of law and in this capacity takes on the role of the accuser in the criminal justice process. The defendant must nevertheless be protected against the exercise of arbitrary power by the state and the onus is on the latter to prove the case. There is thus a presumption of innocence until proven guilty.

The criminal justice process is thus characterised as an obstacle course, where each successive stage of the process is designed as a formidable impediment to carrying the defendant along to the next stage. In contrast to the crime control approach, the due process model is strongly opposed to informal, non-adjudicative fact finding because this could possibly result in a judicial error being made. Consequently, there is an insistence on formal, adjudicative fact finding, for example rules of evidence. In practice, this means that cases are publicly heard by an impartial tribunal and evaluated only after the accused has had the opportunity to discredit the case against them. The decision is never final as there is always the possibility of human error.

The basic difference between the two models is the dichotomy between reliability and efficiency. Due process focuses on the prevention and elimination of mistakes while crime control accepts the probability of mistakes in order to repress crime. The former rejects absolute efficiency as it is identified as producing maximum tyranny and this is replaced with the notion of reliability. Packer (1969: 165) observes that the criminal justice process 'resembles a factory that has to devote a substantial part of its input to quality control. This necessarily cuts down on quantitative output.' There is, moreover, awareness that the power inherent within the criminal justice process is open to abuse and because of this control of the system needs to be maintained. Thus the due process model requires a finding of legal guilt rather than factual guilt, which dictates that a person is guilty only when factual determinations are made in a regular procedural fashion and by authorities who have been given the power to do so. The defendant is thus protected by rules and safeguards and if these are not adhered to then is found not guilty.

The due process model adheres to the principles of fairness and the protection of the individual from the power of the state and it is essential that all those enmeshed in the system have access to equal resources and be given every opportunity to discredit the case against them. The criminal justice process is thus as much about protecting the factually innocent as convicting the guilty. Hence the phrase: it is better that ten guilty people go free than that one innocent person be convicted.

The criminal justice process models of Michael King

Michael King has developed Packer's two models of the criminal justice process and extends them to six 'process models', although the first two are identical to those of his predecessor which warrant no further discussion here, and again all six are ideal types.

The underlying assumption of the *medical model* is that people are not – in a perspective resonant of the predestined actor model of crime and criminal behaviour – responsible for their actions. In terms of this third model, people are seen as the product and, in some cases, the victim of events outside their control. In other words, people are determined by events over which they have no control. The criminal justice process is thus concerned with treating defendants by providing them with the qualities necessary to control their future behaviour and in so doing reforming them into law-abiding citizens. Guilt and punishment have no place in the process and, in fact, the latter can actually be harmful to the individual. Involvement in crime for such individuals is simply an occasion for social intervention with the major function of the criminal justice process being rehabilitation which King (1981: 20) defines as 'the restoration of the defendant to a state of mental and social health whereby s/he will be able to cope with the demands society makes of him/her and refrain from the conduct which causes further intervention to be necessary'.

The court thus resembles a clinic where diagnosis and prognosis take place and treatment programmes and a cure are defined. This is done by experts who collect information about the background of the defendant which is then analysed to allow a recommendation of the appropriate treatment to be made.

The fourth model – the *bureaucratic model* – depicts the criminal justice process as being neutral in the conflict between the state and the accused and rules out any form of discrimination against individuals or groups. This neutrality is achieved by working within a system of predetermined rules of procedure and evidence which limits or even excludes any discretionary decision-making, therefore resulting in rational decisions being reached. King observes a clear link with the due process model but, at the same time, notes a different emphasis. Whereas the due process model is primarily concerned with the protection of the individual from the arbitrary power of the state, the bureaucratic model is concerned to process defendants according to standard procedures.

The bureaucratic model is also concerned with the distribution of resources in a plural environment where there are conflicting interests, and more specifically is concerned with the economic use of resources. The emphasis is on speed and efficiency which requires the use of time-saving methods to process cases and the model thus discourages time-wasting by the use of sanctions such as reduced sentences for guilty pleas. Furthermore, to prevent duplication and, therefore, inefficiency the model dictates that each agency has a clear delineation of its role and there is a clear division of labour between agencies which takes account of the particular skills and resources available in each as well as any limitations. This bureaucratic model stresses the importance of records, as they provide a readily accessible and reliable source of information on what has happened on previous occasions.

King (1981: 24) argues that his fifth model – the *status passage model* – emphasises:

> the function of the criminal courts as institutions for denouncing the defend-
> ant, reducing his social status and promoting solidarity within the community.
> The reduction of social status in the offender results . . . not only in the
> stigmatisation of the defendant as a person with a tarnished moral character,
> but also in the enhancement of social cohesiveness among law-abiding
> members of the community by setting the defendant apart from the
> community and by emphasising the difference between him and law abiding
> citizens.

The court thus acts as a condemner, degrading and denouncing the defendant, resulting in a downgrading of the status of the individual within society and reaffirming the moral values of the community, thus enhancing solidarity. It follows that the court process itself, as a status degradation ceremony, is all-important and thus the ritualised aspects of this process are paramount. The sentencing of an offender is the culmination of the process of denunciation and degradation and the process prior to this is a preparation for it. The ceremony is conducted in public in order to facilitate the loss of status of the defendant in the eyes of the community and in this way is compatible both with the radical conflict and carceral society models of criminal justice development.

According to the sixth model – the *power model* – the criminal justice process is an unequivocal instrument of the ruling class, promoting its interests and perpetuating its dominance over other sections of society, and as such can be unambiguously conceptualised in the context of the radical conflict model. In performing this function, the criminal justice process is unjust, discriminatory and oppressive towards predominantly the working class and ethnic minority groups. It is nevertheless recognised, from this perspective, that in a liberal capitalist state the criminal justice process is characterised by due process which does obstruct the interests of the ruling class and there is therefore a gap between the letter and the practice of the law. It is observed that this reality must be hidden otherwise it may result in popular dissatisfaction and the eventual overthrow of the existing order. This concealment is achieved by perpetuating a facade of due process while, at the same time, permitting the use of coercive methods of control, and by permitting flexibility and discretion in the interpre-tation of rules so that they appear to permit fair play while leaving considerable scope for discrimination and repression. Therefore, the impression of due process actually permits the ruling class to dominate not through force but by consent – in reality, *our* consent – and in this way is clearly evocative of the left realist hybrid model of criminal justice development.

King further classifies the six models into two distinct categories, the 'participant' and the 'social' approaches. He groups three of his models – the due process, crime control and medical models – in terms of the *participant approach* which he argues provides ideal types for identifying and categorising the attitudes and perspectives of the various criminal justice agencies and individuals who work in them. To varying degrees they reflect the values and perspectives of one or more of the regular participants in the criminal justice process. King argues that the due process perspective is likely to be held by defence lawyers, the crime control perspective is likely to be adhered to by the police, and probation personnel are likely to adhere to the medical model. He qualifies this observation by stating that not all personnel in a particular agency will view the process from one perspective. Moreover, individuals may not adhere to any particular one of these perspectives but may select certain components from each of them, depending on the particular individual or the case. It moreover follows that any one participant may change their perspective over time.

The other three models – the bureaucratic, status passage and power models – constitute the social approach and these are very different in their origins and the questions for which they can provide answers. The models are analytical and theoretical and originate from social theories which seek to explain the structure of society, the interrelationships between social institutions within this configuration and forces that are present either to produce or resist change. As a result, these models do not attempt to explain particular perspectives of individuals or agencies or to provide a framework for reform but attempt to explain the totality of the process. King nevertheless argues that they are only able to offer a partial explanation: their contribution is that they explain why the criminal justice process pursues certain goals, why there is a gap between the rhetoric and the reality of the law, and highlight aspects of the system that have previously been ignored.

Further criminal justice process models

Bottoms and McClean (1976) have subsequently outlined the *liberal bureaucratic* model which they argue characterises the criminal justice process. They argue that this perspective is typically, but not exclusively, held by humane and enlightened clerks to the justices in England and Wales and may well describe similar court administrators in other jurisdictions. It differs from the crime control model by seeing the overriding function of the criminal justice process to be not the repression of criminal behaviour but the protection of individual liberty and the need for justice to be done and seen to be done. This is similar to the due process model where formal adjudicative procedures are of paramount importance but departs from that model in one important respect. As we have seen, the due process model proposes that the criminal justice process is an obstacle course, with each stage an impediment to further progress and which through necessity reduces quantitative output. On the other hand:

> the liberal bureaucrat is a practical man [*sic*]; he realises that things need to be done, systems have to run. It is right that the defendant shall have substantial protections; crime control is not the overriding value of the criminal justice system but these protections must have a limit. If this were not so, then the whole system of criminal justice . . . would collapse. Moreover, it is right to build in sanctions to deter those who might otherwise use their 'due process' rights frivolously, or to 'try it on'; an administrative system at State expense should not exist for this kind of time-wasting.
>
> (Bottoms and McClean, 1976: 229)

The liberal bureaucratic model thus has the twin aims of protecting the rights of the defendant *and* administrative efficiency with the latter being of overriding importance. Bottoms and McClean (1976: 230) show that the police primarily adhere to crime control model values but the values of the liberal bureaucratic model are 'everywhere to be found in the actual operation, and even in some of the formal rules, of English courts'. Defence lawyers also act in terms of this model and the provision of defence counsel – the 'sacred tenet' of the due process model – is no guarantee of the operation of the values of due process where the dominant structure of the court system is liberal bureaucratic. Lawyers must work within the system and furthermore:

> The same applies to other Due Process rights formally available under our system. Hence the legal system is able to maintain the formal semblance of a due process model, while in fact being largely committed to a liberal bureaucratic model.
>
> (Bottoms and McClean, 1976: 231)

Bottoms and McClean argue that the values of the liberal bureaucratic model necessarily reinforce crime control values by the emphasis on efficiency, through, for example, lighter sentences if a defendant pleads guilty. It thus actually has the effect of promoting one of the central tenets of crime control. Consequently:

> despite the superficially apparent similarity of the value-systems underlying the liberal bureaucratic and the due process models, in practice the liberal bureaucratic model offers much stronger support to the aims of the crime control model than the due process model.
>
> (Bottoms and McClean, 1976: 232)

Blumberg (1967) had previously reached a similar conclusion when he had portrayed the criminal justice process as operating in terms of a *bureaucratic due process* model. This model characterises the system as superficially adhering to due process but promoting the primary goals of excellence and efficiency through the pursuit of guilty pleas. Due process is thus an ideology which provides a veil for the operation of bureaucratic due process. In this way, the ideology of due process shifts attention away from, and prevents routine examination of, the realities of the criminal justice process.

Blumberg is thus arguing that there is a difference between the rhetoric and the practical operation of the criminal justice process because procedure is reshaped by bureaucratic organisations. The rhetoric is one of due process while in reality the agencies which work within the system rework the rules so that they are consistent with bureaucratic values of efficiency, high production and the maximisation of individual careers. This happens because due process criteria introduce an element of chance and uncertainty which is not tolerated under the bureaucratic principles of the organisational environment of agencies. Consequently, bureaucratic due process represents the practices which agencies have devised to reduce elements of chance in their respective working environments. Blumberg also argues that at each stage of the process it is assumed, wrongly, that any oversights will be reviewed when the defendant has their day in court. As a result, the screening agencies move defendants along to their trial under conditions of maximum efficiency at the expense of any safeguards. In reality, the defendant's day in court (the trial), where it is assumed that any irregularities will be detected, rarely happens because the majority of defendants plead guilty with thus no review of the case undertaken. Consequently, safeguards are withheld because of administrative pressures for efficiency in the mistaken belief that they will be resolved at the trial. In short, due process is undermined by the drive for efficiency.

Blumberg argues that the system is hence one of 'justice by negotiation' which means that a public trial, a major tenet of due process, is a formality, as justice (a guilty plea) has been negotiated at a previous stage. Justice by negotiation has the additional benefit of avoiding public scrutiny. Moreover, the court functions as a closed community that conceals the nature of its operations not only from outsiders but from some of the participants themselves which facilitates evasions of due process requirements. Furthermore, it socialises its members and participants into following its objectives that are not part of the official goals of justice or due process. Within this structure, the occupational and career commitments of individuals take precedence over official goals. In short, the whole system, although paying lip-service to due process ideals, works towards the primary bureaucratic goal of maximum efficiency through the instrument of negotiated justice.

The genesis of Doreen McBarnet's (1985) later analysis arose from the paradox that:

> all the rhetoric of justice we are familiar with presents a picture of a system of criminal justice bending over backwards to favour the defendant rather than the prosecution. . . . The whole flavour of the rhetoric of justice is summed up in the idea that it is better for ten guilty men to go free than one innocent man to be wrongly convicted. Why then the paradox that the vast majority of cases processed through a criminal justice system so geared to favouring the accused result in a finding of guilt?
>
> (McBarnet, 1985: 1–2)

McBarnet argues that only one side of the question of how the criminal justice process works in relation to the principles of law has been analysed, that of the operation of justice. The hypothesis of the analysis always seems to be

> concerned with why people who routinely operate the law also routinely depart from principles of justice . . . in either or both of two ways – violating the principle of equality before the law by being more likely to arrest, convict, or sentence [certain groups][,] [and/or] violating the principle of a criminal justice system geared to safeguarding the accused by routinely subverting the rights . . . [of the accused]. So we are presented with a picture of how social and human factors undermine the workings of a criminal justice system geared to constraining state officials and favouring the accused.
>
> (McBarnet, 1985: 3)

It has not:

> focused on the system itself, seen its aims as problematic rather than to be taken for granted, treated rules as a significant factor explaining its practices, or seen its assumptions and rhetoric, its concept of necessity, fairness and civil liberty, as requiring analysis and explanation too. The net result is that research into how the criminal law works overlooks the most obvious element, the law itself.
>
> (McBarnet, 1985: 23–24)

McBarnet is thus arguing that the actual law has been ignored with its nature and role in the criminal justice process assumed. The assumption is that the law incorporates rights of the accused and the problem has simply been to consider why and how the police or the court subvert, negate or abuse them. Thus:

> In . . . studies of criminal justice then, 'law' stands merely as a supposed standard from which the enforcers of law routinely deviate; legal procedures are simply assumed to incorporate civil rights. The 'law in action' is scrutinised but what the 'law in the books' actually says is simply taken as read, it remains unproblematic and unexplored.
>
> (McBarnet, 1985: 5)

McBarnet argues that the law cannot be assumed to incorporate the principles of due process and it is thus necessary to analyse the law itself not just the people who operate it and this changes the focus of attention away:

> from the routine activities of petty officials of the state to the top of the judicial and political hierarchies where rules are made and sanctions operated, switching our question from the effectiveness or otherwise of rules and sanctions . . . to the intentions themselves. . . . Shifting the focus to the political and judicial elites also shifts the focus to the very core of the operation of

the state. . . . To question whether the law in fact incorporates the rhetoric of justice is to question the ideological foundations of the state.

(McBarnet, 1985: 8)

McBarnet concludes that there is a distinct gap between the substance and the ideology of the law:

A wide range of prosecution evidence can be legally produced and presented, despite the rhetoric of a system geared overwhelmingly to safeguards for the accused, precisely because legal structure, legal procedure, legal rulings, not legal rhetoric, govern the legitimate practice of criminal justice, and there is quite simply a distinct gap between the substance and the ideology of the law.

(McBarnet, 1985: 155)

It is observed that the ideology of the law is clearly due process but its substance actually works for crime control. Packer's dichotomy between due process and crime control is thus a false one and the former is indeed necessary for the latter to work. McBarnet argues that the gap between the substance and the administration of the law does not occur simply because individuals or agencies subvert the law, but both in its substance and procedure it allows, facilitates and upholds the deviation from the substance of the law. In short, the substance of the law provides rhetoric of due process but operates in the interests of crime control.

McConville, Sanders and Leng (1991) disagree with this analysis on two accounts. First, they argue that *both* the law and the low-level officials within the system should be studied, and second, they observe that the system is characterised by both due process and crime control philosophies simultaneously. The authors argue that the gap between the 'law in action' and the 'law in books' can be only partly explained by the law itself for it enables itself to be subverted because of the discretion it allows for interpretation. The malleability of the law allows it to be undermined so that many practices of criminal justice agents are perfectly lawful and only offend due process values. This is nevertheless only a partial explanation, as some of the practices of criminal justice agents do actively break the law while others are not condoned. McConville *et al.* (1991: 175–176) observe 'concentrating on the elasticity of the law should not blind us to the fact that malleability is finite' and they argue that both the law and the agents who operate it should be studied as 'the law tells us what the police can do, it does not tell us what the police do. Although this does not exempt the law and its controllers from scrutiny, the [petty officials] also cannot be exonerated from responsibility.'

McBarnet thus assumes that the rhetoric of the law is 'due process' but McConville *et al.*, in contrast, argue that we cannot make that assumption, observing that the fundamental principles of criminal justice can be seen 'as constituting, or deriving from, both due process and crime control ideologies'. Both due process and crime control are seen to have always co-existed together uncomfortably with both the law and practice favouring crime control but their relative importance changes over time. They observe that, 'if we are now in an era of retreat from due process . . . this may be connected to the massive post-war extension to suspects and defendants of legal advice and representation – to the actual utilisation . . . of due process' (McConville *et al.*, 1991: 180).

McConville *et al.* (1991) conclude by stating that the rhetoric, substance and the practical operation of the criminal justice process should be investigated at all levels from petty officials to the structure of society, for without this a full explanation of the gap between the 'law in books' and the 'law in action' is unachievable.

Andrew Ashworth (1994) observes and discusses five objections to Packer's dichotomous models. First, he observes that there is no clear explanation of the relationship between the models. Packer (1969: 154) thus proposes that 'their polarity is not absolute' but does not explain how it is not. Second, the use of the term crime control assumes that the pre-trial process has the ability to influence the crime rate but the evidence suggests that this is not the case (see Hough, 1987). Third, there is an underestimation of the importance of managing resources in the criminal justice process. Fourth, there is no discussion of the role of victims. Fifth, 'internal critiques' can be made of the models and the example cited is that of speed which is seen to be an essential part of the crime control model but which can also be important to the due process model. As Ashworth (1994: 42) explains, 'delays are also a source of considerable anxiety and inconvenience, and occasionally prolonged loss of liberty, to defendants. A properly developed notion of due process would surely insist that there be no reasonable delay.'

Ashworth acknowledges that the models do emphasise the complexities of devising a theoretical framework but fail to provide an adequate explanatory tool as they neglect important aspects of the process. He thus introduces a set of 'ethical principles' based on the European Convention of Human Rights which 'ought to shape the way in which officials exercising power within the criminal process should conduct themselves towards citizens' (Ashworth, 1994: 49). Furthermore, ethics and integrity should be an integral part of the criminal justice process which he argues:

> reflects the range of factors that may legitimately impinge on decision making in criminal justice. The temptation to reach for the concept of 'balancing' must be resisted: the first task is to explore the claims of various factors to influence the shape of rules and principles for the criminal justice process.
>
> (Ashworth, 1994: 34)

It is, therefore, important to decide which rights are to be respected and why they should be, and Ashworth (1994: 57–67) proposes the following 12 'ethical rights or principles' which he argues should provide the foundations of the legal process. First, there is the right to be treated with humanity and without degradation. Second, there is the right of victims to compensation. Third, there is the right of innocent persons not to be convicted. Fourth, there is the right to be treated fairly and without discrimination. Fifth, there is the right to be presumed innocent until proven guilty. Sixth, there is the principle of legality which ensures that all rules of law and exceptions from this are clearly stated and available. Seventh, reasonable grounds for arrest and detention must exist. Eighth, there is the right to be brought before a court. Ninth, there is the right to prepare a proper defence. Tenth, the rights of the victim must be respected. Eleventh, there is the right to trial within a reasonable period of time. Twelfth, there is the principle of equality of arms so that defendants have the same access to documents and resources as the prosecution.

Ashworth proposes that these principles establish an important benchmark by which to assess the criminal justice process and they also include elements which had been, hitherto, ignored, such as the rights of victims. It is nevertheless difficult to see how this approach provides us with anything new as many of the principles form part of the other models. There is also no discussion as to how conflicts between the rights of victims, suspects and defendants will be resolved.

Concluding comments

It is clear that criminal justice policy is highly politicised and has a tendency to change rapidly in accordance with political thinking and ideology. Policy trends in the past 20 years have been in the direction of a hardening of attitudes towards offenders which has resulted in the erosion of the rights of suspects and defendants with more being sent to prison than ever before. The roots of these policies can be traced to a backlash against the use of diversion and community alternatives to prison and the legal protections afforded to suspects, defendants and offenders in the past, which have been perceived as resulting in an ever-increasing crime rate and too many guilty people going unpunished. The question inevitably arises as to in whose interest these changes have occurred and thus returns us to a brief reconsideration of the four models of criminal justice development.

It is clear that the development and establishment of the criminal justice process can be partially explained by the orthodox social progress model of criminal justice development, not least because the motivation of progressive benevolence can be identified as having a not insignificant role, but the harder-line law and order perspective that has become more orthodox cannot be explained by this model. It is thus also very clear that there are very significant sectional interests involved and this is explained by the radical conflict model which proposes that such developments have occurred in the interests of business and capitalism. At the time of writing, Kenneth Clarke, the current Justice Secretary in the UK, has called for a substantial reduction in the number of offenders incarcerated in prison and his argument has been articulated in the language of liberal humanitarianism but, at the same time, it can be clearly located in the context of a government facing unprecedented economic problems seeking a more cost-effective long-term criminal justice strategy.

It is nevertheless apparent that the situation is more ambiguous and complex than proposed by either the orthodox social progress or radical conflict model and our attention thus turns to the carceral surveillance society model where it is recognised that power is both diffuse and pervasive throughout society with agents and experts at all levels of the social world having both access to and control of power of differing levels of magnitude not least because of the discretion that their roles provide from the front-line police officer to the judge.

The left realist hybrid model significantly recognises our interest and collusion in the creation of the increasingly pervasive socio-control matrix of the carceral surveillance society and, in this context, our self-interest in the successful administration of a criminal justice process which is widely perceived to have a major impact on law and order thus providing us with some protection from the criminal and dangerous elements in our society which threaten our well-being. A rightward shift in criminal justice policy has thus occurred with considerable support from a very fearful general public (Hopkins Burke, 2004a) and these are important issues which require consideration in the ambiguous context of international law and human rights.

International law

International law is the term commonly used for referring to laws that govern the conduct of independent nations in their relationships with each other and differs from other legal systems in that it primarily concerns provinces rather than private citizens and can be used to refer to three distinct legal disciplines. First, public international law governs the relationship between provinces and international entities, either as an individual or as a group, and includes specific legal areas such as treaty law, law of sea, international criminal law and international humanitarian law. Second, private international law, or conflict of laws, addresses the questions of (1) in which legal jurisdiction a case may be heard and (2) which jurisdiction(s) apply to the issues in the case. Third, supranational law, or the law of supranational organisations, concerns regional agreements where the laws of nation-states are held inapplicable when conflicting with a supranational legal system.

The sources of international law are the materials and processes out of which the rules and principles regulating the international community have developed and these have been influenced by a range of political and legal theories. Thus, during the twentieth century, it was recognised by the legal positivists, whom we encountered in the fourth chapter, that a sovereign state could limit its authority to act by consenting to an agreement according to the principle *pacta sunt servanda*.[3] This consensual view of international law was reflected in the Statute of the Permanent Court of International Justice 1920, and is preserved in Article 7 of the Statute of the International Court of Justice 1946.

Public international law (or international public law) concerns the relationships between the entities or legal persons which are considered the subjects of international law, including sovereign nations, the legal status of the Holy See, international organisations (including especially intergovernmental organisations such as the United Nations), and in some cases, movements of national liberation (wars of national liberation) and armed insurrectional movements. Norms of international law have their source in either (1) custom, or customary international law (consistent provincial practice accompanied by *opinio juris*[4]), (2) globally accepted standards of behaviour (peremptory norms known as *jus cogens* or *ius cogens*[5]), or (3) codifications contained in conventional agreements, generally termed treaties. Article 13 of the United Nations Charter obligates the UN General Assembly to initiate studies and make recommendations which encourage the progressive development of international law and its codification. Evidence of consensus or state practice can sometimes be derived from intergovernmental resolutions or academic and expert legal opinions. These are sometimes collectively termed soft law.

International law has existed since the Middle Ages but much of its modern corpus began developing from the mid-nineteenth century. In the twentieth century, the two World Wars and the formation of the League of Nations (and other international organisations such as the International Labor Organization) all helped to accelerate this process and established much of the foundations of modern public international law. After the failure of the Treaty of Versailles and the Second World War, the League of Nations was replaced by the United Nations, founded under the UN Charter. The UN has also been the locus for the development of new advisory (non-binding) standards, such as the Universal Declaration of Human Rights. Other international norms and laws have been established through international agreements, including the Geneva Conventions on the conduct of war or armed conflict, as well as by agreements implemented by other international organisations such as the ILO, the World Health Organization, the World Intellectual Property Organization, the International Telecommunication Union, UNESCO, the World Trade Organization, and the International Monetary Fund. The development and consolidation of such conventions and agreements has proven to be of great importance in the realm of international relations.

Conflict of laws, often called 'private international law' in civil law jurisdictions, is less international than public international law and is distinguished from the latter because it governs conflicts between private persons, rather than states. It concerns the questions of which jurisdiction should be permitted to hear a legal dispute between private parties, and the law of which jurisdiction should be applied, therefore raising issues of international law. Today corporations are increasingly capable of shifting capital and labour supply chains across borders, as well as trading with overseas corporations. This increases the number of disputes of an inter-state nature outside a unified legal framework, and raises issues of the enforceability of standard practices.

International legal theory

International legal theory comprises a variety of theoretical and methodological approaches used to explain and analyse the content, formation and effectiveness of public international law and institutions and to suggest improvements. Some approaches centre on the question of compliance: why states follow international norms in the absence of a coercive power that ensures compliance. Other approaches focus on the problem of the formation of international rules: thus why it is that states voluntarily adopt international legal norms that limit their freedom of action, in the absence of a world legislature. Other perspectives are policy oriented: they elaborate theoretical frameworks and instruments to criticise the existing rules and make suggestions on how to improve them. Some of these approaches are based on domestic legal theory, others are interdisciplinary, while others have been developed especially to analyse international law.

Many early international legal theorists were concerned with the axiomatic truths that were thought to rest in the natural law we encountered in the fourth chapter. Natural law writer Francisco de Vitoria, a professor of theology at the University of Salamanca, examined the questions of the just war, the Spanish authority in the Americas, and the rights of the Native American peoples.

Hugo Grotius, a Dutch theologian, humanist and jurist, played a key role in the development of modern international law and in his *De jure Belli ac Pacis Libri Tres (Three Books on the Law of War and Peace)*, published in 1625, he drew upon the Bible and from the just war theory[6] developed by St Augustine and argued that nations as well as persons ought to be governed by universal principles based on morality and divine justice. Influenced by domestic contract law, he argued that relations among polities ought to be governed by the law of peoples, the *jus gentium*, established by the consent of the community of nations on the basis of the principle of *pacta sunt servanda*, that is, on the basis of the observance of commitments. Christian von Wolff (1679–1754) later contended that the international community should be a world superstate (*civitas maxima*), having authority over the component member states. Emmerich de Vattel (1714–1767) nevertheless rejected this view and argued, in contrast, for the equality of states as articulated by eighteenth-century natural law. In *Le droit des gens*, Vattel suggested that the law of nations was composed of custom and law, on the one hand, and natural law, on the other.

During the seventeenth century, the basic tenets of the Grotian or eclectic school, especially the doctrines of legal equality, territorial sovereignty, and independence of states, became the fundamental principles of the European political and legal system and were enshrined in the Peace of Westphalia 1648.[7]

The early school of legal positivism emphasised the importance of custom and treaties as sources of international law and early positivist scholar Alberico Gentili used historical examples to posit that positive law (*jus voluntarium*) was determined by general consent. Another positivist scholar, Richard Zouche, published the first manual of international law in 1650. Legal positivism became the dominant legal theory during the eighteenth century and found its way into international legal philosophy. At the time, Cornelius van Bynkershoek asserted that the bases of international law were customs and treaties commonly consented to by various states; John Jacob Moser emphasised the importance of state practice in international law; Georg Friedrich von Martens published the first systematic manual on positive international law, *Précis du droit des gens moderne de l'Europe*.

During the nineteenth century, positivist legal theory became an even more dominant paradigm because of the rise of nationalism and Hegelian philosophy.

International commercial law became a branch of domestic law; private international law separate from public international law. Positivism narrowed the range of international practice that might qualify as law, favouring rationality over morality and ethics. The Congress of Vienna 1815 marked the formal recognition of the political and international legal system based on the conditions of Europe.

Modern legal positivists consider international law to be a unified system of rules that emanates from the will of states and propose that it is an 'objective' reality that must be distinguished from law 'as it should be'. Classic positivism demands rigorous tests for legal validity: extralegal arguments, that is, arguments that have no textual, systemic or historical basis on the law, are deemed irrelevant to legal analysis. There is thus only hard law, no soft law (Simma and Paulus, 1999), and critics of positivist international legal theory concentrate on its rigidity, its focus on state consent, without allowing for any interpretation, and the fact that it does not allow moral judgements regarding the conduct of a state as long as it follows international norms.

Legal scholars have drawn from the four main schools of thought in the areas of political science and international relations, that is, realism, liberalism, institutionalism, and constructivism, to examine, through an interdisciplinary approach, the content of legal rules and institutions, to explain why and how legal institutions came to be established and why they are effective (Abbot, 1999). These methods have led some scholars to reconceptualise international law in general (Slaughter *et al.*, 1998).

Realism contends that, in an anarchic international system, states are locked in a perpetual struggle for survival that obliges them to maximise their relative power in order to preserve their territory and existence. Since international cooperation is possible only inasmuch as it responds to the self-interest of the states concerned in maximising their power and prospects for survival, states do not pursue cooperation on the basis of normative commitments (Morgenthau, 1940). Realist legal scholars argue that states only adopt international legal norms that either enhance their power, formalise the subordination of weaker states, or that they intend to violate deliberately to their own advantage (Bradford, 2004). International law may thus address only peripheral matters that do not impact on the power or autonomy of the states. Consequently, for the realist, international law is a 'tenuous net of breakable obligations' (Hoffmann, 1956).

Within the realist approach, some scholars have proposed an 'enforcement theory', according to which international legal norms are effective insofar as they 'publicise clear rules, enhance monitoring of compliance, and institutionalise collective procedures for punishing violations, thereby enhancing the deterrent and coercive effects of a stable balance of power' (Bradford, 2004: 8). Thus, the role of reciprocity and sanctions is underlined. Morrow (2008: 1), for example, notes that:

> International politics in modern times generally recognizes no authority above the nation-state. Agreements among states are enforceable only by the agreeing states themselves. This assumption of anarchy poses a paradox for

agreements to limit violence during wartime. . . . Reciprocity serves as the main tool to enforce agreements in international politics. Enforcement of an agreement is devolved to the parties themselves. Damaged parties have the option to respond with retaliatory sanctions to a violation of an agreement. The threat of reciprocal sanctions may be sufficient to deter violations, and so agreements can be enforced in international politics.

Some scholars utilise liberal international relations theory to argue that the stance of states towards international law is determined by their domestic politics and, in particular, by the aggregation of the preferences of key domestic individuals and groups toward the rule of law. Thus, democratic states with representative govern-ments are more likely than non-democratic states to accept the legal regulation of both domestic and international politics, and, as a consequence, they are more likely to accept and to observe international law. Furthermore, democratic societies are linked by a complex net of interstate, transnational and transgovernmental relations so that both their foreign policy bureaucracies and their civil societies are interested in promoting and strengthening transnational cooperation through the creation and observance of international legal norms (Bradford, 2004). Thus, the adoption of, and the compliance with, international legal norms among democractic states should be easier and more peaceful than the observance of international law among non-democratic states. A.-M. Slaughter (1995: 532) observes that:

> Agreements concluded among liberal States are more likely to be concluded in an atmosphere of mutual trust, a precondition that will facilitate any kind of enforcement. In particular, however, the assumptions that these are agree-ments reached with the participation of a network of individuals and groups in the participating States, and that these States are committed to the rule of law enforced by national judiciaries should lead to more 'vertical' enforce-ment through domestic courts. This mode of enforcement contrasts with the traditional 'horizontal' mode involving State responsibility, reciprocity, and countermeasures.

The rational choice and game theory approach to law applies theories or economics in order to identify the legal implications of maximising behaviour inside and outside of markets. Economics is the study of rational choice under limited conditions and the latter is the assumption that individual actors seek to maximise their preferences. Most of the economic theory employed in this context is neo-classical traditional economics – which includes techniques such as price theory – which evaluates strategic interaction between actors, transaction cost economics, which incorporates costs of identifying actors, negotiating, and costs of enforcing agreements into price theory. Game theory demonstrates how actors who seek to maximise behaviour might fail to take action to increase gain (Forsythe, 2000).

Public choice theory applies economic tools to problems outside of markets and these are used to describe and evaluate laws which are tested for economic efficiency (Ratner, 1998). Economic theories are also used to propose changes in the law and this approach urges the adoption of laws that maximise wealth. A secondary concern is whether or not an actual 'market' context is functioning well. Third, ways to improve the imperfect market are proposed and this approach could be used to analyse general legal questions because it provides highly specified rules and the rationale for using them. This approach nevertheless relies on assumptions that perfect competition exists, and how individuals will behave in order to maximise their preferences. The empirical presence of these conditions is often difficult to determine.

The classic *international legal process* is the method of studying how international law is practically applied to, and functions within, international policy, as well as the study of how it can be improved. O'Connell (1999: 334) observes that 'it concentrates not so much on the exposition of rules and their content as on how international legal rules are actually used by the makers of foreign policy'. ILP was developed in response to the realists from the discipline of international relations who had realised with the beginning of the Cold War exactly how little international law played a role in international affairs. ILP was made a legitimate theory in the 1968 casebook, *International Legal Process*, by Chayes, Ehrlich and Lowenfeldan, in which the American legal process method was adapted to create an international legal process (O'Connell, 1999). ILP describes the way international legal processes work, and the formal and informal ways that foreign offices incorporate international law. It also measures the extent to which individuals are held accountable for abuses in international conflicts and recognises that international law does not force the actions of decision makers but suggests that international law serves as a justification, constraint, and organising device (O'Connell, 1999). Criticism of the lack of normative qualities in its method resulted in the emergence of a new ILP (NLP), which incorporates both law as a process and as the values of each society respectively. Unlike the US legal system, it considers normative values other than democracy, such as 'feminism, republicanism, law and economics, liberalism as well as human rights, peace and protection to the environment' (O'Connell, 1999: 77). The NLP is unique in its flexibility in adapting to the evolution of values and this component of the method is important in order to resolve the changing of legal standards over time. The NLP shows its true departure from the ILP by addressing what happens in the situation of conflict as well as what should be happening.

The New Haven School is a policy-oriented perspective on international law with its intellectual antecedents in the sociological jurisprudence of Roscoe Pound and the reformist ambitions of the American Legal Realists.[8] From this perspective, jurisprudence is a theory about making social choices. The primary jurisprudential and intellectual tasks are the prescription and application of policy in ways that maintain community order and simultaneously achieve the best possible approximation of the social goals of the community (Reisman, 2004). These normative social goals or values of the New Haven approach include the production of wealth, of enlightenment, of skill, of health and well-being, of affection, of respect and rectitude. The New Haven Approach draws heavily upon the older methodology of Transnational Legal Process (TLP) and seeks to encompass both the New Haven Approach and TLP. The key elements of the new approach are described as follows: the 'scholarship often takes a normative stand', it 'often takes a flexible approach to the actors of international law' and it 'adopts a practice-oriented study of the norms and processes of international law in action on the ground' (Dickinson, 2007).

Critical Legal Studies (CLS) emerged in the USA during the 1970s and is a continuing method of analysing international law from a highly theoretical perspective which proposes that the nature of international law is limited because it is determined by language, which is biased and embedded in the conventional structures of politics and power (Shaw, 2003). From this perspective it is argued that structures of power can be found within the binaries that exist in legal language (for example, man vs woman, majority vs minority) (Steinberg and Zasloff, 2006). These scholars recognise the political aspect of international law and argue that universality is impossible (Shaw, 2003). Criticism of this method suggests that this radical practice is impossible to put into practical application but has nevertheless been successful in promoting other approaches to international law, such as feminist and cultural relativist, which follow its deep analysis of language and the imbalances that are thus revealed.

The central case approach is a method of looking at human rights situations which recognises the existence of certain universal rights (Cheng, 2004). The analysis of a human rights issue commences by the construction of a hypothetical ideal situation in which rights are applied and which provides a standard against which to compare an actual situation. The central case approach then investigates to what extent, and in what ways, the actual situation deviates from the ideal (or the central case) (Cheng, 2004). The central case approach allows for more complexity than the traditional binary method of analysis where human rights are seen to be simply violated or upheld hence failing to allow for degrees of severity which creates a deceptively simplistic view of a situation (Cheng, 2004). It is an approach that could be effective in preventing human rights abuses if used by decision-makers because political and social situations are taken into account in addition to specific human rights abuses which enables it to detect trends in human rights abuses and the underlying reasons behind these. The depth of a central case analysis exposes the different degrees of human rights abuses that occur, allowing policy makers to focus on the most severe cases and patterns of abuse with more urgency while it provides an accurate and flexible picture of situations in a state of change. Whereas a binary appraisal would conclude whether a human right had been violated at one point in time, the central case approach can detect shifting political and social conditions and patterns that give a more nuanced view of the state of human rights (Cheng, 2004).

Feminist legal theory criticises current legal vocabulary and practice by arguing that it is patriarchal, presenting men as the norm and women as a deviation from this. Feminist theorists propose to change legal language to make it more inclusive of women, or to rethink law completely, so it is possible to promote broader social goals of justice and equality. Feminist methods seek to expose the biases from which international law is written and particularly the notion that women are more vulnerable than men and need special protection under the law. Feminist theorist Hilary Charlesworth (2010) criticises the dialogue of women as victims in need of protection from both men and international law and argues that the irony of the dominant language is that while it aims to protect women, the emphasis is placed on the protection of her honour and not on her social, cultural and economic rights.

Lesbian, Gay, Bisexual, and Transgender/Transsexual (LGBT) International Law Theory is a critical school of thought that continues to develop as the shortcomings of international law become increasingly recognised and seeks the integration of queer theory[9] into international law theory. While human rights conventions have recently begun to generalise in regard to equality and its recipients, in the past, any discussions of sexual orientation and gender identity have been largely untouched. LGBT International Law Theory centres on the inclusion and awareness of LGBT rights (and protection of persons), as well as the integration of queer theory within the realm of international law. As LGBT theory has become more prominent in scholarly works, international courts and international law organisations (in particular, the European Union Council and the United Nations) have considered workplace discrimination on the basis of sexuality, issues stemming from the definition of family in regard to homosexual unions, the position of transsexuals in the question of sexual orientation, the need for recognition of LGBT rights in regard to general health advocacy and the HIV/AIDS crisis, the inclusion of an LGBT advocacy group within the UN (with adviser status), and the ongoing active persecution of people engaging in homosexual acts, among other issues (Sanders, 2005). Nancy Levit (2000) argues that the challenges for gay legal theory are twofold: first, to move away from the frailties of both formal equality and anti-subordination theories, and second, to develop ways of representing sexual minorities that will make them more acceptable, if not valuable, in a broader cultural context.

Third World Approaches to International Law (TWAIL) is a further critical approach to international law that is not a 'method' in the strict sense of questioning 'what the law is'. Rather, it is an approach to law that is unified by a particular set of concerns and analytical tools with which to explore them and draws primarily from the history of the encounter between international law and colonised peoples. TWAIL shares many concepts with post-colonial studies, feminist theory, critical legal studies, Marxist theory and critical race theory. TWAIL scholarship prioritises the study of the power dynamic between the First World and Third World and the role of international law in legitimising the subjugation and oppression of Third World peoples. TWAIL scholars try to avoid presenting the 'Third World' as a unified, coherent entity but rather use the term to indicate peoples who have the shared experience of underdevelopment and marginalisation. Contemporary TWAIL scholarship has it origins in works of jurists such as Georges Abi-Saab, F. Garcia-Amador, R.P. Anand, Mohammed Bedjaoui, and Taslim O. Elias. Over the years, several Western scholars have been sympathetic to the position of the Third World and have made important contributions to this body of scholarship, and these include scholars such as C.H. Alexandrowicz, Richard Falk, Nico Schrijver and P.J.I.M. De Waart.

International human rights law

International human rights law refers to the body of international law designed to promote and protect human rights at international, regional and domestic levels. It is a body of law primarily composed of international treaties and customary international law but other human rights instruments include Declarations, Guidelines and international principles.

International human rights law can be enforced on either a domestic, regional or international level. States that ratify human rights treaties commit themselves to respecting those rights and ensuring that their domestic law is compatible with international legislation. Customary peremptory norms of international law that relate to human rights are considered binding on all nations, although the status of such norms is often disputed. When domestic law fails to provide a remedy for human rights abuses parties may be able to resort to regional or international mechanisms for enforcement.

International human rights law is related to, but is not the same as, international humanitarian law which regulates armed conflicts and refugee law. War crimes, crimes against humanity, and genocide may be regulated by international human rights law but each has a substantial body of independent international law. The Universal Declaration of Human Rights (UDHR) is a declaration that does not form binding international human rights law, although some legal scholars cite it as evidence for customary international law and it has more broadly become an authoritative human rights reference. The UDHR has nevertheless provided the basis for subsequent international human rights instruments that form binding international human rights law.

Besides the adoption of the two wide-covering Covenants – the International Covenant on Civil and Political Rights and the International Covenant on Economic, Social and Cultural Rights in 1966 – a number of other treaties have been adopted at the international level. These are generally known as *human rights instruments* and some of the most significant include: the Convention on the Elimination of All Forms of Racial Discrimination (CERD) which was adopted in 1965 and came into force in 1969; the Convention on the Elimination of All Forms of Discrimination Against Women (CEDAW) which came into force in 1981; the United Nations Convention Against Torture (CAT) which was adopted in 1984 and came into force in 1987; the Convention on the Rights of the Child which was adopted in 1989 and came into force in 1990; the International Convention on the Protection of the Rights of All Migrant Workers and Members of their Families (ICRMW) which was adopted and came into force in 1990; and the Convention on the Rights of Persons with Disabilities (CRPD) which came into force in 2008.

There are three key regional human rights instruments which have established human rights law on a regional basis: the African Charter on Human and People's Rights for Africa which was adopted in 1981 and which came into force in 1986;

the American Convention on Human Rights for the Americas which was adopted in 1969 and which has been in force since 1978; and the European Convention on Human Rights for Europe which was adopted in 1950 and has been in force since 1953.

The Organization of American States and the Council of Europe, like the UN, have also adopted (but, unlike the UN, later) separate treaties (with weaker implementation mechanisms) containing catalogues of economic, social and cultural rights, as opposed to their aforementioned conventions dealing mostly with civil and political rights. The European Social Charter for Europe 1961 has been in force since 1965 and a complaints mechanism created by the 1995 Additional Protocol has been in force since 1998. The Protocol of San Salvador to the ACHR for the Americas 1988 has been in force since 1999.

There is currently no international court to administer international human rights law; however, quasi-judicial bodies exist under some UN treaties (for example, the Human Rights Committee under ICCPR). The International Criminal Court (ICC) has jurisdiction over the crime of genocide, war crimes and crimes against humanity, while the European Court of Human Rights and the Inter-American Court of Human Rights enforce regional human rights law. Although these same international bodies also hold jurisdiction over cases regarding international humanitarian law, it is crucial to recognise that the two frameworks constitute distinctly different legal regimes. The United Nations Human Rights Bodies do have some quasi-legal enforcement mechanisms which include the Treaty Bodies attached to the current seven active treaties, and the Human Rights Council complaints procedures, known as the 1235 and 1503 mechanisms.

The enforcement of international human rights law is nevertheless the responsibility of the nation-state and it is the primary responsibility of the state to make human rights a reality. In practice, many human rights are very difficult to legally enforce due to the absence of consensus on the application of certain rights, the lack of relevant national legislation or of bodies empowered to take legal action to enforce them.

In over 110 countries national human rights institutions (NHRIs) have been established to protect, promote or monitor human rights with jurisdiction in a given country. Although not all NHRIs are compliant with the Paris Principles, the number and influence of these institutions is increasing. The Paris Principles – which list a number of responsibilities for national institutions – were defined at the first International Workshop on National Institutions for the Promotion and Protection of Human Rights in Paris on 7–9 October 1991, and adopted by the United Nations Human Rights Commission Resolution 1992/54 of 1992 and the General Assembly Resolution 48/134 of 1993.

Universal jurisdiction is a controversial principle in international law whereby states claim criminal jurisdiction over persons whose alleged crimes were committed outside the boundaries of the prosecuting state, regardless of nationality, country of residence, or any other relation with the prosecuting country. The state backs its claim on the grounds that the crime committed is considered a crime against all, which any state is authorised to punish. The concept of universal jurisdiction is therefore closely linked to the idea that certain international norms are *erga omnes*, or owed to the entire world community, as well as the concept of *jus cogens*. In 1993 Belgium passed a *law of universal jurisdiction* to give its courts jurisdiction over crimes against humanity in other countries, and in 1998 Augusto Pinochet, the former President of Argentina, was arrested in London following an indictment by a Spanish judge under the universal jurisdiction principle. The principle is supported by Amnesty International and other human rights organisations as they believe certain crimes pose a threat to the international community as a whole and the community has a moral duty to act, but others, including Henry Kissinger (2001: 25), argue that:

> Widespread agreement that human rights violations and crimes against humanity must be prosecuted has hindered active consideration of the proper role of international courts. Universal jurisdiction risks creating universal tyranny – that of judges.

At first sight the orthodox social progress model of criminal justice development provides an appropriate explanation of the growth of international law and human rights legislation. It nevertheless becomes increasingly apparent that such developments are very much influenced by the economically, industrially and politically powerful societies, often to the detriment of the less powerful, but always to the advantage and advance of global capitalism. Further reflection clearly demonstrates that these developments have been very much part of the growth of a global carceral surveillance society but it is the left realist hybrid model that enables us to recognise the explanatory validity of all three models while, at the same time, locating our motivated interest in the growth of a class-based, ethnically dominant, imperialist international and human rights law which has helped reinforce and preserve our way of life in the modern Western world, invariably to the detriment and disadvantage of others in other less fortunate societies in the world.

6   Punishment in modern society

This chapter discusses the philosophy and theory of punishment in modern societies and locates this debate in the context of the four models of criminal justice development that provide the theoretical underpinnings of this text. It is important to remember that all too often punishment is considered to be a distinct and separate entity from the understanding of penology but it is impossible to legitimately understand one without the other, for imprisonment is, next to capital punishment, the harshest and certainly one of the most commonly used sentences. Without the acknowledgement of penal realities, justifications for punishment become mere intellectual debate. Trying to make sense of familiar concepts such as 'making the punishment fit the crime', is not strictly a theoretical question and these are not just philosophical matters of concern to academia. These questions have great practical relevance within the criminal justice process generally and the penal system specifically. By bringing the two together, locating penal trends in theory, and grounding theory in policy, the totality becomes greater than the sum of its parts.

According to an old Muslim legend, there was once a rich king who left his servant in charge of his kingdom and in receipt of his riches, while he went on a long journey. Upon returning to his kingdom he found to his dismay that his servant had stolen some of his treasures. The rich king took the servant in front of the judge for sentencing. The judge ordered that both the servant and the king should be punished; the servant because he had broken the law, and the king because, by leaving such a great temptation in the hands of a person with so few possessions and possibly weak character (both realities which the king should have been able to assess), the king was in fact causing the man harm (Ellis and Ellis, 1989).

Interpreted broadly, this ancient parable highlights some of the most persistent questions in the philosophy of punishment and penology. Contemporary urban industrial modern societies appear to be overrun with crime and deviance and it is thus questionable who exactly should be considered culpable and punished. Should primary or even sole responsibility rest with the individual who has committed the act, the offender, or might we ask whether an indictment should be read against the social institutions which have created a society which has produced so many criminals?

These issues are at the heart of the philosophy of punishment and this chapter will consider the main justifications for its implementation and what theorists from different disciplines consider to be the main ingredients for 'justice' to be seen to be done. We have seen previously in this book that neither philosophers nor criminologists have reached a consensus on whether or not, or to what extent, individuals have free will, and to what extent their actions are determined by the numerous social, psychological, physiological and economic forces which act upon and influence their behaviours (Hopkins Burke, 2009). Perhaps even more important is the reality that theorists, administrators and practitioners of the criminal justice process, as well as the electorate, cannot agree on the purpose of punishing criminals. Depending on who is speaking, at what time, about which offender, who has committed which crime, the goals of punishment alter, and in many cases conflict with and contradict each other.

The purpose of punishment

> Punishment is an institution in almost every society. Only very small and very isolated communities are at a loss about what to do with transgressors and even they recognise the punishment of children by parents. Punishment, however, has different names. When imposed by English-speaking courts it is called 'sentencing'. In the Christian Church it is 'penance'. In schools, colleges, professional organisations, clubs, trade unions, and armed forces its name is 'disciplining' or 'penalising'. It is an institution which is exemplified in transactions involving individuals, transactions which are controlled by rules, laying down what form it is to take, who may order it, and for what.
>
> (Walker, 1991: 1)

The fact that punishment is common in most societies is well documented through anthropological, philosophical, sociological and historical studies but important questions remain. First, exactly what is the purpose of punishment? Second, why do we punish at all, what purpose does it serve, if any? Third, what is it about the breaking of rules, be they familial, group, societal, religious, national or universal, that makes us want to respond with punishment? We nevertheless need to keep in mind that the main aspect we will consider is that of legal punishment.

Punishment can be defined as a deliberately negative response to an action that is deemed wrongful, inappropriate or criminal – it is rule-breaking behaviour followed by a possibly unpleasant and definitely unwanted infliction – often referred to as 'pain and suffering' imposed on an offender. Primoratz (1989) and others find this view too narrow, especially in the context of an increasingly optimistic discourse concerning humanitarian prisons. Punishment thus need not inflict pain, physical or mental.

Walker (1991) cites seven features of punishment. First, it involves the infliction of something which is assumed to be unwelcome to the recipient. Second, the infliction is intentional and applied for a reason. Third, those who order it are regarded – by the members of the society, organisation or family – as having the right to do so. Fourth, the occasion for the infliction is an action or omission that infringes a law, rule or custom. Fifth, the person punished has played a voluntary part in the infringement, or at least his or her punishers believe or pretend to believe that he or she has done so. Sixth, the punisher's reason for punishing is such as to offer a justification for doing so. Seventh, it is the belief or intention of the person who orders something to be done, and not the belief or intention of the person to whom it is done, that settles the question of whether it is punishment. Walker proposes that it is these 'seven points' that establish the main tenets of punishment: it is thus unpleasant and deliberate, carried out by an authorised human agency (the criminal justice system) because a rule or a law has been broken.

The notion of why we need – and what constitutes a legitimate – rule in modern societies has its origins in the social contract theories we encountered in the first chapter. Such theories were predominantly a product of the European Enlightenment during the seventeenth and early eighteenth centuries and sought to explain the ways in which people form political states in order to maintain social order. The notion of the social contract implies that the people give up sovereignty to a government, or other authority, in order to receive or maintain social order, through the rule of law, which can be conceptualised as an agreement by the citizens of the state on a set of rules by which they are governed. Compliance can be enforced by the fear of punishment, but only if entry into the contract and the promise to comply with it has been freely willed, given and subsequently broken.

Later sociological theories, such as functionalism (see Durkheim, 1933, originally 1893; 1965, originally 1895) or Marxism (see the discussion of the victimised actor model of crime and criminal behaviour in the third chapter), provide explanations of the basic need for acceptable parameters in society, and the great importance to the individual of knowing what those boundaries are, and what can happen when they transgress. It is formal norms and sanctions, in the form of the criminal law, that is our main focus here.

Durkheim's analysis of social change emphasises the importance of social solidarity as the core of society, be it mechanical or organic (Durkheim, 1933).[1] It is observed that rules form a major part of social solidarity, setting out the norms, mores and laws, and it is to this end that punishment becomes so crucial. The existence of the law, and therein punishment, maintains social solidarity (Durkheim, 1965) and does so in the following ways. First, it represses and controls a certain degree of deviation from social norms. Second, it regulates the interactions of the diverse subcultures in existence in complex societies. Third, it provides restitution for those who have been wronged – or, in our contemporary language, victims. Fourth, it clearly delineates between those who are law-abiders and those who are law-breakers.

Just as Durkheim felt that crime was a normal and thus necessary function, in organic societies the act of punishment is viewed by most conventional theorists as being not only normal and functional but necessary and just, and thus can be clearly conceptualised in the context of the social progress model of criminal justice development where these processes are seen to be introduced on a fair, humanitarian basis, developed and refined in the interests of all in society. There are no, or at least limited, sectional interests unfairly influencing policy and its implementation. The radical conflict model, in contrast, proposes that rules or laws are introduced and enforced ultimately in the interests of those with economic and hence political power in capitalist society. The carceral society model develops that radical thesis further by acknowledging the multiple ambiguities and diffusion of power in complex societies and recognises the role and material interests of experts and front-line practitioners with professional discretion in the introduction of laws and their enforcement. The left realist hybrid model significantly recognises the partial validity of each of the other three models but also identifies the interest of the general public in the development of laws and their enforcement. These models need to be kept in mind as we continue our discussion.

The rational actor and predestined actor models of crime and criminal behaviour that we encountered in the third chapter have both informed theories of punishment. We saw how rational actor model theorists propose that people who commit crime do so because they have the freedom to choose how to act. This assumption of 'free will' implies that individuals are responsible for the consequences of their behaviour and it thus logically follows that people can be controlled through fear, in particular, the fear of pain. Punishment by the state, an institution based on a 'social contract' among its citizens, thus became the primary means to instil fear and prevent criminal behaviour. Beccaria, the founder of the Classical school and the rational actor model of crime and criminal behaviour, argued that the primary motivation of the individual is to avoid pain while pursuing pleasure and, to that end, rationality and responsibility characterised human action. Beccaria claimed that punishment should be based on the harm that the criminal act caused to the social contract rather than that suffered by the victim, while the offence was to be judged by the consequences of the act rather than the intentions of the offender. Moreover, in making the punishment proportional to social harm, arbitrary sentences by judges would be limited, while implicit in this perspective are the twin notions that (a) similar crimes should be punished in a similar fashion and (b) mitigating circumstances should not affect the punishment to be inflicted. The punishment should fit the crime committed, not the person committing it (Hopkins Burke, 2009).

Neo-Classicism, an intermediate stage between the Classical school and the later positivist school or predestined actor model of crime and criminal behaviour, was to view the offender as only partially rational, though still accountable for their actions, but was to significantly take into consideration mitigating circumstances. Classicism, in stressing the rational nature of the offender, denied individual differences but this focus on the criminal act, rather than the actor, had led to difficulties in implementation. In assessing responsibility, it was increasingly acknowledged that allowances needed to be made for individuals with limited responsibility, such as children or those with clear mental health difficulties. Neo-Classicists significantly do not excuse the actions of the offender but merely take into account the circumstances surrounding the crime and the characteristics of the particular offender in determining the type and level of punishment.

This revised variant of the rational actor model was eventually to bring about two very important changes in the way punishment was used in the criminal justice process. First, a place was created for experts in fields other than law and in this way social scientists, such as psychologists, and medical experts, such as psychiatrists, became involved in the criminal justice process. These individuals provided additional information regarding the offender, such as possible mitigating circumstances and expert opinion on how he or she might react to specific punishments. Second, the range of available punishments was extended.

The positivists who introduced the predestined actor model of crime and criminal behaviour systematically eliminated the idea of free will and substituted it with the concept of 'determinism'. They proposed that punishment has no place in the criminal justice process and that it should be replaced by the concept of 'treatment' as it was argued that individuals cannot legitimately be held responsible for something which is outside their control. Thus, rather than trying to reduce crime by relying on punishment and deterrence through the criminal justice process, predestined actor adherents sought to discover the root causes of crime, through the use of scientific methods, in order to eliminate the conditions that produce it. Positivists thus argue that crime can only be understood if the focus is on criminal behaviour as opposed to the criminal law (Hopkins Burke, 2009).

These two different models of criminal behaviour, with their conflicting views of the offender and their motivation or rationale for committing crime, have a clear and significant influence on the role of punishment. There is nevertheless no easy linear progression through the theories and their different justifications for punishment.

Utility and retribution are the two main justifications for punishment. In general, most of the theories that we will encounter below are either reductive in perspective (utilitarian) or retributive (deserts-based). First, utilitarian justifications are concerned with the good of society as a whole and, in this case, punishment is seen to be useful as it decreases the frequency with which people infringe the law and its primary goal is, thus, to reduce crime. Second, retributive justification is simply concerned with the fact that the offender has done something wrong and thus deserves to be punished. Often referred to as revenge, retribution focuses on the harmfulness of the act, the blameworthiness of the actor and the severity of the punishment.

Utilitarianism

> All punishment is mischief. . . . If it ought at all to be admitted, it ought only to be admitted in as far as it promises to exclude some greater evil.
>
> (Bentham, 1970, originally 1789: 15)

Bentham, like Beccaria, considered the behaviour of human brings to be motivated by two and only two masters, pain and pleasure. Thus, utility exists when pleasure, which for utilitarians means benefit, advantage, good or happiness, is maximised and pain is minimised. This form of utilitarianism is called 'act utilitarianism' and is one of the clearest and most influential of all utilitarian theories. 'Rule utilitarianism' proposes that rules of conduct, including the criminal laws of society, should be formulated with regard to what will best serve the general welfare of society, and once formulated, the laws should be enforced strictly and consistently, without exception.

Utilitarianism is a 'goal-based theory' which assesses actions in terms of their propensity to generate and maximise happiness (Davies and Holdcroft, 1991). Often defined as 'the greatest good for the greatest number', a particular punishment, whether for a group or individual, has utility if it benefits the greater consensus, for example, society. Implicit in this idea is that in order to achieve utility one must first understand what is good. Once defined, what is good automatically becomes what is right. In order to evaluate what is good, two or more actions must be compared and evaluated, thus what is good, and therefore right, depends on the consequences of the action.

Utilitarian perceptions of punishment are thus consequentialist. Human actions should be evaluated in terms of their consequences and this is the only way to ensure that decisions which are made are rational, objective and clear. Although punishment inherently means that someone will experience unhappiness or unpleasantness, the act of punishing has utility if it is inflicted to lessen or exclude a greater 'evil'. The utilitarian thus views crime as being 'an evil' which will lead to greater 'evil' if left unpunished and punishment is therefore essential.

Ten (1987) observes that many utilitarians see the main beneficial effects of punishment to be in terms of crime reduction and proposes that punishing offenders will have at least some, if not all, of the following three positive effects: first, it will deter offending behaviour both on an individual and general level; second, it will reform or rehabilitate offenders; and third, incapacitate those who are incarcerated. Deterrence, incapacitation and rehabilitation are thus used by utilitarians as justifications for punishment. Bentham argued that the wrong inflicted by crime could not be rectified but future crimes could be prevented by the infliction of punishment and that is its main purpose. By punishing a particular individual their future behaviour can be influenced by one or more of the following three factors: first, by disabling the individual from being able to further commit that wrong; second, by eliminating the desire of the individual to offend; third, by modifying the behaviour of the individual through fear.

For the utilitarian, the appropriate amount of punishment imposed should be only as much as it takes to bring about the above effects: it must be harsh enough to outweigh the consequences of committing the crime again. In other words, the costs must outweigh the benefits of crime. Proportionality of punishment is thus important to the utilitarian. The punishment must not be too lenient but it also must not be too severe, otherwise offenders would find it unacceptable and would thus not be encouraged to change their behaviour.

Punishment is justified because it secures positive consequences but there are also limitations to utility. Bentham (1970) observes that punishment can be groundless, inefficacious, unprofitable and needless. First, it is groundless if and only if: (a) the act committed has produced no pain, and there is, therefore, no utility in prohibiting the act; (b) the act committed, though against the law because in general the act causes pain, does not in this instance; (c) the act committed, although it causes harm, was necessary to prevent a greater harm, or for securing a greater good. Punishment is inefficacious if and only if: (a) the rule or law is retroactive to the act; (b) the pain caused was committed unconsciously, unintentionally, under duress, or in ignorance of the law; or (c) the actors are under the influence of drugs, juveniles or insane. Punishment is unprofitable if and only if the pain of the punishment is greater than the act it is meant to prevent. It is needless if, and only if, preventive effects could be obtained by less punitive measures such as social policy or education.

It is the basis of utilitarianism that all people are equal in society and have the same bargaining power but this is clearly not the case. Moreover, the theory rests on the assumption that there is a consensus in society about what is good and what is right and this is again a highly questionable assumption in contemporary society. The social consensus may not actually exist but rules are nevertheless introduced for the benefit, or contrary to the benefit, of a particular group, or type of individual, as suggested by the radical conflict model of criminal justice development.

The justification of utility is the consequences of punishment where deterrence is perceived to be the main positive effect. It can, on the other hand, be considered a major obstacle – indeed, some would say a terminal one – for deterrence has not been proven to be a valid consequence of the dominant form of punishment, imprisonment (Primoratz, 1989; Ten, 1987; Walker, 1991). This leaves the utilitarian justification of punishment to be flawed or at least in relation to conventional offenders.

Utilitarianism has also been criticised for its claim that if a majority of people can be convinced that an innocent person is guilty, punishing that individual would have utility as a warning to others. This would be clearly unjust as punishment can only be considered legitimate 'when it is deserved' (Bradley, 1962).

Utility leaves very little room for 'mercy' and/or mitigating circumstances. Smart (1969: 224–225) observed that for the utilitarian mitigation can never be legitimate, there is no point, for the statement 'I shall act mercifully' can only mean 'I shall impose a penalty less than the one which will produce the most good', which in turn can only mean 'I shall impose a penalty less than the one which will produce most good because this action is the one which will produce most good'. Furthermore, a subsequent pardon can only have utility if the rule of law is not completely justified in utilitarian terms.

Deterrence

The central justification for punishment favoured by utilitarians is thus the concept of deterrence where the primary aim is to increase the costs of involvement in criminality to the offender. By making the negative consequences of crime greater than the available rewards, the potential offender is deterred and stops offending.

The basis of deterrence is thus the product of a cost/benefit analysis and as Walker (1991: 13) observes 'people are deterred from actions when they refrain from them because they dislike what they believe to be the possible consequences of those actions'.

There are a number of reasons why people might be deterred and Grasmick and Green (1980) identify three external and internal forces which may make crime less desirable for some people. First, there is moral commitment to society and the internalisation of legal norms through the process of socialisation. Second, there is social disapproval and the fear of informal sanctions by peers. Third, there is the threat of punishment and the fear of physical, mental or material pain or deprivation. To these three forces should be added a fourth, that of physical obstacles which prevent the practical commission of a crime. It is, nevertheless, only the third of these forces that may relate to deterrence in the legal sense. Walker (1991) also pertinently observes that a person may be deterred from committing an act in one place but go on to commit the act elsewhere, or at a later date, which is usually referred to as the displacement of crime.

There are two types of deterrence. *General deterrence* is when the general population is deterred from committing crime due to the awareness of both the threat of punishment and the knowledge of particular individuals who have been punished. It involves calculating penalties on the basis of what might be expected to deter others from committing similar acts. *Specific* or *individual deterrence* is when an individual who has committed a crime is deterred from committing further offences by the punishment that they have experienced. In other words, the experience of punishment has resulted in the individual concluding that the costs of the crime outweigh the benefits. If deterrence is the primary rationale for punishment, then, it is the case that repetition of offences is more important than the seriousness of the offence and a distinction would be made between first offenders and recidivists. It would also mean that the court would need detailed information about the character and circumstances of the offender and their prior record so that the court could calculate the sentence that is necessary to deter. Walker (1980: 68) observes that:

> The reason for the distinction [between general and individual deterrence] is the assumption that people who have not experienced, say, the penalty for a crime may well be more or less responsive to the threat than those who have. Essentially, however, general and individual deterrence are attempts to do the same thing: the difference is merely that the former relies on imagination, the latter on memory.

In the case of both general and specific deterrence people are seen as responsible, rational, calculating individuals who weigh up the costs and benefits of offending in accordance with the rational actor model of crime and criminal behaviour. For deterrence to be effective, a hierarchy of penalties is needed so that the punishment can reflect the seriousness of the crime; for example, if the penalty for armed robbery was a mandatory life sentence as it is in the case of murder, then armed robbers would have nothing to lose by shooting and killing a person during a robbery. A hierarchy of punishment established in terms of progressive severity offsets the greater gain to potential offenders of becoming involved in more serious criminal acts and as a consequence will deter them from involvement and protect the victim from greater harm.

The aim of general deterrence is thus to create a fear of punishment in others and as part of this process it may sometimes be necessary for the innocent to be punished in order to achieve the greater social impact. The outcome is that the imposition of punishment is problematically not restricted to those who have been properly convicted of an offence. In other words, the innocent may be punished because justice needs to be seen to be done and in such cases the punishment inflicted is greater than that which is proportional and deserved. This is also an objection that can be made against the use of exemplary sentences where the offender is punished not for their own past behaviour but for the possible future behaviour of others. Thus, in such instances, excessive punishment is justified by reference to the greater social good and the avoidance of greater future harm with individuals used as a means to an end with no respect for their moral worth and autonomy.

The success of general deterrence is very difficult to evaluate and this is partly because it has the potential to achieve an impact over differing time periods which makes it hard to measure. In the long term, deterrence may occur through the perpetuation of the fear of punishment for certain types of conduct. It is, nevertheless, difficult, if not impossible, to disentangle the effects of punishment from the influence of other factors such as moral education and social reinforcement of the law. In the medium term, legislation may influence social behaviour by increasing certain maximum penalties or the introduction of minimum penalties such as those for drunken driving. Exemplary sentences may have more short-term effects when imposed on one or two offenders who are given disproportionately severe sentences in order to deter others from committing the same crime but again this is morally difficult to defend.

Commonsense logic suggests that punishment does have general deterrent effects but its influence on criminal behaviour is difficult to gauge as many crimes are not discovered. It is also impossible to discover how often the threat of legal punishment rather than some other motivation, such as detrimental effects on social standing and respectability, deters people from offending. It is moreover difficult to establish the effect of marginal deterrence, that is, how much extra deterrence is gained or lost by varying the severity of the punishment, and this is, of course, a very important issue when setting the varying levels of sanctions. Finally, it is impossible to separate the deterrent effects of punishment from other influences such as the family. Disentangling these variables is complex yet nevertheless crucial to the understanding of deterrence (see Conklin, 1977; Braithwaite and Geis, 1982).

Few studies have genuinely identified the existence and extent of the general deterrent effects of legal sanctions. For example, in 1973 a young street robber – or 'mugger' to use the popular terminology – from Birmingham in the UK was sentenced to 20 years' detention amid enormous publicity. Despite the imposition of this exemplary sentence there was no apparent effect on the incidence of mugging offences in his home town or in other areas (Baxter and Nuttall, 1975; Beyleveld, 1980). This does not mean that general deterrent effects never occur but that it is difficult to establish in what situations and to what extent they occur. There is, however, some strong support for the existence of general deterrence as a universal restraining influence where the absence of a punishment structure seems to reduce overall observance of the law. For example, the police strikes in Melbourne 1918 and Liverpool 1919 resulted in the overall offence rates increasing significantly (Beyleveld, 1980). Furthermore, during the Second World War when the Germans deported the entire Danish police force for several months, the rates of theft and robbery rose spectacularly (Christiansen, 1975; Beyleveld, 1980).

Deterrence nevertheless tends to emphasise the importance of the severity of the punishment while not addressing issues of the certainty and immediacy of punishment. When faced with 'a crime problem' legislators often increase penalties in the belief that severity is the overwhelming deterrent. Judges, faced with a wave of high profile and/or particularly distressing offences, may hand down exemplary sentences in order to 'make an example' of particular offenders or offences, with the outcome being very harsh long sentences. Research has nevertheless been able to show that in certain cases, severity can be a crucial factor in deterring offenders. King (1972: 116) cites a comment by a safecracker, 'a law was passed which made using nitro-glycerine on a safe a forty year prison term, automatically. So everybody quit using it.' Safes continued to be cracked but different methods were used.

The above example demonstrates that the severity of the sentence can in some circumstances affect criminal behaviour but it is important to note that if punishments are too harsh then there may well be unintended consequences. In Britain in the early nineteenth century, where as we have seen previously in this book, over 200 crimes were punishable by death, juries often acquitted offenders rather than send them to the gallows for what they felt were relatively minor offences (Kalven and Zeisel, 1966).

The comprehensive body of literature on conventional street criminals emphasises the other two factors of certainty and immediacy, and illustrates that altering penalties has little impact on crime rates (Walker, 1991). As Felson (1998: 10) graphically illustrates:

> Consider what happens when you touch a hot stove. You receive a quick, certain, but minor pain. After being burned once, you will not touch a hot stove again. Now think of an imaginary hot stove that burns you only once every 500 times you touch it, with the burn not hurting until five months later. Psychological research and common sense alike tell us this imaginary stove will not be as effective in punishing us as the real stove.

The effectiveness of deterrents, on both an individual and general level, has been tackled empirically by many researchers (for examples see Zimring and Hawkins, 1973; Gibbs, 1975; Beyleveld, 1978, 1980; Bishop, 1984) but many of the studies of deterrence seek an answer to the implicit question of what makes people refrain from committing a criminal act. Harshness of punishment might well seem a reasonable answer, for exactly how many of us would like to be treated harshly? Criminologists have nevertheless emphasised the importance of detection (Beyleveld, 1978, 1980) and indeed this was recognised centuries ago by Beccaria (1963, originally 1764: 58) who stated that 'the certainty of a punishment, even if it be moderate, will always make a stronger impression than the fear of another which is more terrible but combined with the hope of impunity'.

Beyleveld (1980) argues that the notion of general deterrence refers less to the actual or objective conditions that exist than to the conditions potential offenders believe to exist; for example, the perceived likelihood of being detected is more important than the severity of the sentence. Subjective assessments of the likelihood of being caught vary between offenders and are dependent upon optimism, skill and circumstances. The risk of detection is thus more important because if offenders believe that they will not be caught the probable penalty will have no effect. However, even if the likely penalty does play a part, subjective assessment is important and this will include the type of punishment as well as its length or value.

Concentration on the deterrent effects of the severity of punishment also assumes that offenders and potential offenders are aware of the sanctions that are likely to be imposed. Beyleveld (1980) conducted self-report studies and found that knowledge of sanctions was inaccurate and the probability of being caught was overestimated. Moreover, it was found that the average person on the street has no conception of the likely penalty for particular offences.

The notion of risk is important here as some offenders who commit crime are simply not concerned with the probable punishment if caught because they see it as an occupational hazard. Moreover, deterrence theory is based on the assumption that defendants are rational creatures who calculate the risk involved by weighing up the 'pros' and 'cons' of committing particular acts, but this does not allow for the prevalence of opportunistic crime or crimes that are committed in the heat of the moment. Bennett and Wright (1984), for example, found that burglars in their study rarely thought of the risk of punishment because either (a) they never thought that they would be caught, or (b) they saw punishment as an occupational hazard, or (c) they did not think of the consequences, or (d) the rewards were rarely known in advance. Gill and Matthews (1994; see also Matthews, 1996) conducted a study of convicted bank robbers and interestingly found that none of their research subjects had even considered the possibility that they would be caught before setting out on their criminal enterprises, even though all had previous criminal convictions.

In summary, the evidence for the general deterrence effect of punishment is inconclusive. It seems that general deterrence works selectively and only has an impact on some people while it is not only the severity of the punishment that is important but its certainty and immediacy.

The ability of punishment to deter offenders from reoffending is very difficult to measure and this is mainly because of the extent of crime that goes unreported and undetected. Thus, the fact that an offender has not been reconvicted does not mean that they have not reoffended. It may just mean that they have not been caught. Despite this caveat, the main way in which deterrence is measured is by examining reconviction rates. The majority of offenders are reconvicted within two years of the completion of their sentence and the evidence suggests that reconviction rates vary very little for different types of offences (Davies *et al.*, 1995), while there is some evidence to suggest that punishment actually increases the likelihood of reoffending (Brody, 1976; West, 1982). This relates to the idea that prisons are 'universities of crime' which provide offenders with the opportunity to meet others and learn the 'tricks' of the trade. It also relates to ideas of labelling, as punishment labels and stigmatises offenders making it more difficult to stop offending because other legitimate opportunities are closed to them (Hopkins Burke, 2009).

A further criticism of the notion of individual deterrence is that it underestimates mitigating or 'extra-legal' factors. Thus, in other words, it does not differentiate between the impact of the punishment and other factors such as age, family ties and social bonds (see Hirschi, 1969). If we take mitigating factors such as abuse in the home, unemployment, the need for conformity in certain spheres or indeed extra-legal characteristics that may affect the chances of being arrested, such as ethnicity, gender, attitude, personal hygiene and so forth, deterrence is difficult to establish. These factors become particularly important when we consider that most offenders, however persistent, stop offending by the age of 25.

Incapacitation

Incapacitation has become a high profile and popular justification for punishment during the past 30 years because it removes offenders from society so preventing them from committing offences in the future. Selective incapacitation means that offenders who are identified as the most likely to commit further offences, if they were to be released, continue to be incarcerated or their liberty is restricted in some other way. Although incapacitation is the least philosophically sound justification for punishment, for the individual 'in the street', the issue of being protected from the dangerous and/or criminal classes may well be the most important justification of all for punishment and is a significant issue recognised by the left realist hybrid model of criminal justice development.

Incapacitation usually refers to the physical detention or execution of an individual in order to prevent them from committing crime and placing the public in danger. It is most commonly linked with custodial sentences although treatment centres and curfew orders also incapacitate an offender. Incapacitation is simply restraint and whether the individual reforms in that time period is not the purpose or a main concern. The rationale for this form of punishment has been most succinctly argued by a Catholic priest: 'I am concerned that people who assault human lives should be safely contained like nuclear waste so their destruction in our midst will stop' (Byrne, 1979: A23).

Right realist James Q. Wilson (1983) argues that incapacitation is a plausible and desirable justification for punishment based on the possible effectiveness of the following three assumptions: (1) some offenders are recidivists; (2) offenders are not immediately replaced by other criminals upon being imprisoned; (3) prison does not increase crime by changing offenders in ways that outweigh the reductive effects of incapacitation. He argues that the first assumption is a truism and is supported by empirical data (see Brody and Tarling, 1980) and only in the case of organised crime, prostitution and the movement of drugs, would this assumption be false. Wilson acknowledges that the third assumption is open to debate but believes that the one does not outweigh the other. Incapacitation can be viewed as a cynical approach to punishment as it is an acknowledgement that 'nothing works' but at least it means that society will be safe from those who commit crime and in that way it can be argued that prison does work.

Incapacitation requires the identification of offenders who are likely to do serious harm in the future and in this way it is bound up with ideas of 'dangerousness' and risk to the public. Von Hirsch (1984) argues that three things are necessary to ensure that incapacitation is an effective penal strategy: (1) a definition of dangerousness; (2) valid prediction methods; and (3) a known link between dangerousness and violence. The Floud Report 1981 reviewed the law and practice relating to 'dangerous offenders'. It failed to arrive at a definition of dangerousness but nevertheless came up with the notion of acceptable and unacceptable risk:

> There is no such psychological or medical entity as a dangerous person. It is not an objective concept. Dangers are unacceptable risks. . . . Risk is, in principle, a matter of fact; but danger is a matter of judgement or opinion – a question of what we are prepared to put up with. People tolerate enormous risks without perceiving them as dangers, when fears are not aroused or when it suits their convenience.
>
> (Floud and Young, 1981: 213)

Walker (1991) supports this argument and proposes that the label dangerous should not be applied to people, only situations, actions or activities, observing the very low reconviction rate for offenders convicted of murder or violence, although we should note that they do tend to serve increasingly long sentences.

Incapacitation involves predicting the likelihood of the offender reoffending. Various facts about the offender are recorded, such as previous arrests and convictions, social and employment history, prior drug use, and those factors most strongly associated with recidivism are identified and used as a predictive instrument, the most usual being past behaviour. Various studies nevertheless suggest that there is a limited capacity to predict future offending and indeed the evidence shows that forecasts tend to overpredict (Brody and Tarling, 1980; Greenwood, 1984). The Floud Report 1981 found that statistical forecasting can identify groups of offenders who are at a higher than average risk of reoffending but the incidence of 'false positives' is high. The latter are offenders who are classified as potential recidivists but who never reoffend and, there is, therefore, a tendency to over-predict, which is especially high when forecasting serious criminality. The Floud Report found that between 55 per cent and 70 per cent of those classified as risks were mistakenly identified which means that predictions were more likely to be wrong than right (Floud and Young, 1981).

The basic problem is that a system of selective incapacitation conceals erroneous confinements while, at the same time, creating incorrect releases. This occurs because offenders who are wrongly identified and confined have little or no chance of demonstrating that they would not have reoffended if released while those released who go on to commit further offences are brought to the attention of the public. In this way, incapacitation is a self-fulfilling prophecy which results in more and more offenders being confined (Von Hirsch, 1984).

As a result of the identified problems with prediction, the Floud Report 1981 argued that the burden of risk needed to be spread. Thus, non-convicted dangerous people should be entitled to remain at liberty and any risk to potential victims should be accepted by society; however, once a person had been convicted of seriously harming others they would subsequently be held responsible for any risk they posed. A limited use of 'protective sentencing' was thus proposed so that sentences that exceed the proportionate term were limited to instances where only severe harm was predicted.

Scott (1977) argues that one way to overcome the problems of 'false positives' is to concentrate not on the offender and their past behaviour but on particular offences. In other words, if an offender commits certain offences they should be preventatively detained. This method of prediction was to become increasingly important and this is demonstrated by legislation that was to subsequently remove the right to bail for defendants charged with murder, manslaughter and rape with previous convictions for such offences.

One of the most fundamental arguments against the use of incapacitation is that it is inconsistent with the principles of proportionality. Thus, to extend the punishment of an offender beyond what he or she deserves is problematic and perhaps immoral, even if the prediction of dangerousness can be shown to be accurate. A closely associated problem arises with the use of a bifurcatory punishment policy where the 'serious or dangerous' offender is treated differently and more harshly than the 'ordinary' (hence non-dangerous) offender (Bottoms, 1983). The Floud Report 1981 reinforced this policy as 'the rational response to indications of welcome changes in penal policy' (cited in Bottoms, 1983). This dual approach nevertheless not only encounters practical difficulties of implementation but also permits the unjustified blaming of individuals labelled dangerous.

A practical difficulty in considering incapacitation as a justification for punishment has to be the issue of prison overcrowding which in the past has led to some of the most high profile classic criminal justice academic texts and research studies (for examples see Bottoms and Preston, 1980; Fitzgerald and Sim, 1982; Rutherford, 1988; King and McDermott, 1989), not to mention prison riots (Woolf, 1991). The incapacitation of more offenders might lead to further increases in overcrowding and thus the costs of incarceration, in conditions of high security, would be very high. Furthermore, prisons might well become 'dustbins' for 'dangerous offenders' and this could well result in increased control problems due to the high number of long-term prisoners, some serving indeterminate sentences, who have nothing to lose by being disruptive. There is also some evidence to suggest that long-term prison sentences result in deterioration in the mental health and the community ties of offenders which, together with the possible effects of institutionalisation, may result in difficulties when the person is finally released (King and McDermott, 1989).

Incapacitation has a certain 'gut level' appeal which is often heard expressed by the populist sentiment 'lock 'em up and throw away the key'. Attempting to justify incapacitation, predicting human behaviour to an acceptable degree, as well as dealing with problems within the prison, which will eventually become displaced to the outside world, is a much harder task.

Determinism

Determinism became a paradigmatic orthodoxy during the late nineteenth and early twentieth centuries and has its theoretical foundations in the mechanistic, positivistic worldview of modern science – which was heavily based on empirical evidence – and which was so influential in the creation of the predestined actor model of crime and criminal behaviour. Determinism is not a theory of punishment but rather a way of viewing the offender, but its relevance is in its compatibility with theories of punishment.

Early causal determinism (which was popular prior to the 1930s) basically proposes that every event in nature, including human thoughts, words and deeds, has a cause that is both necessary and sufficient. Given event A, there is a subsequent event B that cannot fail to result from event A; correlatively, event B could not occur without event A having caused it. Therefore, event A is necessary and sufficient to cause event B (Franklin, 1969). This rather confusing relationship is often referred to as 'for every action there is an equal and opposite reaction'. The causal determinist admits that individuals do have the power to make choices but believes that this power is strictly limited because each person has been caused to make the choices that he or she makes. Past experiences, the environment, and so on all have a starting point for the determinist and every action is viewed as being traceable, ultimately to the point of birth, perhaps before (Davis, 1971).

Later causal determinism (popular from the 1930s through to the 1960s) proposed that individuals are not able to express free will at any time. The new determinists, Hospers, Foot and Hobart, felt that although it was an empirical impossibility that every action had a necessary and sufficient cause, it was not essential to prove this for determinism to have relevance (Foot, 1957). This new strand of causal determinism asserted that even if some events result from chance, and therefore were not caused, it can still be illustrated that all events are ultimately attributable to either causal or chance factors beyond the control of the individual (Hospers, 1932).

The central argument for causal determinists is that for any given action or decision to occur there are only three possibilities and at no point does free will ever enter into the equation. First, if the event happens by chance then there is no free will. Second, if it is caused by external factors then no free will is involved. Third, if it is the choice of the individual then there are only three possible reasons why that could be the case: either (a) A is caused to occur by the agent themselves, resulting from a choice that the individual has made; or (b) A is caused by some external factor or factors; or (c) A is not caused by anything at all and it is a chance event. The argument thus becomes completely circular and free will is theoretically never an option.

Few people today consider the actions of human beings to be totally determined but if human action is in some way predetermined, albeit in a limited sense, then this would greatly affect the level of punishment that can be legitimately imposed. Determinism has nevertheless unfortunately been historically discussed in an 'all or nothing fashion'. Much of the controversy surrounding determinism focuses on the apparent limitlessness of the concept which, taken to a logical conclusion, would mean that offenders can be completely excused from any blame and responsibility for their actions. Such a position would be politically unacceptable in any society with pretensions to be a democracy or otherwise.

Rehabilitation

Rehabilitation is a combined French and Latin word, with its origins in the French *re*, which means 'return' or 'repetition', and the Latin word *habilis*, which means 'competent'. Return to competence. In the context of punishment, rehabilitation is aimed at reforming the character of the offender so preventing reoffending. The intention is to cure offenders of their criminal tendencies by changing their personality, outlook, habits or opportunities so that they are less inclined to commit crime.

Rehabilitation became the dominant perspective and purpose of 'corrections' policy in both the USA and the UK during the first 60 years of the twentieth century. This dominance followed a gradual movement away from a purely punitive philosophy toward the ideal of rehabilitation and thus signalled a move away from the ideas of the rational actor model of crime and criminal behaviour towards the predestined actor model. In this way, notions of determinism were to take over from ideas of free will, and the role of 'positive science' was emphasised. Its rise was accompanied by the belief that the human sciences – psychology, psychiatry, sociology, economics and medicine – would soon be able to discover the root causes of crime. Human motivation is not a rational function but is caused by antecedent factors in the environment and heredity of the person, as we saw in the third chapter.

Rehabilitation is thus based on the ideas of determinism, individualism and pathology where crime is seen to be caused by something outside the control of the offender. From this perspective, the criminal justice process should concentrate on the offender rather than the offence and this idea was to be juxtaposed with a medical model that proposed that criminals were to be 'treated' in order to prevent reoffending. The level of treatment that was required, rather than the seriousness of the offence, was to determine the type and length of sentence. Experts from the developing sciences of psychiatry, physiology and sociology were used to classify and diagnose the level of treatment necessary and to recommend the sentence required to achieve a 'cure'.

The state now had an obligation to intervene in the lives of its citizens who had committed crime in order to cure them of their criminal tendencies (Hudson, 1987). As crime was caused by something outside of the control of the individual, the role of the state was to prevent these causes. The dominance of rehabilitation as a paradigmatic orthodoxy was to coincide during the 1950s and 1960s with the expansion of the role of the state in general and the welfare state in particular. In these circumstances, a consensus was to develop which proposed that crime was a problem that could be overcome if the state directed more resources to the treatment of offenders (Hudson, 1987).

Rehabilitation reached its peak of popularity in 1967 with the publication of two official reports, one in the USA (President's Commission on Law Enforcement and the Administration of Justice, 1967) and one in the UK (Royal Commission on the Penal System in England and Wales, 1967), both of which took a social democratic perspective and argued that crime was the result of some form of deprivation and the solution was to increase state activity in the areas of crime prevention and the rehabilitation of offenders. Both reports were very optimistic about what could be done if the resources were made available.

Thus, by 1967, the main tenets of rehabilitation were in place. First, individualised sentences were promoted where the type and level of punishment were to be customised to the needs of the individual and not purely determined by the nature of the offence. Second, where prison was found to be necessary indeterminate sentences were proposed and release would subsequently depend upon the progress of the individual in response to a 'cure'. It was accepted that the decision to release an offender should not lie with the judiciary but with penal administrators and experts who had day-to-day contact with the inmate and could judge the optimum release time. Third, treatment programmes such as group therapy, counselling and educational and vocational training were expected to be available to offenders both inside and outside prison. Fourth, the principles of diagnosis, classification and treatment were accepted as the best ways of dealing with offenders. In short, offenders were to be treated as individuals.

Rehabilitation was seen as progressive and humanitarian and its aim was to return offenders to the community as law-abiding citizens, and the underlying principle of this approach apparently theoretically explained by the politically neutral social progress model of criminal justice development was 'to return the offender to society not with the negative vacuum of punishment induced fear, but with affirmative and constructive equipment; physical, mental and moral law abidingness' (Wiehofen, 1971: 261, quoted in Hudson, 1987: 13).

The rehabilitative approach was nevertheless to come under increasing attack following the rediscovery of the rational actor model of crime and criminal behaviour by the emerging political 'new right' during the 1970s. Three fundamental criticisms can be identified. First, the fact that rehabilitation was founded on determinism meant there was an unequivocal assumption that people had no choice in their behaviour and were manipulated and controlled by circumstances outside their control, which was seen to be disrespectful of the individual (Hudson, 1987). Second, it was argued that individuals had a right to retain their personality even if this conflicted with the views of the state or fellow citizens. Third, rehabilitation enabled the state to intervene in the lives of people to a greater extent than was considered to be legitimately permissible and involved the manipulation of individuals.

There were further factors involved in the demise of rehabilitation as a paradigmatic orthodoxy. First, there was the rise of labelling theory and the victimised actor model of crime and criminal behaviour, which proposed that treatment and intervention could actually produce rather than reduce criminal behaviour. Second, there was the rapidly increasing crime rate and disturbances in prisons, which resulted in serious doubts about the competence of the state to successfully tackle these problems. Third, there was an identified need to reduce public expenditure along with mounting arguments supporting the 'rolling back of the state' proposed by the political 'new right'.

Criticisms of rehabilitation focused on three concerns which together formed a formidable attack. First, the civil libertarian critique concentrated on the nature and extent of the intervention in the lives of people who were the subjects of rehabilitation. It was argued that indeterminate sentences were open to abuse by the penal authorities, and as a result, they subverted any potential help or treatment that was proposed. Offenders felt obliged to participate in and accept any treatment that the authorities considered necessary, which could include, for example, the use of drugs, while they invariably felt unable to complain or protest as this might compromise their release date.

Indeterminate sentences also resulted in injustice, for those who were released were not necessarily those who were reformed but those who had conformed to the system. Some offenders who had committed petty crimes spent long periods in incarceration because they did not conform while others who had committed serious offences were released after short periods because they played the rehabilitation game. The system of indeterminate sentences also led to high levels of anxiety and discontent among prisoners as they were unable to plan for the future, either in or out of prison, especially as no reasons were given to them for the decisions that were made.

Second, lawyers observed that concentrating attention on the individual offender rather than on the offence that had been committed had led to huge disparities in the sentences that had been administered. Moreover, these sentences were invariably based on the uncorroborated opinion of experts rather than the objective facts or circumstances of the case. An individualised approach to sentencing also opened up the system to the whims of individual judges and other criminal justice professionals. Basically, it permitted the abuse of discretion and the system was brought into disrepute.

Third, the 'new right' law and order lobby argued that the treatment approach was both ineffective at reducing crime and, at the same time, soft on crime, not least because it advocated the use of prison only as a last resort. These arguments were supported by a wave of widely publicised evaluation studies that purported to show that community corrections were no more or less effective than custodial sentences, and expensive treatment programmes were no more successful than simple incarceration or non-therapeutic sentences such as fines. The most famous and widely (mis)cited is Martinson (1974) who, it is claimed, said 'nothing works'. In reality he had argued that 'nothing, or almost nothing works' but his conclusions were widely acceptable because they were compatible with the re-emerging belief in retributive justifications for punishment that were being sponsored by the political 'new right'.

Two important observations can be made about the 'nothing works' argument. First, research studies purporting to show that 'nothing works' have been heavily criticised because of doubts about the methodology used (see Brody, 1976) and there is now a widespread consensus of opinion that some forms of treatment do work for certain groups of offenders in some circumstances. It is nevertheless only effective when it is applied to certain types of offenders, or when it is adapted to the particular requirements of the individual, or if it is aimed at modifying specific aspects of behaviour, for example, addiction or aggressiveness (Hudson, 1987). Second, it can be argued that treatment programmes were never fully implemented while evaluations of partial schemes are of limited value (Cullen and Gilbert, 1982; Hudson, 1987). These two observations were to lead to the emergence in recent years of a 'what works' agenda based on evidence-based practice.[2]

In response to the extensive criticisms of rehabilitation, subsequent attempts were made to reaffirm its core principles under the guise of the 'new rehabilitation' or 'state-obligated rehabilitation' which accepts and attempts to rectify some of the criticisms of 'old style' rehabilitation while maintaining its main principles (Palmer, 1975; Gendreau and Ross, 1979; Gottfredson, 1979; Cullen and Gilbert, 1982; Hudson, 1987). The revised model advocates that the criminal justice process should not only punish offenders but, at the same time, seek to redress some of the social injustices, or at least ensure that sentencing does not increase social inequality. It nevertheless does not propose that the sole aim of the penal system should be rehabilitation but rather that it should work in conjunction with the other aims of desert, deterrence, reparation and reintegration. Yet rehabilitation is considered to be important because it is the only strategy that obligates the state to care for the needs and welfare of the offender. By punishing the offender humanely and compensating them for the social disadvantages that led to their criminal behaviour, they are considered to be less likely to reoffend. In this way, it is the only available penal strategy that will reduce the likelihood of reoffending and thus meet the primary aim of preventing crime. A purely punitive approach will not reduce crime because it does nothing to tackle the causes of crime. Therefore, state-obligated rehabilitation is based on the assumption that personal and social circumstances in some way contribute to crime. Pat Carlen (1989: 22) observes that 'the aim of judicial intervention into offenders' lives should be to help them create living conditions in which they are more likely to choose to be law abiding in the future'.

The crucial difference between old-style rehabilitation and the new-style state-obligated rehabilitation is that in the case of the latter, the state is obliged to provide rehabilitative programmes in order to reduce crime in society. This obligation would cover both community and prison sanctions unless the 'offender and the court agreed that the rehabilitative element would be redundant in a particular case' (Carlen, 1989: 20). Rehabilitation would involve offenders coming to accept that their behaviour was wrong and also acknowledging that the state subsequently treated them justly. It is a perspective founded on concepts of social justice, which means that sentences administered must take into account the likely impact of the disposal and its feasibility in terms of individual offenders. It is therefore recognised that the social circumstances and context affect both the impact that the sentence will have and its feasibility. The latter questions whether or not an extremely disadvantaged offender is able to complete any demanding non-custodial order. Social circumstances are related in two ways: first, the life-style of the offender, and second, the lack of communal public facilities may mean that offenders willing to comply with an order are unlikely to fulfil their obligations, for example, because there are no child-care facilities.

Under a system of state-obligated rehabilitation, imprisonment is considered to be an extreme form of punishment and would only be used in exceptional circumstances, with community sentences advocated as a substitute because this allows reintegration and not exclusion. When found to be necessary, it is argued that prison should be a positive experience and not just about humane containment and minimum standards. It should have the twin objectives of punishing the offender for what they had already done and preventing reoffending by the provision of decent living conditions, training in life skills, work release, education and training.

State-obligated rehabilitation is about rights: the right of the state to punish and the rights of offenders not to be punished unduly harshly, by the use of determinate sentences fixed by desert while taking account of social circumstances. It is therefore a perspective that realises and counters the problems of old-style rehabilitation by advocating determinate sentences while, at the same time, taking into account the social circumstances of the offender by considering sentence impact and feasibility. By incorporating notions of desert, sentence inconsistency is also overcome while, at the same time, the argument is clearly made that not only society but also the offender must consider the sentence to be just. In addition, this perspective counters the argument that rehabilitation is soft on crime as the sentence administered is appropriate to the seriousness of the offence. A humanitarian approach is nevertheless preserved with a desire to help rather than to hurt, to reintegrate rather than to segregate, 'to promote good rather than to impede evil' (Carlen, 1989: 20).

Retribution

> When someone who delights in annoying and vexing peace-loving folk
> receives at last a right good beating . . . everyone approves of it and considers
> it as good in itself even if nothing further results from it; nay even he who
> gets the beating must acknowledge in his reason, that justice has been done to
> him, because he sees the proportion between welfare and well-doing.
>
> (Kant, 1956, originally 1788)

In the eighteenth century, prior to Beccaria and the rise of the rational actor
model of crime and criminal behaviour, philosophers such as Immanuel Kant
(1724–1804) had predominantly supposed that law-breakers should be punished
in proportion to their moral desert, even if this was to produce more harm than
good in the long term. Though it is this period that is in particular associated with
the notion of retribution, its theoretical foundations can be traced back to the
mythologies of ancient Greece and Rome (Walker, 1991).

Hegel (1965, originally 1822) argued that people have two wills. The first, the
'arbitrary will', is completely free of all external forces and is subject to instincts,
urges and passions. The second, the 'true will', is subject to the general will of
others. When in conflict, the arbitrary will of the individual may suppress the true
will, leading the person to become involved in criminal activity. It is at this point
that proponents and supporters of the notion of retribution as a justification for
punishment feel that it is just, right and necessary to punish, and perhaps to do so
severely. Moberly (1968: 72) succinctly summarises this position:

> It is felt to be unfair that a man's grievous fault should make no difference to
> the treatment he receives and that he should be treated just as favourably as if
> he had done no wrong. It is reasonable that we should do unto others as we
> would wish them to do unto us. But conversely, it is fitting and proper that,
> what others are to do to us, should be affected for better or worse by the
> quality of what we have done to them.

The retributive perspective proposes that punishment is just because it is deserved,
it fulfils a balance of reciprocity, and can be seen to have similarities to the doctrine
of *lex talionis*, more commonly referred to as 'an eye for an eye, a tooth for a
tooth'.[3] The similarity here lies in the idea of reciprocity but retributive theory
does not insist on a one-to-one ratio. The idea is that the offender has taken an
unfair advantage which can and must be taken away from them by a penalty.
Retribution is often thought to be the same thing as revenge but Nozick (1981)
disputes this view and lists five characteristics that distinguish between the notions
of revenge and retribution. First, retribution is carried out to atone for a wrong,
while revenge may be exacted for an injury, harm or slight, and need not be a
wrong. Second, retribution sets an internal limit to the amount of punishment that
is considered to be proportionate to the seriousness of the wrong, whereas revenge

need set no limits. Third, revenge is personal. Fourth, revenge involves a particular emotional tone, pleasure in the suffering of another, which is missing in the case of retribution. Fifth, revenge need not be general in that it does not commit the person to seeking vengeance again in similar circumstances. Ten (1987) adds a further distinguishing characteristic, noting that whereas retributive punishment is only inflicted on the wrongdoers, revenge is sometimes inflicted on an innocent person near to the incident.

Supporters of retribution argue that individuals who violate the law deserve to be punished because they have intentionally hurt others. Thus, in accordance with the rational actor model of crime and criminal behaviour, offenders are considered to be responsible and rational people and punishment is, therefore, the natural and appropriate response to crime. Walker (1985: 108) observes that:

> Essentially, retribution consists of the deliberate infliction of death, suffering, hardship, or at least, inconvenience, not because of any hoped for benefit such as the reduction of misbehaviour but simply because the misbehaviour deserves it.

From this perspective, the primary justification for punishment is that offenders deserve to be punished and in proportion to the harm they have wilfully inflicted on the victim and on society. The emphasis is therefore on what the person has done in the past and not what they may do in the future. There is a moral obligation to impose punishment if harm has been caused but if there is none, punishment would not be necessary. One of the main problems with this approach is how to accurately measure the harm and thus the level of punishment that can be legitimately inflicted.

Just deserts

Retribution, as a justification for punishment, has become increasingly important since the 1970s with the emergence and the prominence given to the idea of 'desert'. With the demise of the rehabilitative ideal, particularly in the USA, the 1970s witnessed an atmosphere of rising panic and desperation with the recognition that the medical model had done nothing to slow the ever-increasing crime rate. In 1976 the penological vacuum was filled with a resurgence of punitive ideologies, strongly influenced by the now classic text commissioned by the Committee for the Study of Incarceration, *Doing Justice* (Von Hirsch, 1976). The justice model or 'just deserts' as it is often called, was developed for the most part by liberals and radicals who argued that the extraordinarily long sentences imposed under the guise of rehabilitation were unacceptable. Consistency in sentencing and the notion of the rational offender, which were central to the concept of retribution, were viewed to be vastly superior to the deterministic perspective on which the rehabilitative ideal was founded.

The main difference between desert and retribution theories is that the latter inflicts punishment on the law-breaker for reasons of morality, while the former does so for purposes of utility. Proponents of retribution thus seek punishment because the wrongdoer deserves to be punished and consider it inappropriate that a wrong should receive the same response as a right. Proponents of just deserts, on the other hand, are a product of disillusionment with retribution (Walker, 1991) and, in their case, punishment is not imposed because of moral duty but out of utility, punishing law-breakers maximises good. Walker (1980:24) summarises this position most succinctly: 'certain things are simply wrong and ought to be punished. And this we do believe.'

The benefactor of punishment, from the just deserts perspective, is society in general, and its imposition satisfies the public for a variety of reasons. Von Hirsch acknowledges the utilitarian inclinations of his theory although he explains that the state has an obligation to respond to wrongdoing, as well as satisfying the public consensus. Just deserts is thus a mixture of both duty and utility, with a particularly strong commitment to utilitarian considerations. Cavadino and Dignan (2006) observe that the just deserts theory is really a 'compromise theory' of retribution. Like a purist variant of the latter, there is a strong emphasis on 'making the punishment fit the crime' by linking proportionality with seriousness and culpability. However, while retribution views culpability as matching the severity of the punishment in some sort of one-to-one ratio, just deserts emphasises that the penalty inflicted should not exceed that which is proportional to the blame-worthiness of the offender. For punishment to be justified as well as appropriate, it must thus be deserved (Von Hirsch, 1976). Furthermore, 'punishment connotes censure. Penalties should comport with the seriousness of crimes, so that the reprobation visited on the offender through his penalty fairly reflects the blame-worthiness of his conduct' (Von Hirsch, 1985: 35).

Just deserts theory proposes an intuitive connection between crime and punishment and there is thus a moral justification for the administration of the latter. Von Hirsch (1985) nevertheless argues that crime prevention is a further justification. Punishment must involve some sort of disincentive to engage in certain conduct and there must be an element of general deterrence. Deterrence nevertheless requires the concept of desert to limit the severity of the punishment so that the individual is not excessively punished for the sake of greater social gain.

'Just deserts' is thus based on the principle of proportionality and the intention is that this should produce consistency with sentences proportional to the serious-ness of the criminal conduct as measured by the harm done by the act and the blameworthiness of the offender (Von Hirsch, 1976). Just deserts thus concentrates on the act and not on the offender, their circumstances, known past, and not on what may happen in the future. A major outcome of the incorporation of just deserts into policy was the replacement of indeterminate sentences with deter-minate ones, and right across the USA, legislators began to alter penal codes so that the latter became mandatory and 'limited the extent to which they could be varied in aggravating or mitigating circumstances' (Walker, 1991: 9).

Just deserts emphasises the importance of due process and the rights of offenders and victims. This is partly a reaction to the wide discretionary powers previously given to the criminal justice process when rehabilitation was the dominant orthodoxy and which deserts theorists argue resulted both in excessive leniency and harshness in individual cases and feelings of injustice on the part of offenders who were treated differently from each other. To overcome this problem, a deserts-based punishment system requires written schedules to be produced to show the appropriate punishments for various offence categories which could then be regularly applied and consistently interpreted. The outcome would be the restoration of due process to the criminal justice system and the protection of the rights of offenders from excessive punishment and a consistent approach to all cases and offenders with the importance of extra-legal factors limited.

'Just deserts' is not a unitary theory and there are some areas of disagreement among proponents and supporters. The first of these focuses on whether or not there should be a system of early release in place. Sentences imposed under the just deserts model should be determinate and based on what was known at the trial about the offence and this, according to Von Hirsch, debars any system of early release as this would entail an element of indeterminacy. Others, such as Ashworth (1992), argue that a system of early release is essential in order to preserve good order in prisons.

The second disagreement centres on the need to construct a scale of penalties proportionate to the seriousness of the offence. Concepts such as seriousness, blameworthiness and severity of penalties are not objective realities and thus require subjective interpretation in order to produce a ranking of penalties which fit particular crimes. For example, the quantification of harm is a complex and changing process as illustrated by offences such as domestic violence and drunk driving which have in recent years come to be perceived as serious offences where previously this was not the case. The concept of a scale of penalties suggests an inherent consensus of opinion on the ranking of offences but there are still several areas of disagreement. First, there is no agreement on matters of mitigation and the relevance of the presence or absence of harm, particularly in the case of attempted crimes. Second, there is no agreement on the ranking of corporate crime, consensual crime and lifestyle offences. Moreover, the very concept of a tariff scale raises the issue of who it is who decides on the rank ordering of offence seriousness and the corresponding appropriate sentences. Many penologists argue that it should be a representative body whose task it is to allocate penalties according to seriousness (Ashworth, 1997).

Although the seriousness of the offence is the most important consideration, mitigating and aggravating factors may be taken into account. There has nevertheless been debate about the role which the past record of the offender should play in sentencing decisions but according to just deserts principles each offence should be treated in isolation without the prior record of the offender having any bearing on the punishment. If the prior record of the offender were taken into consideration it would result in the use of social protection disposals which are inconsistent with desert rationale. Von Hirsch (1985) nevertheless argues that previous convictions should be taken into consideration because the offender should be aware of the harm caused by his or her previous actions.

In other words, repeat offending does have a bearing on the culpability of the offender. In practice, it is argued that first offenders should receive mitigation and thus, lighter sentences, as it is recognised that human beings are fallible.

A popular objection to the just deserts model is the perception that retribution is nothing more than a rationalisation of revenge. Whereas the utilitarians at least work towards positive future change, deterrence, rehabilitation and retribution focus on past actions. Retribution emphasises the act committed and is not particularly concerned with crime prevention; its concerns are solely punitive, without the utilitarian consideration that any future good may arise from the punishment.

Hudson (1987) argues that the just deserts model is wrong in principle as it compares like with unlike and simply ignores the social causes of crime. Treating everybody the same when they clearly are not, results in injustice and discrimination. Proponents argue that the strength of the model is that it is non-discriminatory but the administration of the same penalties to different offenders inflicts diverse levels of punishment because of differential individual characteristics and circumstances. For example, a fine of £100 would be an inconvenience to a person who earns £50,000 a year but may result in considerable hardship for a person in receipt of welfare benefits.

Walker (1991) observes that just deserts theory also ignores the unintended consequences of punishment such as stigma, loss of employment or accommodation, and the impact on the family of the offender. Thus, the totality of the sentence and the extent of suffering involved may exceed that which was intended, while the incidental impact of punishment will vary between different offenders, and this is again contrary to the concept of proportionality.

Other criticisms of the just deserts model revolve around its implementation. Thus, just how do you measure harm, seriousness, the severity of the sentence and blameworthiness? Moreover, how do you deal with multiple offences and the fact that the offender has subsequently repented or made amends to the victim? How does the notion of 'making the punishment fit the crime' become quantifiable in real terms?

Just deserts theory was to become the dominant justification for punishment and its ascent to this status can be accounted for by its being in the right place at the right time. It had been (supposedly) shown that rehabilitation did not work as it had not reduced the level of crime despite the rapid expansion of state intervention in the punishment process. At the same time, there was a need to reduce public expenditure clearly linked with the increasing political importance of crime, that is, the need to be seen to be taking a tough stance on crime.

Although the principles of just deserts were to form the dominant basis of sentencing policy, many commentators argue that the ideas were hijacked by the right-wing law and order lobby and that the justice model was never implemented in its purist form because of political manipulation and it thus became negatively associated with harsh and severe penalties (Hudson, 1987). Proponents of just deserts theory argue that this does not necessarily need to be the case and Von

Hirsch himself argues that the just deserts model applied properly should result in less harsh sentences.

Reparation

> If reparation were more consistently pursued we should have a much more civilised and morally acceptable penal system than the present one.
>
> (Cavadino and Dignan, 2006: 43)

Reparation refers to the idea of 'repairing' the damage that has been done through the commission of an offence. The reparation may be to the victim or to the community and the intention is not only to redress the balance between the offender and victim or society, but that offenders should also be made aware of the harm they have caused and, therefore, acknowledge their law-breaking behaviour. In being brought face-to-face with the consequences of their actions it is hoped that offenders will see the error of their ways.

Reparation is an integral part of the community service order which was originally introduced in 1972 and where the punishment is designed to 'pay back the community'. Unpaid work at an approved community agency or organisation is the usual form of reparation administered under this type of order but it may also involve the payment of compensation either to the victim or the community. The notion of reparation is focused on the victim and the harm that the victim has suffered. It seeks not only to redress the balance, but to illustrate to the offender directly the harm that they have caused (see Cavadino and Dignan, 2006).

Restitution

> Restitution recognises rights in the victim, and this is a principal source of its strength. The nature and limit of the victim's right to restitution at the same time defines the nature and limit of the criminal liability. In this way, the aggressive action of the criminal creates a debt to the victim.
>
> (Barnett, 1985: 222)

Restitution, like reparation, is focused on redressing the balance of a 'wrong' but the philosophical underpinnings of the theories are nevertheless slightly different. Restitution views a crime as being an offence by one individual that has been perpetrated on another, which has led to the rights of the latter individual being taken away, violated or in some way lessened. The focus is on the individuals involved, not society or the social contract.

Restitution in its pure form does not even focus on 'punishment' as such and there is no feeling that the offender deserves to suffer, or that he or she must be deterred, reformed, incapacitated or treated. If these factors were to be achieved through an act of restitution then that would be a favourable outcome but not the intention. Restitution can be seen as simply the righting of a wrong.

Punitive restitution, on the other hand, involves the same considerations as the purist variant but also encompasses the idea of punishment. Restitution in this form views the offender as having to compensate the victim in a way that is entirely burdensome on the offender and they must suffer while paying their debt.

Both reparation and restitution – but in particular the latter – become more difficult goals when the offence committed has nothing to do with property but with, for example, violence against the person or a sexual offence. In these instances it becomes seriously problematic to practically redress the balance (see Barnett, 1985).

The politics of punishment

The importance and priority afforded to different justifications of punishment varies, and sometimes radically changes, over time and this is invariably a consequence of often significant changes in the political climate. One of the practical difficulties for the criminal justice process in locating and implementing effective penological and punishment policies is that crime has become such a politicised issue. 'Law and order' has become an overloaded phrase that conjures up visions of dangerousness, security, protection and divisions between 'us and them'.

The criminal justice process imposes a wide variety of sentences, all of which prioritise different justifications for punishment. The outcome is that the imposition of punishment has multiple justifications and this is a situation made even more complex by the fact that the importance of issues relating to crime, offenders and imprisonment has resulted in the philosophies of punishment being used as justifications for implementing policies, regardless of their proven effectiveness.

The concluding comments to the previous chapter on the criminal justice process are equally relevant here. The development of different justifications for punishment can be partially explained by the social progress model of criminal justice development because yet again we can identify the role of the well-meaning progressive humanitarian in the various changes that have occurred and indeed there is considerable ambiguity as to what exactly constitutes humanitarianism and benevolence in the area of punishment, which makes the situation even more complex. It nevertheless is again abundantly clear that there are sectional interests involved not least with the rise of the 'law and order' agenda and subsequent social order legislation explained by the radical conflict model and its proposal that these developments have occurred in the interests of global capitalism.

Yet again, the situation is more ambiguous and complex than apparent at first sight with the carceral surveillance society model alerting us to the reality of a diffusion of power and the role of experts in colonising and promoting agendas of their own, but it is the left realist hybrid model which significantly recognises the interest of the general public in such changes. Tougher perspectives on punishment can be seen to clearly reflect the wider interests of many in society who legitimately seek protection from those criminal and disorderly elements in their midst which are seen to threaten their security and well-being. They are thus easily persuaded by politicians to endorse a tougher line against miscreants in their midst in the apparent interests of all (Hopkins Burke, 2004a).

7 Youth justice in modern society

The contemporary youth justice system in England and Wales was established by the New Labour flagship criminal justice legislation, the Crime and Disorder Act 1998, and was in many ways the culmination and coming together of often contrasting and conflicting themes that had been in existence and incrementally developed over a period of a century and a half. This chapter observes that in order to theorise the establishment of the contemporary system – or why it is that it came into existence in the form that it did – it is essential to locate the discussion in an historical context because essentially the debates, discourses and political solutions that emerged in the past are very similar to those of the present time. It is thus impossible to make legitimate sense of the contemporary era without reflection on the past. Fears about rising crime rates among children and young people have been periodically repeated throughout history in all modern societies with the present continuously compared unfavourably with the peaceful days of a halcyon non-existent golden age (Humphries, 1981; Pearson, 1983). The emphasis on 'appropriate parenting' in contemporary society is also nothing new and the notion that 'the family' is in 'crisis', and/or that parents are 'failing', is a 'cyclical phenomenon with a very long history' (Day-Sclater and Piper, 2000: 135), while the 'parenting theme' (Gelsthorpe, 1999) has enjoyed and continues to enjoy prominence. It is therefore essential to consider the issue of delinquent and indeed disorderly children and young people, and the nature of the official response that has evolved to deal with these issues, in an historical context.

This chapter revisits the four models of criminal justice development in modern society in order to make theoretical sense of the always contentious and topical issue of the involvement of children and young people in criminality and the subsequent response of the criminal justice authorities to their transgressions. It commences with a brief discussion of the historical development of the concept of young people in the modern era – from their social construction as children and adolescents – and considers the various, varied strategies that were introduced in order to educate, discipline, control and construct them in the interests of myriad different interest groups, not least, but not exclusively, industrial capitalism, and examines their deviance, 'offending behaviour' and the consequential societal juvenile justice response from the beginnings of industrial modernity to the present day.

Young people, discipline, control

It is thus important to consider the issue of delinquent children and youth in an historical context because the way we view childhood and the misdemeanours of the young today is very much a product of the modern world and the social construction of this important element of humanity in the interests of particular groups. In the pre-modern era, childhood was not considered to be a distinct period of development in the way that it is now. The role and status of children was ambiguous and because of the nature of the pre-industrial, predominantly agrarian and rural subsistence economy, they were of little significance or importance and often a drain on limited material resources (Malthus, 1959, originally 1798).[1] It was a situation that was to be nevertheless significantly reversed with the emergence of modern industrial societies where for the first time in history an abundant, fit, healthy populace was to become an essential asset. From that time onwards children were to become increasingly nurtured, pampered and disciplined in the interests of a society that needed them (Hopkins Burke, 2008).

Our modern conception of childhood began to develop in western Europe during the sixteenth century with the emergence of a small recognisable middle class and its demand for a formalised education for its sons (Aries, 1962). Previously, the apprenticeship system had been the main form of education and preparation for adult life had involved children from all social groups being sent into the homes of other families equal to their own particular social status. The idea of education now began to embrace formal schooling, a shift that reflected increasing attachment to the child, with middle-class parents choosing to keep their children close to them (Aries, 1962; Hoyles and Evans, 1989). During the eighteenth century, the contemporary conception of a house emerged and became established among the wealthier classes with the establishment of separate and specialised rooms (Aries, 1962) and it was at this time that the child came to be seen as an irreplaceable and unique individual, the centre of the family, and started to assume great importance in society (Hoyles and Evans, 1989). It is nevertheless important to recognise that this evolution in the concept of childhood occurred mainly in the statistically tiny upper and middle class. The poor – who made up a substantial proportion of the population – continued to live like medieval families into the early nineteenth century (Aries, 1962). However, it was to be these newly emergent middle-class attitudes to childhood that were to provide the dominant template of acceptable, and increasingly enforceable, child socialisation from the nineteenth century onwards.

Childhood came to be increasingly viewed as a time of innocence and dependence, with protection, training and appropriate socialisation paramount. Youth, in contrast, came to be seen as an age of deviance, disruption and wickedness (Brown, 1998) and this perception was strongly linked to the discovery of the pseudo-scientific concept of adolescence. Many researchers (Gillis, 1974; Hendricks, 1990a, 1990b; Jenks, 1996; Brown, 1998) follow Aries (1962) and argue that adolescence was 'discovered' during the Victorian era and from that time onwards it became identified as a cause of delinquency (Gillis, 1974: 171). Clearly, prior to that time when there was little differentiation between children and adults, the problem of youth or adolescent offending simply could not exist.

It was the rapid growth of industrial modernity in the early nineteenth century – at the same time as the emerging distinction between child and adult – that led eventually to fewer young people in the workplace and, with more spare time on their hands, they took to hanging out together on the streets. The social construction of the notions of adolescence, acceptable youthful behaviour, and juvenile delinquency or 'hooliganism' (see Pearson, 1983) became increasingly apparent from that time onwards. The social commentators of the time had their own middle-class conceptions of what should constitute acceptable youthful behaviour and the incremental criminalisation of working-class youth began as early as 1815 with the creation of the Society for Investigating the Causes of the Alarming Increase of Juvenile Delinquency in the Metropolis (Pinchbeck and Hewitt, 1981; Muncie, 2004).

The term 'adolescence' itself was constructed by the professional middle classes in accordance with the work of the influential early US psychologist G. Stanley Hall (1906), who described this stage of development in biologically determinist terms as one of 'storm and stress' in which instability and fluctuation were normal and to be expected. His notion of 'normal adolescent demeanour' was ominously based on the 'unspontaneous, conformist and confident' white middle-class youths with whom he came into contact and this model was again soon prescribed as the desirable model for young people of all social classes (Griffin, 1997). Significantly, the marginalisation of whole cross-sections of young people – especially the working class, girls and ethnic minority groups – became implicit from that time on with the social construction of a notion of adolescence acceptable to middle-class sensibilities. Although theories of 'delinquency' were to broaden their approach during the twentieth century, as we saw in the second chapter, the ways in which adolescence is perceived continue to be heavily influenced by the 'storm and stress' model (Newburn, 2002).

Contemporary notions of childhood and adolescence were thus socially constructed at the outset of industrial modernity and children and their families were subsequently disciplined and controlled, not least in the interests of an industrial capitalism which required a fit, healthy, increasingly educated, trained and obedient workforce. Reality was nonetheless more complex than proposed by proponents of the radical conflict model, while the orthodox social progress perspective which proposes these disciplinary strategies to be merely the actions of motivated entrepreneurial philanthropists with genuine concerns about poor urban children and young people is, while at least partially accurate, also too simplistic. Many of these philanthropists – or 'moral entrepreneurs' (Becker, 1963) – clearly had little idea of the actual or potential long-term consequences of their actions and would probably have been most troubled had they done so. For there was a significant identifiable failure to take into account the complexities of power and the outcomes of strategies promoted by agencies at the mezzo level of the institution, which often enjoy autonomy from the political centre, and those implemented by individual practitioners working at the micro level of the front-line who often enjoy considerable professional discretion.

It is the carceral surveillance society thesis where strategies of power are seen to be pervasive throughout society, with the state only one of the points of control and resistance (Foucault, 1971, 1976), that enables us to make theoretical sense of the situation. This model proposes that there are numerous 'semi-autonomous' realms and relations – such as communities, occupations, organisations, families – in civil society where surveillance and control are present but where the state administration is technically absent and, moreover, these arenas are often nego-tiated and resisted by their participants in ways over which, even now, the state has little jurisdiction.

It is the left realist hybrid model (Hopkins Burke, 2004a, 2004c, 2008) which provides, as we have seen, a variation on the carceral surveillance society thesis and which, while accepting the premise that disciplinary strategies are invariably implemented by moral entrepreneurs, professional agents and practitioners who have little idea how their often humble discourse contributes to the grand overall disciplinary control matrix, does, at the same time, significantly recognise that there are other, further, interests involved and these are significantly *ours* and in this context those of *our* predecessors. The bourgeois child tutelage project of the nineteenth and early twentieth centuries can clearly be viewed in that context, and the accounts of two scholars of young people and criminality, Anthony Platt and Victor Bailey, help support this thesis.

Platt's (1969) study of the child-saving movement in the USA in the late nineteenth century was concerned with the ways in which certain types of youthful behaviour came to be defined as 'delinquent' and argued that 'the child savers . . . brought attention to . . . and, in doing so, invented – new categories of youthful behaviour which had been hitherto unappreciated' (1969: 3–4). Platt argues that the movement was related to the changing role of middle-class women who were attempting to rebuild the moral fabric of society. While the changes were of instrumental significance in that they legitimated new career opportunities for these women, they were also symbolic in that they preserved their prestige in a rapidly changing society and institutionalised certain values and ways of life for women, children and the family. Platt characterises the 'child savers' as disinterested reformers because they regarded their cause as a matter of conscience and morality, and not one which would improve their economic or class interests even though their subjective actions contributed to that objective reality.

Bailey (1987) is concerned with developments in juvenile justice during the first half of the twentieth century and reconstructs the social and ideological back-ground of those who promoted reform during that period. He observes how, during the 1920s, a consensus of opinion emerged around the issue of the causes of young offending, which brought together 'social workers, magistrates, penal reform groups, associations of penal practitioners, and the administrators and inspectors of the Children's Branch' who collectively favoured 'the social conception of delinquency' (Bailey, 1987: 66). This consensus for reform could nevertheless be located in deeper socio-political conditions, not least the new welfarist brand of liberalism which had flourished at the turn of the twentieth century. This, Bailey observes, was a generation of middle-class men and women whose ideas had

formed the social policies of the Liberal governments of 1906–1914 and they therefore inherited not only a social philosophy which recognised social inequalities
and their structural roots, but also a political and legal framework in which the
scope for state intervention and administrative action was considerably extended
and which again we should observe contributed almost subconsciously to the
increasing disciplinary control matrix.

The left realist hybrid model accepts that all the above accounts – radical conflict,
orthodox social progress, carceral surveillance society – are at least partially
legitimate for there were, and indeed *are*, a multitude of motivations for both the
implementation and willing acceptance of the increasing surveillance and tutelage
of young people. The moralising mission of the entrepreneurial philanthropists and
the reforming zeal of the liberal politician and administrator, invariably implemented with the best of humanitarian intentions, were consistently compatible with
those of the mill and mine-owners and a government which wanted a fit healthy
fighting force, but, at the same time, also coincided with the ever increasing
enthusiasm for self-betterment among the great majority of the working class that
has been described from differing sociological perspectives as 'embourgeoisement'
(Goldthorpe, 1968–1969) and 'the civilising process' (Elias, 1978, 1982). Those
who were resistant to that moralising and disciplinary mission – the 'rough working
class' of the Victorian era – have subsequently been reinvented in academic and
popular discourse as the socially excluded underclass of contemporary society, with
the moral panics of today a reflection of those of the past and demands for action
remarkably similar. These theoretical observations should be considered in the
context of the following history of the development of the juvenile, and latterly
youth, justice system in England and Wales which while substantively different
from that in other modern societies nevertheless shares significant themes.

From justice to welfarism

The story of the development of the juvenile justice system is – for at least the first
three-quarters of the twentieth century – one of a far from smooth linear transition
from a predominantly justice/punishment to a welfare/treatment model response
and it is a tale told in the context of repeated concerns and panics from widespread
groups throughout society about the extent of offending by children and young
people, accompanied with simultaneous demands that something should be done
about this perceived problem.

It should be noted that before the nineteenth century there was no special
provision for young offenders who were treated no differently from adults and
could be sent to adult prisons, hanged or transported to the colonies. Children were
considered to be adult above the age of 7 and were held criminally responsible for
their behaviour. Thus, on one day alone in 1814 five children between the ages of
8 and 12 were hanged alongside each other for offences of petty theft (Pinchbeck
and Hewitt, 1973: 352) and this event was by no means exceptional. Moreover,
this harsh treatment of juveniles made perfect sense in a world where childhood
was not viewed as a particularly important stage of life in the eyes of working-

class parents, employers or the law. During the nineteenth century children nevertheless gradually emerged as a distinctive category in relation to both criminal behaviour and legal control with the nature of the response initially located predominantly in the context of the then contemporary justice/punishment model orthodoxy summarised in Table 7.1.

The early stages of a welfare/treatment model approach, which was to prioritise health and social care in the lives of children and young people, were starting to emerge and a tension between this and the justice/punishment model was to become widely apparent from that time onwards. Voluntary reformatories had been opened by the Philanthropic Society in the early part of the century but it was the Youth Offenders Act 1854 which introduced state-recognised Reformatories and Certified Industrial Schools which came to replace prison terms for many young offenders and provide a basic education plus a trade. The Industrial Schools Act 1857 later introduced better provision for the care and education of vagrant, destitute and disorderly children perceived to be in danger of becoming criminals (Newburn, 1995), while the Education Act 1870 led to the establishment of industrial day schools and truant schools at the same time as introducing universal elementary state education for all children. In the language of the twenty-first century, these were early attempts to integrate or reintegrate children and young people into ways of life or lifestyles that were perceived to be appropriate by influential groups in society.

There were again wide-ranging motivations for the introduction of this early arguably welfarist legislation and, in particular, there was pressure from politically powerful religious, philanthropic and penal-reform groups apprehensive about the brutality of conditions in adult prisons and their impact on young offenders. However, by the end of the century these concerns had spread well beyond these groups to the wider general public, not least because of media campaigns which had been encouraged by the commonly observable extensive social disorganisation and drunkenness, while there were simultaneous anxieties about the declining standard of parenting and family socialisation (Davis, 1990; Humphries, 1981; Pearson, 1983).

The Summary Jurisdiction Act 1879 was to go further and reduce both the number of children held in prison – who were now to be tried by magistrates

Table 7.1 The justice/punishment model of youth justice

- Based on the rational actor model of criminal behaviour notions that young people have free will and choose to offend in the same way that adults do.
- Young offenders should thus be held responsible for their actions and be punished if they transgress.
- The level of punishment inflicted should be commensurate with the seriousness of the offence committed.
- Offenders should be punished for the offence committed and not on the basis of who they or their families are or the social conditions in which they live.

Source: Adapted from Hopkins Burke, 2008: 49

– and the penalties available to the judiciary; meanwhile the Gladstone and Lushington Committees were subsequently to introduce alternatives to custody. The Children Act 1908 established specialised juvenile courts which were given powers to deal with both the delinquent and destitute[2] and these involved a mixture of welfare and punitive strategies but, at the same time, remained essentially criminal courts and the idea that the child offender was a wrongdoer was to continue to be the dominant orthodoxy for much of the twentieth century (Gelsthorpe and Morris, 1994).

Platt (1969) has pertinently observed that the arrival of the juvenile court was to herald the appearance of another social construction of youthful humanity, the 'juvenile delinquent'. Previously, there had been simply 'young offenders', to whom varying degrees of responsibility could be ascribed in accordance with the dominant rational actor model philosophy. Juvenile delinquents, in contrast, and in accordance with the newly emerging predestined actor model orthodoxy, were significantly perceived to be different from their non-delinquent peers. Pitts (2003: 73) observes that:

> It was not simply that they behaved differently: they were different in the way they thought, how they felt, in the beliefs and attitudes they held and, indeed, in their very biogenetic constitution. Thus, the juvenile court did not simply assume powers to sentence children and young people to a new, distinctively juvenile, range of penalties and facilities; it also shaped its disposals in accordance with the relationships the new sciences of human behaviour had proposed between the present demeanour of the delinquent and their future needs.

Platt (1969) observes that we need to look beyond the apparently neutral rhetoric of benevolence and the concerns of the 'child savers' for 'salvation', 'innocence' and 'protection' that were undoubtedly the motivations of the middle-class women involved and which can be clearly conceptualised in the context of the orthodox social progress model of criminal justice development. The ideologies of welfare were to enable constant and pervasive supervision of children and young people and allow the state to intervene directly into any element of working-class life that was considered to be immoral or unruly. Thus, regardless of the benevolent original intentions of the child savers, the outcome was that troublesome adolescents could now be defined by the new 'professional' bodies of experts – psychiatrists, social workers and the philanthropists – as 'sick' or 'pathological' with the result that young people came to be imprisoned 'for their own good', had very limited legal rights and were subjected to lengthy periods of incarceration. Morris and Giller (1987: 32) note that most reforms were either implicitly or explicitly coercive and that in reality 'humanitarianism and coercion are essentially two sides of the same coin'.

The Probation of Offenders Act 1907 was to introduce community supervision as an alternative to custody and the following year the use of imprisonment for children under the age of 14 came to an end.[3] The Prevention of Crime Act 1908 established specialised detention centres where rigid discipline and work training could be provided in a secure environment with the first of these at Borstal in Kent, which gave its name to numerous similar establishments. There was a mixture of discipline and training in these establishments with several placing an emphasis on education and later a few were to adopt a therapeutic approach (Hood, 1965).

The welfare/treatment model, which is summarised below in Table 7.2, was becoming increasingly influential and this is demonstrated by the Children and Young Persons Act 1933 which increased the age of criminal responsibility from 7 to 8 and directed magistrates to take primary account of the welfare of the child. This latter clause heralded an important victory for the welfare lobby but highlighted a fundamental contradiction in youth justice policy that has continued to the present day. The justice/punishment and welfare/treatment models appear to be inevitably incompatible, with the former emphasising full criminal responsibility and punishment and the latter the needs of the individual child and welfare treatment.

Crime levels among young people increased throughout the 1930s and accelerated throughout the Second World War where seismic social conditions were identified as being highly significant in the formative years of a whole generation (Newburn, 2002). The 'black-out', evacuation, the closure of schools and youth clubs, were all blamed for much delinquency and this notion of family disruption or dysfunction has remained a dominant approach to explaining criminality among young people (Bailey, 1987).

The Criminal Justice Act 1948 was introduced in the aftermath of the war and in the context of the post-war Labour government and the creation of the welfare state. The legislation placed a number of restrictions on the use of imprisonment but at the same time it introduced detention centres and attendance centres which appeared to reflect a more punitive approach (Morris and Giller, 1987), but concern about the 'welfare' of juveniles was also evident and the legislation sought to end the placement of neglected children in approved schools alongside offenders. Local authority children's departments were also established with their own resources for residential care and trained staff to oversee fostering and adoption (Harris and Webb, 1987).

Table 7.2 The welfare/treatment model of youth justice

- Based on the predestined actor model of criminal behaviour notions that young people, like adults, are not fully responsible for their actions because of biological, psychological and social factors.
- Treatment and rehabilitation is thus advocated rather than punishment.
- Cases are to be preferably dealt with by welfare professionals and experts and not the criminal justice system.
- Later variants of the model recommend limited or non-intervention in accordance with the principles of the victimised actor model of criminal behaviour.

Source: Adapted from Hopkins Burke, 2008: 51

Pitts (2003) observes that the reforms of 1907/1908 had established the right of young offenders to be dealt with differently from adults while the reforms of 1933 and 1948 were concerned with elaborating the nature of that difference. The new political consensus favoured the prescriptions of the welfare/treatment model and because the 'welfare' of young offenders was considered to be paramount it was proposed that the issue should be dealt with, wherever possible, by experts in the care and protection of children and young people. There was, however, resistance to this shift in youth justice emphasis from Conservative politicians, senior police officers, magistrates and judges, who wished to retain a strong element of retribution in the youth justice system and who favoured the prescriptions of the justice/punishment model.

Bailey (1987) nevertheless observes the ambiguities of welfarism itself and it is here possible to identify the beginnings of the progressive critique that was to become so significant during the 1970s and early 1980s. The 'social conception of delinquency' which had become so influential during the inter-war period had made good sense to the many administrators and reformers with experience of boys' club or settlement work. From this perspective offending behaviour was seen as a symptom of wider social and personal conditions, in particular, weak parental control, poor character-training and a lack of opportunity. Furthermore, such explanations suggested practical solutions to the problem – a change of environment, exercises in self-control, occupational training, or the personal influence of suitable adult role-models – all of which could be provided through an improved Borstal system and probation services. In themselves, a series of explanations, justifications and solutions that were in future years to encourage periodic crackdowns on wayward youth and the introduction of 'short, sharp, shocks' to direct them back to the path of righteousness.

The argument between the proponents of two apparently incompatible models of intervention, the justice/punishment and the welfare/treatment models, was to continue into a post-war period characterised by a constant rise in recorded youth crime and where it was increasingly suggested that the approved school system was unable to cope with some of the hardened young offenders that were appearing before the courts (Newburn, 1995).

The Ingleby Report 1960 focused on the perceived conflict between the judicial and welfare functions of the juvenile court and proposed an immediate increase in the age of criminal responsibility from 8 to 12 with only welfare proceedings brought below that age (Morris and Giller, 1987). The subsequent Children and Young Persons Act 1963 increased the age of criminal responsibility to 10 as a compromise.

These debates were central to the introduction of the Children and Young Persons Act 1969 which advocated a rise in the age of criminal responsibility to 14 and proposed alternatives to detention in the guise of treatment, non-criminal care proceedings and care orders. Diversion was emphasised and it was proposed that all offenders under 14 should be dealt with via care and protection, rather than criminal justice proceedings. The police were encouraged to use cautions and only refer juveniles to court as a last resort following consultation with the social services. The expanding role of the social worker was reflected in the provision for care orders and it was to be they rather than magistrates who would make the key decision as to whether the young person would be sent to a residential institution or left at home.

The Children and Young Persons Act 1969 was proclaimed by its supporters to be a decisive instance of 'decriminalising' penal policy but it was never fully implemented, not least because of the election of a Conservative government in 1970 opposed to the social welfare philosophy of the legislation. Two central features of twentieth-century juvenile justice policy were nevertheless to culminate in this legislation: first, increasing attention was given to assessing the suitability of the family situation of the offender; and second, the distinction between the offender and the neglected child was increasingly obscured. Significantly, the notion of the 'responsible individual' enshrined in the justice/punishment model of intervention was to be replaced by the concept of the 'responsible family' with the outcome being increasing state intervention in family life and socialisation under the guise of protecting children considered to be living in 'undesirable' surroundings.

These welfare/treatment model developments appear at first sight to be progressive and humane but nevertheless came to be criticised from various standpoints right across the political spectrum. Clark (1975) argued, from a radical conflict model perspective, that we were simply witnessing a continuation of dominant nineteenth-century concerns to ensure the stable reproduction of future generations of labour power. The only change was that this process would now be achieved by the reformation of whole families rather than by isolating their 'wayward' children. Morris, Giller, Szwed and Geach (1980) and Taylor, Lacey and Bracken (1979) criticised the treatment philosophy and the family pathology model of the causes of delinquency inherent in the 1969 legislation as simply justifications for exercising greater coercive intervention in the lives of 'delinquent' children and their families. They argued that a social work understanding of delinquency, given its dominant grounding in psychoanalytical theories, would only reinforce the principle of individual pathology and ignore the material and social inequality that is inherent in society. Taylor *et al.* (1979), observing that more children came to be incarcerated during the 1970s than at any time previously, argued that the rights of children would be better upheld by returning to principles of eighteenth-century liberal criminal justice. It was argued that a welfare-orientated juvenile justice system based on the discretion of social work and medical 'experts' erodes the rights of children to natural justice.

In some respects such arguments mark a return to the early nineteenth-century rational actor principles of viewing the juvenile as a young adult and, from this perspective, it is argued that children are the best judges of their own interests and should be free to exercise their own choice from the age of 10 years on. Such legalistic arguments for the concept of 'juvenile responsibility for law-breaking' were also ideologically effective in the arguments for order and control promoted by the Conservative government that came to power in 1979.

Youth justice and populist Conservatism

The Conservative government elected in 1979 had promoted itself as being prepared to take a vigorous stance against crime. Conservative intellectual Sir Keith Joseph made explicit reference to the need to reject 'fashionable socialist opinion' and in particular focused his attention on a perceived need to amend the Children and Young Persons Act 1969. The outgoing Labour government was depicted as being anti-police, condoning law-breaking, and as having ineffective policies for crime control. In short, they were seen as being soft on crime. After the election, the Home Secretary expanded places in detention centres for what were referred to as 'young thugs' and a regime of 'short, sharp, shocks' was introduced. A subsequent White Paper, Young Offenders (Home Office, 1980), and the resulting legislation, the Criminal Justice Act 1982, attacked the welfare approach of the Children and Young Persons Act 1969 and there was a significant move away from predestined actor notions of treatment and lack of personal responsibility with a return to rational actor notions of punishment and individual and parental responsibility. In accordance with this rediscovery of the rational actor model, there was also a significant move away from executive decision-making (social workers) and a return to judicial decision-making (courts) and away from the belief in the 'child in need' to what Tutt (1981) termed 'the rediscovery of the delinquent'. The Criminal Justice Act 1982 was nevertheless 'not an unremittingly punitive statute' (Cavadino and Dignan, 1997) for it essentially introduced restrictions on the use of custody for all those under 21 and this, in itself, was an indication of the apparent ambiguity of Conservative government youth justice policy and its outcomes during the following years.

Thus, juvenile justice policy introduced by the populist Conservatives during the period 1979–1997 appears at first sight to be founded on incompatible contradictions and inconsistencies. The Criminal Justice Act 1991 was to espouse an 'anti-custody' ethos, while the government was subsequently to announce the introduction of 'new' secure training units in 1993 and the Criminal Justice and Public Order Act 1994 introduced new tougher sentences for young offenders. Some argued that these apparently contradictory measures were the response of a government which had lost confidence in the ability of the 'experts' to find solutions to the problem of youth offending and was merely reacting to crises as they arose. The situation was nonetheless more ambiguous.

During the 1980s, the 'welfare' approach to youth justice was to come under increasing attack, not just from the right-wing political, law-and-order lobby influenced by 'right realist' criminological thinking and the rediscovery of the rational actor model, but also from proponents of a 'progressive' 'back to justice' policy. In particular, faith in the ability of the social worker to diagnose the causes of delinquency and to treat these with non-punitive methods was increasingly questioned by these 'progressives'. Empirical justification came with the publication of Robert Martinson's (1974) influential paper, which purported to show that rehabilitation programmes in prison simply 'do not work', and, in doing so, persuaded a lot of influential people that the whole rationale for the existence of welfare-oriented intervention strategies was questionable. Moreover, the discretion of social work judgements was criticised as a form of arbitrary power with many young people observed to be the subject of apparently non-accountable state procedures, with their liberty often unjustifiably denied (Davies, 1982). It was further argued that the investigation of social background is an imposition and social work involvement not only preserves explanations of individual pathology but also undermines the right to natural justice. Such an approach, it was now argued, might place the child or young person in double jeopardy and unintentionally accelerate movement up the tariff.

With the experience of the 1970s, in which the numbers of custodial sentences had increased dramatically in the aftermath of the implementation of an at least nominal welfare treatment system, through a process of net-widening, where more and more children and young people were recruited into the system at a younger age, ostensibly for their own good, the progressive new justice proponents argued for a return to notions of 'due process' and 'just deserts' along with moves to decriminalise certain (for example, victimless) offences and a general shift towards using alternatives to custody (Rutherford, 1978). As Taylor, Lacey and Bracken (1979: 22–23) observed:

> Under English law the child enjoys very few of the rights taken for granted by adults under the principles of natural justice. The law's reference to the child's 'best interests' reflects the benevolent paternalism of its approach. Essentially as far as the courts are concerned, the 'best interests' principle empowers social workers, psychologists, psychiatrists and others to define on the basis of their opinions what is good for the child. . . . (The law) does not require that the experts should substantiate their opinions or prove to the court that any course of action they propose will be more effective in promoting the best interests of the child than those taken by the parent or by the child acting on his own behalf. . . . A child may find that his/her arguments against being committed to care are perceived as evidence of their need for treatment, as a sign, for example, that they have 'authority problems'.

A justice/punishment model solution was now proposed and there was to be a return to the use of determinate sentences based on the seriousness of the offence rather than the profile of individual offenders. The Criminal Justice Act 1982 was consequently to introduce criteria to restrict the use of both care proceedings and custodial orders while juveniles were now to be legally represented. Custodial orders were to be made only where it could be established that the offender had failed to respond to non-custodial measures, for the protection of the public, or where the offence was serious. At first sight, there appeared to be little consistency in the use of these strategies. Thus, the legislation had been clearly introduced with the objective of helping to 'restore the rule of law' (Pitts, 1996) but had, at the same time, placed restrictions on the use of custody. This apparent inconsistency can be nonetheless explained with reference to a legislative strategy which Bottoms (1974) terms 'bifurcation' and which involves separating the response to serious offenders from that of minor offenders with the outcome being that the former are dealt with much more harshly than the latter who are considered to be relatively non-problematic.

The late 1980s was proclaimed by some to be a 'successful revolution' in juvenile justice policy not least because of the significant reduction in the numbers of young people and juveniles incarcerated during the period (Hagell and Newburn, 1994). A crucial factor in this reduction was projects developed as alternatives to custody within the DHSS Intermediate Treatment Initiative where local authority practitioners were required to evolve a 'new style of working' with far less focus on the emotional and social care needs of offenders and more on the nature of the offence. Magistrates were consequently persuaded that intermediate treatment schemes were no longer 'soft options', but 'high tariff' criminal justice disposals implemented by inter-agency juvenile panels comprising representatives from the welfare agencies, the youth service, police and education departments.

Perhaps the most notable development during this period was the repeatedly affirmed government commitment to community-based diversionary schemes. Diversion had increased in the years following the introduction of the Children and Young Persons Act 1969 but by the 1980s there was growing recognition that custody was extremely expensive with the vast majority of those released re-offending. Treatment in the community was no less effective and certainly far cheaper (Cavadino and Dignan, 1997).

Pratt (1989) now proposed that the justice/punishment and welfare/treatment models of juvenile justice intervention had been superseded by an apparently depoliticised 'corporatist model' in which a partnership of social workers, youth workers, health workers, police and magistrates cooperated to produce a cost-effective mechanism for the processing of adjudicated offenders. The process was furthered by the Criminal Justice Act 1991 which sought to provide a national consistency to local initiatives and expand the use of diversionary strategies for juveniles to include young adults. The anti-custody ethos was justified with the promise of more rigorous community disposals which were not alternatives to custody but disposals in their own right.

'Punishment in the Community' was now the favoured option but this required a significant change in focus for the juvenile court and the practices of probation and social work agencies. For probation it meant a shift in emphasis away from the traditional approach of 'advise, assist and befriend' the offender towards tightening up the conditions of community supervision and community service work. For the court system it meant the abolition of the juvenile court (which had previously dealt with criminal *and* care cases) and the creation of separate youth courts and family courts to deal with these issues separately.

The impact of these decarcerative measures was nonetheless shown to be fragile when, in 1991, the Home Secretary hastily established a new offence of 'aggravated vehicle taking' carrying a maximum five-year sentence. Two years later, the establishment of 'new' secure training units was announced amidst a furore of media and political debate about a small group of 'persistent young offenders', 'bail bandits'[4] and to appease the public outcry following the James Bulger case where two 10-year-old children were found guilty of abducting and killing a two-year-old child. Prime Minister John Major insisted that 'we should understand a little less and condemn a little more' and comments from police, judges and MPs that official figures showing a decrease in juvenile offending were quite simply 'wrong' also signalled a renewed tough stance on the part of government and a repoliticisation of youth crime (Pitts, 2003). Within weeks of becoming Home Secretary in 1993, Michael Howard commenced a process of revising juvenile justice policy and secure training centres were to be rethought along the lines of US-style 'boot camps' to provide tougher and more physically demanding regimes aimed at knocking criminal tendencies out of young offenders.

The notion that Conservative juvenile justice policies had amounted to a 'successful revolution' is worthy of closer examination. There was certainly no lack of enthusiasm for the apprehension and incapacitation of offenders and an acknowledgment that the latter need not mean imprisonment. Perhaps the most significant component was the policy and legislative strategy of 'bifurcation' (Bottoms, 1977), identified above, where a twin-track approach to justice had sought to identify those young people who had briefly stumbled in the pursuit of an 'upward option' of increased commitment to education and training (Cohen, 1972) and provide them with the impetus and support to overcome their offending behaviour. The persistent and more serious offenders considered to be worthy of a punitive intervention could easily be identified as primarily belonging to those sections of working-class youth who had failed to take advantage of the economic changes that had transformed Britain during the previous 20 years. This group had taken an ostensibly 'downward option' of ignoring the need for improved education and training (Cohen, 1972) and had drifted into a non-skilled, unemployable underclass location. At the peak of industrial modernity there had been informal mechanisms whereby these offenders had been reintegrated back into the fold as Pitts (1996: 280) pertinently observes:

> In the 1960s it was not uncommon for young people in trouble to avoid a custodial sentence by joining the armed forces. For their part, probation officers would often cite the rehabilitative powers of 'going steady', which usually involved getting a 'steady' job in order to 'save up to get married' and 'put a few things away in the bottom drawer'.

Excluded now from legitimate employment opportunities and presenting themselves as unattractive propositions to young women as long-term partners these young men found themselves 'frozen in a state of persistent adolescence' (Pitts, 1996: 281) with important implications for their involvement in crime because the evidence suggests that 'growing up' means growing out of crime (Rutherford, 1992). Stripped of legitimate access to adulthood these young men now found themselves trapped in a limbo world somewhere between childhood and adulthood long after the 'developmental tasks' of adolescence had been completed (Pitts, 1996). Having failed to heed the warnings provided by the welfare and juvenile justice system persistent young offenders were to be targeted with a much harsher intervention than those considered non-problematic. The new multi-agency forum managerialism was simply about identifying the two categories of offender and setting in motion a twin-track response.

The notion of a new political consensus is more suspect. Conservatives and Labour were in agreement over the need for realism but there was a substantial difference in their interpretation of that reality (Hopkins Burke, 1999c). Conservative juvenile justice policy had been for many young people particularly strong on 'the stick' but rather weak on 'the carrot'. There were many complexities and ambiguities to government policy during the period and the closely connected twin concerns of political expediency and pragmatism had led repeatedly to apparent changes in direction but in summary the perceived solution to the problem of offending by children and young people was to catch more of them and send out a clear message that they would get caught and punished. Significantly, the latter did not have to mean incarceration or, indeed, serious punishment, nor did they all have to be treated the same.

The purpose of 'the stick' was to make young people take responsibility for their actions and become fully aware of the consequences of any illegal transgressions. The latter group of persistent and more serious offenders were, however, seriously over-represented among the ranks of those sections of working-class youth who had drifted into a non-skilled, unemployable underclass location. For a fundamental outcome of *laissez-faire* economic and social policy during that period had been the creation of a socially excluded underclass. Youth justice policies, in particular, and welfare policies, in general, had, at best, done nothing to alleviate that situation, and, at worst, had managed to exacerbate the problem. This author has elsewhere termed this the 'excluded tutelage' model of youth justice (Hopkins Burke, 1999c, 2008) and it is summarised below in Table 7.3.

Vivian Stern of NACRO, writing in 1996, observes that while other European countries favoured the reintegration of offenders back into the community and saw this as central to social and criminal justice policy, Home Office press releases and Conservative government ministers 'use the language of conflict, contempt, and

Table 7.3 The excluded tutelage model of youth justice

- The solution to the youth crime problem involves catching more young offenders in order to deter others.
- This involves a twin-track approach to justice that differentiates between: those who have briefly transgressed and can be provided with the support to overcome their offending behaviour, and the more persistent and serious offenders considered more worthy of a punitive intervention.
- The latter group predominantly consists of members of those sections of working-class youth who have drifted into a non-skilled, unemployable underclass location.
- There is a failure of government non-interventionist socio-economic policies to significantly address the social exclusion of this group of young people.

Source: Adapted from Hopkins Burke, 2008: 78

hatred . . . doing good is a term of derision, and seeking to help offenders means that you do not care about the pain and suffering of victims' (Stern, cited in Brown, 1998: 74). It was the intention of New Labour criminal justice and social policy to seek the reintegration of this socially excluded underclass back into mainstream inclusive society.

Youth justice and New Labour

Central to New Labour political thought is the 'third way' (Giddens, 1998) political philosophy of communitarianism which emerged in the USA during the 1980s in response to what its proponents perceived to be the limitations in liberal theory and practice.[5] From this perspective it is argued that the individual rights vigorously promoted by traditional liberals should be balanced with social responsibilities not least because autonomous individual selves do not exist in isolation but are shaped by the values and cultures of the communities in which they live (see Emanuel, 1991; Glendon, 1991; Etzioni, 1993, 1995a). In a pamphlet written shortly after he became Prime Minister of the UK, Tony Blair (1998: 4) demonstrated his communitarian or 'third way' credentials:

> We all depend on collective goods for our independence; and all our lives are enriched – or impoverished – by the communities to which we belong. . . . A key challenge of progressive politics is to use the state as an enabling force, protecting effective communities and voluntary organisations and encouraging their growth to tackle new needs, in partnership as appropriate.

The most familiar and resonant of the 'abstract slogans' used by Blair in the promotion of the importance of community was the idea that rights entail responsibilities and this is taken from the influential work of Etzioni (1993). In contrast to the traditional liberal idea that members of a society may be simply entitled to unconditional benefits or services, communitarians propose that the responsibility to care for each individual should be seen as lying first and foremost with the individual themselves. For Blair and his sociological guru Anthony Giddens (1998) the concept of community is invoked very deliberately as residing in *civil society*: in lived social relations, and in 'commonsense' conceptions of our civic obligations. The 'third way' is presented as avoiding the full-on atomistic egotistical individualism entailed by the Thatcherite maxim that 'there is no such thing as society', and on the other hand, the traditional social-democratic recourse to a strong state as the tool by which to realise the aims of social justice, most notably that of economic equality. For Blair, 'the grievous 20th century error of the fundamentalist Left was the belief that the state could replace civil society and thereby advance freedom' (Blair, 1998: 4). The state has a role to play, he readily accepts, but as a facilitator, rather than a guarantor, of a flourishing community life.

Dissenters have nevertheless observed that the implementation of the New Labour agenda in fact seemed to take rather a different course. Its character appeared to be rather more authoritarian – and thus centred more on the usage of the state apparatus to deliver particular outcomes – than is suggested by the rhetorical appeal to the relatively autonomous powers of civil society to deliver progress by itself (see Driver and Martell, 1997; Jordan, 1998).

The communitarian credentials of the New Labour government elected in 1997 could be clearly identified in its flagship criminal justice legislation, the Crime and Disorder Act 1998, which established the Youth Justice Board (YJB) and the contemporary youth justice system. The latter brought together staff and wider resources from the police, social services, the Probation Service, education and health, in the delivery of youth justice services, in Youth Offending Teams (YOTs), with the principal statutory aim of preventing offending by young people.

Two major criminological theoretical influences on New Labour youth justice policy can be identified as being left realism and reintegrative shaming. The former has its origins in the election of the populist Conservatives in 1979 and the subsequent response of a group of radical criminologists on the political left in the UK who were concerned that the debate on crime control had been lost to the political right. These 'new realists' argued for an approach to crime that recognised both the reality and impact of crime – not least on poor people who were significantly over-represented among the ranks of its victims – but which also addressed the socio-economic context in which it occurred (Lea and Young, 1984). Inasmuch as the 'right realists' – who had provided at least a partial intellectual justification for the new conservative criminal justice perspective – had focused their efforts on targeting the offender in traditional rational actor fashion, 'left realists', with their intellectual foundations in both the predestined actor and victimised actor traditions, emphasised the need for a 'balance of intervention' and willingness to take seriously and consider significant elements of all theoretical perspectives (Hopkins Burke, 2009) and thus provided the foundations of the left realist hybrid model of criminal justice development.

The significance of left realism can be summarised briefly for the purposes of our discussion here: first, there is recognition of the necessity and desirability of offenders taking responsibility for their actions, and second, it is acknowledged that account must be taken of the circumstances in which the crime took place. As we have seen, since the beginning of a distinctive juvenile justice response in the mid-nineteenth century there had always been a tension between the apparently incompatible polar opposites of the justice/punishment and welfare/treatment models of intervention. The contemporary youth justice system was consequently introduced with the intention of developing a model of intervention which addresses both justice and welfare issues and it is a generic criminological approach that was to become popularised by the oft quoted sound-bite of Tony Blair, made when he was Shadow Home Secretary in 1994, 'tough on crime, tough on the causes of crime' (Hopkins Burke, 2008).

John Braithwaite (1989) provides a radical reinterpretation and reworking of the labelling theory tradition with his notion of reintegrative shaming. He argues that Western societies have a long established tradition of *negative shaming*, where young offenders become social outcasts, and consequently turn to others sharing their plight for succour and support, with the inevitable ultimate outcome, we might observe, being the creation in contemporary socio-economic conditions of a criminally susceptible underclass living outside respectable society (Hopkins Burke, 2008). In contrast, his notion of *reintegrative shaming* involves a closely linked two-part strategy for constructive intervention in the life of the offender. First, the offending activities of the individual are shamed with some form of reparation made to the victim and the community, while some form of punishment is administered where this is felt to be appropriate, but, second, rituals of reintegration are subsequently undertaken to restore the individual to an inclusive society which values their role and person. This theoretical perspective can be summarised by the notion 'shame the act, not the person' which has become a dominant orthodoxy in middle-class child socialisation strategies.

Reintegrative strategies are usually termed restorative justice and have become central to the contemporary youth justice system in the UK. These *de facto* communitarian-style interventions seek to balance the concerns and interests of victim and community with the need to reintegrate the young person into society and thus enable all parties with a stake in the justice process to participate (Marshall, 1999). These interventions have been shown to be effective elsewhere in modern societies by reducing reoffending by young people (Sherman and Strang, 1997; Nugent *et al.*, 1999; Street, 2000), especially by violent young people (Strang, 2000), and have provided greater satisfaction for victims (Wynne and Brown, 1998; Umbreit and Roberts, 1996; Strang, 2001). Moreover, compliance with reparation has been found to be generally higher in restorative schemes than through the courts (Marshall, 1999).

It is this notion of reintegration back into the community that enables us to explain the approach to youth justice favoured by New Labour, as part of the generic social policy strategy, and which enables us to distinguish its policies from those of its populist Conservative predecessors, and this author has previously termed this the 'reintegrative tutelage' model of youth justice, which is summarised in Table 7.4 below.

Table 7.4 The reintegrative tutelage model of youth justice

- Based on the left realist notion that crime requires a comprehensive solution and there must be a 'balance of intervention' which tackles both the offence and the social context in which it occurred.
- Young people who commit crime must face up to the consequences of their actions and take responsibility for them (rational actor model of criminal behaviour).
- An effective intervention needs to address the causes of offending as well as punishing the offender (predestined actor model).
- It is part of a wider set of educative and welfare strategies that seek to reintegrate socially and economically sections of society.

Source: Adapted from Hopkins Burke, 2008: 79

Reflections on the management of contemporary youth crime

It is evident from self-report studies that have been undertaken in recent years that most young people in contemporary society are not involved in criminality of any kind (Communities that Care, 2002; Flood-Page *et al.*, 2000; MORI, 2001, 2002, 2003), while the great majority of those who do offend continue to 'grow out' of it (MORI, 2003) regardless of the virtually continuous 'moral panics' that suggest the very opposite to be true. The evidence we have of the relationship between young people and criminality in the contemporary world would thus seem to contradict popular perceptions. Indeed, if we consider the notion of the 'fear of crime'[6] from the perspective of the young person, what might be the most worrying, if perhaps ironic, observation about the crime statistics, is that young people are the group more likely to be victims of crime (Furlong and Cartmel, 1997; Home Office, 2002). Yet, as NACRO (2001) has observed, British public perceptions tend to overstate the extent of crime attributable to young people: thus whilst 28 per cent believe that young people are responsible for more than half of all offences and a further 55 per cent believe that responsibility for crime is shared equally between adults and children, in fact at the beginning of the millennium, 76 per cent of detected crime was committed by persons over the age of 18, and those over 21 were responsible for almost 60 per cent. Furthermore, to locate these findings in their proper context, trend data from the British Crime Survey shows quite clearly that offending by young people is significantly, and incrementally, in decline (Hopkins Burke, 2008).

It is also significant that many young people do not appear to possess a liberal 'let them grow out of it' attitude to the criminal behaviour of their peers. The left realist hybrid model of criminal justice development recognises our material interests in the creation of the social control matrix and crucially among those who wish to see a rigorous intervention in the lives of those socially excluded young people who are over-represented among the numbers of persistent offenders are both *ourselves* as parents and perhaps more importantly our children themselves. It is the latter who want protection from what they widely perceive to be the dangerous threatening elements in their age group. Thus, a survey conducted by IPO-MORI for the Youth Justice Board showed that 60 per cent of young people between 10 and 17 years of age wanted to see more police on the beat as the best way to protect them from becoming a victim of crime at the hands of other young people while 38 per cent called for harsher punishments for those in their age group who offend (Hopkins Burke, 2008).

The decline in youth crime reflects a similar decrease in crime overall in society (Young, 1999) and the available evidence suggests that these changes were in progress before the introduction of the contemporary youth justice system and it is difficult to disentangle the possible causes and the impact of particular policies. Hopkins Burke (2008) nevertheless observes the real possibility that increasing numbers of young people have simply desisted from involvement in offending behaviour in recent years because it is no longer a 'cool' or rational choice in a changed socio-economic context where the only hope of legitimate material success is the adoption of an 'upward' strategy of educational attainment and the pursuit of careers and where the possession of a criminal record is a significant if not insurmountable obstacle.

Improved education opportunities and provision was clearly a significant cornerstone of the New Labour 'reintegrative tutelage' project but taking advantage of these opportunities has been problematic for many young people and this includes those not necessarily members of a socially excluded underclass. Fergusson *et al.* (2000) argue that contemporary 'quasi-market' systems actively encourage instability in the trajectories of a substantial minority of young people in pursuit of post-age-16 education and training. Powerful pressures are generated which force young people, who are often ill-informed and unable to identify or pursue a preferred option, to make particular rational choices while the market draws them into particular modes of participation. The outcome is often unsuitable options pursued with little commitment and which are short-lived.

In reality, there is a significant blurring of boundaries between many of those who have taken a conscious 'upward solution' of education and career pursuit progression and those who have taken a 'downward solution' of *laissez-faire* non-participation albeit invariably by default (Hopkins Burke, 2008). There is thus a significant group in the middle who are sufficiently motivated to take an upward trajectory but who are unable to acquire sufficient cultural capital[7] to obtain a stable successful economic location. Such young people have significantly weakened social bonds to society (see Hirschi, 1969) and are very much at risk of being absorbed into the readily available and invariably welcoming offending subcultures on the street (Hopkins Burke, 2008).

The New Labour reintegrative tutelage project consequently appears to be established on fragile socio-economic foundations with the economy unable to provide accessible legitimate *sustainable* opportunities for increasingly large sections of young people, particularly in a period of a major economic downturn. In these circumstances, the notion of restorative justice on which the contemporary youth justice strategy is based is equally problematic. Supporters argue that the reinvigoration of community through restorative justice mechanisms can facilitate strong bonds of social control (Strang, 1995) but, as Crawford and Clear (2003) observe, alternative justice systems, through necessity, presuppose an existing degree of informal control upon which mutuality, reciprocity and commitment can be reformed and, problematically, the appeal to revive or transform community has arisen at exactly the time when it appears most absent, when Durkheimian anomie or normlessness is the norm in society (see Durkheim, 1933) and where there is no evidence of a possible improvement in the situation.

Young people have become significant targets in the battle against crime and disorder, social disorganisation, and most notably, antisocial behaviour (Squires and Stephen, 2005). This zealous focus on antisocial behaviour consequently 'signals exclusion and rejection' (Burney, 2005: 2) and instead of empowering and uniting the community, it ostracises certain families or individuals, whilst also pitting the community against the individual, as the former effectively has to police the latter to make sure they comply with the requirements of the Anti-Social Behaviour Order (ASBO).[8] This allows for the development of resentment and division rather than the creation of a strong inclusive community.

Thus, when a young person becomes the subject of an ASBO, the community in which they live may be informed through the local newspapers or through the distribution of leaflets and this publicity includes information regarding the restrictions placed on the activities of the individual and a photographic image, so that the person is easily recognised. Not only is this contrary to the long established principle in youth justice established by the Children and Young Persons Act 1933 which places significant restrictions on the naming of a young person involved in criminal proceedings but it is also a classic example of 'disintegrative, rather than reintegrative, shaming because it does nothing constructive for the individual to ensure their reintegration into the community, but serves to alert a mistrusting community to their misbehaviour and places them under the surveillance of their neighbours' (Fionda, 2005: 243).

Jamieson (2005) observes that the authoritarian penal populism of the 'respect' agenda introduced by New Labour – of which the anti-social behaviour order agenda is such a central part – has a particular electoral appeal to contemporary society. The punitive emphasis of responses to 'anti-social' and criminal behaviour provides an opportunity to reassure the public that firm measures are in place to deal with such behaviours. Jamieson observes that while such interventionist measures may well provide some respite from troublesome behaviour in the short term – and may even serve to deter involvement – the denigration inherent in the derogatory rhetoric and punitive emphasis of that agenda promotes profoundly negative portrayals of the parents, children and young people primarily targeted (Burney, 2005; Squires and Stephen, 2005). The danger of this contemporary approach is that it not only encourages intolerance and hostility, but also serves to obscure the often complex and diverse needs underlying 'parenting deficits' (Etzioni, 1993; Dennis and Erdos, 1992), 'anti-social' and 'criminal' behaviour and is thus entirely incompatible with the aims and objectives of the reintegrative tutelage project.

Conclusions

The development of a juvenile/youth justice system to specifically target the apparently perpetual social problem of criminal behaviour by children and young people can be at least partially explained by the orthodox social progress model of criminal justice development because it is obvious that many – if not virtually all – of those involved in this element of the much wider and ever increasing surveillance and disciplinary project targeted at children and young people throughout the modern period have done so with the best of benevolent and invariably humanitarian intentions, even though there is some dispute over definitions of these terms which seem to change over time. It is nevertheless clear that the increasing development of an intrusive and pervasive child surveillance system has occurred in the final instance in the interests of a capitalist economy (radical conflict model) which has come under increasingly competitive economic pressures in contemporary neo-liberal Western societies. There is a pressing cost-effective demand to both discipline and control a fast-expanding, increasingly superfluous sub-population of society, while the role of the expert, front-line professional and practitioner in the construction of that all-seeing, all-encompassing disciplinary surveillance matrix is also very apparent regardless of any humanitarian intention.

It is nevertheless the left realist hybrid model which demonstrates how we the general public have a socially constructed interest in the control of out-groups of young people – and indeed their elders – who are the contemporary 'folk devils' that apparently threaten our well-being. It is this concern about these groups of young people that has helped to bring about an enforced mechanical social solidarity and not always unknowing commitment to the carceral surveillance society and its containment project.

The commitment of the great majority in society to the mainstream social project and their willing support of the surveillance of supposedly high risk, high threat groups such as disaffected, dispossessed and disillusioned young people will be further considered in the following, final chapter of this book.

8 Conclusions

The future of criminal justice

It has been the central aim of this book to explain from different theoretical perspectives why it is that the various components of the 'criminal justice system', or 'process', function in the way that they do and in whose interest it operates. Four different and invariably competing, but sometimes complementary, models of criminal justice development have been outlined in order to achieve that aim.

The first, the orthodox social progress model, proposes that the development of modern societies, their laws and criminal justice systems, is the product of incremental enlightenment, benevolence and a consensual society, where the great majority of the population share the same core values, and are fairly uncritically accepting of an increasingly progressive humanitarian response to crime and disorder which is widely perceived to be in the interests of everyone. A revisionist variant of the model tells a less idealist account where developments occur as functional solutions to immediate social changes and problems as they arise, but this, nevertheless, remains a liberal model where it is still assumed that things can be improved if we learn the appropriate lessons from history and research.

The second, the radical conflict model, challenges the notion of consensus and recognises, in contrast, a society characterised by conflict where the developing criminal justice system has been used throughout the modern era to successfully support the needs of capitalism by allowing for the continued repression of un-cooperative members of the working class and increasingly other outsider groups while continuing to give the impression that the changes introduced have been fair, humane and progressive. A revisionist variant of this model nevertheless recognises that while the reformers may well have acted out of political self-interest they might have had benevolent motives as well.

The third, the carceral surveillance society model, considers that both the social progress and radical conflict models are too simplistic. While the carceral surveil-lance approach is complementary to the radical conflict model, it is recognised that power is both diffuse and pervasive in society. Agents and experts at all levels of the social world have access to, and control of, significant elements of power, and although this is invariably exercised in the overall interests of the capitalist class in the final analysis, those involved in its application at a local, micro and mezzo level are not always aware of their contribution to the 'grand design'. Indeed, often, as a result of their discretion, independence and relative autonomy in the social world, these agents pose significant challenges to the totality through their control of localised 'expertise' which needs to be overcome, or at least accommodated, to ensure the reproduction of a successful capitalist society.

The fourth, the left realist hybrid model, does not completely dismiss any of the other three models but instead recognises that each has significant strengths and, thus, produces a synthesis of the three, while additionally recognising the interest and collusion of the general public in the creation of the increasingly pervasive socio-control matrix of the carceral society. It is thus observed that since at least the beginning of the modern era the general public has always had a material interest in social progress and such concerns have conveniently coincided with the requirements of capitalist society not least while it has managed to provide them with an incrementally improved standard of living. In short, it is proposed that there are further interests involved in the creation and expansion of the disciplinary control matrix other than those of capitalism and its various agents and these are significantly ours and those of our predecessors. This hybrid model accepts that all of the other accounts offered – social progress, radical conflict and carceral society – are to some extent legitimate for there were and are a multitude of motivations for both implementing and accepting the increasing surveillance and control of a potentially dangerous population on the streets and elsewhere in an increasingly risk-ridden world from which we all require protection.

Chapters 2–7 of this book considered those theories that have sought to explain the various substantive elements of the criminal justice system or process and each of these have also been considered in the context of the four models of criminal justice development.

The second chapter considered those criminological theories that have sought at various times to explain the nature of crime and criminal behaviour during the modern era. Three models of criminal behaviour were identified. The first, the rational actor model, can be broadly conceptualised in the context of the social progress model of criminal justice development and proposes that human beings choose to become involved in criminality because they are rational creatures who calculate the rewards to be obtained from illegality after taking into account the likelihood of getting caught and punished.

The second, the predestined actor model, fundamentally rejects the rational actor emphasis on free will and replaces it with the doctrine of determinism. This model can still be conceptualised in terms of the orthodox social progress model of criminal justice development and indeed many people working within this tradition would consider this to be an issue of neutral science beyond the realms of the political. From this *positivist* standpoint, criminal behaviour is explained in terms of factors, either internal or external to the human being, that cause, or *determine,* people to act in ways over which they have little or no control. The individual is thus in some way predestined to be a criminal.

The third, the victimised actor model, proposes, with increasingly radical variations, that the criminal is in some way the victim of an unjust and unequal society and this clearly can be conceptualised in terms of the radical conflict model of criminal justice development. From this perspective, it is argued that it is the behaviour and activities of the poor and powerless sections of society that are targeted and criminalised while the dubious activities of the rich and powerful are either simply ignored or not even defined as criminal. With reflection, it would nevertheless seem to be increasingly the case that the activities of the rich and powerful are not being ignored in contemporary Western societies which are coming under immense competitive economic pressure from the developing world. In these changed circumstances it is becoming significantly clear that these dubious activities threaten the very fabric of Western-style competitive capitalism.

There followed a discussion of attempts in recent years at theoretical integration where the intention is to identify commonalities in two or more theories in order to produce a synthesis that is superior to any one individual theory. Different integrated theories can be located in the context of any of the models of criminal justice development but in general the intention of developing a more powerful explanatory criminological tool tends to place them predominantly in the context of the apolitical orthodox social progress model.

The third chapter considered the philosophers of law who are concerned with providing a general philosophical analysis of law and legal institutions. Three categories of modernist legal philosophy are identified. The first, analytic jurisprudence, provides an analysis of the essence of law in order to differentiate it from other systems of norms such as ethics. The second, normative jurisprudence, involves the examination of normative, evaluative and otherwise prescriptive issues about the law, such as restrictions on freedom, obligations to obey the law, and justifications for punishment. Both of these categories can be broadly conceptualised in the context of the orthodox social progress model. The third category, critical theories of law, which includes critical legal studies and feminist jurisprudence, can be widely conceptualised in the context of the radical conflict model. Indeed, it is possible to see the incrementally increasing body of legislation which has, in recent years, placed significant restrictions on our freedoms and civil liberties, in the context of the carceral society *and* left realist hybrid models.

Finally, there was a consideration of Islamic jurisprudence, or Sharia law, which is increasingly providing a significant radical challenge to the Western tradition of legal philosophy in contemporary post-industrial societies and indeed, in its more radical forms, modernity itself, although moderate proponents are, in contrast, seeking an accommodation within a pluralist West.

The fourth chapter considered the policing of modern societies and explored the incremental development from the beginnings of the professional police force or service. At first sight, it might appear ostensibly obvious that the history of the public police service can best be explained by the orthodox social progress model but advocates of the radical conflict perspective argue that from the beginning of modernity the emphasis has always been on surveillance, discipline and control of the rough and dangerous working-class elements in the interests of capitalism. It was nevertheless recognised that from the perspective of the carceral surveillance model, policing is both pervasive and insidious throughout contemporary fragmented society. Thus, 'hard' and 'soft' policing styles – and these can involve not only the public police service, but the private security industry and social work agencies – are all part of the contemporary all-seeing multi-agency corporate crime industry. It is, moreover, recognised from a left realist hybrid model perspective that crime and public disorder have always been a real problem for ordinary people and the respectable working class have always required protection from the criminal elements in their midst whether these are termed the 'rough working classes', as in the past, or a socially excluded underclass, as in contemporary society.

The fifth chapter considered the legal process in modern society which has its foundations in the very beginning of modern society, which was to introduce increasingly bureaucratised criminal justice institutions and a rationalised process for responding to criminality. Again, at first sight, it appears that these develop-ments can best be conceptualised in the context of the social progress model but it becomes increasingly apparent that the criminal justice process has a control function in society and there are clearly interest groups involved. Our attention is thus alerted to the radical conflict model and the argument that this progress has occurred in the interests of capitalism, the carceral surveillance society model which recognises the role of apparently neutral agents and experts in introducing these changes and the left realist hybrid model which significantly recognises our interest and collusion in the creation of the increasingly pervasive socio-control matrix.

The sixth chapter discussed the philosophy and theory of punishment in modern societies and again this is located in the context of the four models of criminal justice development. Punishment is viewed by most theorists as being both necessary and just and it is a viewpoint that can be clearly conceptualised in the context of the social progress model, but radical conflict model proponents observe that rules or laws are introduced and enforced ultimately in the interests of the rich and powerful in capitalist society. The carceral society model of course develops that thesis and recognises the multiple ambiguities and diffusion of power in complex societies and the role and material interests of experts and front-line practitioners with professional discretion in the introduction of laws and their enforcement. The left realist hybrid model goes further and recognises the partial validity of each of the other three models but also identifies the interest of the general public in the development of laws and significantly their enforcement.

The seventh chapter considered the development of a separate criminal justice system in modern society to deal with children and young people and it was observed that in order to theorise the establishment of the contemporary system it is essential to locate the discussion in an historical context because the debates, discourses and political solutions that emerged in the past are very similar to those of today. Contemporary notions of childhood and adolescence were thus socially constructed at the outset of industrial modernity and children and their families were subsequently disciplined and controlled not least in the interests of an industrial capitalism which required a fit, healthy, increasingly educated, trained and obedient workforce. Reality was nevertheless again more complex than that proposed by the radical conflict model, while the orthodox social progress perspective which proposes these disciplinary strategies to be the actions of motivated entrepreneurial philanthropists with genuine concerns about poor urban children and young people is, while at least partially correct, also too simplistic.

Many of these philanthropists clearly had little idea of the actual or potential long-term consequences of their actions while, at the same time, there is an identifiable failure to recognise the complexities of power and the outcomes of strategies promoted by agencies that often enjoy autonomy from the political centre and front-line practitioners who often take advantage of considerable discretion. It is the carceral surveillance society model which enables us to make theoretical sense of these developments and the left realist hybrid model which, while accepting the premise that disciplinary strategies are invariably implemented by moral entre-preneurs, professional agents and practitioners who have little idea how their often humble discourse contributes to the grand overall disciplinary control matrix, does, at the same time, significantly recognise that there are other, further, interests involved and these are significantly *ours* and in this context those of *our* prede-cessors. It is, furthermore, a theoretical perspective with particular relevance to the contemporary era.

Criminal justice in an age of moral uncertainty

Increasing doubts began to emerge about the sustainability of the modernist project which had provided the socio-economic and political conditions for the develop-ment of the criminal justice system and process that we have examined in this book during the last decades of the twentieth century. In an increasingly fragmented and diverse social world this is a situation that some have come to refer to as the *post*modern condition (see Lyotard, 1984; but also Baudrillard, 1988; Bauman, 1989, 1991, 1993).

Three significant characteristics can be identified which distinguish the post-modern from the modern. First, there is an aversion to 'metadiscourses' or those grand self-legitimating political or social theories that seek to explain all social phenomena in terms of their body of knowledge and beliefs. Second, there is an awareness of the indeterminacy of knowledge and consequently the impossibility of absolute truth. Third, there is an enthusiasm for eclecticism and variety that has been derived from art, architecture and literature but which has come to have much stronger intellectual reverberations (Hopkins Burke, 2009).

In the crucial interlinked spheres of the economy, the political system and culture, increasingly diverse and fragmented social structures began to emerge. Thus, in the sphere of economics there was rejection of the mass production-line technology of high modernism in favour of both flexible working patterns and a more compliant labour force, which, in turn, involved a weakening of trade unions, greater reliance on peripheral and secondary labour markets, the development of a low-paid and part-time, often female, labour force, and the shift towards a service, rather than manufacturing, economy. On the side of capital-owning and controlling interests, there was a greater emphasis on enterprise and entrepre-neurialism, corporate restructuring and the growth of small businesses acting as subcontractors to larger firms.

In the political sphere, the postmodern condition is complex and difficult to categorise in traditional terms but the diversity of interests that have become apparent in Western societies has placed strains on conventional representative democratic systems with the inability of long-standing political parties to represent myriad interest groups as diverse as major industrialists and financiers, small business proprietors, the unemployed and dispossessed, wide-ranging gender and sexual preference interests, environmentalists and the homeless.

Modernity was essentially an era characterised by moral certainty where there was a confidence in the explanatory power of grand social and political theories to solve the problems of humanity. There might well be competing theories – for example, the many criminological theories introduced in this book – but the devotees of each of these had confidence in the fundamental capacity of their doctrine to solve the crime problem although this might entail revisions to the theory, the incorporation of concepts from other theoretical perspectives and indeed other models of criminal behaviour. Societies characterised by the postmodern condition are, in contrast, characterised by moral ambiguity, a condition which involves a terminal loss of certainty with absolutely no assurance, or even expectation, that it will ever return.

Thus, whereas modernists have attempted to develop large-scale theories to explain society in terms of enduring, identifiable social structures, postmodernists emphasise the redundancy and futility of such efforts and contest the very idea or possibility of objective truth. The social sciences – since their very inception in modern societies – had made efforts to transcend the relativity of social situations and identify 'what is going on' systematically and objectively, while philosophers had attempted to establish some rational standpoint from which reality could be described. Postmodern writers have, on the other hand, celebrated the failure of the modern project to establish rational foundations for knowledge and have themselves embraced the trend towards human diversity and social fragmentation, arguing that there is no objective reality behind the plethora of social meanings.

The idea of the postmodern can appear to be an extremely negative and nihilistic vision for if there is no such thing as the 'truth of the human condition' it is difficult to formulate an argument in support of basic human rights, or to locate legitimate foundations for law, if the human experience is seen to be simply reflexive and relative. The relativism implied by the postmodern condition thus denies the possibility of truth, and hence of justice, in anything other than a purely subjective form, which inevitably consigns us to the prospect of conflict.[1]

The schizophrenia of crime

This author has previously devised the term 'the schizophrenia of crime' to refer to the apparently contradictory duality of attitude to criminal behaviour that has become endemic in contemporary societies characterised by the postmodern condition (Hopkins Burke, 2007, 2009). Thus, on the one hand, we can observe a widespread public demand for a rigorous intervention against criminality that has made the 'war against crime' a major populist political issue and, indeed, it is in this context that we can observe an extensive expansion in situational crime prevention strategies epitomised by the ubiquitous existence of closed-circuit television cameras (Hopkins Burke, 2004b), a whole raft of crime control legislation that has placed increasing restrictions on our civil liberties and human rights (Hopkins Burke, 2004c) and the introduction of rigorous 'zero-tolerance-style' policing interventions (see Hopkins Burke, 1998b, 2002, 2004a) that have occurred not as the outcome of the coercive strategies of a totalitarian regime but in response to overwhelming public demand in a liberal democratic society (Hopkins Burke, 2004b). '*We* want it, *we* demand it, and *we* get it' (Hopkins Burke, 2007) even though as individuals we are invariably unaware of the ultimate implications for our freedom as proposed by the left realist hybrid model of criminal justice development.

Thus, on the other hand, we can observe that criminality has become widespread to the virtual point of universality, with many people having committed criminal offences at some stage in their life, a great many continuing to do so, and even more having an extremely ambiguous attitude to the whole idea of criminality. This of course does not mean that these people get caught and are processed by the criminal justice process. There is much empirical evidence to show that white-collar, corporate and business crime is extremely widespread and when one considers, for example, recreational drug use (far from the sole prerogative of an unemployed underclass) (see Winlow and Hall, 2006), crimes of disorder and incivility associated with alcohol use (extremely extensive in any location urban or rural in the UK, particularly during weekend evenings) (Hobbs *et al.*, 2000, 2005) and driving cars beyond the legal speed limit (virtually compulsory through peer group pressure on motorways) (Hopkins Burke, 2007), the notion of the virtual universality of criminality is not as implausible as it may at first seem.

The 'schizophrenia of crime' thesis is influenced by Mike Presdee's concept of 'second lives' where he observes that the usually law-abiding and often pillars of straight society enjoy alternative part-time existences involving 'walking on the wild-side' (Presdee, 2000). There is thus, as Jock Young (1999, 2001) has observed, a considerable 'blurring of boundaries' between the criminal and the legal and, significantly, in our perceptions and understandings of these supposedly polarised opposite behaviours, that enables us to make some sense of this duality of attitude in a world where crime has become both normal and indeed non-pathological.

Crime as normal and non-pathological

For many years the crime rate in advanced (post)industrial societies rose ever upwards. It has fallen in the last decade in the UK, and more so in the USA, but that fall has been from unprecedented very high levels and crime rates continue to be significant. David Garland (1996) has nevertheless pertinently observed that as crime has come to be ever more frequent it has ceased to be an exceptional or pathological event, which surprises us when it occurs, but has become instead a standard, normal, background feature of our lives.

This blurring of boundaries between the legal and illegal has become no more apparent than in the realms of organised crime, corporate crime and legitimate business. Ruggiero (2000) thus observes that organised crime has become a branch of big business and is simply the illegal sector of capital. Castells (1998) notes that by the middle of the 1990s the 'gross criminal product' of global organised crime had made it the twentieth richest organisation in the world and richer than 150 sovereign states, while De Brie (2000) notes that the total world gross criminal product is estimated at a phenomenal 20 per cent of world trade.

Ruggiero (1997) also observes that legitimate business both actively seeks relations with criminal organisations and adopts methods akin to those of organised crime. Thus, immigrant smuggling eases labour supply problems in a variety of manufacturing sectors such as clothing and food, construction and agriculture and in 'dirty economies' where semi-legal employment is interspersed with employment in more directly criminal activity. Moreover, as De Brie (2000) notes, the global sphere of multinational corporations enables the export of the most brutal aspects of cheap labour to convenient locations in the southern hemisphere.

At the same time, the legal financial sector can go out of its way to attract criminal investments. Kochan and Whittington (1991) note that the closure of the Bank of Credit and Commerce International in 1991 shows how private banks and investment traders openly tout for legal and illegal funds without being too concerned about the distinction between the two. Moreover, legitimate capital has started to use the same tactics as organised crime. Thus, while drugs cartels launder their profits through 'offshore' banking facilities, legitimate capital enhances its power over governments to reduce tax burdens not only with the threat to relocate employment but also by adopting some of the tactics and resources of organised crime (Shelley, 1998). At the same time, for many states criminality acts as a buffer against poverty and economic collapse. Cocaine production, for example, acts as a counter to the impoverishment of thousands of Latin American peasant farmers, reducing the impact of falling world prices for agricultural products and raw materials in these areas. Thus, in a world where the boundaries between criminals and non-criminals and legal and illegal activities become increasingly difficult to disentangle, the classic crime control methods of modernity have become increasingly problematic.

New modes of governance

The concept of governance in contemporary political theory signifies, 'a change in the meaning of government, referring to a *new* process of governing; or a *changed* condition of ordered rule; or the *new* method by which society is governed' (Rhodes, 1997: 46). In criminology and criminal justice the concept has been used to signify changes in the control of crime and to acknowledge similar objects of control such as incivility, harm, safety and security. The principal feature of the concept of governance is a rupture with traditional modernist perceptions that locate the state at the centre of the exercise of political power.

In this new Foucauldian conceptualisation, which has significant links with the carceral surveillance society model of criminal justice development, power is not simply possessed by the state to be wielded over civil society but is tenuous, unresolved and the outcome of struggles between coalitions of public and private, formal and informal actors. These struggles are rooted in the central paradox of power: thus, when actors possess the potential to govern they are not powerful because they are not actually governing, but neither are they powerful when they govern because they are dependent on others to carry out their commands (Clegg, 1989).

This all implies a new complex and fragile process of governing through negotiation, bargaining and other relationships of exchange rather than through command, coercion or normative appeals for support. Thus, in order to accomplish and sustain political authority, would-be political leaders have to appreciate their 'power-dependence' on others and recruit and retain sufficient supporters to maintain a governing coalition (Rhodes, 1997). A criminal justice example is the attempt to control crime through partnerships of statutory, commercial and voluntary organisations (Crawford, 1997). This multi-agency approach has accompanied official recognition of the limits to the capacity of the state to reduce crime, in particular the insufficiency of criminal justice, and the consequent need to enrol expertise and resources from non-state actors including the 'responsibilisation' of private citizens for their own security (Garland, 2001).

This idea of 'joined-up' government to confront multi-faceted and complex problems such as, for example, youth offending, through multi-agency partnerships employing a broad spectrum of social policy interventions, represents a definite break with the methods of modernist public administration. It challenges the specialisation of government into discrete areas of functional expertise and, in so doing, defines new objects of governance. Youth offending, for example, ceases to be defined only in terms of 'criminality' and thus subject to the expertise of criminal justice professionals but becomes a problem of education, health and, in terms of contemporary terminology, one of 'social exclusion' and 'anti-social behaviour' (Hopkins Burke, 2008).

For most of the twentieth century crime control was dominated by the 'treatment model' prescribed by the predestined actor model of crime and criminal behaviour and was closely aligned to the powerful and benevolent state which was obliged to intervene in the lives of individual offenders and seek to diagnose and cure their criminal behaviour. It was to be the apparent failure of that interventionist modernist project epitomised by chronically high crime rates and the apparent failure of criminal justice intervention that led to a rediscovery of the rational actor model and an increased emphasis on preventive responses.

Crime and the risk society

Garland (1996) observes that the new governmental style is organised around economic forms of reasoning and thus reflects those contemporary rational actor theories which view crime to be simply a matter of opportunity and which require no special disposition or abnormality. In other words, anyone can do it. The subsequent and logical outcome has been a shift in policies from those directed at the individual identified offender to those directed at managing 'criminogenic situations' and these include 'unsupervised car parks, town squares late at night, deserted neighbourhoods, poorly lit streets, shopping malls, football games, bus stops, subway stations and so on' (Garland, 1999: 19).

Feeley and Simon (1994: 180) identify a paradigm shift in the criminal justice process from the 'old penology' to the 'new penology', with the former having been concerned with the identification of the individual criminal for the purpose of ascribing guilt and blame, the imposition of punishment and treatment, while the latter is 'concerned with techniques for identifying, classifying and managing groups assorted by levels of dangerousness', based not on individualised suspicion, but on the probability that an individual may be an offender because they belong to a particular category or group. Justice is thus becoming 'actuarial', its interventions increasingly based on risk assessment, rather than on the identification of specific criminal behaviour, and we are therefore witnessing an increase in, and the legal sanction of, such practices as preventive detention, offender profiling and mass surveillance (Norris and Armstrong, 1999).

The past 20 years have witnessed an ever-increasing use of surveillance technologies designed to regulate groups as part of a strategy of managing danger and these include the omnipresent city-centre surveillance systems referred to above, the testing of employees for the use of drugs (Gilliom, 1994) and the introduction of the blanket DNA testing of entire communities (Nelken and Andrews, 1999). The introduction of these new technologies often tends to be justified in terms of their ability to monitor 'risk' groups who pose a serious threat to society, but, once introduced, the concept of dangerousness is broadened to include a much wider range of offenders and suspects (see Pratt, 1999). Thus, the National DNA Database was originally established in the UK as a forensic resource to help identify those involved in serious crimes, such as murder and rape, but an amendment to the Criminal Justice and Public Order Act 1994 allowed samples to be taken without consent from any person convicted or *suspected* of a recordable offence (Home Office, 1999).

Some identify these trends as indicative of a broader transition in the social structural formation from that of an industrial society towards a risk society (Beck, 1992). This concept is not intended to imply any increase in the levels of risk that exist in society but rather refers to a social formation which is organised in order to respond to risks. As Giddens (1998: 3) observes, 'it is a society increasingly preoccupied with the future (and also with safety), which generates the notion of risk'; while Beck (1992: 21) identifies 'a systematic way of dealing with hazards and insecurities induced and introduced by modernisation itself'.

Human beings have always been subjected to certain levels of risk but modern societies are exposed to a particular type which is the outcome of the modernisation process itself and as a result this has led to changes in the nature of social organisation. Thus, there are risks such as natural disasters that have always had negative effects on human populations but these are produced by non-human forces. Modern risks, in contrast, are the product of human activity and Giddens (1998) refers to these two different categories as *external* and *manufactured* risks. Risk society is predominantly concerned with the latter.

Because manufactured risks are the product of human agents there is the potential to assess the level of risk that is being or about to be produced. The outcome is that risks have transformed the very process of modernisation. Thus, with the introduction of human caused disasters such as Chernobyl (in the Ukraine)[2] and the Love Canal Crisis (in New York City)[3] public faith in the modernist project has declined, leaving only limited trust in industry, government and experts (Giddens, 1990). The increased critique of modern industrial practices has resulted in a state of reflexive modernisation with widespread consideration given to issues of sustainability and the precautionary principle that focuses on preventative measures to reduce risk levels. Contemporary debates about global warming and the future of the planet should be seen in the context of debates about the risk society.

Ericson and Haggerty (1997: 450) argue that in the area of criminal justice we are witnessing a transformation of legal forms and policing strategies that reflects the transition to the risk society:

> Risk society is fuelled by surveillance, by the routine production of knowledge of populations useful for their administration. Surveillance provides biopower, the power to make biographical profiles of human populations to determine what is probable and possible for them. Surveillance fabricates people around institutionally established norms – risk is always somewhere on the continuum of imprecise normality.

In these circumstances, policing becomes increasingly more proactive rather than reactive and, given that risk assessment is probabilistic rather than determinist, it requires the assignment of individuals and events to classificatory schemes which provide differentiated assessment of risk, and calls for management strategies. Returning to the predestined actor tradition, offenders are now classified as 'prolific' rather than merely opportunistic and having been designated as such, the individual becomes a candidate for targeting by more intensive forms of technical or human surveillance. The emphasis on risk makes everyone a legitimate target for surveillance and 'everyone is assumed guilty until the risk profile assumes otherwise' (Norris and Armstrong, 1999: 25).

Many of the programmes of practical action which flow from strategies of 'risk management' in the criminal justice system are increasingly addressed not to central-state agencies such as the police, 'but *beyond* the state apparatus, to the organisations, institutions and individuals in civil society' (Garland, 1996: 451; see also O'Malley, 1992, Fyfe, 1995). Following the demise of the Keynesian Welfare State that had epitomised for many the high point in modernity in advanced capitalist nations (Hopkins Burke, 1999a), the emphasis on individuals managing their own risk finds converts from all parts of the political spectrum (Barry *et al.*, 1996). Thus, Pat O'Malley (1992) has written of the emergence of a new form of 'prudentialism' where insurance against future risks becomes a private obligation of the active citizen. Responsibilisation strategies are thus designed to offload the responsibility for risk management from central government on to the local state and non-state agencies, hence the increasing emphasis on public/ private partnerships, inter-agency cooperation, inter-governmental forums and the rapid growth of non-elected government agencies. The composition of such networks allows the state to 'govern-at-a-distance' – to utilise the norms and control strategies of those formerly autonomous institutions identified by Foucault (1971, 1976) – while leaving 'the centralised state machine more powerful than before, with an extended capacity for action and influence' (Garland, 1996: 454).

It is thus in this context that this author has previously directed our attention not just to the increasing pervasiveness of the generic concept of policing in society in its various 'hard' and 'soft' guises (Hopkins Burke, 2004c) including the development of the contemporary youth justice system (Hopkins Burke, 2008) but also significantly to our own contribution in the legitimisation of this state of affairs and, in this neo-Foucauldian hybrid left realist variation on the carceral surveillance society model, proposes that in a complex fragmented dangerous global risk society it is *we* the general public, regardless of class location, gender or ethnic origin, that have a significant material interest in the development of the grand overall disciplinary control matrix that increasingly controls us all in contemporary society. The recent work of the French sociologist Loïc Wacquant provides significant empirical support for the left realist hybrid model of criminal justice development.

Loïc Wacquant and the government of insecurity

Loïc Wacquant (2009) observes that the significant punitive trend in penal policies that has occurred in advanced societies over the past two decades cannot simply be explained in terms of traditional criminal justice discourse. In an analysis significantly compatible with the new modes of governance and risk society theses he argues persuasively that these changes have instigated the introduction of a new 'government of social insecurity' which is targeted at shaping the conduct of the men and women caught up in the turbulence of economic deregulation in advanced societies and the conversion of welfare into a mechanism which leads people towards precarious employment. He observes that within this apparently 'liberal-paternalist' apparatus, the prison has been restored to its original purpose at the beginning of modernity, which is to discipline and control those populations and territories which are resistant to the emerging new economic and moral order, while at the same time ritually reasserting the resilience of the dominant groups. It was in the USA that this new politics and policy of marginality, which brings together restrictive 'workfare' and expansive 'prison-fare', was invented, in the aftermath of the social and racial upheaval of the 1970s that was to instigate the neo-liberal revolution, in response, that has transformed the socio-economic situation of the USA and which has subsequently spread to Europe, in general, and the UK, in particular. Crucial to this disciplinary-tutelage agenda in the USA has been the need to control an increasingly economically excluded but enduringly problematic and potentially dangerous black population.

Racial inequality and imprisonment in contemporary USA

Wacquant (2001) observes three significant realities about racial inequality and imprisonment in contemporary USA. First, for the first time in US history, African Americans make up a majority of those entering prison each year. Second, the rate of incarceration for this ethnic group has soared to levels unknown in any other society and is higher now than the total incarceration rate in the Soviet Union at the height of the Gulag and in South Africa at the peak of the anti-apartheid struggle. Thus, since the beginning of this millennium, nearly 800,000 black men have been held in custody in federal penitentiaries, state prisons and county jails, which is one male out of every 21, and one out of every nine between 20 and 34. An additional 68,000 black women have been incarcerated, a number higher than the *total* carceral population of any one major western European country at the time.[4] Over one-third of African American men in their twenties find themselves behind bars, on probation or on parole and, at the core of the formerly industrial cities of the north, this proportion often exceeds two-thirds. Third, the ratio of black to white imprisonment rates has steadily grown over the past 40 years, rising from approximately 5:1 to 8.5:1. In 10 US states, African Americans are imprisoned at more than 10 times the rate of European Americans and in the District of Columbia blacks are 35 times more likely than whites to be put behind bars (Donziger, 1996; Mauer, 1997).

Wacquant (1998a) argues that to understand these phenomena, we first need to break out of the narrow 'crime and punishment' paradigm and examine the broader role of the penal system as *an instrument for managing dispossessed and dishonoured groups*, and second, it is necessary to take a longer historical view on the shifting forms of ethno-racial domination in the USA. It is by doing so that we can identify the astonishing increase in black incarceration in the past 40 years to be the outcome of the obsolescence of the ghetto as a device for caste control and the correlative need for a substitute apparatus for keeping (unskilled) African Americans in a subordinate and confined position, physically, socially and symbolically.

Wacquant agrees with George Rusche – who provides the earliest version of the radical conflict model – that it is the official mission of crime control to be part of the complete system of strategies, including social policies, which are aimed at regulating the poor, but takes a more sophisticated carceral surveillance society model perspective. He thus does *not* follow Rusche in: (1) assuming a *direct* link between brute economic forces and penal policy; (2) the reduction of economic forces to the sole state of the *labour market*, and still less the supply of labour; (3) limiting the control function of the prison to the lower *classes*, as distinct from other subordinate categories (ethnic or national, for instance); and (4) omitting the complex *symbolic* effects that the penal system exercises by drawing, dramatising and enforcing group boundaries (see Rusche, 1980).

Wacquant (2001) observes that in the case of black Americans, the symbolic function of the carceral system is paramount. Thus, in the post-Civil Rights era, the remnants of the traditional black ghetto and an expanding carceral system have become linked in a single schema that entraps large numbers of younger black men, who simply move back and forth between the two institutions. This carceral mesh is seen to have emerged from two sets of convergent changes: first, there are the sweeping economic and political forces that have reshaped the mid-century 'Black Belt' to *make the ghetto more like a prison*, and second, the 'inmate society' has broken down in ways that *make the prison more like a ghetto*. Wacquant (2001) argues that the resulting symbiosis between ghetto and prison enforces the socio-economic marginality and symbolic taint of an urban black sub-proletariat. Moreover, by producing a racialised public culture that vilifies criminals, it plays a pivotal role in remaking 'race' and redefining the citizenry.

A more extensive analysis shows that this increasing use of imprisonment to sustain the caste division in American society is part of a broader 'upsizing' of the state's penal sector, which, together with the drastic 'downsizing' of its social welfare sector, aims to enforce a regime of flexible and casual wage labour as a norm for unskilled segments of the post-industrial working class (Wacquant, 1998b). This emerging *government of poverty* weds the 'invisible hand' of a deregulated labour market to the 'iron fist' of an omnipresent punitive apparatus. It is anchored not by a 'prison industrial complex', as political opponents of the policy of mass incarceration maintain (Gordon, 1999), but by a system of gendered institutions that monitor, train and neutralise populations recalcitrant or superfluous to the new economic and racial regime. Thus, men are handled by its penal wing while (their) women and children are managed by a revamped welfare-workfare system designed to reinforce and enhance casual employment.

Wacquant (2001) thus argues that the massive expansion in the use of imprisonment is but one component of a more comprehensive restructuring of the US state to suit the requirements of neo-liberalism but, at the same time, observes that ethnicity plays a special role in this emerging system. The USA far surpasses all advanced nations in the international trend towards the penalisation of social insecurity and while the dismantling of welfare programmes has been accelerated by a cultural and political conflation of blackness and undeservingness (Gilens, 2000), so the 'great confinement' of the rejects of market society – the poor, mentally ill, homeless, jobless and useless – can be articulated as a welcome 'crackdown' on *them*, those dark-skinned criminals from a pariah group still considered to be alien to the national body. The handling of the 'underclass' question by the prison system at once reflects, reworks and reinforces the racial division of US society and plays a key role in the fashioning of a post-Keynesian US state.

Four peculiar institutions

Wacquant (2001) observes that the task of defining, confining and controlling African Americans in the USA has been successively administered by four 'peculiar institutions': (1) slavery, (2) the Jim Crow system, (3) the urban ghetto, and latterly (4) the organisational complex formed by the remnants of the ghetto and the expanding carceral system. The first three served, each in its own way, both to extract labour from African Americans and to demarcate and ultimately seclude them so that they would not 'contaminate' the surrounding white society that viewed them as irrevocably inferior and vile.

Wacquant observes that these two goals of *labour extraction* and *social seclusion* are nevertheless in tension: thus, extracting labour from a group requires regular communication with its constituent members, which may blur the boundaries separating 'us' from 'them'; while, at the same time, social isolation can make efficient labour extraction more difficult to achieve. When the tension between exploitation and exclusion reaches the point where it threatens to undermine either of them, the institution is re-stabilised through *physical violence:* the customary use of the lash and ferocious suppression of slave insurrections on the plantation, terroristic vigilantism and mob lynchings that occurred in the South in the years following the Civil War, and periodic bombings of Negro homes and pogroms against ghetto residents (such as the six-day riot that shook up Chicago in 1919)[5] ensured that blacks kept to their appointed place in each era (Wacquant, 2001).

Wacquant (2001) observes that the built-in instabilities of un-free labour and the anomaly of caste partition in a formally democratic and highly individualistic society, such as the USA, guaranteed that each of these peculiar institutions would eventually be undermined by its internal tensions as well as by black resistance and external opposition, and be inevitably replaced by its successor regime. Moreover, at each new stage, the apparatus of ethno-racial domination became less total and less capable of encompassing all elements of the social life of the pariah group. Wacquant observes that as African Americans became differentiated along class lines and attained full formal citizenship, the institutional complex charged with keeping them 'separate and unequal' grew more differentiated and diffuse, allowing a rapidly increasing middle class of professionals and salary earners to *partially* compensate for the negative symbolic capital of blackness through their high-status cultural capital and proximity to centres of political power. Lower-class blacks, on the other hand, remained burdened by the triple stigma of 'race', poverty, and presumed immorality, while the new middle class had an often expert interest as 'moral entrepreneurs' (Becker, 1963) in the control and indeed suppression of the unskilled and dispossessed elements of their own ethnic group which can be explained by both the highly compatible carceral surveillance society and left realist hybrid models of criminal justice development.

This historical schema should not therefore be seen as an inescapable forward march towards ethno-racial equality as might be suggested by the social progress model. Wacquant observes that each new phase of racial domination entailed retrogression as well as progress and notes that while it is true that there has been a civilising of racial domination – in the sense of the term used by Norbert Elias (1978, 1982) – it remains the case that each regime has to be evaluated in light of the institutional possibilities it harbours, not simply by contrast to its predecessor(s), and in this way can be explained by the radical conflict model.

Carceral recruitment and authority

Wacquant observes that the prison today further resembles the ghetto for the simple reason that an overwhelming majority of its occupants originate from the racialised core of the major cities in the USA, and return there upon release, only to be soon caught again and incarcerated for ever-longer periods, in a self-perpetuating cycle of escalating socio-economic marginality and legal incapacitation. Thus, in the late 1980s, three out of every four inmates serving sentences in the entire state of New York came from *seven black and Latino neighbourhoods* of New York City and these also happened to be the poorest areas of the city. Ellis (1993) observes that every year these segregated and dispossessed districts provide a fresh contingent of 25,000-odd inmates, while 23,000 ex-convicts are discharged, most of them on parole, back into these devastated areas. Moreover, the reality that 46 per cent of the inmates of New York state prisons come from neighbourhoods served by the 16 worst public schools[6] of the city ensures that their clientele will continue to be replenished.

The contemporary prison system and the ghetto not only display a similarly skewed recruitment and composition in terms of class and caste but the former also duplicates the authority structure characteristic of the latter in that it places a population of poor blacks under the direct supervision of whites, in this case, lower-class whites. In the communal ghetto of the post-war era, black residents chafed under the rule of white landlords, white employers, white unions, white social workers and white policemen (Clark, 1965). Likewise, in the new millennium, the convicts of New York City, Philadelphia, Baltimore, Cleveland, Detroit and Chicago, who are overwhelmingly African American, serve their sentences in establishments staffed by officers who are overwhelmingly white.

The convergent changes that have 'prisonised' the ghetto and 'ghettoised' the prison in the aftermath of the civil rights revolution suggest that the astonishing increasing over-representation of blacks behind bars does not stem simply from the discriminatory targeting of specific penal policies such as the War on Drugs (Tonry, 1995) or from the sheer destabilising effects of the increased penetration of ghetto neighbourhoods by the penal state (Miller, 1997). Wacquant notes that these two factors are clearly relevant but argues that they fail to capture the precise nature and full magnitude of the transformations that have interlocked the prison and the (hyper)ghetto into a *single institutional mesh* suited to fulfil anew the mission historically imparted to America's 'peculiar institutions'. The 'blackening' of the carceral population has thus closely followed the demise of the Black Belt as a viable instrument of caste containment in the urban-industrial setting.

Wacquant observes that perhaps the most important effect of this institutional mesh is the revival and consolidation of the centuries-old *association of blackness with criminality* and devious violence. The massively disproportional incarceration of blacks supplies a powerful commonsense authorisation for 'using colour as a proxy for dangerousness' (Kennedy, 1997: 136), while, in recent years, the courts have consistently authorised the police to employ race as 'a negative signal of increased risk of criminality' (Kennedy, 1997: 143) and legal scholars have rushed to endorse it as 'a rational adaptation to the demographics of crime' (Kennedy, 1997: 146) and all of this has been justified by the blackening of the prison population. The conflation of blackness and crime in collective representation and government policy (the other side of this equation being the conflation of blackness and welfare) thus reactivates the notion of 'race' by giving a legitimate outlet to the expression of anti-black hostility in the form of the vigorous public condemnation of criminals and prisoners.

Wacquant observes that a second major effect of the penalisation of the 'race question' has been to depoliticise it. Thus, reframing problems of ethno-racial division as issues of criminality and law enforcement automatically delegitimises any attempt at collective resistance and redress. Established organisations that speak for African Americans cannot directly confront the crisis of hyper-incarceration for fear that this might reinforce the very conflation of blackness and crime in the minds of the general public. This thus fuels the crisis and in doing so has silenced sub-proletarian revolt.

By assuming a central role in the contemporary government of race and poverty at the crossroads of the deregulated low-wage labour market, a revamped 'welfare-workfare' apparatus designed to support casual employment and the vestiges of the ghetto, the overgrown US carceral system has become a major engine of symbolic production in its own right. Just as bondage imposed 'social death' on imported African captives and their descendants (Patterson, 1982), mass incarceration induces civic death for those it ensnares.

Wacquant (2001) observes that inmates in the USA today are the targets of three forms of significant social exclusion. First, they are denied access to valued cultural capital. At a time when university degrees are becoming a prerequisite for employment in the (semi-)protected sector of the labour market, inmates have been made ineligible for higher-education grants. The exclusion started with drug offenders in 1988, continued with convicts sentenced to death or lifelong imprisonment without the possibility of parole in 1992, and ended with all remaining state and federal prisoners in 1994. This expulsion was passed by Congress for the sole purpose of accentuating the symbolic boundary between criminals and 'law-abiding citizens' in spite of overwhelming evidence that prison educational programmes drastically cut recidivism as well as help to maintain carceral order.

Second, prisoners are systematically excluded from social redistribution and public aid in an age when work insecurity makes access to such programmes more essential than ever for those dwelling in the lower regions of the socio-economic hierarchy. Laws deny welfare payments, veteran's benefits and food stamps to anyone in detention for more than 60 days.

Third, convicts are banned from political participation via 'criminal dis-enfranchisement' practised on a scale and with vigour unimaginable in any other country. All but four states deny the vote to mentally competent adults held in detention facilities; 39 states forbid convicts placed on probation from exercising this political right; and 32 states also disenfranchise parolees. In 14 states, ex-felons are barred from voting even when they are no longer under criminal justice supervision, for life in 10 of these states. The result is that nearly 4 million Americans have temporarily or permanently lost the ability to cast a ballot, including 1.47 million who are not behind bars and another 1.39 million who have served their sentences in full (Fellner and Mauer, 1998). A mere quarter-century after acceding to full voting rights, one black man in seven nationwide is banned from the electoral booth through penal disenfranchisement and seven states permanently deny the vote to more than one-quarter of their black male residents.

Wacquant (2009) observes that this triple exclusion, the prison and the criminal justice system contribute to the ongoing reconstruction of the 'imagined community' of Americans around a polar opposition. On the one hand, there are praiseworthy 'working families', implicitly white, suburban and deserving; on the other hand, there is a despicable 'underclass' of criminals, loafers, and leeches, by definition dark-skinned, undeserving and personified by the dissolute teenage 'welfare mother' and the dangerous street 'gang banger'. The former are exalted as the living incarnation of genuine American values: self-control, deferred gratification, subservience of life to labour. The latter are condemned as the loathsome embodiment of their abject desecration, the 'dark side' of the 'American dream' of affluence and opportunity for all, believed to flow from morality anchored in conjugality and work. And the line that divides them is increasingly being drawn, materially and symbolically, by the prison.

Conclusions: living in penal society

In summary, Wacquant (2009) argues that the social policy of transition from welfare to workfare that is incrementally taking place in advanced neo-liberal societies needs to be analysed in conjunction with the rise of prisonfare, that is, the mass incarceration of certain categories of the population perceived to be problematic. Workfare and prisonfare are from this perspective simply two sides of the same coin: they are the areas where the neo-liberal state can still assert its authority once depleted of its economic and social policy functions. The combination of workfare and prisonfare is seen to fulfil both economic and symbolic functions for the neo-liberal punitive state (for workfare and prisonfare are both punishments) as it fights the crisis of legitimacy that pervades all developed democracies as the state progressively loses its capacity to establish successful economic policies in an increasingly competitive world and thus has little choice but to abandon social justice and redistribution strategies. Wacquant argues that with the assistance of the media, public attention is directed away from the massive transfer of wealth to the top of the social stratification structure towards designated 'incorrigible' deviants who can be blamed for our lack of economic competitiveness: welfare cheats and parasites, criminals and paedo-philes, against whom the ever-more intrusive mechanisms of the carceral surveillance society are rigorously applied.

Wacquant argues that this neo-liberal crusade is based on a series of falsifications that are perpetuated and dispersed throughout society, mostly, again, through the media. Thus, the USA is said to be spending enormous quantities of money on welfare whereas it has never accounted for more than one per cent of the federal budget; or crime continues to rise, perpetrated by ever younger and more dangerous 'predators', whereas the reality is that criminality has been on the decline for a long time irrespective of the policies implemented. Americans nevertheless still believe that there is more crime. We should note that the situation is similar in the UK and other countries in continental Europe.

The increasing regulation of the poor is the major outcome of these policies but there is not a large-scale conspiracy as suggested by the radical conflict model of criminal justice development for such an undertaking would require much more competent coordination and centralisation than is available in the USA and probably any other advanced liberal democratic society. The perceived outcome is in reality the logical conclusion of separately adopted neo-liberal strategies: liberalisation/privatisation in the economic domain, the shrinking of the state in the name of efficiency, and the desocialisation of waged labour (along with waves of outsourcing and off-shoring), along with a moral cultural outlook on social deviance devised by politicians and 'experts' who may or may not be aware of their contribution to the pervasive socio-control matrix of the carceral surveillance society. Such economic policies are bound to be devastating for certain, usually poorer segments of the population, who then need to be controlled for their individual moral failings, largely depicted in terms of a lack of self-control and responsibility.

The victims of neo-liberal policies are thus targeted as irresponsible, unproductive individuals who need tutelage and discipline and that is a job which is left to the state with recourse to partnerships with private sector agencies such as private welfare/child welfare administrations and private prisons. In this sense, in this punitive environment, structural conditions leave the most vulnerable members of society to fend for themselves even though their ghettoisation prevents them from improving their conditions. They are then blamed for their failure to get out of this situation. There is, of course, one form of economic activity which would lead to better material outcomes for the dispossessed poor and that is the illegal economy and Wacquant (2009) observes that is where the policies of the War on Drugs in the USA have worked to prevent those deprived of socialised wage labour from taking this one exit from poverty, leaving them, of course, in prison, serving large sentences for which there is no parole.

Wacquant (2009) observes that this double regulation of poverty (through workfare and prisonfare) has been exported to Europe, starting with the liberalisation of the state through Thatcherism in the UK, the Kohl years in Germany and the Chirac years in France. Even the various left-of-centre parties, such as the socialist parties in western Europe, are seen to have embraced the law-and-order view of the state and neo-liberal economic 'reforms'.

The mechanisms and discourse used for targeting, marginalising and controlling the poor and dispossessed differ in each country and there are important different historical and cultural factors in each society. Thus, while black Europeans are significantly over-represented among the 'clientele' of the criminal justice systems of their particular countries, there are important variations in the mechanisms of control that reflect historical differences with the USA. A comparison between the USA and UK provides a useful case study.

Racism is endemic in both the USA and the UK and while there are significant similarities in the socio-economic position of black people in both countries there are also important differences. The first difference is that the USA has had a large black population for over 300 years, while in contrast the great majority of black emigration to the UK occurred following the Second World War. In the case of the USA large numbers of black people were taken to that country in chains, having been sold as slaves, and thus clearly posed a serious physical threat to the white population that required techniques of control and containment which may well have become more sophisticated and 'civilised' in recent years but still nevertheless reflect the origins of this sizeable ethnic minority. Although the British were heavily involved in the slave trade to the USA and the Caribbean – and indeed much of the latter became British colonies – the black population which emigrated to Britain from the Caribbean during the 1950s was invited because of a labour shortage. Many of those involved in the first wave had fought in the British military during the war and considered Britain to be the motherland. On arrival in the UK they experienced racism with many similarities to the USA during the 'Jim Crow' era but this was never officially sanctioned – as had been the case in the USA, in the South, in particular, and indeed a prominent member of the Conservative government, Enoch Powell, was forced to resign because of a widely condemned racist speech although his views were extremely popular with large sections of the white working class at the time. Policies to integrate the black population into mainstream UK society have been pursued by all subsequent governments although racism remains significant and many black people remain jobless, in receipt of welfare and overly represented as the clients of the criminal justice system and inmates of the prison estate. Clearly, Wacquant's account of the disciplining and tutelage of the contemporary black population has significant resonance in the UK but there are crucial differences. Black people with origins in the Caribbean are far more integrated into mainstream British society with high levels of inter-'marriage' with white people whereas in the USA there are far fewer such instances in a society which to many visitors appears to be characterised by apartheid.

Many black people in the UK are the targets of tutelage and discipline strategies – with many integrated into the penal society mesh that resembles that identified by Wacquant in the USA – but as part of a socially excluded, economically excluded underclass that incorporates people from different ethnic groups but which, at the same time, is as invidious and pervasive in its own way as the system the other side of the Atlantic. It is just different.

This concluding chapter is a consideration of the possible future of criminal justice in advanced societies and what is becoming increasingly apparent is that the socio-control matrix of the carceral society continues to expand incrementally in close parallel with progressively more insurmountable economic pressures. The outcome is that more and more groups are being absorbed into the net of surveillance and tutelage as the inevitably failing liberal economies of advanced societies come under intense pressure to make significant cuts in services and the real incomes of its citizenry. At the time of writing, public sector employment in the UK is coming under immense pressure with government policy seeking a substantial reduction in services and jobs, all of which is 'justified' by a media vilification of people who were once known, and indeed respected, as public servants. It is a long time since that descriptive language has been widely used.

The future thus looks bleak with the carceral surveillance model of criminal justice development having increasing explanatory relevance. We should nevertheless not underestimate our own contribution to this state of affairs with those people lucky enough to still have reasonable jobs and futures – and that number is decreasing rapidly – being encouraged to buy into the language of vilification and exclusion. It is thus the left realist hybrid model of criminal justice development that makes most sense of these developments. There are those involved in these processes who do things for the best of humanitarian motives (social progress model), but these strategies and interventions are clearly taking place in the interests of capitalism or the market economy (radical conflict model), at least in the final analysis. It is thus the central proposition of this book that it is the left realist hybrid model that provides the most comprehensive explanation or theory of the development of the criminal justice system or process and, moreover, significantly indicates the direction in which we are going.

Notes

1 Introduction: modernity and criminal justice

1 A social construction or social construct is any institutionalised entity or object in a social system 'invented' or 'constructed' by participants in a particular culture or society that exists because people agree to behave as if it exists or follow certain conventional rules. Social status is an example of a social construct (see Clarke and Cochrane, 1998).

2 This author has conducted interviews with numerous practitioners in different criminal justice – and indeed, other public sector – agencies in very different situations during the course of the past 20 years. Virtually all have considered the solution to the problems of their particular agency to be the almost mythical further resources. Just give us the resources and we will deliver is the message.

3 Materialist philosophy proposes that matter and energy are the only objects existing within the universe, and mental and spiritual phenomena are explainable as functions of the nervous system of people.

4 In Marxist theory, a failure to recognise the instruments of one's oppression or exploitation as one's own creation, as when members of an oppressed class unwittingly adopt views of the oppressor class.

5 The theory of the influence of economics: the belief that the economic organisation of a society determines the nature of all other aspects of its life.

6 Jock Young (1999) has argued that most 'Marxism' is little more than a form of functionalism which replaces the interests of 'society' with those of the 'ruling class'.

2 Explaining crime and criminal behaviour

1 A more extensive discussion of the models and theories contained in this chapter can be found in Hopkins Burke (2009).

2 We should note that no society is entirely mechanical or organic with any social formation being in a state of development between the two extremes. Indeed, there may well be many pockets of intense mechanical solidarity in highly developed organic societies. Hopkins Burke (2009) provides a more detailed account.

3 The philosophy of law and legal ethics

1 Saint Thomas Aquinas (also Thomas of Aquin or Aquino; (c. 1225–1274) was an Italian priest of the Roman Catholic Church in the Dominican Order and an immensely influential philosopher and theologian in the tradition of scholasticism known as Doctor Angelicus and Doctor Communis. He is frequently referred to as Thomas because 'Aquinas' refers to his residence rather than his surname. He was the foremost classical proponent of natural theology and the father of the Thomistic school of philosophy and

theology. His influence on Western thought is considerable, and much of modern philosophy was conceived as a reaction against, or as an agreement with, his ideas, particularly in the areas of ethics, natural law and political theory.

2 Sir William Blackstone (1723–1780) was an English judge, jurist and legal professor who produced the historical and analytic treatise on the common law entitled *Commentaries on the Laws of England*, first published in four volumes 1765–1769. It had an extraordinary success, reportedly bringing the author £14,000, and still remains an important source on classical views of the common law and its principles.

3 Cognitivism is the view that there exists knowledge or the capability of acquiring knowledge, relative to some field of inquiry. Non-cognitivism is the opposite, arguing that knowledge in the relevant field cannot be acquired. The concept is usually expressed in debates about two areas: ethics and the existence of gods.

In ethics, non-cognitivism takes the position that when people express moral judgements, they are not making claims of knowledge or making propositions which can possibly have any cognitive, epistemic, or truth value. They are, instead, simply making a statement about their emotions (subjectivism) or they are making a raw expression of emotion (emotivists). Non-cognitivists will often focus on the social function of ethical discourse, pointing out how it serves to negotiate social disagreements and construct both social boundaries and social cohesion, rather than describe factual states of affairs in the world.

4 This formulation states that we should never act in such a way that we treat humanity, whether in ourselves or in *others*, as a means only but always as an end in itself. This is often seen as introducing the idea of 'respect' for persons, for whatever it is that is essential to our humanity.

5 Syllogistic reasoning is a logical argument involving three propositions. It is a formal deductive argument that consists of a major premise, a minor premise and a conclusion. An example is, 'All birds have feathers, penguins are birds, therefore penguins have feathers'.

6 The Qur'an is the holy book of Islam revealed in stages to the Prophet Muhammad over a period of 23 years. Qur'anic revelations are regarded by Muslims as the sacred word of God and are intended to correct any errors in previous holy books such as the Old and New Testaments. The Qur'an was revealed to the Prophet Muhammad by God in Arabic and although early variants are known to have existed, Muslims believe that the text we have today was established shortly after the death of the Prophet by the Caliph Uthman.

7 Muslims believe that Islam is a faith that has always existed and that it was gradually revealed to humanity by a number of prophets, but the final and complete revelation of the faith was made through the Prophet Muhammad in the seventh century CE. Muhammad was born in Mecca in Saudi Arabia in 570 and was a deeply spiritual man who often spent time in meditation on Mount Hira. The traditional story of the Qur'an tells how one night in 610 he was meditating in a cave on the mountain when he was visited by the angel Jibreel who ordered him to recite. Once Jibreel mentioned the name of Allah, Muhammad began to recite words that he came to believe were the words of God.

8 Muslims regard abortion as wrong and haram (forbidden), but many accept that it may be permitted in certain cases. All schools of Muslim law accept that abortion is permitted if continuing the pregnancy would put the mother's life in real danger. This is the only reason accepted for abortion after 120 days of the pregnancy. Different schools of Muslim law hold different views on whether any other reasons for abortion are permitted, and at what stage of pregnancy if so. Some schools of Muslim law permit abortion in the first 16 weeks of pregnancy, while others only permit it in the first 7 weeks. However, even those scholars who would permit early abortion in certain cases still regard abortion as wrong, but do not regard it as a punishable wrong. The more advanced the pregnancy, the greater the wrong.

9 Capital punishment remains widespread for acts of treason against the state throughout modernist Western societies and in the USA has been incrementally reintroduced in most states since 1976.

4 Policing modern society

1 In Britain, seizure of common land and change to private property, or the changing of open-field systems (farming in strips apportioned over two or three large fields) to enclosed fields owned by individual farmers. The enclosed fields were often used for sheep. This process began in the fourteenth century and became widespread in the fifteenth and sixteenth centuries. It caused poverty, homelessness and rural depopulation, and resulted in revolts in 1549 and 1607. A further wave of enclosures occurred between about 1760 and 1820 during the agrarian revolution.
2 The Gordon Riots were an anti-Catholic uprising against the Papists Act of 1778. The Popery Act of 1698 had imposed a number of penalties and disabilities on Roman Catholics in England and the 1778 legislation had removed some of these. The uprising became an excuse for widespread rioting and looting and was the most destructive to occur during the eighteenth century in London.
3 For a more detailed analysis see Henry (1993).
4 Felson's work is based on the USA but the general idea transfers well across the Atlantic.
5 The political right, usually not opposed to zero tolerance policing itself, was to point to the successful increase in incarceration – or incapacitation to use their favoured terminology – of a large number of young males as a central reason for this decline in the crime figures.
6 Post-structuralism is a school of thought that emerged partly from within French structuralism in the 1960s, and which was a reaction against structuralist pretensions to scientific objectivity and comprehensiveness. The term covers the philosophical deconstruction practised by Jacques Derrida and his followers, along with the later works of the critic Roland Barthes, the psychoanalytic theories of Jacques Lacan and Julia Kristeva, the historical critiques of Michel Foucault, and the cultural-political writings of Jean-François Lyotard and Gilles Deleuze. These thinkers emphasised the instability of meanings and of intellectual categories (including that of the human 'subject'), and sought to undermine any theoretical system that claimed to have universal validity, denouncing such claims as 'totalitarian'.
7 Turk (1969) describes the control of legal images and living time as a form of a more subtle exercise in social control. Legal systems have formal laws, breaches of which are legally punishable, and there are established procedures for exercising those laws. There are also degrees of discretion as to how that law is exercised. Turk argues that it is the subtle interplay of the formal and informal that allows the powerful to manipulate the legal system in their own interests while still preserving an image of due process and impartiality. The concept of the control of living time suggests that people will become accustomed to forms of domination and control, especially if it is maintained and legitimised over generations. New generations will gradually forget that social control conditions were ever any different from those with which they are familiar.

5 The legal process in modern society

1 Beccaria was an Italian mathematician and the author of *Dei delitti e delle pene (On Crimes and Punishment)* (1963, originally 1764), an extremely influential book translated into 22 languages and which had an enormous impact on European and US legal thought.

2   Ideal type (German: *Idealtyp*) is also known as pure type and is a typological term most closely associated with the anti-positivist sociologist Max Weber (1864–1920). For Weber, the conduct of social science depends upon the construction of hypothetical concepts *in the abstract*. The 'ideal type' is therefore a subjective element in social theory and research; one of many subjective elements which necessarily distinguish sociology from natural science. An ideal type is formed from characteristics and elements of the given phenomena, but it is not meant to correspond to all of the characteristics of any one particular case. It is not meant to refer to perfect things, moral ideals nor to statistical averages but rather to stress certain elements common to most cases of the given phenomena. It is also important to pay attention that in using the word 'ideal' Max Weber refers to the world of ideas (German: *Gedankenbilder*) and not to perfection; these 'ideal types' are thus idea-constructs that help put the chaos of social reality in order.

3   In its most common sense, the principle refers to private contracts, stressing that contained clauses are law between the parties, and implies that non-fulfilment of respective obligations is a breach of the pact. The general principle of correct behaviour in commercial praxis – and by implication the bona fide – is a requirement for the efficacy of the whole system, so the eventual disorder is sometimes punished by the law of some systems even without any direct penalty incurred by any of the parties. With reference to international agreements, every treaty in force is binding upon the parties to it and must be performed by them in good faith.

4   Opinio juris sive necessitatis (an opinion of law or necessity) or simply opinio juris (an opinion of law) is the belief that an action was carried out because it was a legal obligation. This is in contrast to an action being the result of different cognitive reaction, or behaviours that were habitual to the individual. This term is frequently used in legal proceedings such as a defence for a case. Opinio juris is the subjective element of custom as a source of law, both domestic and international, as it refers to beliefs. The other element is state practice, which is more objective as it is readily discernible. To qualify as state practice, the acts must be consistent and general international practice.

5   A peremptory norm (also called jus cogens or ius cogens, Latin for 'compelling law'), is a fundamental principle of international law which is accepted by the international community of states as a norm from which no derogation is ever permitted. There is no clear agreement regarding precisely which norms are jus cogens or how a norm reaches that status, but it is generally accepted that jus cogens includes the prohibition of genocide, maritime piracy, slaving in general (to include slavery as well as the slave trade), torture, and wars of aggression and territorial aggrandisement.

6   Just War Theory (or *Bellum iustum*) is a doctrine of military ethics of Roman philosophical and Catholic origin, studied by moral theologians, ethicists and international policy makers, which holds that a conflict can and ought to meet the criteria of philosophical, religious or political justice, provided it follows certain conditions.

7   The term Peace of Westphalia denotes a series of peace treaties signed between May and October of 1648 in Osnabrück and Münster. These treaties ended the Thirty Years' War (1618–1648) in the Holy Roman Empire, and the Eighty Years' War (1568–1648) between Spain and the Dutch Republic.

8   Legal realism is a family of theories about the nature of law developed in the first half of the twentieth century in the USA (*American legal realism*) and Scandinavia (*Scandinavian legal realism*). The essential tenet of legal realism is that all law is made by human beings and is therefore subject to human foibles, frailties and imperfections.

9   Queer theory is a field of critical theory that emerged in the early 1990s out of the fields of LGBT studies and feminist studies. It is a kind of interpretation devoted to queer readings of texts. Heavily influenced by the work of Eve Kosofsky Sedgwick and Judith Butler, queer theory builds both upon feminist challenges to the idea that gender is part

of the essential self and upon gay/lesbian studies' close examination of the socially constructed nature of sexual acts and identities. Whereas gay/lesbian studies focused its inquiries into 'natural' and 'unnatural' behaviour with respect to homosexual activity, queer theory expands its focus to encompass any kind of sexual activity or identity that falls into normative and deviant categories.

6 Punishment in modern society

1 Durkheim (1893) proposed that the types of social solidarity correlate with types of society and introduced the terms 'mechanical' and 'organic solidarity' as part of his theory of the development of societies. In societies with high levels of mechanical solidarity, cohesion and integration are founded on the homogeneity of individuals: people feel connected through similar work, educational and religious training and lifestyle. Mechanical solidarity normally operates in 'traditional' and small-scale societies. Organic solidarity comes from the interdependence that arises from specialisation of work and the complementarities between people which is a development that occurs in 'modern' and 'industrial' societies and is a social cohesion based on the dependence individuals in more advanced societies have on each other. Although individuals perform different tasks and often have different values and interests, the order and very solidarity of society depends on their reliance on each other to perform their specified tasks. Organic here is referring to the interdependence of the component parts. Thus, social solidarity is maintained in more complex societies through the interdependence of its component parts (for example, farmers produce the food to feed the factory workers who produce the tractors that allow the farmer to produce the food).
2 The concept of evidence-based practice should be seen as a response to concerns that professional practice is not always based on the 'best evidence' or is minimally informed by research knowledge (Carew, 1979; Rosen, 1994). As such, it is proposed that it can assist practitioners to identify, call upon and utilise the 'best' research in their daily practice.
3 'Eye for an eye' is a quotation from several passages of the Hebrew Bible in which a person who has injured the eye of another is instructed to give the value of his or her own eye in compensation. It defined and restricted the extent of retribution in the laws of the Torah.

7 Youth justice in modern society

1 Malthus (1959) had famously argued during the nineteenth century that, if unchecked, population would grow geometrically while, at the same time, agricultural product would increase only arithmetically. Disaster, it was argued, had only been averted by the three periodical population controls of famine, plague and war and, therefore, in such a world children – or more accurately, little people – were of little intrinsic value to society and invariably an economic liability.
2 The first Juvenile Court had been introduced 10 years previously in Chicago in 1898.
3 This was at a time when the age of criminal responsibility was 7 and the school leaving age 12.
4 Offenders committing further offences while on bail.
5 Significantly, diverse strands in social, political and moral thought, arising from very different locations on the political spectrum – such as Marxism (Ross, 2003) and traditional 'one-nation' conservatism (Scruton, 2001) – can be identified within the body of communitarian thought.
6 The notion fear of crime refers to the fear of being a victim of crime as opposed to the actual probability of being a victim of crime. The fear of crime, along with fear of the streets and the fear of youth, is said to have been in Western culture for 'time immemorial'.

7 Cultural capital (French: *le capital culturel*) is a sociological concept that has gained widespread popularity since it was first articulated by Pierre Bourdieu. Bourdieu and Jean-Claude Passeron first used the term in 1973 in *Reproduction in Education, Society and Culture* (Bourdieu and Passeron, 1990). In this work he attempted to explain differences in children's outcomes in France during the 1960s. It has since been elaborated and developed in terms of other types of capital in *The Forms of Capital* (1986); and in terms of higher education, for instance, in *The State Nobility* (1996). For Bourdieu, capital acts as a social relation within a system of exchange, and the term is extended 'to all the goods material and symbolic, without distinction, that present themselves as rare and worthy of being sought after in a particular social formation' (cited in Harker, 1990: 13) and cultural capital acts as a social relation within a system of exchange that includes the accumulated cultural knowledge that confers power and status.

8 An Anti-Social Behaviour Order or ASBO is a civil order made against a person who has been shown, on the balance of evidence, to have engaged in anti-social behaviour in the United Kingdom and the Republic of Ireland. The orders, designed originally by former Prime Minister Tony Blair in 1998, were intended to be imposed after minor incidents that would not ordinarily warrant prosecution. The orders restrict behaviour in some way, by prohibiting a return to a certain area or shop, or by restricting public behaviour such as swearing or drinking. Many see the ASBO as connected with young delinquents. In July 2010, new Home Secretary Theresa May announced her intention to reform anti-social behaviour measures for England and Wales with the abolition of ASBOs in due course in favour of alternative 'community-based' social control policies.

8 Conclusions: the future of criminal justice

1 We should note that many commentators and theorists deny the existence of postmodern society – which for such a social formation to exist would require some substantive rupture with the modernist social formation – and thus emphasising the continuities and following the influential social theorist Anthony Giddens (1990, 1991) use the term late modernity. The term *postmodern condition* is thus used by this author, although we might note that the equally distinguished social theorist Norbert Elias (1978, 1982) had previously observed that we live in a period of late barbarism.

2 The Chernobyl disaster was an accident at the Chernobyl Nuclear Power Plant on April 26, 1986, consisting of an explosion at the plant and subsequent radioactive contamination of the surrounding geographic area (see Davidson, 2006).

3 Love Canal is a neighbourhood in Niagara Falls, New York, the site of the worst environmental disaster involving chemical wastes in the history of the USA (see Mazur, 1998).

4 Because males compose over 93 per cent of the US state and federal prison population and 89 per cent of jail inmates, and because the disciplining of women from the lower class and caste continues to operate primarily through welfare and workfare, his analysis focuses solely on men. But a full-fledged analysis of the distinct causes and consequences of the astonishing growth in the imprisonment of black (and Hispanic) women is urgently needed, in part because the penal confinement of women has immensely deleterious effects on their children.

5 From July 27 to August 2, 1919, a race riot broke out in Chicago. When it was over 38 people were dead, 537 injured and about 1000 rendered homeless. The incident that sparked the riot was the drowning of a black youth after he drifted onto a white area of a beach, on a hot, 96 degree day. The reasons for the riot, however, lie with segregation, vicious racism, and the organised activities of white gangs, many of which were

sponsored by Chicago's political machine. Most of the rioting, murder, and arson were concentrated in the Black Belt.

6 In the USA public schools are what the name suggests, free schools provided by the state. In the UK the term is used to describe fee-paying private education.

References

Abbot, K.W. (1999) 'Symposium on Method in International Law: International Relations Theory, International Law and the Regime Governing Atrocities in Internal Conflicts', *American Journal of International Law*, 93 (2): 361–378.

Abram, K.M. (1989) 'The Effect of Co-occurring Disorders on Criminal Careers: Interaction of Antisocial Personality, Alcoholism, and Drug Disorders', *International Journal of Law and Psychiatry*, 12: 122–136.

Adler, F. (1975) *Sisters in Crime: The Rise of the New Female Criminal*, New York: McGraw-Hill.

Aichhorn, A. (1925) *Wayward Youth*, New York: Meridian Books.

Akers, R.L. (1985) *Deviant Behaviour: A Social Learning Approach*, 3rd edn, Belmont, CA: Wadsworth.

Akers, R.L. (1992) 'Linking Sociology and Its Specialities', *Social Forces*, 71: 1–16.

Akers, R.L. (1997) *Criminological Theories: Introduction and Evaluation*, Los Angeles, CA: Roxbury.

Akers, R.L., Krohn, M.D., Lanza-Kaduce, L. and Radosevich, M. (1979) 'Social Learning and Deviant Behaviour: A Specific Test of a General Theory', *American Sociological Review*, 44: 635–655.

Althusser, L. (1969) *For Marx*, London: Allen Lane.

Altman, A. (1986) 'Legal Realism, Critical Legal Studies, and Dworkin', *Philosophy and Public Affairs*, 15 (2).

Anderson, P. (1968) 'Components of the National Culture', *New Left Review*, 161, January–February 1987, reprinted in P. Anderson (1992) *English Questions*, London and New York: Verso.

Ansari, Z.I. (1992) 'The Contribution of the Qur'an and the Prophet to the Development of Islamic Figh', *Journal of Islamic Studies*, 3 (2): 141–171.

Aries, P. (1962) *Centuries of Childhood: A Social History of Family*, trans. Robert Baldick, New York: Alfred A. Knopf.

Armstrong, D. (2005) 'A Risky Business? Research, Policy, Governmentality and Youth Offending', *Youth Justice*, 4 (2): 100–116.

Ashworth, A. (1992) *Sentencing and Penal Policy*, London: Weidenfeld & Nicolson.

Ashworth, A. (1994) *The Criminal Process*, Oxford: Oxford University Press.

Ashworth, A. (1997) 'Sentencing', in M. Maguire, R. Morgan and R. Reiner (eds) *The Oxford Handbook of Criminology*, Oxford: Clarendon Press.

Aubert, W. (1952) 'White Collar Crime and Social Structure', *American Journal of Sociology*, 58: 263–271.

Audit Commission (1996a) *Tackling Crime Effectively*, London: Audit Commission.

Audit Commission (1996b) *Misspent Youth: Young People and Crime*, London: Audit Commission.

Audit Commission (1999) *Annual Report on the Police and Fire Services*, London: Audit Commission.

Austin, J. (1995, originally 1833) *The Province of Jurisprudence Determined*, Cambridge: Cambridge University Press.

Bailey, V. (1987) *Delinquency and Citizenship: Reclaiming the Young Offender 1914–48*, Oxford: Clarendon Press.

Baldwin, J.D. (1990) 'The Role of Sensory Stimulation in Criminal Behaviour, with Special Attention to the Age Peak in Crime', in L. Ellis and H. Hoffman (eds) *Crime in Biological, Social, and Moral Contexts*, New York: Praeger.

Bandura, A. and Walters, R.H. (1959) *Adolescent Aggression*, New York: Ronald Press.

Barnett, R. (1985) 'Restitution: A New Paradigm of Criminal Justice', in J. Murphy (ed.) *Punishment and Rehabilitation*, 2nd edn, London: Wadsworth Publishing.

Barry, A., Osborne, T. and Rose, N. (1996) *Foucault and Political Reason: Liberalism, Neo-Liberalism and Rationalities of Government*, London: UCL Press.

Baudrillard, J. (1988) *Selected Writings*, Stanford, CA: Stanford University Press.

Bauman, Z. (1989) *Modernity and the Holocaust*, Cambridge: Polity Press.

Bauman, Z. (1991) *Modernity and Ambivalence*, Cambridge: Polity Press.

Bauman, Z. (1993) *Postmodern Ethics*, Oxford: Blackwell.

Baumhart, R.C. (1961) 'How Ethical are Businessmen', *Harvard Business Review*, 39: 156–176.

Baxter, R. and Nuttall, C. (1975) 'Severe Sentences: No Deterrent?' *New Society*, 2 January: 11–13.

Beccaria, C. (1963, originally 1764) *On Crimes and Punishments*, London: Bobbs-Merrill.

Beck, U. (1992) *Risk Society*, London: Sage.

Becker, G.S. (1968) 'Crime and Punishment: An Economic Approach', *Journal of Political Economy*, 76 (2): 169–217.

Becker, H. (1963) *Outsiders: Studies in the Sociology of Deviance*, New York: Free Press.

Bennett, T. and Wright, R. (1984) *Burglars on Burglary*, Aldershot: Gower.

Bennett, T., Holloway, K. and Williams, T. (2001) *Drug Use and Offending: Summary Results From the First Year of the NEW-ADAM Research Programme*, Findings 148, London: Home Office.

Bentham, J. (1970, originally 1789) *An Introduction to the Principles of Morals and Legislation*, ed. J.H. Burns and H.L.A. Hart, London: Athlone Press.

Bequai, A. (2002) *How to Prevent Computer Crime: A Guide to Forensics and Technology*, San Diego, CA: Academic Press.

Bernard, T.J. (1983) *The Consensus-Conflict Debate*, New York: Columbia University Press.

Beyleveld, D. (1978) *The Effectiveness of General Deterrents Against Crime: An Annotated Bibliography of Evaluative Research*, Cambridge: Cambridge Institute of Criminology.

Beyleveld, D. (1980) *A Bibliography on General Deterrence Research*, London: Saxon House.

Bishop, D. (1984) 'Legal and Extralegal Barriers to Delinquency: A Panel Analysis', *Criminology*, 22 (August): 403–419.

Bix, B. (1995) 'Conceptual Questions and Jurisprudence', *Legal Theory*, 1 (4): 465–479.

Bix, B. (1996) *Jurisprudence: Theory and Context*, Boulder, CO: Westview Press.

Blackstone, W. (1979) *Commentaries on the Law of England*, Chicago, IL: University of Chicago Press.

Blair, T. (1998) *The Third Way: New Politics for the New Century*, London: The Fabian Society.

Blumberg, A. (1967) *Criminal Justice*, Chicago, IL: Quadrangle Books.

Blumstein, A. and Wallman, J. (eds) (2000) *The Crime Drop in America*, New York: Cambridge University Press.

Bottomley, A.K., James, A., Clare, E. and Liebling, A. (1996) 'The Wolds Remand Centre – An Evaluation', Home Office Research Findings No. 32, London: Home Office.

Bottoms, A. (1974) 'On the Decriminalization of the Juvenile Court', in R. Hood (ed.) *Crime, Criminology and Public Policy*, London: Heinemann.

Bottoms, A. (1977) 'Reflections on the Renaissance of Dangerousness', *The Howard Journal*, 16 (2): 70–96.

Bottoms, A.E. (1983) 'Neglected Features of Contemporary Penal Systems', in D. Garland and P. Young (eds) *The Power to Punish*, London: Heinemann.

Bottoms, A.E. and McClean, J. (1976) *Defendants in the Criminal Process*, London: Routledge.

Bottoms, A.E. and Preston, R.H. (eds) (1980) *The Coming Penal Crisis: A Criminological and Theological Exploration*, Edinburgh: Scottish Academic Press.

Bourdieu, P. (1986) *The Forms of Capital*, English version in J.G. Richardson *Handbook for Theory and Research for the Sociology of Education*, London: Sage.

Bourdieu, P. (1996) *The State Nobility*, London: Sage.

Bourdieu, P. and Passeron, J.-C. (1990, originally 1973) *Reproduction in Education, Society and Culture*, London: Sage.

Bowlby, J. (1952) *Maternal Care and Mental Health*, 2nd edn, Geneva: World Health Organization.

Bowling, B. (1998a) Review of N. Dennis (ed.) 'Zero Tolerance: Policing a Free Society', *British Journal of Criminology*, 38 (2): 318–321.

Bowling, B. (1998b) *The Rise and Fall of New York Murder*, Paper presented to the University of Cambridge/Police Research Group Seminar, 'Police and Crime Reduction', 3 March 1998.

Box, S. (1981) *Deviance, Reality and Society*, 2nd edn, London: Rinehart & Winston.

Box, S. (1983) *Crime, Power and Mystification*, London: Sage.

Box, S. (1987) *Recession, Crime and Punishment*, London: Macmillan.

Box, S. and Hale, C. (1983) 'Liberation and Female Criminality in England and Wales', *British Journal of Criminology*, 23 (1).

Bradford, W. (2004) 'In the Minds of Men: A Theory of Compliance with the Laws of War', Available at SSRN: http://ssrn.com/abstract=555894

Bradley, F.H. (1962) 'The Vulgar Notion of Responsibility in Connection with the Theories of Free Will and Necessity', *Ethical Studies*, 2nd edn, Oxford: Oxford University Press.

Braithwaite, J. (1979) *Inequality, Crime and Public Policy*, London: Routledge & Kegan Paul.

Braithwaite, J. (1984) *Corporate Crime in the Pharmaceutical Industry*, London: Routledge.

Braithwaite, J. (1989) *Crime, Shame and Reintegration*, Cambridge: Cambridge University Press.

Braithwaite, J. and Geis, G. (1982) 'On Theory and Action for Corporate Crime Control', *Crime & Delinquency*, 28 (April): 292–314.

Brake, M. (1980) *The Sociology of Youth Cultures and Youth Sub-cultures*, London: Routledge & Kegan Paul.

Brake, M. (1985) *Comparative Youth Culture*, London: Routledge.

Brantingham, P.J. and Brantingham, P.L. (eds) (1981) *Environmental Criminology*, Beverly Hills, CA: Sage.

Bratton, W.J. (1997) 'Crime is Down in New York City: Blame the Police', in N. Dennis (ed.) *Zero Tolerance: Policing a Free Society*, London: Institute for Economic Affairs.

Brody, S. (1976) *The Effectiveness of Sentencing*, Home Office Research Study No. 35, London: HMSO.

Brody, S. and Tarling, R. (1980) *Taking Offenders out of Circulation*, Home Office Research Study No. 64, London: HMSO.

Brown, S. (1998) *Understanding Youth and Crime*, Buckingham: Open University Press.

Bunyan, T. (1976) *The Political Police in Britain*, London: Julian Friedmann Publishers.

Bunyan, T. (1978) *The History and Practice of the Political Police in Britain*, London: Quartet.

Burgess, E.W. (1928) 'The Growth of the City', in R. Park, E.W. Burgess and R.D. McKenzie, *The City*, Chicago, IL: University of Chicago Press.

Burke, E. (1790) *Reflections on the Revolution in France*, London: J. Dodsley.

Burney, E. (2005) *Making People Behave: Anti-social Behaviour, Politics and Policy*, Cullompton: Willan Publishing.

Burt, C. (1945) *The Young Delinquent*, London: University of London Press.

Burton, J. (1990) *The Sources of Islamic Law: Theories of Abrogation.* Edinburgh: University of Edinburgh Press.

Burton, J. (1994) *An Introduction to the Hadith*, Edinburgh: University of Edinburgh Press.

Burton, R.V., Maccoby, E. and Allinsmith, W. (1961) 'Antecedents of Resistance to Temptation in Four-year-old Children', *Child Development*, 32: 689.

Byrne, H.J. (1979) 'Society Needs Draconian Justice', *The New York Times*, 20 October, A23, in J.E. Conklin (1986) *Criminology*, 2nd edn, Basingstoke: Macmillan.

Campbell, B. (1993) *Goliath: Britain's Dangerous Places*, London: Methuen.

Carew, R. (1979) 'The Place of Knowledge in Social Work Activity', *British Journal of Social Work*, 19 (3): 349–364.

Carlen, P. (1983) *Women's Imprisonment*, London: Routledge & Kegan Paul.

Carlen, P. (1989) 'Crime, Inequality and Sentencing', in P. Carlen and D. Cook (eds) *Paying for Crime*, Milton Keynes: Open University Press.

Carrington, B. and Wilson, B. (2002) 'Global Clubcultures: Cultural Flows and Late Modern Dance Music Cultures', in M. Cieslik and G. Pollock (eds) *Young People in Risk Society: The Restructuring of Youth Identities in Late Modernity*, Aldershot: Ashgate.

Carter, D. (1997) 'International Organized Crime: Emerging Trends in Entrepreneurial Crime', in P. Ryan and G. Rush (eds) *Understanding Organized Crime in Global Perspective*, Newbury Park, CA: Sage.

Castells, M. (1998) *End of Millennium (The Information Age: Economy Society and Culture III)*, Oxford: Blackwell.

Cavadino, M. and Dignan, J. (1997) *The Penal System: An Introduction*, London: Sage.

Cavadino, M. and Dignan, J. (2006) *The Penal System: An Introduction*, 4th edn, London: Sage.

Chambliss, W.J. (1975) 'Toward a Political Economy of Crime', *Theory and Society*, 2: 152–153.

Charlesworth, H. (2010) *Fault Lines of International Legitimacy*, Cambridge: Cambridge University Press.

Chayes, A., Ehrlich, T. and Lowenfeld, A. (1968) *International Legal Process: Materials for An Introductory Course*, London: Little Brown.

Cheng, T.-H. (2004) 'The Central Case Approach to Human Rights', *Pacific Rim Law and Policy*, 13 (237): 245–262.

Christiansen, K.O. (1968) 'Threshold of Tolerance in Various Population Groups Illustrated by Results from the Danish Criminologic Twin Study', in A.V.S. de Reuck and R. Porter (eds) *The Mentally Abnormal Offender*, Boston, MA: Little, Brown.

Christiansen, K.O. (1975) 'On General Prevention from an Empirical Viewpoint', in National Swedish Council of Crime Prevention, *General Deterrence: A Conference on Current Research and Standpoints, 2–4 June 1975*, Stockholm: National Swedish Council for Crime Prevention: 60–74.

Christie, N. (1977) 'Conflicts as Property', *British Journal of Criminology*, 17 (1): 1–15.

Christie, N. (1993) *Crime Control as Industry: Towards Gulags, Western Style?* London: Routledge.

Cicourel, A. (1968) *The Social Organisation of Juvenile Justice*, New York: Wiley.

Clapham, B. (1989) 'A Case of Hypoglycaemia', *The Criminologist*, 13: 2–15.

Clark, J. (1975) *Ideologies of Control of Working Class Youth*, University of Birmingham: Centre for Contemporary Cultural Studies.

Clark, K.B. (1965) *Dark Ghetto: Dilemmas of Social* Power, Middletown, CT: Wesleyan University Press.

Clarke, J. and Cochrane, A. (1998) 'The Social Construction of Social Problems', in E. Saraga (ed.) *Embodying the Social Construction of Difference*, London: Routledge/ Open University.

Clarke, R.V.G. (1987) 'Rational Choice Theory and Prison Psychology', in B.J. McGurk *et al.* (eds) *Applying Psychology to Imprisonment: Theory and Practice*, London: HMSO.

Cleckley, H. (1976) *The Mask of Sanity*, 2nd edn, St Louis, MO: C.V. Mosby.

Clegg, S. (1989) *Frameworks of Power*, London: Sage.

Clinard, M.B. (1952) *The Black Market: A Study of White Collar Crime*, New York: Holt, Rinehart & Winston.

Cloninger, C.R. and Gottesman, I.I. (1987) 'Genetic and Environmental Factors in Antisocial Behaviour Disorders', in S.A. Mednick, T.E. Moffit and S. Stack, *The Causes of Crime: New Biological Approaches*, Cambridge: Cambridge University Press.

Cloward, R.A. and Ohlin, L.E. (1960) *Delinquency and Opportunity: A Theory of Delinquent Gangs*, New York: Free Press.

Cohen, A.K. (1955) *Delinquent Boys: The Culture of the Gang*, New York: Free Press.

Cohen, L.E. and Felson, M. (1979) 'Social Inequality and Predatory Criminal Victimization: An Exposition and Test of a Formal Theory', *American Sociological Review*, 44: 588–608.

Cohen, P. (1972) 'Sub-Cultural Conflict and Working Class Community', *Working Papers in Cultural Studies*, No.2, Birmingham: CCCS, University of Birmingham.

Cohen, P. (1979) 'Policing the Working Class City', in B. Fine, R. Kinsey, J. Lea, S. Picciotto and J. Young (eds) *Capitalism and the Rule of Law*, London: Hutchinson.

Cohen, S. (1973) *Folk Devils and Moral Panics: The Creation of the Mods and Rockers*, London: Paladin.

Cohen, S. (1980, new edition) *Folk Devils and Moral Panics*, Oxford: Martin Robertson.

Cohen, S. (1985) *Visions of Social Control*, Cambridge: Polity Press.

Collins, J.J. (1986) 'The Relationship of Problem Drinking in Individual Offending Sequences', in A. Blumstein, J. Cohen, J. Roth and C. Visher (eds) *Criminal Careers and 'Career Criminals'*, Vol. 2, Washington, DC: National Academy Press.

Collins, J.J. (1988) 'Alcohol and Interpersonal Violence: Less than Meets the Eye', in

A. Weiner and M.E. Wolfgang (eds) *Pathways to Criminal Violence*, Newbury Park, CA: Sage.

Collins, R. (1975) *Conflict Sociology*, New York: Academic.

Colvin, M. (2000) *Crime and Coercion: An Integrated Theory of Chronic Criminality*, New York: St Martin's Press.

Communities that Care UK (2001) 'Risk and Protective Factors Associated with Youth Crime and Effective Interventions to Prevent it', Youth Justice Board Research No. 5, London: Youth Justice Board.

Communities that Care (2002) 'Youth at Risk? A National Survey of Risk Factors, Protective Factors and Problem Behaviour Among Young People in England, Scotland and Wales', London: Communities that Care.

Comte, A. (1976, originally 1842) *The Foundations of Sociology* (readings edited and with an introduction by K. Thompson), London: Nelson.

Conklin, J.E. (1977) *'Illegal but not Criminal': Business Crime in America*, New York: Prentice-Hall.

Connell, R.W. (1987) *Gender and Power*, Cambridge: Polity.

Connell, R.W. (1995) *Masculinities*, Cambridge: Polity.

Constitutional Rights Foundation (2009) *The Origins of Islamic Law*, online at: http://www.crf-usa.org/terror/islam_law.htm

Cornish, D.B. and Clarke, R.V.G. (1986) *The Reasoning Criminal*, New York: Springer-Verlag.

Cornwell, R. (2002) 'Shocked and Angry: The Prophet Whose Warnings Over Wall Street Were Ignored', *The Independent*, 1 July.

Cortes, J.B. and Gatti, F.M. (1972) *Delinquency and Crime: A Biopsychological Approach*, New York: Seminar Press.

Crawford, A. (1996) 'Alternatives to Prosecution: Access to, or Exits from Criminal Justice?', in R. Young and D. Wall (eds) *Access to Criminal Justice: Legal Aid, Lawyers and the Defence of Liberty*, London: Blackstone Press.

Crawford, A. (1997) *The Local Governance of Crime: Appeals to Community and Partnerships*, Oxford: Clarendon Press.

Crawford, A. and Clear, T.R. (2003) 'Community Justice: Transforming Communities through Restorative Justice?' in E. McLaughlin, R. Fergusson, G. Hughes and L. Westmarland, *Restorative Justice: Critical Issues*, London: Sage/Open University.

Critchley, T.A. (1978) *A History of Police in England and Wales*, London: Constable.

Crowther, C. (1998) 'Policing the Excluded Society', in R. Hopkins Burke (ed.) *Zero Tolerance Policing*, Leicester: Perpetuity Press.

Crowther, C. (2000a) *Policing Urban Poverty*, Basingstoke: Macmillan.

Crowther, C. (2000b) 'Thinking About the "Underclass": Towards a Political Economy of Policing', *Theoretical Criminology*, 4 (2): 149–167.

Crowther, C. (2007) *An Introduction to Criminology and Criminal* Justice, Basingstoke: Palgrave Macmillan.

Cullen, F. and Gilbert, K. (1982) *Reaffirming Rehabilitation*, Cincinnati: Anderson.

Currie, E. (1997) *Confronting Crime: An American Challenge*, New York: Pantheon.

Dahrendorf, R. (1958) 'Out of Utopia: Toward a Reconstruction of Sociological Analysis', *American Journal of Sociology*, 67 (September): 115–127.

Dahrendorf, R. (1985) *Law and Order*, London: Stevens.

Dale, D. (1984) 'The Politics of Crime', *Salisbury Review*, October.

Dalgard, S.O. and Kringlen, E. (1976) 'Norwegian Twin Study of Criminality', *British Journal of Criminology*, 16: 213–232.

Dalton, K. (1961) 'Menstruation and Crime', *British Medical Journal*, 2: 1752–1753.

Dalton, K. (1964) *The Pre-menstrual Syndrome and Progesterone Therapy*, London: Heinemann Medical.

Damer, S. (1974) 'Wine Alley: The Sociology of a Dreadful Enclosure', *Sociological Review*, 22: 221–248.

Darwin, C. (1871) *The Descent of Man*, London: John Murray.

Davies, B. (1982) 'Juvenile Justice in Confusion', *Youth and Policy*, 1 (2).

Davies, H. and Holdcroft, D. (1991) *Jurisprudence: Text and Commentary*, London: Butterworths.

Davies, M., Croall, H. and Tyrer, J. (1995) *Criminal Justice*, Harlow: Longman.

Davis, J. (1990) *Youth and the Condition of Britain*, London: Athlone Press.

Davis, W. (1971) *The Freewill Question*, New York: Nijhoff.

Day-Sclater, S. and Piper, C. (2000) 'Re-moralising the Family? Family Policy, Family Law and Youth Justice', *Child and Family Law Quarterly*, 12(2): 135–151.

De Brie, C. (2000) 'Thick as Thieves', *Le Monde Diplomatique* (April) http://www.monde-diplomatique.fr/en/2000/04/05debrie

Delgado, R. and Stefanic, J. (1997) *Critical White Studies: Looking Beyond the Mirror*, Philadelphia, PA: Temple University Press.

DeLuca, J.R. (ed.) (1981) *Fourth Special Report to the US Congress on Alcohol and Health*, Rockville, MD: National Institute on Alcohol Abuse and Alcoholism.

Dennis, N. (ed.) (1997) *Zero Tolerance: Policing a Free Society*, London: Institute of Economic Affairs.

Dennis, N. and Erdos, G. (1992) *Families Without Fatherhood*, London: Institute of Economic Affairs.

Dennis, N. and Mallon, R. (1997) 'Confident Policing in Hartlepool', in N. Dennis (ed.) *Zero Tolerance: Policing a Free Society*, London: Institute of Economic Affairs.

Department of Health (2005) *Smoking, Drinking and Drug Use among Young People in England in 2004*, London: Department of Health.

Devlin, P. (1965) *The Enforcement of Morals*, Oxford: Oxford University Press.

Dickinson, L. (2007) 'Commentary: Toward a "New" New Haven School of International Law?' *Yale Journal of International Law*, 32: 547–552.

Dobash, R.E. and Dobash, R.P. (1992) *Women, Violence and Social Change*, London: Routledge & Kegan Paul.

Donzelot, J. (1980) *The Policing of Families: Welfare versus the State*, London: Hutchinson.

Donziger, S.R. (1996) *The Real War on Crime: The Report of the National Criminal Justice Commission*, New York: Harper Perennial.

Downes, D. (1966) *The Delinquent Solution*, London: Routledge & Kegan Paul.

Downes, D. and Rock, P. (1998) *Understanding Deviance*, 3rd edn, Oxford: Oxford University Press.

Driver, S. and Martell, L. (1997) 'New Labour's Communitarianisms', *Critical Social Policy*, 52: 27–46.

Dugdale, R.L. (1877) *The Jukes*, New York: Putnam.

Durkheim, E. (1933, originally 1893) *The Division of Labour in Society*, Glencoe, IL: Free Press.

Durkheim, E. (1951, originally 1897) *Suicide*, New York: Free Press.

Durkheim, E. (1964, originally 1915) *The Elementary Forms of Religious Life*, Glencoe, IL: Free Press.

Durkheim, E. (1965, originally 1895) *The Rules of Sociological Method*, trans. S.A. Solovay and J.H. Mueller, ed. G.E.G. Caitlin, London: Free Press.

Dworkin, G. (1972) 'Paternalism', *The Monist*, 56.

Dworkin, R. (1977) *Taking Rights Seriously*, Cambridge, MA: Harvard University Press.

Dworkin, R. (1982) '"Natural" Law Revisited', *University of Florida Law Review*, 165.

Dworkin, R. (1986) *Law's Empire*, Cambridge, MA: Harvard University Press.

Edmunds, M., Hough, M. and Turnbull, P.J. (1999) *Doing Justice to Treatment: Referring Offenders to Drug Treatment Services*, Drugs Prevention Initiative Paper No. 2, London: Home Office.

Eduardo, F. (2000) 'International Money Information Network for Money Laundering Investigators', *Journal of Money Laundering Control*, New York: Cambridge University Press.

Eduardo, F. (2002) 'Combating Money Laundering and Financing of Terrorism', *International Monetary Fund*, 39 (3): 126–139.

Elias, N. (1978) *The Civilising Process, Vol. 1: The History of Manners*, Oxford: Blackwell.

Elias, N. (1982) *The Civilising Process, Vol. 2: State-Formation and Civilisation*, Oxford: Blackwell.

Elliot, D., Ageton, S. and Canter, J. (1979) 'An Integrated Theoretical Perspective on Delinquent Behaviour', *Journal of Research in Crime and Delinquency*, 16: 126–149.

Ellis, E. (1993) *The Non-Traditional Approach to Criminal Justice and Social Justice*, New York: Community Justice Center.

Ellis, L. (1990) 'The Evolution of Violent Criminal Behaviour and its Non-Legal Equivalent', in L. Ellis and H. Hoffman (eds) *Crime in Biological, Social and Moral Contexts*, New York: Praeger.

Ellis, L. and Crontz, P.D. (1990) 'Androgens, Brain Functioning, and Criminality: The Neurohormonal Foundations of Antisociality', in L. Ellis and H. Hoffman (eds) *Crime in Biological, Social, and Moral Contexts*, New York: Praeger.

Ellis, R.D. and Ellis, C.S. (1989) *Theories of Criminal Justice: A Critical Reappraisal*, London: Longman.

Emanuel, E. (1991) *The Ends of Human Life: Medical Ethics in a Liberal Polity*, Cambridge, MA: Harvard University Press.

Emsley, C. (1996) *The English Police: A Political and Social History*, Harlow: Longman.

Emsley, C. (2001) 'The Origins and Development of the Police', in E. McLaughlin and J. Muncie (eds) *Controlling Crime*, London: Sage/Open University.

Emsley, C. (2002) 'The History of Crime and Crime Control Institutions', in M. Maguire, R. Morgan and R. Reiner (eds) *The Oxford Handbook of Criminology*, 3rd edn, Oxford: Oxford University Press.

Emsley, C, (2009) *The Great British Bobby*, London: Queraus Books.

Ericson, R.V. and Haggerty, D. (1997) *Policing the Risk Society*, Oxford: Clarendon Press.

Etzioni, A. (1961) *A Comparative Analysis of Complex Organisations*, Glencoe, IL: Free Press.

Etzioni, A. (ed.) (1991) *New Communitarian Thinking: Persons, Virtues, Institutions and Communities*, Charlottesville: University of Virginia Press.

Etzioni, A. (1993) *The Spirit of Community: The Reinvention of American Society*, New York: Touchstone.

Etzioni, A. (ed.) (1995a) *New Communitarian Thinking: Persons, Virtues, Institutions and Communities*, 2nd edn, Charlottesville: University of Virginia Press.

Etzioni, A. (1995b) *The Parenting Deficit*, London: Demos.

Eysenck, H.J. (1970) *Crime and Personality*, London: Granada.

Eysenck, H.J. (1977) *Crime and Personality*, 3rd edn, London: Routledge & Kegan Paul.

Fagan, J. (1990) 'Intoxication and Aggression', in M. Tonry and J.Q. Wilson (eds) *Crime and Justice: A Review of Research*, 13, Chicago, IL: University of Chicago Press.

Farnsworth, M. (1989) 'Theory Integration versus Model Building', in S.F. Messner, M.D. Krohn and A.E. Liska (eds) *Theoretical Integration in the Study of Deviance and Crime*, Albany, NY: State University of New York Press.

Farrington, D.P. (1992) 'Juvenile Delinquency', in J.C. Coleman (ed.) *The School Years*, 2nd edn, London: Routledge.

Farrington, D.P. (1994) 'Introduction', in D.P. Farrington (ed.) *Psychological Explanations of Crime*, Aldershot: Dartmouth.

Farrington, D.P. and Morris, A.M. (1983) 'Sex, Sentencing and Reconviction', *British Journal of Criminology*, 23 (3).

Feeley, M. and Simon, J. (1994) 'Actuarial Justice: The Emerging New Criminal Law', in D. Nelken (ed.) *The Futures of Criminology*, London: Sage.

Feeney, F. (1985) 'Interdependence as a Working Concept', in D. Moxon (ed.) *Managing Criminal Justice*, London: Home Office.

Feinberg, J. (1979) 'Civil Disobedience in the Modern World', *Humanities in Review*, 2: 37–60.

Feinberg, J. (1985) *Offense to Others*, Oxford: Oxford University Press.

Feldman, M.P. (1977) *Criminal Behaviour: A Psychological Analysis*, Bath: Pitman Press.

Fellner, J. and Mauer, M. (1998) *Losing the Vote: The Impact of Felony Disenfranchisement in the United States*, Washington, DC: Human Rights Watch and The Sentencing Project.

Felson, M. (1998) *Crime and Everyday Life*, 2nd edn, Thousand Oaks, CA: Pine Forge.

Fergusson, R., Pye, D., Esland, G., McLaughlin, E. and Muncie, J. (2000) 'Normalised Dislocation and the New Subjectivities in Post-16 Markets for Education and Work', *Critical Social Policy*, 20 (3): 283–305.

Ferrell, J. (1996) *Crimes of Style: Urban Graffiti and the Politics of Criminality*, Boston, MA: Northeastern University.

Ferrell, J. (1997) 'Criminological *Verstehen*: Inside the Immediacy of Crime', *Justice Quarterly*, 14: 3–23.

Ferrell, J. (1998) 'Against the Law: Anarchist Criminology', *Social Anarchism*, 25: 5–23.

Ferrell, J. (1999) 'Cultural Criminology', *Annual Review of Criminology*, 25: 395–418.

Ferrell, J. and Sanders, C.R. (eds) (1995) *Cultural Criminology*, Boston, MA: Northeastern University Press.

Ferri, E. (1895) *Criminal Sociology*, London: Unwin.

Fielding, N. (1988) *Joining Forces*, London: Routledge.

Findlay, M. (2000) *The Globalisation of Crime*, London: Cambridge University Press.

Finnis, J. (1980) *Natural Law and Natural Rights*, Oxford: Clarendon Press.

Fionda, J. (2005) *Devils and Angels*, Oxford: Hartley Publishing.

Fishbein, D.H. and Pease, S.E. (1990) *The Dynamic of Drug Abuse*, Boston, MA: Allyn & Bacon.

Fitzgerald, M. and Sim, J. (1982) *British Prisons*, Oxford: Basil Blackwell.

Flanzer, J. (1981) 'The Vicious Circle of Alcoholism and Family Violence', *Alcoholism*, 1 (3): 30–45.

Flood-Page, C., Campbell, S., Harington, V. and Miller, J. (2000) *Youth Crime Findings from the 1998/99 Youth Lifestyles Survey*, Home Office Research Study 209, London: Home Office.

Floud, J. and Young, W. (1981) *Dangerousness and Criminal Justice*, London: Heinemann Educational Books.

Fogelson, R. (1977) *Big City Police*, Cambridge, MA: Harvard University Press.

Foot, P. (1957) 'Free Will as Involving Determinism', *Philosophical Review*, 66: 439–50.

Forsythe, D. (2000) *Human Rights in International Relations*, Cambridge: Cambridge University Press.

Foucault, M. (1971) *Madness and Civilisation: A History of Insanity in the Age of Reason*, London: Tavistock.

Foucault, M. (1976) *The History of Sexuality*, London: Allen Lane.

Foucault, M. (1977) *Discipline and Punish – the Birth of the Prison*, London: Allen Lane.

Foucault, M. (1980) *Power/Knowledge: Selected Interviews and Other Writings 1972–77*, ed. C. Gordon, Brighton: Harvester Press.

Franklin, R.L. (1969) *Freewill and Determinism*, London: Routledge.

Freud, S. (1920) *A General Introduction to Psychoanalysis*, New York: Boni & Liveright.

Freud, S. (1927) *The Ego and the Id*, London: Hogarth.

Friedlander, K. (1947) *The Psychoanalytic Approach to Juvenile Delinquency*, London: Kegan Paul.

Friedlander, K. (1949) 'Latent Delinquency and Ego Development', in K.R. Eissler (ed.) *Searchlights on Delinquency*, New York: International University Press: 205–215.

Fuller, L.L. (1958) 'Positivism and Fidelity to Law', *Harvard Law Review*, 630.

Fuller, L.L. (1964) *The Morality of Law*, New Haven, CT: Yale University Press.

Furlong, A. and Cartmel, F. (1997) *Young People and Social Change*, Buckingham: Open University Press.

Füsser, K. 'Farewell to "Legal Positivism": The Separation Thesis Unravelling', in R.P. George (1996) *The Autonomy of Law: Essays on Legal Positivism*, Oxford: Clarendon Press.

Fyfe, N.R. (1995) 'Law and Order Policy and the Spaces of Citizenship in Contemporary Britain', *Political Geography*, 14 (2): 177–189.

Garfinkel, H. (1984) *Studies in Ethnomethodology*, Oxford: Basil Blackwell.

Garland, D. (1996) 'The Limits of the Sovereign State: Strategies of Crime Control in Contemporary Society', *British Journal of Criminology*, 34 (4): 445–471.

Garland, D. (1999) '"Governmentality" and the Problem of Crime', in R. Smandych (ed.) *Governable Places: Readings on Governmentality and Crime Control*, Aldershot: Ashgate.

Garland, D. (2001) *The Culture of Control*, Oxford: Oxford University Press.

Garofalo, R. (1914) *Criminology*, Boston, MA: Little, Brown.

Gatrell, V. (1980) 'The Decline of Theft and Violence in Victorian and Edwardian England', in V. Gatrell, B. Lenman and G. Parker (eds) *Crime and the Law: The Social History of Crime in Europe Since 1500*, London: Europa.

Geis, G. (1968) *White-collar Crime: The Offender in Business and the Professions*, New York: Atherton.

Gelsthorpe, L. (1999) 'Parents and Criminal Children', in A. Bainham, S. Day Sclater and M. Richards (eds) *What is a Parent? A Socio-legal Analysis*, Oxford: Hart.

Gelsthorpe, L. and Morris, A. (1994) 'Juvenile Justice 1945–1992', in M. Maguire, R. Morgan and R. Reiner, *The Oxford Handbook of Criminology*, Oxford: Clarendon Press.

Gendreau, P. and Ross, B. (1979) 'Effective Correctional Treatment: Bibliotherapy for Cynics', *Crime and Delinquency*, 25 (October): 463–489.

Gibbens, T.C.N. (1963) *Psychiatric Studies of Borstal Lads*, Oxford: Oxford University Press.

Gibbons, D.C. (1970) *Delinquent Behaviour*, Englewood Cliffs, NJ: Prentice-Hall.

Gibbs, J. (1975) *Crime, Punishment, and Deterrence*, New York: Elsevier.

Giddens, A. (1990) *The Consequences of Modernity*, Cambridge: Polity Press.

Giddens, A. (1991) *Modernity and Self-Identity*, Cambridge: Polity Press.

Giddens, A. (1998) *The Third Way*, Cambridge: Polity Press.

Gilens, M. (2000) *Why Americans Hate Welfare: Race, Media, and the Politics of Anti-Poverty Policy*, Chicago, IL: University of Chicago Press.

Gill, O. (1977) *Luke Street: Housing Policy, Conflict and the Creation of the Delinquency Area*, London: Macmillan.

Gill, M. and Matthews, R. (1994) 'Robbers on Robbery: Offender Perspectives', in M. Gill (ed.) *Crime at Work: Studies in Security and Crime Prevention, Vol. 1*, Leicester: Perpetuity Press.

Gilliom, J. (1994) *Surveillance, Privacy and the Law: Employee Drug Testing and the Politics of Social Control*, Michigan: University of Michigan Press.

Gillis, G.R. (1974) *Youth and History*, London: Academic Press.

Glendon, M.A. (1991) *Rights Talk: The Impoverishment of Political Discourse*, New York: Free Press.

Glueck, S. and Glueck, E. (1950) *Unravelling Juvenile Delinquency*, Oxford: Oxford University Press.

Goddard, H.H. (1914) *Feeblemindedness: Its Causes and Consequences*, New York: Macmillan.

Goldson, B. and Muncie, J. (2006) *Youth Crime and Justice*, London: Sage.

Goldthorpe, J.H. (1968–1969) *The Affluent Worker in the Class Structure*, 3 vols, Cambridge: Cambridge University Press.

Goodwin, D., Schulsinger, F., Hermansen, L., Guze, S. and Winokur, G. (1973) 'Alcohol Problems in Adoptees Raised Apart from Alcoholic Biological Parents', *Archives of General Psychiatry*, 28: 238–243.

Gordon, A.F. (1999) 'Globalism and the Prison Industrial Complex: An Interview with Angela Davis', *Race and Class*, 40: 145–157.

Goring, C. (1913) *The English Convict: A Statistical Study*, London: HMSO.

Gottfredson, M.R. (1979) 'Treatment Destruction Techniques', *Journal of Research in Crime and Delinquency*, 16 (January): 39–54.

Gottfredson, M.R. (1984) *Victims of Crime: The Dimension of Risk*, Home Office Research Study No. 81, London: HMSO.

Gottfredson, M.R. and Hirschi, T. (1990) *A General Theory of Crime*, Stanford, CA: Stanford University Press.

Gramsci, A. (1977–1978) *Selections from the Political Writings*, London: Lawrence & Wishart.

Grasmick, H.G. and Green, D.E. (1980) 'Legal Punishment, Social Disapproval and Internalization as Inhibitors of Illegal Behaviour', *Journal of Criminal Law and Criminology*, 71 (Fall): 325–335.

Greenwood, P. (1984) 'Selective Incapacitation: A Method of Using Our Prisons More Effectively', *NIJ Reports* (January): 4–7.

Griffin, C. (1997) 'Representations of the Young', in J. Roache and S. Tucker (eds) *Youth in Society*, London: Sage.

Gross, E. (1978) 'Organisations as Criminal Actors', in J. Braithwaite and P. Wilson (eds) *Two Faces of Deviance: Crimes of the Powerless and the Powerful*, Brisbane: University of Queensland Press.

Guerry, A.M. (1833) *Essai sur la Statisque Morale de la France*, Paris: Crochard.

Hagan, J. (1989) *Structural Criminology*, New Brunswick, NJ: Rutgers University Press.

Hagan, J., Gillis, A.R. and Simpson, J. (1985) 'The Class Structure of Gender and Delinquency: Toward a Power-Control Theory of Common Delinquent Behavior', *American Journal of Sociology*, 90 (2): 1151–1178.

Hagan, J., Gillis, A.R. and Simpson, J. (1987) 'Class in the Household: A Power-Control Theory of Gender and Delinquency', *American Journal of Sociology*, 92 (4): 788–816.

Hagan, J., Gillis, A.R. and Simpson, J. (1990) 'Clarifying and Extending Power-Control Theory', *American Journal of Sociology*, 95 (4): 1024–1037.

Hagell, A. and Newburn, T. (1994) *Persistent Young Offenders*, London: Policy Studies Institute.

Hall, G.S. (1906) *Youth: Its Regime and Hygiene*, New York: Appleton.

Hall, S., Critcher, C., Jefferson, T., Clarke, J. and Roberts, B. (1978) *Policing the Crisis*, London: Macmillan.

Hanmer, J. and Saunders, S. (1984) *Well-Founded Fear*, London: Hutchinson.

Hare, D.R. (1980) 'A Research Scale for the Assessment of Psychopathy in Criminal Populations', *Personality and Individual Differences*, 1: 111–119.

Hare, D.R. (1982) 'Psychopathy and Physiological Activity During Anticipation of an Aversive Stimulus in a Distraction Paradigm', *Psychophysiology*, 19: 266–280.

Hare, D.R. and Jutari, J.W. (1986) 'Twenty Years of Experience with the Cleckley Psychopath', in W.H. Reid, D. Dorr, J.I. Walker and J.W. Bonner (eds) *Unmasking the Psychopath: Antisocial Personality and Related Syndromes*, New York: Norton.

Harker, R. (1990) 'Education and Cultural Capital', in R. Harker, C. Mahar and C. Wilkes (eds) *An Introduction to the Work of Pierre Bourdieu: The Practice of Theory*, London: Macmillan.

Harris, A.P. (1990) 'Race and Essentialism in Feminist Legal Theory', *Stanford Law Review*, 42: 581–616.

Harris, R. and Webb, D. (1987) *Welfare, Power and Juvenile Justice*, London: Tavistock.

Hart, H.L.A. (1963) *Law, Liberty and Morality*, Oxford: Oxford University Press.

Hart, H.L.A. (1994) *The Concept of Law*, 2nd edn, Oxford: Oxford University Press.

Hart, J. (1978) 'Police', in W. Cornish (ed.) *Crime and Law*, Dublin: Irish University Press.

Harvey, D. (1989) *The Condition of Postmodernity: An Enquiry into the Origins of Cultural Change*, Oxford: Blackwell.

Hay, D. (1981) 'Property, Authority and the Criminal Law', in M. Fitzgerald, G. McLennan and J. Pawson (eds), *Crime and Society: Readings in History and Theory*, London: Open University Press/Routledge.

Hay, D., Lindebaugh, P. and Thompson, E.P. (1975) *Albion's Fatal Tree*, London: Allen Lane.

Healy, W. and Bronner, A.F. (1936) *New Light on Delinquency and its Treatment*, New Haven, CT: Yale University Press.

Hebdige, D. (1976) 'The Meaning of Mod', in S. Hall and T. Jefferson (eds) *Resistance Through Rituals: Youth Sub-cultures in Post-war Britain*, London: Hutchinson: 118–143.

Hebdige, D. (1979) *Subculture: The Meaning of Style*, London: Methuen.

Hegel, G.W.F. (1965, originally 1822) *Philosophy of Right*, trans. T.M. Knox, Oxford: Oxford University Press.

Heidensohn, F.M. (1985) *Women and Crime*, London: Macmillan.

Hendricks, H. (1990a) 'Constructions and Reconstructions of British Childhood: An Interpretive Study 1800 to the Present', in A. James and A. Prout (eds) *Constructing and Reconstructing Childhood*, London: Falmer Press.

Hendricks, H. (1990b) *Images of Youth: Age, Class and the Male Youth Problem 1880–1920*, Oxford: Clarendon.

Henry, B. (1993) 'The First Modern Police in the British Isles: Dublin, 1786–1795', *Police Studies*, 16 (4).

Henry, S. and Milovanovic, D. (1996) *Constitutive Criminology: Beyond Postmodernism*, London: Sage.

Henry, S., and Milovanovic, D. (1999) *Constitutive Criminology at Work: Applications to Crime and Justice*, New York: State University of New York Press.

Henry, S., and Milovanovic, D. (2000) 'Constitutive Criminology: Origins, Core Concepts, and Evaluation', *Social Justice*, 27 (2) 260–276.

Henry, S. and Milovanovic, D. (2001) 'Constitutive Definition of Crime: Power as Harm', in S. Henry and M.M. Lanier (eds) *What is Crime? Controversies over the Nature of Crime and What to Do about It*, Lanham, MD: Rowman & Littlefield.

Hibert, C. (1987) *The English Social History 1066–1945*, London: Grafton.

Himma, K.E. (1998) 'Positivism, Naturalism, and the Obligation to Obey Law', *Southern Journal of Philosophy*, 36 (2): 145–161.

Hirschi, T. (1969) *Causes of Delinquency*, Berkeley, CA: University of California Press.

Hirschi, T. (1995) 'The Family', in J.Q. Wilson and J. Petersilia (eds) *Crime*, San Francisco, CA: ICS Press.

Hirschi, T. and Hindelang, M.J. (1977) 'Intelligence and Delinquency: A Revisionist Review', *American Sociological Review*, 42: 572–587.

Hirst, P.Q. (1980) 'Law, Socialism and Rights', in P. Carlen and M. Collinson (eds) *Radical Issues in Criminology*, Oxford: Martin Robertson.

Hobbes, T. (1968, originally 1651) *Leviathan*, ed. C.B. Macpherson, Harmondsworth: Penguin.

Hobbs, D., Hadfield, P., Lister, S., Winlow, S. and Hall, S. (2000) 'Receiving Shadows: Governance and Liminality in the Night-time Economy', *British Journal of Sociology*, 51 (4): 701–717.

Hobbs, D., Winslow, S., Lister, S. and Hadfield, P. (2005) 'Violent Hypocrisy: Governance and the Night-time Economy', *European Journal of Criminology*, 42 (2): 352–370.

Hodge, J. (1993) 'Alcohol and Violence', in P. Taylor (ed.) *Violence in Society*, London: Royal College of Physicians.

Hoffman, B. (1993) *Holy Terror*, Santa Monica, CA: RAND.

Hoffman, M.L. and Saltzstein, H.D. (1967) 'Parent Discipline and the Child's Moral Development', *Journal of Personality and Social Psychology*, 5: 45.

Hoffmann, S. (1956) *Conditions of World Order*, 364.

Holdaway, S. (1983) *Inside the British Police: A Force at Work*, Oxford: Blackwell.

Hollin, C.R. (1989) *Psychology and Crime: An Introduction to Criminological Psychology*, London: Routledge.

Holmes, R.M. and De Burger, J. (1989) *Serial Murder*, Newbury Park, CA: Sage.

Home Office (1980) *Young Offenders*, Cmnd 8045, London: HMSO.

Home Office (1999) *Proposals for Revising Legislative Measures on Fingerprints, Footprints and DNA Samples*, London: Home Office.

Home Office (2002) *British Crime Survey*, London: HMSO.

Home Office (2003) 'Crime in England and Wales Quarterly Update to June 2003', *Crime Statistical Bulletin 13/03*, London: Home Office.

Hood, R. (1965) *Borstal Re-Assessed*, London: Heinemann.

Hooton, E.A. (1939) *The American Criminal: An Anthropological Study*, Cambridge, MA: Harvard University Press.

Hopkins Burke, R.D. (ed.) (1998a) *Zero Tolerance Policing*, Leicester: Perpetuity Press.

Hopkins Burke, R. (1998b) 'A Contextualisation of Zero Tolerance Policing Strategies', in R. Hopkins Burke (ed.) *Zero Tolerance Policing*, Leicester: Perpetuity Press.

Hopkins Burke, R. (1998c) 'Begging, Vagrancy and Disorder', in R. Hopkins Burke (ed.) *Zero Tolerance Policing*, Leicester: Perpetuity Press.

Hopkins Burke, R.D. (1999a) 'Tolerance or Intolerance: The Policing of Begging in Contemporary Society', in H. Dean (ed.) *Begging and Street Level Economic Activity*, Bristol: The Social Policy Press.

Hopkins Burke, R. (1999b) 'The Socio-Political Context of Zero Tolerance Policing Strategies', *Policing: An International Journal of Police Strategies & Management*, 21 (4): 666–682.

Hopkins Burke, R.D. (1999c) *Young Offending and the Fragmentation of Modernity: Models of Youth Justice*, Leicester: Scarman Centre.

Hopkins Burke, R.D. (2000) 'The Regulation of Begging and Vagrancy: A Critical Discussion', *Crime Prevention and Community Safety: An International Journal*, 2 (2): 43–52.

Hopkins Burke, R.D. (2002) 'Zero Tolerance Policing: New Authoritarianism or New Liberalism?' *Nottingham Law Journal*, 11 (1): 20–35.

Hopkins Burke, R.D. (ed.) (2004a) *'Hard Cop/Soft Cop': Dilemmas and Debates in Contemporary Policing*, Cullompton: Willan Publishing.

Hopkins Burke, R.D. (2004b) 'Policing Contemporary Society', in R.D. Hopkins Burke (ed.) *'Hard Cop/Soft Cop': Dilemmas and Debates in Contemporary Policing*, Cullompton: Willan Publishing.

Hopkins Burke, R.D. (2004c) 'Policing Contemporary Society Revisited', in R.D. Hopkins Burke (ed.) *'Hard Cop/Soft Cop': Dilemmas and Debates in Contemporary Policing*, Cullompton: Willan Publishing.

Hopkins Burke, R.D. (2007) 'Moral Ambiguity, the Schizophrenia of Crime and Community Justice', *British Journal of Community Justice*, 5 (1): 43–64.

Hopkins Burke, R.D. (2008) *Young People, Crime and Justice*, Cullompton: Willan Publishing.

Hopkins Burke, R.D. (2009) *An Introduction to Criminological Theory*, 3rd edn, Cullompton: Willan Publishing.

Hopkins Burke, R.D. and Pollock, E. (2004) 'A Tale of Two Anomies: Some Observations on the Contribution of (Sociological) Criminological Theory to Explaining Hate Crime Motivation', *Internet Journal of Criminology*: http://www.flashmousepublishing.com/ Hopkins%20Burke%20&%20Pollock%20%20A%20Tale%20of%20Two%20Anomies. pdf: 18.

Hopkins Burke, R.D. and Sunley, R. (1996) *'Hanging Out' in the 1990s: Young People and the Postmodern Condition*, Occasional Paper 11, COP Series, Scarman Centre for the Study of Public Order, University of Leicester.

Hopkins Burke, R.D. and Sunley R. (1998) 'Youth Subcultures in Contemporary Britain', in K. Hazelhurst and C. Hazlehurst (eds) *Gangs and Youth Subcultures: International Explorations*, New Jersey: Transaction Press.

Hospers, J. (1932) *An Introduction to Philosophical Analysis*, New York: Prentice-Hall.

Hough, M. (1987) 'Thinking about Effectiveness', *British Journal of Criminology*, 27: 70.

Hough, M., Clarke, R.V.G. and Mayhew, P. (1980) 'Introduction', in R.V.G. Clarke and P. Mayhew (eds) *Designing Out Crime*, London: HMSO.

Howard, J. (1777) *The State of the Prisons in England and Wales, with Preliminary Observations, and an Account of some Foreign Prisons*, Warrington: William Eyres.

Hoyles, M. and Evans, P. (1989) *The Politics of Childhood*, London: Journeyman Press.

Hucklesby, A. (1993) 'Unnecessary Legislative Change', *New Law Journal*, 143, 19 February: 233–234, 255.

Hudson, B. (1987) *Justice Through Punishment: A Critique of the Justice Model of Corrections*, Basingstoke: Macmillan.

Humphreys, R.S. (1991) *Islamic History: A Framework for Inquiry*, Princeton, NJ: Princeton University Press.

Humphries, S. (1981) *Hooligans or Rebels?* Oxford: Blackwell.

Hutchings, B. and Mednick, S.A. (1977) 'Criminality in Adoptees and their Adoptive and Biological Parents: A Pilot Study', in S.A. Mednick and K.O. Christiansen (eds) *Biosocial Bases of Criminal Behaviour*, New York: Gardner.

Ignatieff, M. (1978) *A Just Measure of Pain: The Penitentiary in the Industrial Revolution 1750–1850*, London and Basingstoke: Macmillan.

Ignatieff, M. (1983) 'State, Civil Society and Total Institutions: A Critique of Recent Social Histories of Punishment', in S. Cohen and A. Scull (eds) *Social Control and the State: Historical and Comparative Essays*, Oxford: Martin Robertson.

Iman, B. (2001) 'Safiyatu's Conviction Untenable Under Sharia', *Jenda: A Journal of Culture and African Women Studies*, 1 (2). Online at: http://www.jendajournal.com/jenda/vol1.2/iman.pdf

Institute of Alcohol Studies (2005) *Adolescents and Alcohol*, Cambridge: IAS.

Jamieson, J. (2005) 'New Labour, Youth Justice and the Question of "Respect"', *Youth Justice*, 5 (3): 180–193.

Jefferson, T. (1997) 'Masculinities and Crime', in M. Maguire, R. Morgan and R. Reiner (eds) *The Oxford Handbook of Criminology*, 2nd edn, Oxford: Clarendon.

Jenks, C. (1996) *Childhood*, London: Routledge.

Jensen, A.R. (1969) 'How Much Can We Boost IQ and Scholastic Achievement?' *Harvard Educational Review*, 39: 1–23.

Jewkes, Y. (2005) 'The Construction of Crime News', in J. Muncie (ed.) *Criminology, Volume 1: The Meaning of Crime: Definition, Representation and Social Construction*, London: Sage.

Johansen, B. (1993) 'Legal Literature and the Problem of Change', in C. Mallat (ed.) *Islam and Public Law*, London: Graham & Trotman.

Johnson, L. (1992) *The Rebirth of Private Policing*, London: Routledge.

Jones, S. (1993) *The Language of the Genes*, London: Harper Collins.

Jordan, B. (1996) *A Theory of Social Exclusion and Poverty*, Cambridge: Polity.

Jordan, B. (1998) 'New Labour, New Community?' *Imprints*, 3 (2): 113–131.

Judge, T. (1994) *The Force of Persuasion – The Story of the Police Federation*, Surbiton: Police Federation.

Kalven, H. and Zeisel, H. (1966) *The American Jury*, Chicago, IL: Little, Brown.

Kamali, M.H. (1991) *Principles of Islamic Jurisprudence*, Cambridge: Islamic Texts Society.

Kant, I. (1956, originally 1788) *Critique of Practical Reason*, trans. L.W. Beck, London: Bobbs-Merrill.

Kant, I. (1996, originally 1797) *Fundamental Principles of the Metaphysics of Morals*, Cambridge: Cambridge University Press.

Karmen, A. (2004) 'Zero Tolerance in New York City: Hard Questions for a Get-Tough Policy', in R.D. Hopkins Burke (ed.) *'Hard Cop/Soft Cop': Dilemmas and Debates in Contemporary Policing*, Cullompton: Willan Publishing.

Katz, J. (1988) *Seductions of Crime: Moral and Sensual Attractions in Doing Evil*, New York: Basic Books.

Kazdin, A.E. (1987) *Conduct Disorder in Childhood and Adolescence*, Newbury Park, CA: Sage.

Kelling, G.L. and Coles, C.M. (1996) *Fixing Broken Windows*, New York: Free Press.

Kelsen, H. (1967) *Pure Theory of Law*, Berkeley, CA: University of California.

Kelsen, H. (1991) *General Theory of Norms*, Oxford: Clarendon Press.

Kennedy, R. (1997) 'Race, Law and Suspicion: Using Color as a Proxy for Dangerousness', *Race, Crime and the Law*, New York: Pantheon.

Keverne, E.B., Meller, R.E. and Eberhart, J.A. (1982) 'Social Influences on Behaviour and Neuroendocrine Responsiveness in Talapoin Monkeys', *Scandinavian Journal of Psychology*, 1: 37–54.

King, H. (1972) *Box Man: A Professional Thief's Journey*, as told to and edited by B. Chambliss, New York: Harper & Row.

King, M. (1981) *A Framework of Criminal Justice*, London: Croom Helm.

King, R. and McDermott, K. (1989) 'British Prisons 1970–1987: The Ever Deepening Crisis', *British Journal of Criminology*, 29: 107–128.

Kissinger, H. (2001) *Does America Need a Foreign Policy? Toward a Diplomacy for the 21st Century*, New York: Simon and Schuster.

Kitsuse, J.I. (1962) 'Societal Reaction to Deviant Behaviour: Problems of Theory and Method', *Social Problems*, 9: 247–256.

Klinefelter, H.F., Reifenstein, E.C. and Albright, F. (1942) 'Syndrome Characterized by Gynecomastia, Aspermatogenesis without Aleydigism and Increased Excretion of Follicle-Stimulating Hormone', *Journal of Clinical Endocrinology*, 2: 615–627.

Kochan, N. and Whittington, B. (1991) *Bankrupt: The BCCI Fraud*, London: Victor Gollancz.

Koestler, A. and Rolph, C.H. (1961) *Hanged by the Neck*, Harmondsworth: Penguin.

Kolvin, I., Miller, F.J.W., Scott, D.M., Gatzanis, S.R.M. and Fleeting, M. (1990) *Continuities of Deprivation?* Aldershot: Avebury.

Kozol, H.L., Boucher, R.J. and Garofalo, R.F. (1972) 'The Diagnosis and Treatment of Dangerousness', *Crime and Delinquency*, 18: 371–392.

Kretschmer, E. (1946) *Physique and Character*, trans. W.J.H. Sprott, New York: Cooper Square.

Lacey, N. (1998) *Unspeakable Subjects: Feminist Essays in Legal and Social Theory*, Oxford: Hart Publishing.

Lane, R. (1967) *Policing the City*, Cambridge, MA: Harvard University Press.

Langbein, J.H. (1974) *Prosecuting Crime in the Renaissance: England, Germany, France*, Cambridge, MA: Harvard University Press.

Lange, J. (1930) *Crime as Destiny*, London: Allen & Unwin.

Lea, J. and Young, J. (1984) *What is to be Done about Law and Order?* Harmondsworth: Penguin.

Leigh, L. and Zedner, L. (1992) *A Report of the Administration of Criminal Justice in the Pre-Trial Phase in England and Germany*, Royal Commission on Criminal Justice, Research Study No. 1, London: HMSO.

Leiter, B. (1998) 'Naturalism and Naturalized Jurisprudence', in B. Bix (ed.) *Analyzing Law: New Essays in Legal Theory*, Oxford: Clarendon Press.

Lemert, E. (1951) *Social Pathology: A Systematic Approach to the Theory of Sociopathic Behavior*, New York: McGraw-Hill.

Lemert, E. (1972) *Human Deviance, Social Problems and Social Control*, 2nd edn, Englewood Cliffs, NJ: Prentice-Hall.

Lesser, M. (1980) *Nutrition and Vitamin Therapy*, New York: Bantam.

Levit, N. (2000) 'A Different Kind of Sameness: Beyond Formal Equality and Antisubordination Principles in Gay Legal Theory and Constitutional Doctrine', *Ohio State Law Journal*, 61: 860–875.

Lindqvist, P. (1986) 'Criminal Homicide in Northern Sweden, 1970–1981 – Alcohol Intoxication, Alcohol Abuse and Mental Disease', *International Journal of Law and Psychiatry*, 8: 19–37.

Liska, A.E. (1987) *Perspectives on Deviance*, Englewood Cliffs, NJ: Prentice-Hall.

Locke, J. (1970, originally 1689) *Two Treatises of Government*, ed. P. Laslett, Cambridge: Cambridge University Press.

Locke, J. (1975) *An Essay Concerning Human Understanding*, ed. P.M. Nidditch, Oxford: Clarendon Press.

Loeber, R. and Dishion, T. (1983) 'Early Predictors of Male Delinquency: A Review', *Psychological Bulletin*, 94 (1): 68–91.

Lofland, L.H. (1973) *A World of Strangers: Order and Action in Urban Public Space*, New York: Basic Books.

Lombroso, C. (1875) *L'uomo delinquente* (*The Criminal Man*), Milan: Hoepli.

Loveday, B. (1993a) 'Civilian Staff in the Police Force – Competences and Conflicts in the Police Force', Research Paper No. 2, Centre for the Study of Public Order, University of Leicester.

Loveday, B. (1993b) 'Civilian Staff in the Police Service', *Policing*, 9 (Summer).

Loveday, B. (1995) 'Reforming the Police: From Local Service to State Police', *The Political Quarterly*, 66 (2).

Lukács, G. (1970) *Writer and Critic*, London: Merlin Press.

Lyotard, J.-F. (1984) *The Post-Modern Condition: A Report on Knowledge*, Manchester: Manchester University Press.

McBarnet, D. (1985) *Conviction: Law, the State and the Construction of Justice*, London: Macmillan.

McConville, M. and Bridges, L. (eds) (1994) *Criminal Justice in Crisis*, Aldershot: Edward Elgar.

McConville, M., Sanders, A. and Leng, R. (1991) *The Case for the Prosecution*, London: Routledge.

McCord, W., McCord, J. and Zola, I.K. (1959) *Origins of Crime: A New Evaluation of the Cambridge-Somerville Youth Study*, New York: Columbia University Press.

McEwan, A.W. (1983) 'Eysenck's Theory of Criminality and the Personality Types and Offences of Young Delinquents', *Personality and Individual Differences*, 4: 201–204.

McGurk, B.J. and McDougall, C. (1981) 'A New Approach to Eysenck's Theory of Criminality', *Personality and Individual Differences*, 13: 338–340.

McLaughlin, E. (2001) 'Key Issues in Policework', in E. McLaughlin and J. Muncie (eds) *Controlling Crime*, London: Sage/Open University.

Malthus, T.R. (1959, originally 1798) *Population: The First Essay*, Chicago, IL: University of Michigan.

Mannheim, H. (1948) *Juvenile Delinquency in an English Middletown*, London: Kegan Paul, Turner, Trubner & Co. Ltd.

Mannheim, H. (1955) *Group Problems in Crime and Punishment*, London: Routledge & Kegan Paul.

Mark, V.H. and Ervin, F.R. (1970) *Violence and the Brain*, New York: Harper Row.

Marshall, T.F. (1997) 'Seeking the Whole Justice', in S. Hayman, (ed.) *Repairing the Damage: Restorative Justice in Action*, London: ISTD.

Marshall, T.F. (1999) *Restorative Justice: An Overview* (Occasional Paper), London: Home Office.

Martin, D. (1986) *Battered Wives*, 3rd edn, London: Pocket Books.

Martin, D. (2003) 'The Politics of Policing, Managerialism, Modernisation and Performance', in R. Matthews and J. Young (eds) *The New Politics of Crime and Punishment*, Cullompton: Willan Press.

Martinson, R. (1974) 'What Works? – Questions and Answers about Prison Reform', *The Public Interest*, 35 (Spring): 22–54.

Marx, G.T. (2001) 'Police and Democracy', in M. Amir and S. Einstein (eds), *Policing, Security, and Democracy: Theory and Practice*, Huntsville, TX: Office of International Criminal Justice.

Matthews, R. (1996) *Armed Robbery: Police Responses*, Crime Detection and Prevention Series, Paper 78, London: Home Office, Police Research Group.

Matthews, R. and Young, J. (eds) (1986) *Confronting Crime*, London: Sage.

Matthews, R. and Young, J. (eds) (1992) *Issues in Realist Criminology*, London: Sage.

Matza, D.M. (1964) *Delinquency and Drift*, New York: Wiley.

Matza, D.M. (1969) *Becoming Deviant*, Englewood Cliffs, NJ: Prentice-Hall.

Mauer, M. (1997) 'Racial Disparities in Prison Getting Worse in the 1990s', *Overcrowded Times*, 8: 8–13.

Mayhew, H. (1968) *London Labour and the London Poor, Vol. IV: Those That Will Not Work, Comprising Prostitutes, Thieves, Swindlers and Beggars*, New York: Dover Publications.

Mays, J.B. (1954) *Growing Up in the City: A Study of Juvenile Delinquency in an Urban Neighbourhood*, Liverpool: Liverpool University Press.

Mazor, L.J. (1978) 'Disrespect for Law', in R.J. Pennock and J.W. Chapman (eds) *Anarchism*, New York: New York University.

Mead, G. (1934) *Mind, Self and Society*, Chicago, IL: University of Chicago Press.

Mednick, S.A. (1977) 'A Biosocial Theory of the Learning of Law-Abiding Behavior', in S.A. Mednick and K.O Christiansen (eds) *Biosocial Bases of Criminal Behavior*, New York: Gardner.

Mednick, S.A. and Volavka, J. (1980) 'Biology and Crime', in N. Morris and M. Tonry (eds) *Crime and Justice: An Annual Review of Research*, Vol. 2, Chicago, IL: University of Chicago Press.

Mednick, S.A., Gabrielli, T., William, F. and Hutchings, B. (1984) 'Genetic Influences on Criminal Convictions: Evidence from an Adoption Cohort', *Science*, 224.

Mednick, S.A., Moffit, T.E. and Stack, S. (eds) (1987) *The Causes of Crime: New Biological Approaches*, Cambridge: Cambridge University Press.

Mednick, S.A., Pollock, V., Volavka, J. and Gabrielli, W.F. (1982) 'Biology and Violence', in M.E. Wolfgang and N.A. Weiner (eds) *Criminal Violence*, Beverly Hills, CA: Sage.

Melossi, D. and Pavarini, M. (1981) *The Prison and the Factory: Origins of the Penitentiary System*, trans. G. Cousin, London and Basingstoke: Macmillan.

Menard, S. and Morse, B. (1984) 'A Structuralist Critique of the IQ-Delinquency Hypothesis: Theory and Evidence', *American Journal of Sociology*, 89: 1347–1378.

Merton, R.K. (1938) 'Social Structure and Anomie', *American Sociological Review*, 3 (October): 672–682.

Messerschmidt, J.W. (1993) *Masculinities and Crime*, Lanham, MD: Rowman & Littlefield.

Mill, J.S. (1906, originally 1869) *On Liberty*, New York: Alfred A. Knopf.

Mill, J.S. (1963–1984) *The Collected Works of John Stuart Mill*, ed. F.E.L. Priestly, Toronto: University of Toronto Press.

Miller, J.G. (1997) *Search and Destroy: African-American Males in the Criminal Justice System*, Cambridge: Cambridge University Press.

Miller, W.B. (1958) 'Lower Class Culture as a Generalising Milieu of Gang Delinquency', *Journal of Social Issues*, 14: 5–19.

Miller, W. (1999) *Cops and Bobbies*, 2nd edn, Columbus, OH: Ohio State University Press.

Mirrlees-Black, C., Mayhew, P. and Percy, A. (1996) *The 1996 British Crime Survey*, Home Office Statistical Bulletin 19/96, London: Home Office.

Moberly, W. (1968) *The Ethics of Punishment*, London: Faber & Faber.

Moffitt, T.E. (1993a) 'Adolescent-Limited and Life-Course-Persistent Antisocial Behavior: A Developmental Taxonomy', *Psychological Review*, 100: 674–701.

Moffitt, T.E. (1993b) 'The Neuropsychology of Conduct Disorder', *Development and Psychopathology*, 5: 135–151.

Monahan, J. (1981) *Predicting Violent Behaviour*, Beverly Hills, CA: Sage.

Morgan, P. (1978) *Delinquent Fantasies*, London: Temple Smith.

Morgan, R. (1997) 'Swept Along by Zero Option', *The Guardian,* 22 January.

Morgenthau, H.J. (1940) 'Positivism, Functionalism, and International Law', *American Journal of International Law*, 34: 260.

MORI (2000) *Youth Survey 2000*, Research conducted for the Youth Justice Board, London: Youth Justice Board.

MORI (2001) *Youth Survey 2001 for the Youth Justice Board for England and Wales*, London: Youth Justice Board.

MORI (2002) *Youth Survey 2002 for the Youth Justice Board for England and Wales*, London: Youth Justice Board.

MORI (2003) *Youth Survey 2003*, London: Youth Justice Board.

Morris, A. and Giller, H. (1987) *Understanding Juvenile Justice*, London: Croom Helm.

Morris, A., Giller, H., Szwed, E. and Geach, H. (1980) *Justice for Children*, London: Heinemann.

Morris, T.P. (1957) *The Criminal Area: A Study in Social Ecology*, London: Routledge & Kegan Paul.

Morrow, J.D. (2008) 'The Laws of War as an International Institution', Paper presented to Cooperation and Conflict conference at Northwestern University, November 7–8.

Mott, J. (1990) *Young People, Alcohol and Crime*, Home Office Research Bulletin (Research and Statistics Department), 28: 24–28.

Muncie, J. (2004) *Youth and Crime*, 2nd edn, London: Sage.

Muncie, J. (2008) 'The "Punitive Turn" in Juvenile Justice: Cultures of Control and Rights Compliance in Western Europe and the USA', *Youth Justice*, 8: 107.

Murray, C. (ed.) (1990) *The Emerging British Underclass*, London: Institute of Economic Affairs Health and Welfare Unit.

Murray, C. (1994) *Underclass: The Crisis Deepens*, London: Institute of Economic Affairs.

NACRO (2001) *Some Facts about Young People Who Offend*, London: NACRO.

Nelken, D. and Andrews, L. (1999) 'DNA Identification and Surveillance Creep', *Sociology of Health and Illness*, 21 (5): 689–706.

Newburn, T. (1995) *Crime and Criminal Justice Policy*, London: Longman.

Newburn, T. (2002) 'Young People, Crime, and Youth Justice', in M. Maguire, R. Morgan and R. Reiner (eds), *The Oxford Handbook of Youth Justice*, 3rd edn, Oxford: Oxford University Press.

Norris, C. and Armstrong, G. (1999) *The Maximum Surveillance Society: The Rise of CCTV*, Oxford: Berg.

Nozick, R. (1981) *Philosophical Explanations*, Oxford: Oxford University Press.

Nugent, W., Umbreit, M., Winnamaki, L. and Paddock, J. (1999) 'Participation in Victim Offender Mediation Reduces Recidivism', *Connections* (VOM Association), 3 (Summer).

Nye, F.I. (1958) *Family Relationships and Delinquent Behaviour*, New York: Wiley.

O'Connell, M.E. (1999) 'Symposium on Method in International Law', *American Journal of International Law*, 334.

Olwens, D. (1987) 'Testosterone and Adrenaline: Aggressive and Antisocial Behaviour in Normal Adolescent Males', in S.A. Mednick, T.E. Moffit and S. Stack (eds) *The Causes of Crime: New Biological Approaches*, Cambridge: Cambridge University Press.

O'Malley, P. (1992) 'Risk, Power and Crime Prevention', *Economy and Society*, 21 (3): 252–275.

O'Malley, P. and Mugford, S. (1994) 'Crime, Excitement and Modernity', in G. Barak (ed.) *Varieties of Criminology*, Westport, CT: Praeger.

Omerod, D. (1996) 'The Evidential Implications of Psychological Profiling', *Criminal Law Review*, 863.

Packer, H. (1969) *The Limits of the Criminal Sanction*, Stanford, CA: Stanford University Press.

Palmer, T. (1975) 'Martinson Revisited', *Journal of Research in Crime and Delinquency*, 12 (July): 133–152.

Park, R.E. (1921) *Introduction to the Study of Sociology*, Chicago, IL: University of Chicago Press.

Parker, H. (1974) *View From the Boys*, Newton Abbot: David and Charles.

Patterson, O. (1982) *Slavery and Social Death*, Cambridge, MA: Harvard University Press.

Pearson, G. (1983) *Hooligan – A History of Respectable Fears*, London: Macmillan.

Perry, B. (2001) *In the Name of Hate*, London: Routledge.

Persky, H., Smith, K.D. and Basu, G.K. (1971) 'Relation of Psychological Measures of Aggression and Hostility to Testosterone Production in Man', *Psychosomatic Medicine*, 33: 265–275.

Philips, C. (1981) *Report of the Royal Commission on Criminal Procedure*, Cmnd 8092, London: HMSO.

Philips, D. and Storch, R. (1999) *Policing Provincial England, 1829–1856*, Leicester: Leicester University Press.

Piaget, J. (1980) *Adaptation and Intelligence: Organic Selection and Phenocopy*, trans. W. Mays, Chicago, IL: University of Chicago Press.

Pihl, R.O. (1982) 'Hair Element Levels of Violent Criminals', *Canadian Journal of Psychiatry*, 27: 533–545.

Pihl, R.O. and Peterson, J.B. (1993) 'Alcohol/Drug Use and Aggressive Behaviour', in S. Hodgins (ed.) *Moral Disorder and Crime*, Newbury Park, CA: Sage.

Piliavin, I. and Briar, B. (1964) 'Police Encounters with Juveniles', *American Journal of Sociology*, 69: 153–162.

Pinchbeck, I. and Hewitt, M. (1973) *Children in English Society*, Vol. 2, London: Routledge & Kegan Paul.

Pitts, J. (1986) 'Black Young People and Juvenile Crime: Some Unanswered Questions', in R. Matthews and J. Young (eds) *Confronting Crime*, London: Sage.

Pitts, J. (1996) 'The Politics and Practice of Youth Crime', in E. McLaughlin and J. Muncie (eds) *Controlling Crime*, London: Sage/Open University.

Pitts, J. (2003) 'Youth Justice in England and Wales', in R. Matthews and J. Young (eds) *The New Politics of Crime and Punishment*, Cullompton: Willan Publishing.

Platt, A. (1969) 'The Rise of the Child-Saving Movement', *The Annals*, 381.

Plint, T. (1851) *Crime in England*, London: Charles Gilpin.

Pollak, O. (1950, 1961) *The Criminality of Women*, New York: Barnes.

Pollard, C. (1997) 'Zero-Tolerance: Short-Term Fix, Long-Term Liability', in N. Dennis (ed.) *Zero Tolerance: Policing a Free Society*, London: Institute for Economic Affairs.

Posner, R. (1992) *Economic Analysis of Law*, 4th edn, Boston: Little, Brown, & Company.

Pratt, J. (1989) 'Corporatism: The Third Model of Juvenile Justice', *British Journal of Criminology*, 29: 236–254.

Pratt, J. (1999) 'Governmentality, Neo-Liberalism and Dangerousness', in R. Smandych (ed.) *Governable Places: Readings on Governmentality and Crime Control*, Dartmouth: Ashgate.

Presdee, M. (2000) *Cultural Criminology and the Carnival of Crime*, London: Routledge.

Presdee, M. (2004) 'Cultural Criminology: The Long and Winding Road', *Theoretical Criminology*, 8 (3): 275–285.

President's Commission on Law Enforcement and the Administration of Justice (1967) *The Challenge of Crime in a Free Society*, Washington, DC: US Congress.

Price, W.H. and Whatmore, P.B. (1967) 'Behaviour Disorders and Patterns of Crime Among XYY Males Identified at a Maximum Security Hospital', *British Medical Journal*, 1: 533.

Primoratz, I. (1989) *Justifying Legal Punishment*, London: Humanities Press International.

Prinz, R.J., Roberts, W.A. and Hantman, E. (1980) 'Dietary Correlates of Hyperactive Behaviour in Children', *Journal of Consulting and Clinical Psychology*, 48: 760–785.

Pryce, K. (1979) *Endless Pressure: A Study of West Indian Life-styles in Bristol*, Harmondsworth: Penguin.

Pullinger, H. (1985) 'The Criminal Justice System Viewed as a System', in D. Moxon (ed.) *Managing Criminal Justice*, London: Home Office.

Quételet, M.A. (1842) *A Treatise on Man*, Edinburgh: William and Robert Chalmers.

Quinney, R. (1970) *The Social Reality of Crime*, Boston, MA: Little, Brown.

Rada, R. (1975) 'Alcoholism and Forcible Rape', *American Journal of Psychiatry*, 132: 444–446.

Radzinowicz, L. (1948–1986) *A History of English Criminal Law and its Administration from 1750*, 5 volumes: i) (1948) *The Movement for Reform*; ii) (1956) *The Clash Between Private Initiative and Public Interest in the Enforcement of the Law*; iii) (1956) *Cross Currents in the Movement of the Reform of the Police*; iv) (1968) *Grappling for Control*; v) (with R. Hood, 1986) *The Emergence of Penal Policy in Victorian and Edwardian England*, London: Stevens & Sons.

Raloff, J. (1983) 'Locks – A Key to Violence', *Science News*, 124: 122–136.

Ramsay, M. (1996) *The Relationship Between Alcohol and* Crime, Home Office Research Bulletin 38: 37–44, London: Home Office.

Ratner, S.R. (1998) 'International Law: The Trials of Global Norms (in the Frontiers of Knowledge)', *Foreign Policy*, Special Edition: Frontiers of Knowledge, 110: 65–80.

Rawlings, P. (2001) *Policing: A Short History*, Cullompton: Willan.

Rawls, J. (1964) 'Legal Obligation and the Duty of Fair Play', in S. Hook (ed.), *Law and Philosophy*, New York: New York University Press.

Raz, J. (1979) *The Authority of Law: Essays on Law and Morality*, Oxford: Clarendon Press.

Read, S. (1997) 'Below Zero', *Police Review*, 17 January.

Reckless, W. (1967) *The Crime Problem*, 4th edn, New York: Appleton Century Crofts.

Redhead, S. (1990) *The End-of-the-Century Party: Youth and Pop Towards 2000*, New York: St Martin's Press.

Redl, F. and Wineman, D. (1951) *Children Who Hate*, New York: Free Press.

Reiner, R. (2000) *The Politics of the Police*, 3rd edn, Oxford: Oxford University Press.

Reisman, M. (2004) 'The View from the New Haven School of International Law', in *International Law in Contemporary Perspective*, 2nd edn, New York: Foundation Press.

Reith, C. (1956) *A New Study of Police History*, London: Oliver & Boyd.

Rhodes, R.A.W. (1997) *Understanding Governance: Policy Networks, Governance, Reflexivity and Accountability*, Buckingham: Open University Press.

Robb, M. (2003) *Football (Disorder) Act 2000 – Summary and Commentary*, London: Magnacartaplus.

Romeanes, T. (1998) 'A Question of Confidence: Zero Tolerance and Problem-Oriented Policing', in R. Hopkins Burke (ed.) *Zero Tolerance Policing*, Leicester: Perpetuity Press.

Rose, R.M., Bernstein, I.S., Gorden, T.P. and Catlin, S.E. (1974) 'Androgens and Aggression: A Review and Recent Findings in Primates', in R.L. Holloway (ed.) *Primate Aggression: Territoriality and Xenophobia*, New York: Academia Press.

Rosen, Q. (1994) 'Knowledge Use in Direct Practice', *Social Service Review*, 68 (4): 561–577.

Ross, P. (2003) 'Marxism and Communitarianism', *Imprints*, 6 (3): 215–243.

Rothman, D. (1971) *The Discovery of the Asylum: Social Order and Disorder in the New Republic*, Boston, MA: Routledge & Kegan Paul.

Rothman, D. (1980) *Conscience and Convenience: The Asylum and its Alternatives in Progressive America*, Boston, MA: Little, Brown.

Rousseau, J. (1964) *First and Second Discourses*, ed. R.D. Masters, New York: St Martin's Press.

Rousseau, J.-J. (1978) *The Social Contract*, ed. R.D. Masters, New York: St Martin's Press.

Rowe, D.C. (1990) 'Inherited Dispositions toward Learning Delinquent and Criminal Behaviour: New Evidence', in L. Ellis and H. Hoffman (eds) *Crime in Biological, Social and Moral Contexts*, New York: Praeger.

Rowe, D.C. and Rogers, J.L. (1989) 'Behaviour Genetics, Adolescent Deviance, and "d": Contributions and Issues', in G.R. Adams, R. Montemayor and T.P. Gullotta (eds), *Advances in Adolescent Development*, Newbury Park, CA: Sage: 38–67.

Royal Commission on the Penal System in England and Wales (1967) *Report*, London: HMSO.

Ruggiero, V. (1997) 'Trafficking in Human Beings: Slaves in Contemporary Europe', *International Journal of the Sociology of Law*, 25 (3): 231–244.

Ruggiero, V. (2000) *Crimes and Markets: Essays in Anti-Criminology*, Oxford: Oxford University Press.

Runciman, Viscount (1993) *Report of the Royal Commission on Criminal Justice*, Cmnd 2263, London: HMSO.

Rusche, G. (1980) 'Labor Market and Penal Sanction: Thoughts on the Sociology of Punishment', in T. Platt and P. Takagi (eds) *Punishment and Penal Discipline*, Berkeley, CA: Crime and Social Justice Associates.

Rusche, G. and Kirchheimer, O. (1968, originally 1938) *Punishment and Social Structure*, New York: Russell & Russell.

Rutherford, A. (1978) 'Decarceration of Young Offenders in Massachusetts', in N. Tutt (ed.) *Alternative Strategies for Coping with Crime*, Oxford: Blackwell/Martin Robertson.

Rutherford, A. (1988) 'The English Penal Crisis: Paradox and Possibilities', in R. Rideout and J. Jowell (eds) *Current Legal Problems*, London: Stevens.

Rutherford, A. (1992) *Growing Out of Crime*, 2nd edn, London: Waterside Press.

Rutter, M. (1981) *Maternal Deprivation Reassessed*, Harmondsworth: Penguin.

Sanders, A. (1994) 'From Suspect to Trial', in M. Maguire, R. Morgan and R. Reiner (eds) *The Oxford Handbook of Criminology*, Oxford: Clarendon Press.

Sanders, A. and Young, R. (2006) *Criminal Justice*, 4th edn, London: Butterworths.

Sanders, D. (2005) 'Human Rights and Sexual Orientation in International Law', *International Gay and Lesbian Law Association*, 11 November.

Saunders, W. (1984) *Alcohol Use in Britain: How Much is Too Much?* Edinburgh: Scottish Health Education Unit.

Scarman, Lord (1982) *The Scarman Report: The Brixton Disorders, 10–12 April 1981*, Harmondsworth: Penguin Books.

Scarmella, T.J. and Brown, W.A. (1978) 'Serum Testosterone and Aggressiveness in Hockey Players', *Psychosomatic Medicine*, 40: 262–275.

Schalling, D. (1987) 'Personality Correlates of Plasma Testosterone Levels in Young Delinquents: An Example of Person-Situation Interaction', in S.A. Mednick, T.E. Moffit and S.A. Stack (eds) *The Causes of Crime: New Biological Approaches*, Cambridge: Cambridge University Press.

Schlapp, M.G. and Smith, E. (1928) *The New Criminology*, New York: Boni & Liveright.

Schlesinger, P. and Tumber, H. (1994) *Reporting Crime: The Media Politics of Criminal Justice*, Oxford: Clarendon Press.

Schutz, A. (1962) *The Problem of Social Reality*, The Hague: Martinus Nijhoff.

Schwendinger, H. and Schwendinger, J. (1970) 'Defenders of Order or Guardians of Human Rights', *Issues in Criminology*, 7: 72–81.

Scott, P.D. (1977) 'Assessing Dangerousness in Criminals', *British Journal of Criminology*, 131: 127–142.

Scraton, P. (1985) *The State of the Police*, London: Pluto.

Scraton, P. and Chadwick, K. (1996, originally 1992) 'The Theoretical Priorities of Critical Criminology', in J. Muncie, E. McLaughlin, and M. Langan (eds) *Criminological Perspectives: A Reader*, London: Sage.

Scruton, R. (1980) *The Meaning of Conservatism*, Harmondsworth: Pelican.

Scruton, R. (1985) *Thinkers of the New Left*, London: Longman.

Scruton, R. (2001) *The Meaning of Conservatism*, 3rd edn, Basingstoke: Palgrave.

Shah, S.A. and Roth, L.H. (1974) 'Biological and Psychophysiological Factors in Criminality', in D. Glaser (ed.) *Handbook of Criminology*, London: Rand McNally.

Shaw, C.R. and McKay, H.D. (1972, originally 1931) *Juvenile Delinquency and Urban Areas*, Chicago, IL: University of Chicago Press.

Shaw, M.N. (2003) *International Law*, 5th edn, Cambridge: Cambridge University Press.

Shearing, C. (1989) 'Decriminalising Criminology', *Canadian Journal of Criminology*, 31 (2): 169–178.

Sheldon, W.H. (1949) *Varieties of Delinquent Youth*, London: Harper.

Shelley, L. (1998) 'Crime and Corruption in the Digital Age', *Journal of International Affairs*, 51 (2): 605–620.

Sherman, L. and Strang, H. (1997) 'Restorative Justice and Deterring Crime', *RISE Working Papers*, Canberra: Australian National University.

Shockley, W. (1967) 'A "Try Simplest Cases" Approach to the Heredity-Poverty-Crime Problem', *Proceedings of the National Academy of Sciences*, 57: 1767–1774.

Shoenthaler, S.J. (1982) 'The Effects of Blood Sugar on the Treatment and Control of Antisocial Behaviour: A Double-Blind Study of an Incarcerated Juvenile Population', *International Journal for Biosocial Research*, 3: 1–15.

Silverman, E. (1998) 'Below Zero Tolerance: The New York Experience', in R. Hopkins Burke (ed.) *Zero Tolerance Policing*, Leicester: Perpetuity Press.

Sim, J., Scraton, P. and Gordon, P. (1987) 'Introduction: Crime, the State, and Critical Analysis', in P. Scraton, (ed.) *Law, Order and the Authoritarian State: Readings in Critical Criminology*, Milton Keynes: Open University Press.

Simma, B. and Paulus, A.L. (1999) 'Symposium on Method in International Law: The Responsibility of Individuals for Human Rights Abuses in Internal Conflicts: A Positivist View', *American Journal of International Law*, 93: 302 (April).

Simon, R.J. (1975) *Women and Crime*, London: Lexington Books.

Skinner, B.F. (1938) *The Behaviour of Organisms*, New York: Appleton-Century-Crofts.

Skinner, B.F. (1981) 'Selection by Consequences', *Science*, 213: 501–504.

Slaughter, A.-M. (1995) 'International Law in a World of Liberal States', *European Journal of International Law*, 6: 532.

Slaughter, A.-M., Tulumello, A.S. and Wood, S. (1998) 'International Law and International Relations Theory: A New Generation of Interdisciplinary Scholarship', *American Journal of International Law*, 92: 367–397.

Slaughter, P. (2003) 'Of Crowds, Crimes and Carnivals', in R. Matthews and J. Young (eds), *The New Politics of Crime and Punishment*, Cullompton: Willan Press.

Smart, A. (1969) 'Mercy', in H.B. Acton (ed.) *The Philosophy of Punishment*, Basingstoke: Macmillan.

Smart, C. (1977) *Women, Crime and Criminology*, London: Routledge & Kegan Paul.

Smart, P. (1993) *Feminist Jurisprudence*, Oxford: Clarendon Press.

Smith, D.E. and Smith, D.D. (1977) 'Eysenck's Psychoticism Scale and Reconviction', *British Journal of Criminology*, 17: 387.

Smith, D.J. and Gray, J. (1985) *Police and People in London: The PSI Report*, London: Gower.

Smith, M.B.E. (1973) 'Do We Have a Prima Facie Obligation to Obey the Law', *Yale Law Journal*, 82: 950–976.

Spencer, H. (1971, originally 1896) *Structure, Function and Evolution*, readings, ed. and intro. S. Andreski, London: Nelson.

Spergel, I.A. (1964) *Racketsville, Slumtown, Haulburg*, Chicago, IL: University of Chicago Press.

Sprack, J. (1992) 'The Trial Process', in E. Stockdale and S. Casale (eds) *Criminal Justice Under Stress*, London: Blackstones.

Squires, P. and Stephen, D.E. (2005) *Rougher Justice: Anti-social Behaviour and Young People*, Cullompton: Willan Publishing.

Staw, B.M. and Szwajkowski, E. (1975) 'The Scarcity-Munificence Component of Organizational Environments and the Commission of Illegal Acts', *Administrative Science Quarterly*, 20: 345–354.

Steedman, C. (1984) *Policing the Victorian Community*, London: Routledge & Kegan Paul.

Steinberg, R. and Zasloff, J. (2006) 'Power and International Law', *American Journal of Law*, 100 (64): 64–87.

Stenson, K. (2000) 'Some Day Our Prince Will Come: Zero-tolerance Policing and Liberal Government', in T. Hope and R. Sparks (eds) *Crime, Risk and Insecurity*, London: Routledge.

Storch, R. (1975) 'The Plague of the Blue Locusts: Police Reform and Popular Resistance in Northern England 1840–57', *International Review of Social History*, 20: 61–90.

Storch, R. (1989) 'Policing Rural Southern England before the Police: Opinion and Practice 1830–1856', in D. Hay and F. Snyder (eds) *Policing and Prosecution*, Oxford: Clarendon Press.

Strang, H. (1995) 'Replacing Courts With Conferences', *Policing*, 11 (3): 21–30.

Strang, H. (2000) *Victim Participation in a Restorative Justice Process: The Canberra Reintegrative Shaming Experiments*, PhD Dissertation, Law Program, Research School of Social Sciences, Canberra: Australian National University.

Strang, H. (2001) *Repair or Revenge: Victim Participation in Restorative Justice*, Oxford: Oxford University Press.

Street, R. (2000) 'Restorative Justice Steering Group: Review of Existing Research', London: Home Office (unpublished).

Sutherland, E.H. (1940) 'White-collar Criminality', *American Sociological Review*, 5: 1–12.

Sutherland, E.H. (1947) *Principles of Criminology*, 4th edn, Philadelphia, PA: Lippincott.

Sutton, M. (1995) 'Supply by Theft: Does the Market for Second-hand Goods Play a Role in Keeping Crime Figures High?', *British Journal of Criminology*, 38 (3): 352–365.

Sutton, M. (1998) *Handling Stolen Goods and Theft: A Market Reduction Approach*, Home Office Research Study 178, London: Home Office.

Sutton, M. (2004) 'Tackling Stolen Goods Markets is "Root-Level" Situational Crime Prevention', in R.D. Hopkins Burke (ed.) *'Hard Cop/Soft Cop': Dilemmas and Debates in Contemporary Policing*, Cullompton: Willan Press.

Tappan, P.W. (1960) *Crime, Justice and Correction*, New York: McGraw-Hill.

Taylor, D. (1997) *The New Police in Nineteenth-Century England: Crime, Conflict and Control*, Manchester: Manchester University Press.

Taylor, I., Walton, P. and Young, J. (1973) *The New Criminology: For a Social Theory of Deviance*, London: Routledge & Kegan Paul.

Taylor, L., Lacey, R. and Bracken, D. (1979) *In Whose Best Interests: The Unjust Treatment of Children in Courts and Institutions*, London: Cobden Trust/Mind.

Ten, C.L. (1987) *Crime, Guilt and Punishment*, Oxford: Oxford University Press.

Thompson, E.P. (1975) *Whigs and Hunters*, London: Allen Lane.

Thornhill, R. and Palmer, C. (2000) *A Natural History of Rape: Biological Bases of Sexual Coercion*, Cambridge, MA: MIT Press.

Tifft, L. (1995) 'Social Harm Definitions of Crime', *Critical Criminologist*, 7 (1): 9–12.

Tittle, C.R. (1995) *Control Balance: Towards a General Theory of Deviance*, Boulder, CO: Westview Press.

Tittle, C.R. (1997) 'Thoughts Stimulated by Braithwaite's Analysis of Control Balance', *Theoretical Criminology*, 1: 87–107.

Tittle, C.R. (1999) 'Continuing the Discussion of Control Balance', *Theoretical Criminology*, 3: 326–343.

Tittle, C.R. (2000) 'Control Balance', in R. Paternoster and R. Bachman (eds) *Explaining Criminals and Crime: Essays in Contemporary Theory*, Los Angeles, CA: Roxbury.

Tolman, E.C. (1959) 'Principles of Purposive Behaviour', in S. Koch and D.E. Leary (eds) *A Century of Psychology as a Science*, New York: McGraw-Hill.

Tonry, M. (1995) *Malign Neglect: Race, Crime, and Punishment in America*, New York: Oxford University Press.

Trasler, G. (1986) 'Situational Crime Control and Rational Choice: A Critique', in K. Heal and G. Laycock (eds) *Situational Crime Prevention: From Theory into Practice*, London: HMSO.

Turk, A.T. (1969) *Criminality and the Social Order*, Chicago, IL: Rand-McNally.

Tutt, N. (1981) 'A Decade of Policy', *British Journal of Criminology*, 21 (4): 246–256.

Uglow, S. (1995) *Criminal Justice*, London: Sweet & Maxwell.

Umbreit, M. and Roberts, A. (1996) *Mediation of Criminal Conflict in England: An Assessment of Services in Coventry and Leeds*, Rochester, MN: Center for Restorative Justice and Mediation, University of Minnesota.

United Nations Development Programme (UNDP), *Human Development Report 1999: Globalization with a Human Face*, Oxford: Oxford University Press.

Virkkunen, M. (1987) 'Metabolic Dysfunctions Amongst Habitually Violent Offenders: Reactive Hypoglycaemia and Cholesterol Levels', in S.A. Mednick, T.E. Moffit and S.A. Stack (eds) *The Causes of Crime: New Biological Approaches*, Cambridge: Cambridge University Press.

Volavka, J. (1987) 'Electroencephalogram Among Criminals', in S.A. Mednick, T.E. Moffit and S.A. Stack (eds) *The Causes of Crime: New Biological Approaches*, Cambridge: Cambridge University Press.

Vold, G.B. (1958) *Theoretical Criminology*, Oxford: Oxford University Press.

Vold, G.B., Bernard, T.J. and Snipes, J.B. (1998) *Theoretical Criminology*, 4th edn, Oxford: Oxford University Press.

Von Hirsch, A. (1976) *Doing Justice: The Choice of Punishments. Report of the Committee for the Study of Incarceration*, New York: Hill & Wang.

Von Hirsch, A. (1984) 'The Ethics of Selective Incapacitation: Observation on the Contemporary Debate', *Crime and Delinquency*, 30 (April): 175–194.

Von Hirsch, A. (1985) *Past or Future Crimes*, Manchester: Manchester University Press.

Wacquant, L. (1998a) 'Crime et châtiment en Amérique de Nixon à Clinton', *Archives de politique criminelle*, 20: 123–138.

Wacquant, L. (1998b) 'Negative Social Capital: State Breakdown and Social Destitution in America's Urban Core', *The Netherlands Journal of the Built Environment*, 13: 25–40.

Wacquant, L. (2001) 'The New "Peculiar Institution": On the Prison as Surrogate Ghetto', *Theoretical Criminology*, 4: 382–385.

Wacquant, L. (2009) *Urban Outcasts: A Comparative Sociology of Advanced Marginality*, Cambridge: Polity Press.

Wadham, J. (1998) 'Zero Tolerance Policing: Striking the Balance, Rights and Liberties', in R.D. Hopkins Burke (ed.) *Zero Tolerance Policing*, Leicester: Perpetuity Press.

Wadham, J. and Modhi, K. (2003) 'National Security and Open Government in the United Kingdom', in *National Security and Open Government: Striking the Right Balance*, Syracuse University, NY: Campbell Public Affairs Institute.

Walker, N. (1980) *Punishment, Danger and Stigma: The Morality of Criminal Justice*, Oxford: Basil Blackwell.

Walker, N. (1985) *Sentencing – Theory, Law and Practice*, London: Butterworths.

Walker, N. (1991) *Why Punish?*, Oxford: Oxford University Press.

Wasik, M. (2001) *Emmins on Sentencing*, 4th edn, London: Blackstones.

West, D.J. (1967) *The Young Offender*, New York: International Universities Press.

West, D.J. (1969) *Present Conduct and Future Delinquency*, London: Heinemann.

West, D.J. (1982) *Delinquency: Its Roots, Careers and Prospects*, London: Heinemann.

Wilkins, L. (1964) *Social Deviance*, London: Tavistock.

Willis, P. (1977) *Learning to Labour*, London: Saxon House.

Wilmott, P. (1966) *Adolescent Boys in East London*, London: Routledge & Kegan Paul.

Wilson, D., Ashton, J. and Sharp, D. (2002) *What Everyone in Britain Should Know About the Police*, London: Blackstone.

Wilson, F.P. (1963) *The Plague in Shakespeare's London*, London: Oxford University Press.

Wilson, J.Q. (1975) *Thinking About Crime*, New York: Basic Books.

Wilson, J.Q. (1985) *Thinking About Crime*, 2nd edn, New York: Basic Books.

Wilson, J.Q. and Herrnstein, R.J. (1985) *Crime and Human Nature*, New York: Simon and Schuster.

Wilson, J.Q. and Kelling, G.L. (1982) 'Broken Windows', *Atlantic Monthly*, March: 29–38.

Winlow, S. and Hall, S. (2006) *Violent Night: Urban Leisure and Contemporary Culture*, Oxford: Berg.

Witkin, H.A., Mednick, S.A. and Schulsinger, F. (1977) 'XYY and XXY Men: Criminality and Aggression', in S.A. Mednick and K.O. Christiansen (eds) *Biosocial Bases of Criminal Behaviour*, New York: Gardner Press.

Woolf Report (1991) *Prison Disturbances April 1990: Report of the Inquiry*, Cmnd 1456, London: HMSO.

Wootton, B. (1959) *Social Science and Social Pathology*, London: Allen & Unwin.

Wright, M. (1982) *Making Good: Prisons, Punishment and Beyond*, London: Burnett.

Wright, R.A. (1993) 'A Socially Sensitive Criminal Justice System', in J.W. Murphy and D.L. Peck (eds) *Open Institutions: The Hope for Democracy*, Westport, CT: Praeger.

Wynne, J. and Brown, I. (1998) 'Can Mediation Cut Re-offending?' *Probation Journal*, 46 (1).

Young, J. (1971) *The Drug Takers: The Social Meaning of Drugtaking*, London: Paladin.

Young, J. (1994) 'Incessant Chatter: Recent Paradigms in Criminology', in M. Maguire, R. Morgan and R. Reiner (eds) *The Oxford Handbook of Criminology*, Oxford: Clarendon Press.

Young, J. (1997) 'Left Realist Criminology: Radical in its Analysis: Realist in its Policy', in M. Maguire, R. Morgan and R. Reiner (eds) *The Oxford Handbook of Criminology*, 2nd edn, Oxford: Clarendon Press.

Young, J. (1999) *The Exclusive Society: Social Exclusion, Crime and Difference in Late Modernity*, London: Sage.

Young, J. (2001) 'Identity, Community and Social Exclusion', in R. Matthews and J. Pitts (eds) *Crime, Disorder and Community Safety*, London: Routledge.

Young, M. (1991) *An Inside Job: Policing and Police Culture in Britain*, Oxford: Oxford University Press.

Young, M. (1993) *In the Sticks*, Oxford: Oxford University Press.

Zander, M. (1988) *Cases and Materials on the English Legal System*, 5th edn, London: Weidenfeld & Nicolson.

Zimring, F. and Hawkins, G. (1973) *Deterrence*, Chicago, IL: University of Chicago.

Author index

Subject index

Page numbers in *italic* refer to tables

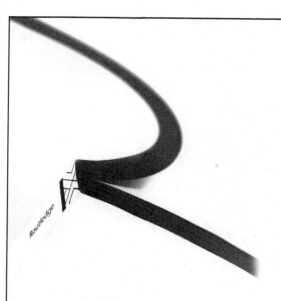